T0384785

Living in Two Worlds

This unique collection of diaries and letters offers a vivid personal account of the experiences of a Jewish couple living parallel lives during the Second World War. While their children left for England just before war broke out, and Siegfried soon followed, Else Behrend was unable to obtain her visa in time, and remained in Germany. This volume includes Else's account of her years of persecution under the Nazi dictatorship, and of her life underground in Berlin, before her eventual daring escape to Switzerland on foot in 1944. Her dramatic story is presented alongside Siegfried's account of his very different experience, living penniless and in isolation in England, as well as some of her letters to her close friend and confidante, Eva. Complemented by QR codes that allow readers to listen to Else's own voice from her 1963 BBC interviews. Published in English for the first time, *Living in Two Worlds* offers an unforgettable and moving insight into the impact of the Second World War on everyday life.

Marita Krauss is Professor of History in the Faculty of Philology and History at the University of Augsburg, Germany. Her previous publications include biographies of the pioneering female doctor Dr Hope Bridges Adams Lehmann (2009) and the dancer Lola Montez (2020).

Erich Kasberger is an independent historian and freelance writer. He previously worked as a history teacher at a grammar school in Munich. He began researching a nearby site which had been an internment camp for Jews, where he established a memorial to Else Behrend-Rosenfeld and to 500 deported Jews. He received an award from the City of Munich for his work on the Rosenfeld family.

Deborah Langton is an independent translator. She previously taught at Munich's Ludwig-Maximilians-Universität, and has translated numerous volumes of fiction and non-fiction from German into English.

Living in Two Worlds

Diaries of a Jewish Couple in Germany and in Exile

Edited by

Marita Krauss

University of Augsburg

and

Erich Kasberger

Translated into English by

Deborah Langton

With a foreword by

Richard Evans

University of Cambridge

CAMBRIDGE
UNIVERSITY PRESS

CAMBRIDGE
UNIVERSITY PRESS

University Printing House, Cambridge CB2 8BS, United Kingdom

One Liberty Plaza, 20th Floor, New York, NY 10006, USA

477 Williamstown Road, Port Melbourne, VIC 3207, Australia

314–321, 3rd Floor, Plot 3, Splendor Forum, Jasola District Centre, New Delhi – 110025, India

103 Penang Road, #05–06/07, Visioncrest Commercial, Singapore 238467

Cambridge University Press is part of the University of Cambridge.

It furthers the University's mission by disseminating knowledge in the pursuit of education, learning, and research at the highest international levels of excellence.

www.cambridge.org
Information on this title: www.cambridge.org/9781316519097
DOI: 10.1017/9781009004756

First published 2022

Printed in the United Kingdom by TJ Books Limited, Padstow, Cornwall

A catalogue record for this publication is available from the British Library.

Library of Congress Cataloging-in-Publication Data
NAMES: Behrend-Rosenfeld, Else R., author. | Krauss, Marita, editor. | Kasberger, Erich, editor. | Langton, Deborah, 1955- translator.
TITLE: Living in two worlds : diaries of a Jewish couple in Germany and in exile / edited by Marita Krauss, University of Augsburg, Germany and Erich Kasberger ; translated into English by Deborah Langton, Independent Scholar ; with a foreword by Richard Evans.
OTHER TITLES: Leben in zwei Welten. English | Diaries of a Jewish couple in Germany and in exile
DESCRIPTION: Cambridge, United Kingdom ; New York, NY : Cambridge University Press, [2022] | "Translated into English from the original work, "Leben in zwei Welten" © 2011 Volk Verlag." | Includes bibliographical references and index.
IDENTIFIERS: LCCN 2021020769 (print) | LCCN 2021020770 (ebook) | ISBN 9781316519097 (hardback) | ISBN 9781009001380 (paperback) | ISBN 9781009004756 (epub)
SUBJECTS: LCSH: Behrend-Rosenfeld, Else R.–Diaries. | Berg am Laim (Concentration camp) | Rosenfeld, Siegfried, 1874-1947–Diaries. | Rosenfeld family. | Holocaust, Jewish (1939-1945)–Germany–Personal narratives. | Exiles–Great Britain–Diaries. | Jews–Germany–Biography. | Munich (Germany)–Biography.
CLASSIFICATION: LCC DS134.42.B45 A3 2022 (print) | LCC DS134.42.B45 (ebook) | DDC 940.53/18092 [B]–dc23
LC record available at https://lccn.loc.gov/2021020769
LC ebook record available at https://lccn.loc.gov/2021020770

ISBN 978-1-316-51909-7 Hardback

CONTENTS

ILLUSTRATIONS

FOREWORD

Else Behrend-Rosenfeld (1891–1970) was a German teacher and social worker, half Jewish and married to a Jew. Siegfried Rosenfeld (1874–1947) was one of a small minority of people classified by the Nazis as Jewish who lived in Germany through the years of Hitler's Third Reich (1933–1945), and survived to tell the tale. The fact that they brought up their children as Christians and did not themselves participate actively in the Jewish religious community offered the Rosenfelds little protection from discrimination and persecution.

Hitler and the Nazis believed that people of Jewish blood all over the world were innately inclined to engage in conspiracies and plots to undermine and ultimately destroy the German or 'Aryan' race. Hence they had to be removed. From the moment they came to power in 1933, the Nazis began to put pressure on Germany's small Jewish community, roughly half a million people, to emigrate, dismissing them from their jobs and removing the economic basis of their existence. By the outbreak of World War II in September 1939, half of Germany's Jews had emigrated, Siegfried Rosenfeld among them.

Those that remained had already been deprived of most of their rights and forced into an existence separate from that of the majority of 'Aryans'. The Nazis' antisemitism became increasingly radical during the war, which brought millions of Eastern European Jews under their control. In 1941 Hitler's paranoid vision came to imagine a world-wide Jewish conspiracy behind Germany's enemies, Britain, then the Soviet Union and finally the United States, and unleashed a campaign of extermination that left some 6 million European Jews dead by the middle of 1945.

The vast majority of ordinary Germans did nothing to prevent or protest against this unfolding campaign of hatred, discrimination and mass murder. Some were convinced by the antisemitic propaganda pumped out by the Nazi media and education system; some were intimidated by the Gestapo and the organs of the police state that made anyone who tried to help Jews liable to arrest and imprisonment: all, however, knew what was going on, and by the summer of 1942 at the latest were aware of the killing fields and extermination camps of the east, informed about them by soldiers and others who had witnessed or learned about them. After Germany's defeat in 1945, ordinary Germans had to come to terms with their collective guilt for what later became known as the Holocaust.

Despite this, small groups of Germans had tried to resist the Nazis. The best-known act of resistance was the attempt by a group of army officers to kill Hitler on 20 July 1944, an attempt that only failed because of chance circumstances. There were other resistance movements as well. The most important secret organisations were linked either to the extreme left Communist Party of Germany or to the moderate, left of centre Social Democrats, who had been the largest political party in Germany before the rise of the Nazis, in the early 1930s, and the mainstay of the democratic Weimar Republic, effectively ruling its largest federated state, Prussia, until 1932.

Both the Rosenfelds were active members of the Social Democratic Party until the Nazis banned it in 1933; Siegfried was a senior official in the Prussian administration but as a Social Democrat and a Jew was sacked by the Nazis soon after they came to power. Despite massive persecution by the Gestapo, small remnants of the party continued underground propaganda work against the regime, and it is to these that Else Behrend-Rosenfeld owed her survival, along with relatives and friends from her university days.

Else Behrend-Rosenfeld's diaries and letters, gathered together for the first time in this book, give a detailed and often moving account of the discrimination and persecution to which she was subjected by the Nazis from 1933 until the end of the war. She recounts the verbal abuse and aggression to which she was subjected by Nazi officials, along with acts of spite and denunciation by ordinary Germans. But she also experienced many acts of kindness and consideration, which led her to doubt the justice of imposing the kind of blanket condemnation of collective guilt on the entire nation that her husband Siegfried, viewing events in the Reich from his British exile, clearly shared. The detail of her diaries enables us to observe the whole variety of attitudes and behaviour of ordinary, non-Jewish, non-Social Democratic Germans towards people like herself, much like that of another Jewish diarist who survived the Third Reich, the literature professor Victor Klemperer.

Perhaps she was lucky. In August 1942, as the mass extermination of Europe's Jewish population by the Nazis was reaching its terrible climax, Else clearly reached the conclusion that her luck was running out, and went first to Berlin and subsequently to Freiburg, southern Germany, concealing her identity and living secretly with a series of courageous men and women who were willing to shelter her. She had entered an even smaller world, one of which we still know relatively little, that of German Jews living underground. Eventually she was placed in the hands of people who engaged on a regular basis in the highly dangerous business of smuggling Jews and others across the Swiss border, and made her way to freedom.

Else Rosenfeld was a gifted writer, and her account of these events and experiences makes for gripping reading. It needs to be remembered, however, that many Jews who tried to live underground were caught and killed; those who survived were a tiny minority. Betrayal, denunciation and hostility were more common than loyalty, discretion and sympathy. Just as important were the experiences of Siegfried Rosenfeld in Britain, eking out a precarious existence in Oxford and then subjected to the privations of internment on the Isle of Man as an 'enemy alien'. It is understandable that the story of Jewish-Germans living in exile from the Third Reich is usually told as a story of achievement, but there were many, like Siegfried, who were broken by the experience.

Richard Evans

INTRODUCTION

Marita Krauss

The story of the Rosenfeld family is at once extraordinary and yet entirely typical of the period. It is a tale of ghettoes, deportations, of certain death and a last-minute reprieve, as well as the grinding misery of exile. Else's diary recounts her life as a Jewish woman in Germany up to 1944, but this volume offers not only a selection of the letters she penned during this period to Eva Schmidt, a close friend since student days and a key player in Else's survival, but also an opportunity to listen to interviews with Else herself, recorded in 1963 by the BBC, all in her own voice and words.

QR Code 1: Rosenfeld, *An Old Lady Remembers*, BBC Radio, April/May 1963

Ever since her diary was first published in 1945, it has formed part of the continuing debate about the conduct of 'ordinary Germans' towards persecuted Jews under the National Socialist (NS) regime.[1] It provides early evidence of the way some Jews managed to live underground.[2] Else Behrend-Rosenfeld draws a clear distinction, as do a number of others among her contemporaries, between those Germans seen as the perpetrators and those who displayed kindness and humanity in helping the persecuted while putting themselves at serious risk.

Siegfried's diary and letters, first published in the German version of this volume, *Leben in zwei Welten* (2011), present an altogether different view of

[1] Bajohr and Pohl, *Massenmord*; Benz, ed., *Überleben*; Kosmala and Schoppmann, eds., *Überleben*; Kosmala and Verbeeck, eds., *Facing the Catastrophe*; Moore, *Survivors*.

[2] Extensively in Lutjens, *Submerged on the Surface*; examples from Strauss, *Over the Green Hill*; Roseman, *Past in Hiding*; Friedländer, *Versuche*; Jalowicz-Simon, *Underground*; Lewyn and Saltzmann-Lewyn, eds., *Versteckt in Berlin*; Orbach and Orbach-Smith, *Soaring Underground*; Kosmala, *Nichts wie raus und durch!*; Zahn, Von einem Quartier zum nächsten, pp. 229–238; further accounts in Benz, ed., *Überleben im Dritten Reich*.

1. Else Rosenfeld, 1940s.

2. Siegfried Rosenfeld, 1940s.

Germany.[3] From the outside and his life in exile, Siegfried's own view of 'Germany – the appalling criminal' seems entirely justified when he first reads Else's diary on publication in November 1945 and thereby learns just what his wife lived through in the seven years they were apart. Siegfried Rosenfeld assesses Germany and its citizens from his various standpoints as refugee, active member of the German centre left, the Social Democratic Party of Germany (SPD), and sharp political observer now engaged with the Social Democrats in exile in Great Britain. He draws on his personal experience as a German soldier in the First World War to make astute observations on the course of this second war. Above all else, he longs for Else's rescue through an Allied victory over Germany. The diaries and letters of this one couple thus demonstrate widely divergent positions in this enormously significant debate.

It is an exception to find such duality in any account of Jewish lives under the Nazi regime. The way in which Else and Siegfried turn to one another through their diary entries, each of them grappling with the years spent apart, is another special feature of this volume. Originally written separately

[3] See Krauss and Kasberger, eds., *Leben in zwei Welten.*

from one another, the diaries have now been interwoven in such a way as to create a dialogue that feels at times like an ongoing exchange of love letters, but written with long months in between when neither knew what was happening to the other.

Historical Background

What happened to the Rosenfeld family represents the wider exclusion and persecution of other political voices under the Nazis over the period from 1933 to 1945, in addition to the more widely recognised expulsion and annihilation of Jews.[4] As active Social Democrats living in Berlin, they fell foul of the first phase of persecution aimed at left-leaning opponents of the National Socialists. Then, as early as 1 April 1933, came the boycott of Jewish businesses, the first of many measures intended to discriminate against Jews by stigmatising them, leaving them disenfranchised, excluded from economic life and eventually robbed, displaced or murdered.[5] Nazi Germany eventually enacted some 2,000 laws against Jews. By the close of 1937, there were 400,000 people in Germany now categorised as being Jewish. In the five years following 1933, as many as 130,000 of them had already emigrated.[6] Under the so-called Nuremberg Laws of 1935, many fully assimilated Germans but with a Jewish family background, such as the Rosenfelds themselves, were declared as Jews, along with anyone indeed practising the Jewish faith. Under the new Reich Citizenship Law, all of these people found themselves downgraded to the status of second-class citizen in Germany and with immediate effect.[7] Shortly thereafter, a Certificate of Aryan Descent, or *Ariernachweis*, became an essential requirement for anyone seeking access to paid employment. The Law for the Restoration of the Professional Civil Service (Gesetz zur Wiederherstellung des Berufsbeamtentums) meant that in 1933 anybody with one Jewish grandparent, as well as any politically undesirable civil servants and their relatives, was suspended from public

[4] Comprehensive documentation can be found in the series Die Verfolgung und Ermordung der europäischen Juden durch das nationalsozialistische Deutschland, published by order of the Bundesarchiv. Volumes 1, 2, 3, 6 and 11 are of particular relevance as they focus on Germany in particular.

[5] Gruner, Einleitung, pp. 13–50; for the Nazi boycott of Jewish businesses, Gruner, *Verfolgung und Ermordung der europäischen Juden*, doc. 17, pp. 100–104 (Call for a Reich-wide boycott, 30.3.1933).

[6] Heim, Einleitung, p. 13, a detailed account of its development.

[7] Gruner, Einleitung, pp. 45f. Also documents 198 and 199 in Gruner, *Verfolgung und Ermordung der europäischen Juden*, pp. 492–494.

duty unless they had been serving soldiers in the First World War. The term 'Jewish' was defined in law by descent, although the only fixed criterion for ruling whether someone was Jewish was the religious affiliation of their grandparents, while the status of 'half' or 'quarter' Jews remained uncertain.[8] Over the period 1933 to 1938 Jews were, both in theory and in practice, successively shut out of the German economy.[9] Many of those impacted chose at first to remain in Germany, either because they considered themselves German or to be simply too old to move.[10] External migration became increasingly difficult when a special tax to stem the likely outflow of capital, first introduced during the Depression years, was further tightened, so that Jewish accounts were blocked. These twin measures meant that the Nazi regime could collect whatever funds remained once these desperate people had been forced to give up their properties.[11]

3. Boycott of Jewish businesses. Using the slogan 'Do Not Buy from Jews', on 1 April 1933 the SA tried to intimidate shoppers into not patronising any Jewish business. This is Bamberger & Hertz in Munich's Kaufinger Straße. Photo: Weiler.

[8] Longerich, *Politik der Vernichtung.*
[9] Heim, Einleitung, pp. 18–20; Gruner, Einleitung, p. 50.
[10] For observations not in favour of emigration, see Jünger, *Jahre der Ungewissheit.*
[11] Gruner, Einleitung, p. 50.

In November 1938, the so-called Night of Broken Glass or Night of the Pogrom (*Kristallnacht*) marked a watershed. Across the Reich, over 1,000 synagogues were burned to the ground, 7,500 Jewish-owned shops were wrecked, and 30,000 Jewish men were carried off to concentration camps and released only when they promised to leave the country. The scale of destruction and the proliferation of arrests and murders in 1938 left even the hesitant in no doubt that the only option was to leave. The Rosenfelds, in Munich throughout the pogrom, were among this number and resolved now to pursue the migration route. Sadly, fewer and fewer countries were willing to take in Jewish refugees, who often arrived without the means to support themselves. A number of organisations stepped in, making great efforts to secure visas and locate in the destination country those individuals prepared to host and sponsor people forced to abandon Germany. Siegfried Rosenfeld had the Quakers to thank for his own visa to Great Britain and his passage out in August 1939. In total, some 300,000 persecuted Jews left Germany before the outbreak of war, very much in line with the Nazi regime's aim of making as many Jews as possible desert the country. The routes to migration were many, and often convoluted. Escape to most other countries in Europe, such as the Netherlands, Czechoslovakia or France, offered no protection in the end, however, as German conquests meant those fleeing had to travel on further still or face internment and deportation even so. Regulations meant that Switzerland and England were often used for transit purposes, and anyone who could do so would move on to the United States, which in the end took a quarter of the 500,000 German-speaking migrants from across the Reich, Austria and Czechoslovakia.[12]

At the outbreak of war, the situation worsened. With the occupation of Poland, many Jewish and non-Jewish Poles died at the hands of the police and the military.[13] The National Socialists were striving towards what they saw as a 'solution to the Jewish question', and one of the many ideas put forward was to resettle all Jews on Madagascar, although this plan was never realised. With Germany's attack on the Soviet Union in June 1941, their plans became yet more radical. In this war of annihilation, over 1 million Jewish men, women and children in eastern Europe were shot dead. All this took place beyond the bounds of the *Altreich* – the German

[12] For more about countries of emigration, methods and statistics, Krohn and Mühlen, eds., *Handbuch der deutschsprachigen Emigration*.

[13] Löw, Einleitung, p. 27 and pp. 28–64.

territories prior to 1938. At the same time, the reign of terror intensified within the Reich itself. Jews were interned or allocated to forced labour, one example being at the flax-processing plant at Lohhof in Munich, where Else herself was set to work.[14] Jews who were either the main tenants in a property or indeed the owners were now forced to run 'Jewish houses' or 'Jewish flats' and to take in Jewish lodgers who had been driven from their homes elsewhere. To put this into practice, a law was required, promulgated as early as April 1939.[15] The enforced removal of Jews into 'Jewish flats' led to their loss of contact with old 'Aryan' friends and neighbours. Opportunities to flee dwindled fast as more and more countries were drawn into the war. An outright ban on emigration was put in place in October 1941. Between 1942 and 1945 only around 8,500 Jews succeeded in getting out of Germany.[16]

The next stage was internment in camps. In summer 1941 transit camps were set up in Munich at Milbertshofen and Berg am Laim, with Else Behrend-Rosenfeld put in place as overall head of housekeeping at the latter. The first two deportations to the East took place in 1940, as well as one to Gurs in France, followed by smaller transports from Vienna and Danzig. Systematic deportation on a larger scale started in October 1941. The first sizeable deportation of 1,000 Jews left Munich in November 1941, bound for Kaunas (Kovno) in Lithuania.[17] Many from the Berg am Laim camp were named on the deportation lists, and Else Rosenfeld describes in her diary the heart-rending farewells that had to be made. All of those taken to Lithuania were shot at Kaunas (Kovno). Only one person survived. After this, there were forty-three further deportations out of Munich to several different destinations.[18] Deportation did not necessarily mean immediate death. Sometimes deportees were held in a succession of different camps before being transported to one of the death camps in operation, such as Auschwitz II, Sobibor, Belzec or Treblinka, where they would be gassed. Across the Reich, 160,000 people were deported and murdered, 3,666 from Munich alone.[19] This represents a fraction of the 6 million Jews who fell victim to the Shoah. Forty of the transports out of Munich went to Theresienstadt, supposedly a 'model camp', although the provision of food and the standard

[14] Strnad, *Flachs für das Reich.*

[15] Gesetz über Mietverhältnisse mit Juden, in *Regierungsblatt I* 1939, p. 864f.

[16] Summary in Benz, Jüdische Emigration, pp. 6–16.

[17] Heusler, Fahrt in den Tod, pp. 13–24.

[18] Ibid., pp. 13f.

[19] Kundrus and Meyer, eds., *Deportation der Juden*; Bundesarchiv, ed., *Gedenkbuch.*

of medical care, accommodation and sanitation were worse than inadequate, and many inmates were subsequently taken to Auschwitz to be murdered. Of the 1,550 men and women deported from Munich to Theresienstadt, a mere 160 returned after the war.[20]

The protection initially afforded to half Jews or quarter Jews, as well as to Jews in a 'mixed marriage' with an Aryan, grew increasingly fragile, and at local levels individuals were repeatedly persecuted or actually deported.[21] Since the passing of the Nuremberg Laws, anyone with one Jewish parent or two Jewish grandparents was categorised as 'Grade One *Mischling*' or 'half Jew', while anyone with one Jewish grandparent became 'Grade Two *Mischling*'.[22] In 1941 and 1942 there were repeated efforts to extend the concept of 'Jew' to any degree of *Mischling*, and the subject of mixed marriages and *Mischling* status was discussed over and over at the Wannsee Conferences. There were plans to forcibly separate couples in a mixed marriage and to subject *Mischlinge* to compulsory sterilisation, or alternatively to put them on the same footing as 'full Jews' and thus make them part of the Nazis' 'Final Solution'. Where a 'half Jew' married a 'full Jew', such as in the case of Else's marriage to Siegfried, the 'half Jew' was then deemed a *Geltungsjude*, in other words a 'full Jew', in spite of actually being a *Mischling*.

Full Jews and *Geltungsjuden* had little or no opportunity to escape deportation. In most cases, those who fled were swiftly tracked down. But there were people who helped those who had decided their only chance was to live under the radar, and these 'silent heroes' are today being increasingly recognised and honoured.[23] In August 1942 Else Rosenfeld left Munich to live underground in Berlin. Around 1,700 Jews managed to survive this way in the capital, out of an estimated 6,500 people living underground in Berlin.[24] These figures are approximations and do not take into account individuals like Else, seeking the anonymity of the city, who came in from elsewhere to join the underground and described themselves as 'U-boats'. In Munich alone, around 500 Jews

[20] Heusler, Fahrt in den Tod, p. 15; for Theresienstadt see for example Weiss, *Und doch ein ganzes Leben*.

[21] Meyer, *'Jüdische Mischlinge'*, pp. 379–382.

[22] For definitions and analysis see ibid., pp. 96–104.

[23] Detailed further in Lutjens, *Submerged*; Wette, ed., *Stille Helden*; Schrafstetter, *Flucht und Versteck*; Strauss, *Over the Green Hill*; Roseman, *Past in Hiding*; Friedlander and Schwerdtfeger, *'Versuche dein Leben zu machen'*; Jalowicz-Simon, *Underground*; Lewyn and Saltzmann-Lewyn, *Versteckt in Berlin*; Orbach and Orbach-Smith, *Soaring Underground*.

[24] Lutjens, *Submerged on the Surface*, pp. 211f.; Lutjens discusses in some detail the figures, which can only ever be viewed as estimates.

survived by living in hiding like this.[25] Across the Reich as a whole, estimates suggest, around 10,000 to 12,000 lived in hiding, of whom about 5,000 survived.[26] This was made possible by the tens of thousands of people across the Reich who became helpers, procuring false papers, providing food, seeking out safe accommodation and planning escapes across the border. Support networks began to take shape.[27] It took an estimated minimum of ten non-Jews to help just one person survive life underground. A wide variety of men and women became helpers, and their reasons for doing so were equally diverse, ranging from the political and the ideological to the compassionate. In many cases, it was the individual in hiding who took the initiative, actively making contact with old friends whenever a different place of shelter was needed for the night. These helpers put themselves at great personal risk. After the war was over, Eva Schmidt, key to Else's survival, confided in a friend that she had felt personally responsible for Else's life, which at times had left her close to despair. She had often felt unable to carry on, but she always did.[28] This help given to the persecuted is, with good reason, defined as 'resistance'.[29] But to be successful, it also needed the courage, determination and ingenuity seen in the fugitives themselves.[30] Chance and luck were decisive factors too. While Else was living in hiding in Berlin between 15 August 1942 and 30 May 1943, there were multiple arrests and deportations of Jews who had been living underground in the city. Then, in late February 1943, all Jews still working in factories in Berlin were rounded up in what became known as the *Fabrikaktion*, and were deported, while the Gestapo and SS raided flats and seized a number of those living in hiding. In Berlin alone, 11,000 Jews were arrested.[31] At first, about 4,000 escaped, but many were recaptured. In the middle of March Else too had to cope with an official check while she was living in hiding at Hans Kollmorgen's home. Towards the end of May she escaped to Freiburg and remained there until April 1944.[32]

[25] Schrafstetter, *Flucht und Versteck*.

[26] Gedenkstätte Stille Helden, Berlin: Silent Heroes Memorial Center, www.gedenkstaette-stille-helden.de/gedenkstaette/ (last accessed 10 November 2020).

[27] Düring, *Verdeckte soziale Netzwerke*.

[28] Conversations on 12 September 2011 with Elke Minckwitz, Weimar, Eva Schmidt's executor and the daughter of Hanna Schadendorf, friend to both Else and Eva, and on the same date with Jens Riederer of the Weimar City Archive.

[29] Lustiger, ed., *Rettungswiderstand*; about those who helped others escape with many further references, Düring, *Verdeckte soziale Netzwerke*.

[30] Benz, *Überleben im Dritten Reich*, p. 12.

[31] Schoppmann, 'Fabrikaktion'.

[32] Lutjens, *Submerged on the Surface*, pp. 215, 220.

One of the most difficult tasks for a support network was the organisation of an escape across the border. This required helpers and helpers' helpers, but most of all money and good contacts in all manner of circles, including the illegal when it came to matters such as false passports or other identity documents. On the German–Swiss border near Schaffhausen, a support network run by Luise Meier and Josef Höfler helped Jews, including Else Rosenfeld, across the border.[33] On the Upper Rhine between Lake Constance and Basel, the German–Swiss border takes a convoluted course, offering reasonable opportunities for making a crossing. Jews were helped to escape by a number of local people, including the head of the Gestapo for Constance himself, Jakob Weyrauch, along with the Roman Catholic priest for Singen, August Ruf.[34] This was a highly risky business, and a number of Jews were caught and condemned to death.[35] Even when they had succeeded in getting across the border, people still could not be sure of safe haven: from 1942 onwards the Swiss authorities sent back as many as 25,000 Jews, while knowing full well that their lives would be endangered once they returned.[36]

Elsewhere within the National Socialist area of control, similar networks were also getting people across the border. Best known among these perhaps was Varian Fry, who, by order of US President Franklin Delano Roosevelt, organised escape routes across the Pyrenees with Lisa Fittko and her husband. Around 2,000 refugees succeeded in crossing the border thanks to this group, including prominent German intellectuals such as Lion Feuchtwanger and Heinrich Mann, who were living in France at the time of the German invasion and crossed into Spain and then onward to Lisbon for passage to the United States.[37] Yad Vashem, the World Holocaust Remembrance Center, has to date honoured more than 27,700 non-Jews by adding them to the list of Righteous among Nations in recognition of the risk they took in helping Jews escape the Nazi regime.[38]

[33] Düring, *Verdeckte soziale Netzwerke*, pp. 90–103; Battel, '*Wo es hell ist*'; Schoppmann, *Fortgesetzte Beihilfe*, pp. 163–178.

[34] Halbauer, Fluchthelfer an Hochrhein, pp. 179f.; Keller, Emigrantenschmuggler, pp. 200–212.

[35] Düring, *Verdeckte soziale Netzwerke*, p. 7.

[36] Since August 1942 Switzerland had been turning back all Jewish refugees; Battel, '*Wo es hell ist*', p. 147; Keller, Emigrantenschmuggler, pp. 198f.

[37] Fittko, *Mein Weg über die Pyrenäen*; Klein, *Flüchtlingspolitik*; Sogos and Fry, 'Engel von Marseille', pp. 209–220; Strempel, Letzter Halt Marseille, pp. 185–196.

[38] Yad Vashem, Righteous among the Nations – Statistics, www.yadvashem.org/de/righteous/statistics.html (last accessed 6 September 2020).

4. Escape organisers: (*from left*) Josef Höfler, Luise Meier, Gertrud Höfler, Elise Höfler. Photo taken around 1952.

Source Documents

The life of the Rosenfeld family post-1933 is richly documented in diaries, letters and other autobiographical material. Else Rosenfeld's diary was first published in 1945 in Switzerland under the title *Verfemt und Verfolgt: Leben einer Jüdin in Deutschland 1933–1944*.[39] It is an exceptionally accurate source and was used as evidence in the post-war Munich denazification hearings.[40] This is not a diary where life was recorded on a daily basis, but one with irregular entries starting in 1939 and then taking a long look back over the period 1933 to 1939, her retrospective being abridged in this volume. After her flight across the border to Switzerland, Else prepared her diary for publication to bear witness to that whole era. The publisher's advance meant she now had some measure of personal freedom. She had, after all, escaped without financial means, with quite literally nothing more than her freedom. Siegfried Rosenfeld's diary, on the other hand, embraces the years 1940 to 1945 and is composed of fragments bearing witness to the wretched misery of

[39] See Behrend-Rosenfeld, *Verfemt und Verfolgt*.
[40] StAM Spruchkammerakten (Denazification Hearings) K 1919: Wegner, Hans.

life in exile, reproduced here as excerpts.[41] Any correspondence between Siegfried and Else after 1942 was made possible by Alice Rosenberg, Siegfried's sister-in-law, who was living in neutral Lisbon during Else's life in hiding. But even then, these letters had to be written in a code of sorts, with only indirect references. These letters have not been available to the editors because some luggage went missing during a family house move in the 1990s. What was saved, however, were 230 letters written by Else during her internment and life in hiding, all addressed to Dr Eva Schmidt, her close friend in Weimar.[42] This friendship had endured since their student days, and continued after the war with reciprocal visits and exchanges of letters.[43] The correspondence passed to us as researchers and editors relates only to the period dealt with in this volume, and was entrusted to us in 2010 by Hanna Cooper, Else Rosenfeld's daughter. The letters give a vivid account of the day's events, often with a sense of urgency, while the diary comes over as more measured. Else had a mission in publishing it, not to serve as accusation the moment the war ended, but rather to show other nations that while crimes had indeed been committed by Germany, those who suffered persecution had at times also found help and support. She wanted to demonstrate that the German 'collective guilt' referred to by the Allies had never in fact existed.

A further source has been the unique autobiographical interviews given by Else to the BBC. Broadcast in England during April and May 1963 as *An Old Lady Remembers*, these were made into twenty-three programmes, each lasting fifteen minutes.[44] Here, Else reflects in detail on her youth in Berlin and the special relationship she had with her father's Jewish family, and, with the perception of hindsight, she formulates evaluations and assessments that go far beyond the scope of the diary. In 1964 the BBC published a book *The Four Lives of Elsbeth Rosenfeld*, based on the radio series,[45] but the original interviews offer a wealth of extra information, along with the

[41] Hanna Cooper (Birmingham, England) gave us the typed version transcribed by Gustel Behrend (Argentina) from Siegfried's handwritten original. First published in 2011 as Krauss and Kasberger, eds., *Leben in zwei Welten*.

[42] As recently as 1984, Eva Schmidt dedicated a book to her dear friend: *Jüdische Familien*; a new edition in 1993 included an obituary of Eva Schmidt with all the key elements of her life: Uta Kühn-Stillmark, Autorin, in Schmidt, *Jüdische Familien*, pp. 139–143. See Glossary of Key People. Thanks to Elke Minckwitz and Jens Riederer, Weimar City Archive, for photographs and information.

[43] Interview with Hanna Cooper, Birmingham, England, 2010; photos of Else Rosenfeld und Eva Schmidt in Icking.

[44] Rosenfeld, *An Old Lady Remembers*, interviewer Charles Parker.

[45] Rosenfeld, *Four Lives.*

priceless addition of Else's own voice. It says so much about her as a person, so we have included QR codes to make available Else's voice and her reflections on the past.

QR Code 2: Early life among Jews and Christians

The many conversations and interviews with Peter and Ursula Rosenfeld, as well as with Hanna Cooper, are also of great importance. A warm relationship between the editors and Else's children was established as early as 1986, but Peter and Ursula have since sadly passed away. Hanna Cooper is now advanced in years. From Hanna, we received documents and photographs, the letters to Eva Schmidt and the BBC recordings. We also talked and corresponded with many other contemporary witnesses, including the son of the Quaker couple Drs Rudolf and Annemarie Cohen, Professor Rudolf Cohen, and with friends of Dr Tilla Kratz in Icking and Dr Eva Schmidt in Weimar, with the daughter of escape route organiser Hugo Wetzstein, and many more. They have all contributed to recreating the world that was Else's life.

Else's diary was first published just before the end of the war, and many names remained disguised to protect those who had helped her. Since secrecy is no longer an issue, real names have been used wherever possible. These helpers, known as 'silent heroes', are a very special group in whom researchers have in recent years taken a great interest.[46] In its turn, Siegfried's diary brings us so much about the network of exiles as well as about internment on the Isle of Man, where German refugees were held as 'enemy aliens' from 1940.[47] We learn about his hand-to-mouth existence in Oxford as an outsider, and of how his children, Peter and

[46] Wette, ed., *Stille Helden*; Kosmala, Stille Helden, 29–34; Schieb, *Möglichkeiten und Grenzen*. See the following for further information: Heim, Meyer and Nicosia, eds., *'Wer bleibt'*; Schilde, Grenzüberschreitende Flucht, pp. 151–190; Kosmala and Schoppmann, eds., *Solidarität und Hilfe*; Schrafstetter, *Flucht und Versteck*.

[47] Seyfert, 'His Majesty's Most Loyal Internees', pp. 155–182; Chappell, *Island of Barbed Wire*; Gillman and Gillman, *Collar the Lot!*; Stent, *Bespattered Page*; Lafitte, *Internment of Aliens*.

Hanna, grew up and made their lives in England, having started out as farmworker and domestic help respectively, only to work their way up from the bottom.

Biographies

Dr Siegfried Rosenfeld was born on 22 March 1874 in Marienwerder, West Prussia, the son of assimilated German Jews. He was raised as a Jew, but stepped away from Judaism in 1891.[48] His education took the classic route of the German middle classes, first at the local grammar school in Marienwerder from 1887; in 1893 he took his final school examination, the *Abitur*, at the Berlin grammar school called zum Grauen Kloster.[49] Afterwards, Siegfried studied law in Berlin and Freiburg, becoming a legal clerk in 1897. He then completed his military service, and in 1899 obtained his doctorate in jurisprudence at Rostock. In 1904 he established himself in Berlin as a lawyer and notary. The following year he joined the SPD. During the First World War he served four years in the territorial reserve.[50] In 1915 he married dentist Gertrud Rewald, also involved with the SPD, but she died after the birth of their daughter Gustel (Eva Gustave). It was through his niece, Dr Hertha Kraus,[51] that he met Else Behrend. She was a good deal younger than him, but they were married in September 1920. Their son Peter was born in 1921, and daughter Hanna in 1922. Siegfried Rosenfeld was elected to the Prussian parliament in 1921 and remained active there until 1933. In 1923, when he was forty-nine, he embarked on a career in the Prussian civil service, working first as a special adviser. On 30 June 1925 he was promoted by Prussian Minister-President Otto Braun, a fellow Social Democrat, first to the rank of *Ministerialrat* in the Prussian Ministry of Justice and later as *Ministerialdirigent*, thus becoming the most senior civil servant in that ministry.[52]

[48] *Biographisches Handbuch der deutschsprachigen Emigration*, vol. I, p. 614.

[49] IFZ MA 1500/50, Fragebogen (Questionnaire) on Siegfried Rosenfeld, completed by his daughter, Gustel.

[50] StAM Staatsanwaltschaften 7863, Special Court Indictment of Siegfried Rosenfeld, 09.08.1934.

[51] More about Dr Hertha Kraus, *Biographisches Handbuch der deutschsprachigen Emigration*, vol. I, p. 391; Schirrmacher, *Hertha Kraus*. See Glossary of Key People.

[52] GStA PK Rep. 90a, Minutes of Ministerial Meeting MF 1035, Agenda item 4, Proposed Promotions: 'Der Hilfsarbeiter im Justizministerium, Kammergerichtsrat Dr Siegfried Rosenfeld, zum Ministerialrat im Justizministerium', 30.6.1925.

QR Code 3: Siegfried's career in the Ministry

Else Behrend had a Christian mother, Gertrud Grosskopf, and a Jewish father, Dr Friedrich Behrend,[53] by profession a long-established family doctor in Berlin. This was considered a *Mischehe*, a mixed marriage, one of 3,215 such marriages in Greater Berlin in 1924.[54] Else arrived on 1 May 1891 in Berlin, the first of what were to be eight children born to the family.[55] The children were baptised and brought up in the Christian faith, as was customary in a mixed marriage.[56] Her father was a central figure in her life, and she identified strongly with him. It was he who helped her come to terms with a birth defect that had left her with a severely weakened left arm. Her upper arm lacked all strength and there was only minimal movement in the forearm. She learned not to allow this to be a handicap. From 1899 to 1901 she attended a Berlin school for girls, 'die Höhere Mädchenschule',[57] where she learned the arts of housekeeping and sewing. At seventeen, she trained as a kindergarten teacher and immediately found work in a large private school for girls. She prepared for the *Abitur* examination by taking a course of study run by the Helene-Lange-Fortbildungskurse,[58] as it was still exceptional for a woman to undertake further study, or indeed employment of any kind. In Prussia, for example, it was 1908 before women were allowed to attend university. Else studied German, history, philosophy and German literature, first in Berlin and then from 1916 at the University of Jena. Initially she wanted to be a teacher, but then gave a lot of thought to social work. Her academic ambition was to

[53] *Biographisches Handbuch der deutschsprachigen Emigration*, vol. II/2, p. 986 and IFZ MA 1500/50, Rosenfeld, Elisabeth (Elsbeth), Fragebogen (Questionnaire). Gertrud Grosskopf, born Berlin 1868, died 6.10.1944 in La Cumbrecita, Córdoba/Argentina.

[54] Meyer, *'Jüdische Mischlinge'*, p. 24.

[55] IFZ MA 1500/50, Rosenfeld, Elsbeth, Fragebogen (Questionnaire).

[56] Meyer, *'Jüdische Mischlinge'*, p. 25.

[57] IFZ MA 1500/50, Rosenfeld, Elsbeth, Fragebogen (Questionnaire).

[58] Helene Lange was probably the leading exponent of the *Abitur* qualification being opened to girls; Gerhard, *Unerhört*, pp. 138–162.

5. Siegfried Rosenfeld, around 1930.

obtain a PhD in history. In Jena, she found a group of friends – clever, active women with lively minds – all a few years younger than her,[59] including Eva Schmidt, Hanna Schadendorf,[60] and Hertha Kraus; all were friendships that were to last a lifetime. Since 1917 it had also been obligatory for students to do voluntary work in support of the war effort.[61] In 1919 Else Behrend completed her doctoral research and was awarded a university prize for her thesis.[62] She was twenty-eight. Following her marriage to Siegfried Rosenfeld and a few years at home with her young family, she was then able to find the role in social work she had always dreamed of. Under the auspices of the Workers' Welfare organisation, Else started in 1926 to work on a voluntary basis at the women's prison in Barnimstrasse, the Königlich-Preußisches Weibergefängnis.

[59] Rosenfeld, *An Old Lady Remembers*, episode 2; and Kühn-Stillmark, Autorin, p. 140.

[60] Hanna Schadendorf was born 02.07.1896 and died 23.02.1987; she was married to the medical doctor Kurt Schadendorf; conversation with their daughter, Elke Minckwitz, 23.03.2011.

[61] Rosenfeld, *An Old Lady Remembers*, episode 3.

[62] Behrend, 'Politischen Ideen', the private archive of Hanna Cooper, 1964, reissue of Else's missing certificate.

6. Else Rosenfeld with her children Peter and Hanna, 1923.

The Rosenfelds and National Socialism

During the late 1920s Siegfried Rosenfeld was already proving a thorn in the side of the National Socialists. His dual function in the Prussian parliament and the Ministry of Justice made him a valued and valuable contact for many in the legal profession. In November 1932 the then fifty-eight-year-old was made to retire on the basis of a temporary injunction valid until 1 May 1933 as part of government austerity measures passed in the Depression to 'simplify and reduce administration costs' ('Verordnung zur Vereinfachung und Verbilligung der Verwaltung').[63] The Prussian Ministry of Justice resurfaces in the exiled Siegfried's diary entry of Christmas 1943, as he reminisces about the building in Wilhelmstrasse, later destroyed by bombing, and along with it, the

[63] Leo Baeck Institute, New York, Ernst Hamburger Collection AR 7034/MF 672, Box 7, Folder 23 Siegfried Rosenfeld 1932–77, copy of a document from the Prussian Ministry of Justice in which Siegfried Rosenfeld is dismissed, 11.11.1932. GStA PK Rep. 90a, Minutes of a Ministerial Meeting MF 1063, session with Reichskommissar von Papen on 27.10.1932, resulting in Rosenfeld's permanent retirement with effect from 01.05.1933. *Biographisches Handbuch der deutschsprachigen Emigration*, vol. I, pp. 614f.

orderly world of justice and tradition that he himself had been so much a part of.[64] When the Nazis came to power, Else was informed that as a 'non-Aryan', her services were now also surplus to requirements at the women's prison.[65]

QR Code 4: Reasons not to leave

In July 1933 the family travelled to Bavaria for a much needed holiday but stayed on. Like many other German Jews, the Rosenfelds had been hoping that the prevailing situation would not continue.[66] After all, there were so many reasons not to leave their country: Siegfried's age, his pension and the children. Their first stop, on what was to become a far longer journey, culminating in exile in England, was Schönau on Lake Königsee. As early as 1934, they were as Jews asked to leave the locality because it lay in Hitler's favourite district, the '*Führerbezirk*' Berchtesgaden. The family moved on to Bayerisch Gmain near Bad Reichenhall, but their landlady, Margarete Winterberg, turned out to be the most scheming of informants, and Siegfried Rosenfeld was arrested on a trumped-up charge.[67] An amnesty on account of the death of President Hindenburg led to the charge against him being dropped. For the next few years the family made their home at Icking, in the Isar Valley.

The Rosenfelds now lived in beautiful surroundings and were once again free to meet up with old friends and make new ones. Evil felt far away. Even so, the outlook felt a little bleaker with every new antisemitic law passed by the government. Gustel, Siegfried's daughter by his first wife, emigrated to Argentina in 1937 and married her childhood sweetheart, Heinz, who just happened to be Else's youngest brother. That same year, Else and Siegfried's other two children, Peter and Hanna, began at the Jewish agricultural training farm at Gross-Breesen, an establishment whose purpose was to provide skills specifically in order to emigrate.[68] In early spring 1939 the two youngsters were able to leave for England with the aid of the Quakers.

64 Siegfried's diary, Christmas 1943.

65 Rosenfeld, *An Old Lady Remembers*, episode 8.

66 Jünger, *Jahre der Ungewissheit.*

67 StAM Staatsanwaltschaften 7863, Special Court trial of Siegfried Rosenfeld, further detail in Else Rosenfeld's diary.

68 Angress, Auswandererlehrgut Groß Breesen, 168–187.

7. Icking in the Isartal, picture postcard, date unknown.

In 1938 the Night of Broken Glass was the turning point when escape became an absolute priority,[69] not only for the Rosenfelds but also for most German Jews still living in Germany.[70] The family had planned to emigrate to Argentina. Six of Else's siblings had already escaped and were settled there, as was Siegfried's daughter Gustel.[71] An increasing number of countries, however, were closing their borders to those suffering persecution. In the BBC radio programmes broadcast in 1963, Else spoke critically of this policy, commenting that America could have taken in every German Jew but didn't want to. Here is what she said:[72]

[69] Steinweis, *Kristallnacht*; for the situation in Munich, Heusler and Weger, *'Kristallnacht'*; Schrafstetter, *Flucht und Versteck*, pp. 28–31.

[70] Also Jünger, *Jahre der Ungewissheit*. Around three thousand Munich residents of Jewish background emigrated between 1933 and 1938, including many practising Jews. About seven hundred left for what they wrongly considered as safe havens in European countries, which, due to later German occupation, did not provide the escape expected. Those who fled to Eastern Europe met the same fate. A similar number were able to reach Palestine or the United States, but as refugees still faced years of difficulty. Up to 1942, a further four thousand Jews managed to escape to other countries.

[71] IFZ MA 1500/50, Rosenfeld, Fragebogen (Questionnaire).

[72] Rosenfeld, *An Old Lady Remembers*, episode 13. Else gave these interviews in English and they are reproduced here word for word. Her actual voice can be heard here by scanning the QR code 1.

8. Else and Siegfried Rosenfeld at Lake Starnberg (part of a larger photo), 1930s.

QR Code 5: Foreign countries and the persecution of Jews

> Even after November '38, when nearly all the people in the other countries realised what happened, the authorities in the other countries didn't help us a bit – in the contrary, there were lots and lots of new regulations which made it extremely difficult for most of us to get out. You know, America at that time could have taken us in all, all the Jews remaining in Germany, it wasn't such a vast number. It would have been a very easy thing to do that – they didn't want to.

In the end, and just a few days before war was declared, it was Siegfried who received a visa to travel to England. He did not want to go without Else, but she persuaded him to leave because he was in greater danger than her.

9. The ruined Ohel Jakob Synagogue in Herzog-Rudolf-Straße, 10 November 1938.

On 25 August 1939 he emigrated to England alone. On 1 September war broke out. Else's visa never came.

War

Following Siegfried's departure, Else found herself an occupation as a welfare worker in the Jewish Community Centre in Munich.[73] Her diary recounts that her role included accompanying children on a Kindertransport bound for England,[74] and she also looked after Jewish adults from Baden and the

[73] Behrend-Rosenfeld, Leben und Sterben, pp. 452–457.

[74] Among the extensive writings about the Kindertransport are: Fast, *Children's Exodus*; Fox and Abraham-Podietz, *Ten Thousand Children*; Watts, *Escape from Berlin*; Hammel, ed., *Kindertransport to Britain*; Baumel-Schwartz, *Never Look Back*.

Palatinate, all staying temporarily in Bavaria on the way.[75] When over 1,000 Jews were deported in February 1940 from Stettin to Poland,[76] she joined forces with Gertrud Luckner, a pacifist, and the Quaker Annemarie Cohen, and together they started the despatch of relief parcels.[77] The content of the letters they received from the ghetto in the small Polish town of Piaski was profoundly shocking, and she had them published after the war as *Lebenszeichen aus Piaski*, or *Signs of Life from Piaski*.[78]

When Else was still based in Icking, she and her friend Dr Tilla Kratz, a teacher, moved into a small house adjacent to the Rosenfeld family's previous home.[79] But then, in June 1941, Else was assigned to forced labour and sent to work at the flax-processing plant at Lohhof.[80]

The heavy physical work involved became too much for her because of her weak arm, so she was instead ordered to take on all aspects of housekeeping at the newly created transit camp for Jews at Berg am Laim[81] in Munich. It was officially called the 'Heimanlage für Juden', or 'residential facility for Jews', and was located at the convent of the Barmherzige Schwestern, the Sisters of Mercy, adjacent to St Michael's Church in Berg am Laim.[82]

Else stayed here until August 1942.[83] She had an extensive range of duties, bearing in mind that up to 350 people were living there at any one time.

QR Code 6: In the ghetto at Berg am Laim

Her previous experience in welfare work helped her to quickly get to grips with the role, and the nuns proved an enormous support to the Jews thus ghettoised in their very midst. Else was able to rely on great friends during

[75] The list of Jewish people deported to Gurs in France in October 1940; Bundesarchiv, ed., Gedenkbuch.

[76] Ibid.

[77] For information about Gertrud Luckner and Annemarie Cohen, see Glossary of Key People.

[78] See Rosenfeld and Luckner, eds., *Lebenszeichen aus Piaski*.

[79] For Tilla Kratz, see Glossary of Key People.

[80] Strnad, *Flachs für das Reich*.

[81] Strnad, *Zwischenstation 'Judensiedlung'*.

[82] Kasberger, 'Heimanlage für Juden Berg am Laim', pp. 341–380.

[83] Else Rosenfeld's diary describes this period in detail, so only the main events are reported here.

this period, including Dr Tilla Kratz and Dr Eva Schmidt, and not least Dr Magdalena Schwarz, the doctor allocated to the Jews interned at Berg am Laim,[84] and the Quaker Dr Annemarie Cohen. In November the first big deportation out of Munich took place. It was sent to Kaunas (Kovno) in Lithuania, taking eighty-five of Else's charges with it. It fell to Else to inform female residents of the deportation order when their names appeared on the list, and she would also help them prepare for departure. At Easter 1942 her own name appeared on the list for deportation.[85] It was only the urgent intervention of the Jewish Community Centre that got her name removed at the eleventh hour, and she went back to Berg am Laim in the short term.

Life in Exile

Siegfried Rosenfeld stayed first in London at the home of a relative,[86] but then found somewhere in Oxford that happened to be near his son, Peter, who was working on a farm an hour or so distant. Hanna, meanwhile, was working as a live-in domestic help in the home of the Bligh family in Reading. Siegfried's early diary entries all centre around this period in his life. On 11 July 1940 Siegfried Rosenfeld was interned as an 'enemy alien' and found himself in the camp at Douglas on the Isle of Man.[87] Peter came to join him shortly thereafter. On 28 September, and after the strangest of times, Siegfried was released from the constricting life of the internment camp, but then lost the stimulating world of discussion, debate and learning he had enjoyed there. The many German intellectuals who found themselves in internment had rendered the oppressive nature of camp life that much more bearable through whole series of organised concerts, lectures and exhibitions.

In September 1940 Siegfried took new lodgings in Oxford and kept himself busy through his own research among the city's well-stocked libraries. He was preparing a paper on the history of Jews in Europe, probably with the intention of securing a grant from one of the academic

[84] For Magdalena Schwarz, see Glossary of Key People.

[85] For more about the deportations out of Munich: Schrafstetter, *Flucht und Versteck*, pp. 44–56.

[86] Rosenfeld, *An Old Lady Remembers*, episode 14; Rudolf Cohen's card index for Siegfried Rosenfeld, with thanks to Rudolf Cohen Jr. See also Zahn, *Annemarie and Rudolf Cohen*, p. 19; Holl, ed., Stille Helfer. Interview with Hanna Cooper, Birmingham, England, September 2010.

[87] Dates in accordance with the diary. For more regarding internment on the Isle of Man, see Chappell, *Island of Barbed Wire*, particularly pp. 45–58; Seyfert, 'His Majesty's Most Loyal Internees', pp. 164–167, 173–177.

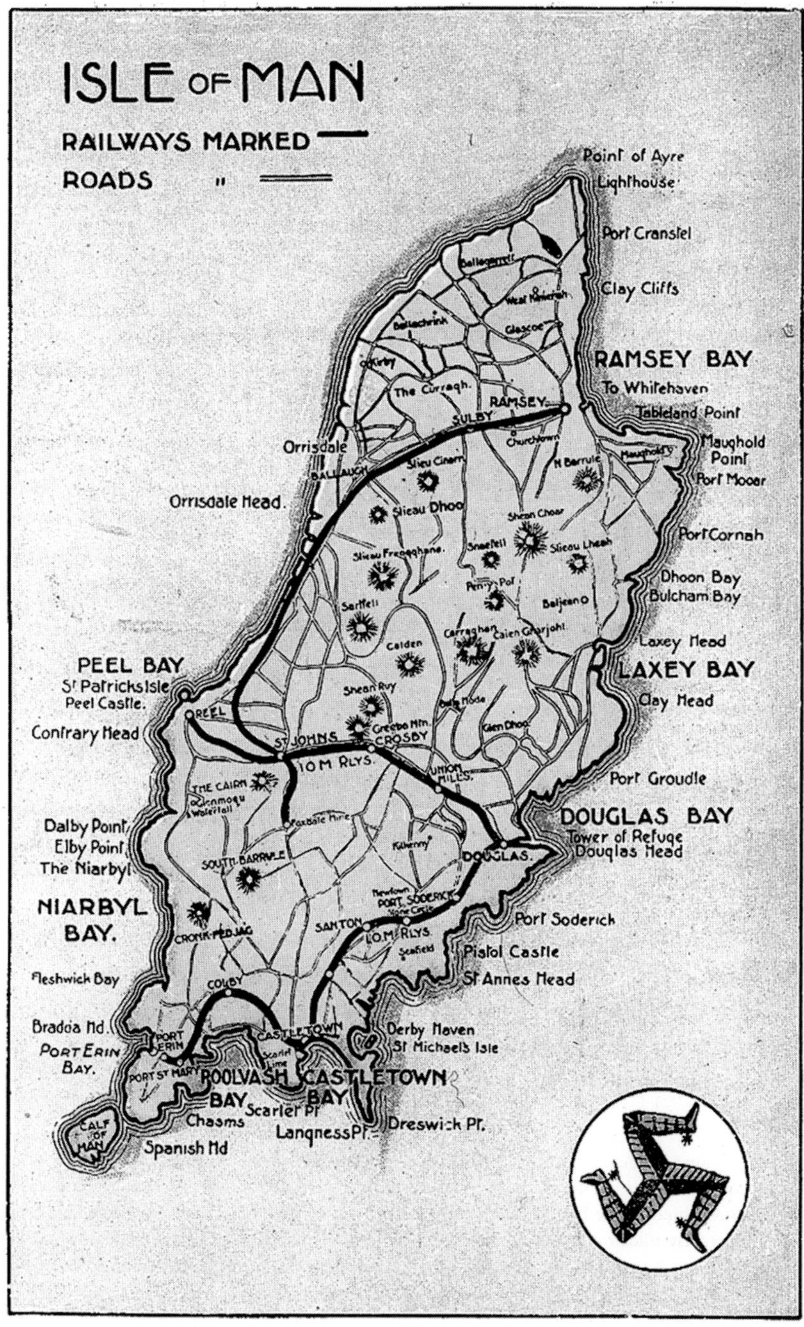

10. The Douglas Internment camp was on the eastern side of the Isle of Man. Colour postcard.

organisations in the United States, but his application was unsuccessful. And as a German alien, he was not permitted to take up any employment that could otherwise be done by a native. This meant he was forced to rely on his children for financial help. Siegfried's one and only concern at this time was to get hold of all the documents required for his family to travel to Argentina and take up residence there, or alternatively, at least to get to Cuba or Santo Domingo.[88] These were the last remaining hopes for saving Else from her existence in Germany. But in the end, they all failed. Siegfried tormented himself more and more with survivor guilt,[89] where typically the sufferer is filled with self-reproach at finding himself in a favourable position while his partner remains in severe danger. This was the period of the first deportations of Jews out of Munich. He wrote in his diary:

> Else's letter dated 31 October leaves me in no doubt that she's going to have to stay in Germany right through to the bitter end. Fate could not be more cruel to us. . . . And yet here am I, in the warmth of my room, working in freedom among people who live their lives without being treated like slaves. I take no pleasure at all in finding myself so much better off than my darling wife. How did it ever come to this? I accept all the blame. I was too slow in planning our own departure once the children had left. I don't know why I didn't do it straight away. The guilt will never leave me.[90]

'*The dream of Cuba has vanished*,' Else wrote for her own part. 'The grief behind those words. Nothing can console me. Whichever way I turn, I come up against the insurmountable.' Siegfried's anxiety for Else left him with a chronic stomach complaint brought on by his poor mental health.

Siegfried eventually found somewhere else to live and moved to an attic room in Oxford.[91] He became actively involved with the Federal Union, an organisation advocating a federal world state.[92] This gave him occasional

[88] Emigration to Argentina was made possible where relatives were already resident in the country and had called for the family to join them; Spitta, Argentinien, p. 145. So far as Cuba went, Siegfried's niece in the United States, Hertha Kraus, who was a Quaker, had managed to obtain the necessary transit visa, but no one could come up with the 1,800 dollars required for entry. See Siegfried Rosenfeld's diary 29.09. and 18.11.1941. For information on the settlements in the Dominican Republic, and on Latin America in general, Mühlen, Lateinamerika, pp. 299f.

[89] For more about survivor syndrome: Bergmann, Jucovy and Kestenberg, eds., *Kinder der Opfer.*

[90] Siegfried's diary, Oxford, 01.12.1941.

[91] Letter from Siegfried Rosenfeld to Hanna, 22.09.1941.

[92] Bosco, *Federal Union.*

contact with exiled SPD members in London and with the Association of Jewish Refugees (AJR), the leading Jewish exile organisation in Great Britain.[93] Like most other people in his position, he reflected a great deal on being German with a strong attachment to the fatherland, and yet also feeling like an outcast with no home country. For those German migrants who had been persecuted for their Jewishness, this was the most painful wrench of all.

In the end, Siegfried could only find work as a junior bookkeeper for a milk delivery firm.[94] Here he was at seventy years old, once a highly regarded German lawyer and politician, entering details of the delivery men's tokens in the main ledger and then totting it all up, a task that was deadly dull but still demanded a high degree of concentration. But always in his mind was Else, as he wondered what was happening to her. He learned months after the event, and even then only from coded letters, that she had gone underground in August 1942. After one year and seven months in the job, he was dismissed because there were others who could do the same work for a lower wage.

Siegfried's frugal existence, the laborious nature of his work, and his eventual physical and psychological collapse demonstrate that living in exile is a far cry from any kind of way out. The few exiles of substantial means, such as Thomas Mann's family, tend to detract from all those who never managed to rebuild an existence to any adequate level.[95] 'He wasn't ever a practical chap.' His wife made this remark of him years later during the BBC interviews, explaining that she had always taken care of the more mundane aspects of their daily life.[96] Once in exile, he had to fall back on his own resources and was quite alone in every respect.[97] Exile may mean one life saved, but only for the lowest of existences.

Living Underground

In mid August 1942 Else Rosenfeld took the decision, reluctantly at first, to live a life in hiding and go underground in Berlin.[98] She was able to live with

[93] Grenville, Association of Jewish Refugees, pp. 89–112. [94] Siegfried's diary, 29.06.1942.

[95] Documented in detail in for example Krohn and Mühlen., eds., *Handbuch der deutschsprachigen Emigration.*

[96] Rosenfeld, *An Old Lady Remembers*, episode 14.

[97] Interview with Hanna Cooper, Birmingham, England, September 2010.

[98] Else's diary, 18.08.1942. For the Jews in hiding in Berlin, Lutjens, *Submerged on the Surface*, pp. 211f.

her sister, Eva Fischer and her non-Jewish husband Georg,[99] and did so until 8 December 1942, by which time her brother-in-law had become quite unable to go on living with the constant fear of discovery.[100]

QR Code 7: Life underground

So she had to leave and, with the help of old friends, found accommodation in the home of entrepreneur Hans Kollmorgen, who ran his own company manufacturing optical instruments. This man was one of the 'silent heroes' of this era.[101] He took her in without having ever met her. In the BBC interviews, she said she had pointed out to him the risk he was taking.[102] She relates how he reacted. 'He laughed and said: Oh, I know quite well, I don't mind all the risks, I take them on gladly. You know, I am an old man – he was sixty-seven – and I think the best thing I can do is just to help as much as possible and take the risks when they come.'[103]

Kollmorgen had been in a position to build up a good stock of food and could provide for Else. As the air raids over Berlin intensified, it remained out of the question for Else or any other Jew living underground to take cover in an air-raid shelter. But air-raid protection wardens nonetheless carried out regular checks, including of people's private homes. Here again, an extract from Else's BBC interviews tells us more.[104] 'I always during the air raids stayed under the big couch hidden and I always waited for the warden to look under the couch with his torch, but he never did. But we couldn't know, how long that would go on.'

[99] In her diary and even in the BBC interviews of 1963 she used the names cousin Erna and her husband Gustav to protect them.

[100] BayHStA LEA 1674 BEG 31409, Rosenfeld, Elisabeth, *Bestätigungsschreiben von Tilla Kratz im Rahmen des Wiedergutmachungsverfahren vom 28.12.1955* and letter from Else Rosenfelds, 21.12.1955.

[101] Wette, ed., *Stille Helden*; Kosmala, Stille Helden, 29–34. See also information available through the Silent Heroes Memorial Center, Berlin.

[102] Rosenfeld, *An Old Lady Remembers*, episode 19; and reports following.

[103] Kollmorgen reportedly said the same thing to Lotte Bamberg; Bamberg, Erinnerung, 804.

[104] Rosenfeld, *An Old Lady Remembers*, episode 19.

QR Code 8: Life underground in the air war

Else remained at Hans Kollmorgen's until 15 March 1943, during which time he also sheltered four other Jewish people, among them Dr Lotte Bamberg.[105] Else then moved to the home of Magdalena Heilmann, widow of Ernst Heilmann, former leader of the SPD party in the Prussian parliament, and she stayed there until 20 May 1943. After that, she was brave enough to travel on false papers to Freiburg and the home of Lotte and Edmund Goldschagg,[106] where she remained until 20 April 1944, after which date, with the support of Luise Meier's escape network, she was at last able to flee.[107] When Else later had to correspond with the post-war authority for Bavaria handling compensation and redress, the Bayerische Landesentschädigungsamt,[108] she wrote: 'If I had ever had any idea that it would be 20 April 1944 before I would escape, and then only by a hair's breadth on such a precarious route, and that I would have to live the whole time before that underground, there is no doubt that I would instead have chosen certain death.'

Rescue and Beyond

On 21 April 1944 the Swiss border guard at Hofen reported 'the capture of a Jewish woman':[109]

> On yesterday's watch, between 20.00 hours and 24.00 hours, the following incident occurred at 21.55. At 21.50 I noticed how the German guard was using his flashlight, carefully shining it around the area to the west of the Customs House. Convinced the man had noticed something suspicious, I just stayed completely quiet and looked in the direction of

[105] Bamberg, Erinnerung, 804. [106] For Edmund Goldschagg, see Glossary of Key People.

[107] Battel, '*Wo es hell ist*'; Schoppmann, 'Fortgesetzte Beihilfe', pp. 163–178.

[108] BayHStA LEA 1674 BEG 31409, Rosenfeld, Elsbeth 20.10.1956.

[109] BAB E 4264–1985/196 vol. 1902, Dossier 22262, Rosenfeld-Behrend Elsbeth. Swiss Border Guard, Customs District II. Head of Post Kpl. Lingried, Matr. 237, Hofen 21.04.1944, 'Aufgreifen einer Jüdin'.

11. Lotte Goldschagg in Gräfelfing, near Munich; she worked at Dornier in Neuaubing, 1940.

> Kreuzhalde. Just then I heard a cry and the sound of someone apparently falling, all from behind our Customs House. I proceeded to the spot and found an elderly lady on the ground, where she had landed after taking a tumble from our surrounding wall.

Else Rosenfeld was lucky. The Swiss did not do what they had previously done with refugees coming in from Germany, namely send them back. Instead they arranged for her to go to hospital at Schaffhausen, where she stayed for two months and was nursed back to relative health and strength.[110] Then in August 1944 she was admitted to a small Swiss internment camp with forty or so other refugees, all older people in need of care and with hardly any Germans among them. She was eventually released for 'private internment' in the home of a rector she was already acquainted

[110] BAB E 4264–1985/196 vol. 1902, Dossier 22262, Rosenfeld-Behrend Elsbeth, *Polizeiabteilung des Eidgenössische Justiz- und Polizeidepartements*, 05.08.1944.

12. Edmund Goldschagg out walking in Freiburg with his ten-year-old son, Rolf, 1940.

with.[111] His parish was the village of Feldis in the Grisons, and at 1,500 metres' altitude, a good place for Else to continue convalescing after what she had been through.

When Siegfried learned that Else had escaped safely to Switzerland, the main source of his anxiety was removed, but within just a few short months his own health broke down. From September 1944 he was cared for in a Quaker home for the elderly, and during this period provided the English authorities with a number of draft papers on the German judiciary.[112] And at last he now had a regular correspondence with Else.

Else was very taken up with trying to understand why she herself had been saved. This made her feel she had a responsibility to tell others what she had experienced and so, with the help of a young woman in Zurich, she got in touch with a publisher, the Büchergilde Gutenberg, and by

[111] Ibid. [112] Siegfried's diary, 12.11. and 30.12.1944.

August 1945 had received a book contract and an advance.[113] Her diary was published in November. She also found a job with an organisation looking after political refugees in Europe. It was 3 March 1946 before she was at last allowed to leave for England. She landed at Croydon Aerodrome, where she was reunited with her husband and their two children. As she told the BBC:

> And I could leave Switzerland on the 3rd of March '46, which was very early. The funny thing was, to get the French visa would take so long that the British visa already was not valid any more, so there was only the one thing: to fly. And it was a peculiar thing to get from Zurich to London in three hours' time ... My husband and my two children met me on the airport of Croydon and that was a moment I shall never forget in my life. I think this made up for a lot of worries and difficulties before that.[114]

QR Code 9: Arrival in England, 1946

Else began a new life in England. Her husband was still very ill and she was fearful she had returned only to see him die, but he made a good recovery. They lived together in London. She herself had taken on the official task of gathering the experiences of German prisoners of war, and this meant her travelling widely in England, Scotland and Wales. Her daughter, Hanna Cooper, recalls:

> The Foreign Office made sure my mother always had a first-class ticket and she would get on the train and sit down. Then, if the ticket inspector came along and said to her 'Madam, this is first class,' my mother, always very quick-witted in German and now seemingly the same in English, answered back, 'Yes, I know, I may not look like first class, but I happen to have a first-class ticket.'

[113] Private archive of Hanna Cooper, the original contract.
[114] Rosenfeld, *An Old Lady Remembers*, episode 22.

13. Else and Siegfried Rosenfeld in Kew Gardens, 1946. Photo: Rose Nicolaier.

Siegfried took an active interest in her work, and both treated each new day together as a day of good fortune. He was involved in correspondence with his SPD colleagues Erich Ollenhauer and Willi Eichler on the matter of future voting rights in Germany.[115] The democratic future of Germany was still a subject very close to his heart. After the war, he remained in contact with senior political figures who had decided to go back to Germany, while Else joined the welfare committee supporting SPD followers in exile and became its treasurer.[116] His letters to Erich Ollenhauer and Wolfgang Heine certainly allow us to speculate as to Siegfried's likely involvement in the rebuilding of Germany had he lived longer. But the years of anguish, when he had no gainful employment and was torn apart by the constant anxiety,

115 Archiv der Sozialen Demokratie der Friedrich-Ebert-Stiftung (hereafter ASD), SPD Party Executive, Chair Kurt Schuhmacher, File 68, letter from Rosenfeld to Erich Ollenhauer, 16.06.46, and from Ollenhauer to Rosenfeld, 17.06.46; ASD from the estate of Willi Eichler, File 90, letter from Rosenfeld to Eichler, 13.05.47, and from Eichler to Rosenfeld, 10.06.47.

116 At the 1947 AGM of the Association of German Social Democrats in Great Britain, Else Rosenfeld was elected treasurer to the London Workers' Welfare Committee; reported and issued by the London Representative of the German Social Democratic Party, No. 96/97 (1947), p. 18.

had taken a permanent toll.[117] Rosenfeld the Prussian politician had not become Rosenfeld the Englishman, although he had mentally distanced himself from Germany. 'I have no proper home and cannot envisage ever finding one. At times my life feels quite futile.' This is part of his diary entry at Christmas 1942.[118] Siegfried Rosenfeld died in December 1947, broken by exile.[119]

Else began to receive funds once more from her husband's pension and, after a lengthy process, a lump sum as compensation. The rebuilding of Germany progressed and Else was still German at heart, so she used some of the money to build herself a little home in Icking. From then on, she spent half the year in Icking and the other half in England with her children. England became her second home, while for the next generation, and indeed the generation after that, it was and still is the primary residence.

To keep herself busy and useful, Else took on voluntary welfare work in a women's prison in Upper Bavaria. As she grew older, she found it hard to accept she had to be less active, something she told the BBC in 1963.[120] Else Rosenfeld died in Birmingham in 1970 at the age of seventy-eight.

Outcomes

An overview of sources related to the Rosenfeld family story paves the way for new findings when looked at in conjunction with current research and the documentation of memories. A special feature of this family's history is the way it throws into stark relief the distinction between those with an outside perception and those with an equally strong, but inside, perception, the exiled having a particular view of Germany, the persecuted a particular view of the Germans.[121] Siegfried Rosenfeld saw Germany as seriously culpable for its conduct of the war, its persecution of the Jews and a

[117] Krauss, *Heimkehr in ein fremdes Land*, pp. 30–49; about exile in Great Britain, Brinson et al., eds., *'England'*; Ritchie, *Exile in Great Britain*, pp. 9–20, and Paucker, Speaking English, pp. 21–32; Ritchie, *German-speaking Exiles*, touching for its everyday perspective on their lives; Malet and Grenville, *Changing Countries*.

[118] Siegfried's diary, Christmas 1942.

[119] *Sozialistische Mitteilungen*, 106, December 1947: 'On 6 December in Room 1 at Broadhurst Gardens, there was a large gathering of members and friends of the Association in honour of guests from Germany. The occasion was led by Gen. W. Sander, who opened with a eulogy to our recently deceased colleague, Siegfried Rosenfeld, who had suddenly passed away at the age of 73 following a heart attack. Prior to his emigration to England, he had been a member of the Prussian state parliament and held high ministerial office in Berlin.'

[120] Rosenfeld, *An Old Lady Remembers*, episode 23.

[121] For further reading on this phenomenon, Krauss, *Heimkehr in ein fremdes Land*, pp. 42–61.

perceived absence of resistance within, and it was not only for personal reasons that he longed for an end to the war and the defeat of Hitler. He believed the comprehensive re-education of Germany to be essential. By contrast, Else focuses more on the aid and support she received from many Germans during her own persecution as a Jewish woman, and herself viewed the Hitler regime more as a kind of alien domination over 'ordinary' Germans. This is how she explained her thoughts to the BBC:

> There was a sort of organisation which stood up against Nazi injustice . . . It was formed by ordinary people, I think, belonging to all political parties. They only in small circles could come together. What they did, and all they could do in that time, I think, was to help people like ourselves, and a surprising number of German people did that.[122]

A defining element in the lives of both husband and wife was having the time and the opportunity to be active. In exile, Siegfried was condemned to a life of passivity from the very start. He was not allowed to work and had to scratch around for money if he wanted to go from Oxford to London to meet up with other politically engaged exiles.[123] And he felt helpless, having to stand by and watch the borders close in on Else. In marked contrast, she was busily occupied until summer 1942 at the transit camp, working to help others, and seeing this as the useful, fulfilling work it clearly was, strengthened her own feelings of self-worth and gave her some distance from the danger she herself was in. She was no victim; instead of surrendering herself to the situation, she was proactive and drew on all her personal resources.

QR Code 10: Courage

When she first went underground in Berlin, like others living in hiding she had to endure the long and demoralising waiting game and did so in constant

[122] Rosenfeld, *An Old Lady Remembers*, episode 9. [123] Siegfried's diary, 18.03.1942.

danger of being found out and having to face the consequences.[124] This in particular affected her psychologically, and she suffered a period of severe depression.[125] But while living in the homes of Hans Kollmorgen, Lene Heilmann and then the Goldschaggs in Freiburg, she actively took on tasks that helped her get back on her feet. With her eventual escape to Switzerland, her life changed fundamentally, and she managed to find a job again in a relief organisation. With her work, the friends who supported her and the people who helped her, she rarely felt alone, while Siegfried had found few friends in England. In her BBC broadcast, Else described this period in their lives as to some extent having been easier for herself than for him.[126]

Another personal characteristic of Else's made possible her survival in Nazi Germany, and that was her willingness to trust others and readiness to expect help and to receive it. Those she describes came from a variety of backgrounds and gave her assistance while placing themselves at serious risk. She had actually wanted to call her book *About the Other Germany*,[127] but Siegfried felt this to be a somewhat exaggerated and subjective viewpoint.[128] A review of the experiences of other Jews who went underground, along with research into the 'silent heroes', whether as helpers or rescuers, does, however, confirm that many individuals were ready to lend practical aid and support,[129] and that those who survived life underground were indeed able to find a succession of helping hands, even amongst people previously unknown to them.[130]

Else also needed a vision and some personal maxim that would provide strength and a plan when under threat. To this end, Margot Friedländer had chosen her mother's parting words: 'Try and make your own life.'[131] She also took this as the title for her memoirs. For many younger women who survived life underground, it was their profound and natural longing to live that carried them through the horror and demands of the times. In Else Rosenfeld's case, it was her heartfelt wish to be reunited with her husband and children that kept her going. But even she fell into despondency before going underground. In this dark hour, she was spurred on by the blessing she received from Sister Theodora at Berg am Laim:

> 'I don't know what will happen, when or whether we'll ever meet again, but please always remember that our thoughts and prayers

124 Examples are Jalowicz-Simon, *Underground*, p. 119; Friedländer and Schwerdtfeger, *'Versuche, dein Leben zu machen'*, p. 121.

125 Else's diary, 17.11.1942.

126 Rosenfeld, *An Old Lady Remembers*, episode 23.

127 Siegfried's diary, 10.12.1945.

128 Ibid.

129 Lutjens, *Submerged on the Surface*; Wette, ed., *Stille Helden*; Schrafstetter, *Flucht und Versteck*.

130 Jalowicz-Simon, *Underground* makes this particularly clear.

131 Friedländer and Schwerdtfeger, *'Versuche dein Leben zu machen'*.

> are with you wherever you may be. We know what difficult times you have gone through and can't see what lies ahead, but feel confident that your circumstances will change for the better.' One thing I did know for sure: her words gave me strength, banished my fear and apprehension, and suddenly I regained my old energy, along with the courage to take the risk![132]

At critical moments like this, Else felt a powerful sense of certainty that everything was going to be all right, which gave her confidence and boosted her inner strength. Later she said that she no longer feared for herself but for the people who helped her and risked so much in doing so.

There has of late been great interest in the networks that helped people survive.[133] Part of the discussion has always been an interest in the type of personality demonstrated by adherents of such networks. One can no longer assume that there is an 'altruistic personality' that qualified someone to be a rescuer, as the experiences of those in hiding put an emphasis on 'the importance of being asked'.[134] People became rescuers in many different ways and with very different motivations, often simply because someone was desperate and asked for help. Alongside individuals who acted independently and were not affiliated with any particular group, there were also well organised and more complex webs of contacts. Examples include Franz Kaufmann and his associates in Berlin, who were close to the Bekennende Kirche, the Protestant church movement so critical of the Nazis. Karl Deibel and his colleagues in Berlin arose initially from the anarchist–communist resistance movement.[135] In Essen, there was the *Bund*, or Union for a Socialist Life, to which Marianne Strauss owed her survival. This group even had a youth wing, all of them centred around the philosopher and educationalist Artur Jacobs and his Jewish wife Dore, a teacher of movement and dance. Their ethics were greatly at odds with Nazi ideology.[136] Another circle, known as Onkel Emil, was more of a band of like-minded close friends who were all hostile to National Socialism but otherwise held a range of political beliefs.[137]

The Quakers were central to Else's own survival networks. Annemarie and Rudolf Cohen organised Siegfried's departure from Germany and remained a loyal support to Else, while Gertrud Luckner arranged the help for Piaski together with Else, and Hella Gorn, from Berlin, was at Else's side

132 Else's diary, 18.08.1942.

133 Düring, *Verdeckte soziale Netzwerke* summarises the research.

134 Varese and Yaish, 'Importance of Being Asked', 307–334.

135 Düring, *Verdeckte soziale Netzwerke*, pp. 74–90, 118–150.

136 Roseman, *Past in Hiding*; Roseman, Surviving Undetected, pp. 465–480; Reichling, Mit Kant gegen die Nazis, pp. 59–63.

137 Düring, *Verdeckte soziale Netzwerke*, pp. 103–117.

for her escape into Switzerland and accompanied her almost to the border itself. She too was a Quaker,[138] as was Siegfried Rosenfeld's niece, Hertha Kraus,[139] who tried hard to secure migration visas for Else and Siegfried as well as conveying their letters and providing contacts. These people were no exception to their faith. The international Quaker community as a whole stood up for persecuted Jews[140] and played a central role in the British government's decision, after the pogrom of 1938, to take in 10,000 Jewish children on the Kindertransport.[141]

QR Code 11: Kindertransport

Another network that became a lifeline for Else was that of an old Social Democrat family, the Heilmanns. Ernst Heilmann, murdered at Buchenwald, had been head of the SPD within the Prussian state parliament.[142] His family in Berlin hid Else for some time, and their son Peter Heilmann and his girlfriend Hella Gorn together obtained a false identity document for Else and established contact with the escape network around Luise Meier.[143] Once in Freiburg, Else lived at the home of Edmund Goldschagg and his family. Prior to 1933 he had worked as a Social Democrat journalist in Munich, then in 1945 became a co-licensee of the *Süddeutsche Zeitung*. Among Social Democrats there was huge potential for resistance work and a readiness to operate at high personal risk. This corresponds with the experience of others in hiding, such as Marianne

138 Zahn, *Annemarie and Rudolf Cohen*; Wollasch, Hilfe für Verfolgte, on Gertrud Luckner, pp. 67–86. On Hella Gorn there is also Strauss, *Over the Green Hill.*

139 Schirrmacher, *Hertha Kraus.*

140 Wriggins, *Picking up the Pieces*; Palmer, *Humanitarian Relief*; Schmitt, *Quakers and Nazis*; Taylor, Missing Chapter; Radcliffe, Bishop Bell, 277–286; Genizi, American Interfaith Cooperation, 347–361.

141 Further reading on the Kindertransport, Oldfield, 'It Is usually She', 57–70; Fox and Abraham-Podietz, *Ten Thousand Children*; Holtman, 'Covert from the Tempest', 107–126; Schmitt, Quaker Efforts; Kieval, Legality and Resistance, 339–366; Watts, *Escape from Berlin*; Hammel, ed., *Kindertransport to Britain*; Association of Jewish Refugees in Great Britain: Refugee Voices.

142 Schröder, Biographien sozialdemokratischer Parlamentarier, Heilmann, Ernst; Heilmann, like Rosenfeld, had been a city councillor in Berlin-Charlottenburg in 1919–1920.

143 Schoppmann, 'Fortgesetzte Beihilfe'; Düring, *Verdeckte soziale Netzwerke*, pp. 90–103.

Strauss and Marie Jalowicz-Simon, who also obtained help from those putting up resistance to whatever degree, often people from leftist factions.[144]

A further group of rescuers, and perhaps the most important, comprised friends and relatives who gave shelter and investigated possible escape routes, passed on letters and messages, and helped identify new lodgings. It was with the help of long-standing women friends in particular that Else came to hide at the home of Hans Kollmorgen. Else's diary describes a network of female postgraduate friends and supporters. At the time, it was very unusual to find a woman who had had the opportunity to study to doctorate level, but there were many highly educated women supporting Else: Dr Eva Schmidt, Dr Hanna Schadendorf and Dr Hertha Kraus, Dr Tilla Kratz and the female medical doctors, Drs Annemarie Cohen and Magdalena Schwarz.[145] Each one of these women helped Dr Else Rosenfeld, often placing themselves at serious risk. Clearly there was a strong sense of solidarity among these clever, well-qualified women to support one of their own when she was in need, so strong that it outweighed the fear of being caught. Not one of these women was in agreement with the NS regime. They were quite the antithesis of the women doing the groundwork for the Nazis.[146]

There are also statements in Else Rosenfeld's diaries and BBC interviews that may help determine when German Jews first started to have a more accurate understanding of the Holocaust.[147] Until July 1942, Else still believed that deportees were destined for inhumane conditions but that they would live. She had a few doubts and fears but hope remained strong. Beyond July 1942, she knew that every deportation ended in death, as she describes to the BBC.

> When I was alone in charge of our ghetto, very soon every week a deportation came and I had to tell the people they had to leave. It was a terrible thing and, you know, I couldn't stand this strain of sending people to their death, which, I have to tell you, I didn't quite realise before the last six weeks. Before that I knew that I would sent

144 Roseman, *Past in Hiding*; Jalowicz-Simon, *Underground.*

145 For Magdalena Schwarz, see Glossary of Key People.

146 Krauss, ed., *Sie waren dabei*; Kompisch, ed., *Täterinnen.*

147 The debate about how much those impacted knew, and about how much the Germans knew about the Shoah is as intense as it ever was. Refer to Longerich, '*Davon haben wir nichts gewusst!*'. Löw emphasises the importance of the Behrend-Rosenfeld writings on this issue in Deutsche Geschichte(n), p. 7. See also Benz, ed., *Juden in Deutschland*; Kosmala, Zwischen Ahnen und Wissen, pp. 135–159; Kaplan, *Mut zum Überleben.* Kaplan had not read Else Rosenfeld's account, makes only one reference to it (p. 377, note 58, 'quoted from'), and on pp. 223f. refers only to the 'barracks at Berg am Laim'. From her personal sources she reaches very different conclusions from Else Rosenfeld in her own detailed account.

> them to an extremely difficult, primitive life, deprived of all necessities which make live a bit easier, of all things which make life pleasant. Nothing of that they would find in Poland or even in Theresienstadt. But I didn't know, except for the last six weeks, that I sent them directly to their death. I couldn't get insensitive to that, it was impossible. It harassed me through nights and days and exhausted me and made my health go. I couldn't forget what happened to them. I saw them all going to the gas chambers, and I had friends amongst them, very near friends. You can't forget this sort of thing – I can't forget it even now. They still appear in my dreams; they still appear in nightmares.[148]

QR Code 12: Deportation

When help was no longer a practical possibility, she changed her mind. Now was the time to go underground.

The Book's Reception and Thereafter

The family history of the Rosenfelds is but one dimension of this story. Else's fate, her diary entries, her talks for prisoners of war and her lectures have reached many people. They have led to further research, the creation of a memorial at Berg am Laim, and the compilation of this volume.

Else Rosenfeld had managed to complete the book version of her diary entries by the middle of 1945, by which time she was living in Feldis in Switzerland. It was published by the Büchergilde Gutenberg in Zurich under the title *Verfemt und Verfolgt: Erlebnisse einer Jüdin in Nazi-Deutschland*. Within a few short months the first print run of 7,000 copies was sold out. The publisher wrote to her on 28 December 1945: 'As soon as we have enough paper back in stock, we shall do another print run and probably of 5,000 copies . . . The refined and objective style in your work, even when depicting such misery, has contributed to the book's

[148] Rosenfeld, *An Old Lady Remembers*, episode 18.

success. We shall be making every effort with foreign publishing houses and will recommend the book for translation.'[149]

Just a year and a half after her escape to Switzerland, after illness and internment, Else Rosenfeld had found success with her book. Plans to have it translated into Hebrew and English and make it known internationally did not come to fruition, but it was to find rapid dissemination throughout a German-language readership. Siegfried Rosenfeld stepped in at this point from England, corresponding with Dr Leo Baerwald, the former chief rabbi of the Jewish community in Munich, to ask for his support. Baerwald wrote back from New York:

> When I left Germany in September 1945, bookshops in the German cities now in the American zone were supposed to be reopening, and this meant Frankfurt, Heidelberg, Munich, Nuremberg and hundreds of other places, big and small. Books of this kind must now be brought out of Switzerland through the recognised channels and made available on the German book market. Centres such as New York offer a further outlet for sales, even for the original German language edition.[150]

Else Rosenfeld's book was widely and thoroughly reviewed by the Swiss press.[151] The critics gave it a unanimously positive response and were in full agreement on its essential features. They liked Else's objective and yet engaging style of writing, immersing the reader 'in her wholly unpolitical presentation and sober honesty' (Maccabi, 28 June 1946). Another piece judged it 'a truly documentary book' (*Die Frau*, Aarau, February 1946).[152] 'This is a simple account, an objective and unsentimental report, filed separately from the brutal everyday life of Jews in Germany. The writer does not impose an opinion on us and does not try to appeal to our sense of sympathy, "only" painting the picture of her private fate' (*Die Weltwoche*, Zurich, 10 May 1946). The critics were also as one in their observation that here was a writer who, unlike many others at the time, was not making a conscious condemnation but had another and very different message. 'This is much more a thank you to everyone who helped than any indictment of those who carried out the persecution'

149 Hanna Cooper, private archive, letter from the Büchergilde Gutenberg to Else Rosenfeld, 28.12.1945.

150 Hanna Cooper, private archive, letter from Leo Baerwald to Siegfried Rosenfeld, 03.01.1946, from New York.

151 On its reception in Germany, Peitsch, *'Deutschlands Gedächtnis'*, pp. 165–177.

152 These book reviews are from Hanna Cooper's private archive.

(*Neues Winterthurer Tagblatt*, 5 June 1946). The picture that Else paints of the people in a country fresh from defeat offers a change of perspective. Almost every review refers to the people who helped – the nuns, the friends, the courageous hosts who offered shelter to all those living underground. 'We can at least gain some hope from the fact that so many Germans showed the self-sacrifice needed to come to the aid of these desperate people, and in doing so, put themselves at serious risk' (*Monatsschrift der Büchergilde*, issue 12, December 1945). The diaries' message captured the imagination, calling into question the vigorously debated post-war theory of the German populace sharing a 'collective guilt'. The book also demonstrates how running serious personal risk and helping those in need requires a person of exceptional qualities. 'A highly educated woman imbued with an unshakeable sense of social duty, capable of self-sacrifice for her fellow creatures, pours every ounce of strength into the fight for others' (*Basler National-Zeitung*, 7 July 1946).

A letter from Rabbi Leo Baerwald to Siegfried Rosenfeld demonstrates how deeply the book touches the reader. Baerwald had had to endure at first hand years of persecution in Munich.

> My wife and I found ourselves in a state of tension as we read the book and were both increasingly moved by its content. This account of those dark years is more raw and haunting than any expert report or novel could ever be. The deep-rooted cunning of the system, and of those who devised and served it, is alive on every page of the book, all the more so given our own familiarity with every part of Munich. We trembled as we read of the gruesome role the city itself played in all those personal destinies, of the good and the evil, of all those well-known faces and features, of our brave friends and the conduct of so many decent ordinary Germans and Christians. Your wife has earned the gratitude and admiration of us all for her extreme courage and for this account, so powerful in its simplicity.[153]

Else Rosenfeld's diaries appeared in two further editions with the Hamburg-based publisher Europäische Verlagsanstalt in 1949 and 1963, and then again in 1988, but this time with the Munich publisher C. H. Beck, at the instigation of Peter Rosenfeld and Hanna Cooper.

[153] Hanna Cooper's private archive, letter from Leo Baerwald to Siegfried Rosenfeld, 03.01.1946, from New York.

This edition emerged from the 1985 school project led by a history teacher, Erich Kasberger, and his students at the Michaeli-Gymnasium, a Munich grammar school in Berg am Laim.[154] The school is located very close to the site of the Jewish transit camp at Berg am Laim, and Erich Kasberger was able to 'rediscover' it together with his students, developing his find into a school history project of a type which was at the time quite exceptional. The outcome of their dedicated work offered an engrossing collection of documentation as well as a public reading, something which stimulated wide discussion in the locality. This was met with both approval and with anonymous letters of a threatening nature, but it was also awarded a prize in the Munich History competition, an initiative started by the city itself for further research into its own past. In partnership with the district council, a proposal was developed for the placing of a memorial at the convent of the Barmherzige Schwestern (Sisters of Mercy). Munich City Council was in agreement with the idea, and so the remaining gateway at the northern entrance to the convent was sealed off by a block of granite, designed by artist Nikolaus Gerhart, as a symbol of the circumstances in which Jews found themselves in the Nazi era: with no way out. The local people then requested that a Star of David be added to the memorial, together with a reference to the years 1941–1943 and a bronze plaque that included a quotation from Else Behrend-Rosenfeld's diaries: '"How much easier it is to live among those suffering injustice than among those who mete it out." Dr. Else Behrend-Rosenfeld, Head of Housekeeping. On this site stood the internment camp for Jews 1941–1943. In Memoriam.'[155]

American historian Dr Gavriel Rosenfeld acknowledges in his book *Munich and Memory* the importance of the discussion that took place locally regarding the design.

> What is most noteworthy about the improvements that were added is that it was the local citizens who were unwilling to accept the timidity of that first memorial. There was obviously a need for a more explicit form of commemoration. It was thanks

[154] History teacher Erich Kasberger and his school's class 11D researched and produced *Jüdische Schicksale* and a second edition of same, *Die nationalsozialistische Gewaltherrschaft*; the work was published in part as Landeshauptstadt München, ed., *Verdunkeltes München: Geschichtswettbewerb* (History Competition) *1985/86*.

[155] These are the words of the inscription on the memorial at Berg am Laim at the gates of the former camp, near the school where co-editor Erich Kasberger served as a long-standing history teacher.

> to this citizen involvement that Berg am Laim managed to avoid the rather formulaic style of other memorials in the city.[156]

The memorial was formally unveiled in July 1987 by Klaus Hahnzog, the mayor of Munich, in the presence of Peter Rosenfeld and Hanna Cooper, Else's children, as well as a gathering of young Israelis who had been especially invited to the ceremony.[157]

Clemens-August-Strasse in Berg am Laim has become a place of remembrance. Every November for the last thirty-three years an event has taken place at the convent and around the memorial itself, supported by groups such as Pax Christi, by church representatives, the local further education college, as well as political parties and individual citizens. Speakers have included leading figures in the work of commemoration, including Max Mannheimer, concentration camp survivor, and the late Hans-Jochen Vogel, former lord mayor of Munich. Further to this, the district council for Berg am Laim wanted to honour deserving Jewish women by renaming streets after them, and this is how Else-Rosenfeld-Strasse came into being in 1997. In the small town of Icking in the Isar valley, where the Rosenfeld family lived until 1939, Else on her own until 1941 and then again after the war, there is also now the Else-Rosenfeld-Weg.

Berg am Laim is only one of the places in Munich where the Jewish victims of the persecution are commemorated and the perpetrators of crimes recorded. There is a rich and varied culture of remembrance, as the following examples will suggest. Gegen Vergessen, für Demokratie (Against Forgetting, For Democracy) is an association founded by Hans-Jochen Vogel, and every November it arranges commemoration of the Night of Broken Glass with a public reading, in the centre and elsewhere, of the names and biographies of all those Jewish citizens from Munich who were deported and murdered. There are contributions from contemporary witnesses, lectures and guided walks following in the footsteps of those who suffered. Munich City Archive compiled the 'Gedenkbuch der Münchner Juden', a book of remembrance of Munich's Jews. The Munich National Socialism Documentation Centre was opened in 2014 and there is a new initiative in Unterschleissheim to create a place of remembrance for the forgotten forced labourers of the Lohhof flax-processing plant. Schools are highly involved in the development work.[158] The nationwide *Stolpersteine*, small brass memorial slabs let into the pavement in front of the homes of

[156] Rosenfeld, *Architektur und Gedächtnis*, pp. 484f.; Rosenfeld, *Munich and Memory*.

[157] Dr Klaus Hahnzog on the dedication of the memorial to the former Residential Facility for Jews at Berg am Laim, 07.07.1987.

[158] Mühlfenzl, Erinnerung an vergessene Verbrechen.

14. Mayor of Munich, Dr Klaus Hahnzog, 7 July 1987, at the dedication of the memorial to the former Residential Facility for Jews at Berg am Laim. Photo: Fritz Neuwirth.

those murdered under the regime, was met with resistance in Munich as the president of the Jewish Community, Dr Charlotte Knobloch, argued that it was unacceptable for others to tread over the names of Jewish victims. As a result, it was decided not to place any *Stolpersteine* on the ground in public places. Since then, another idea has been developed quite independently, namely, the erection of upright columns with commemorative inscriptions.[159] In 2010 the city of Munich launched the Michaela Melián art project *Memory Loops*, creating a virtual memorial using soundtracks that can be called up across the city, 300 in German and 175 in English, using quotations from perpetrators and victims.[160] This project is a touchstone for the future. Individual places of commemoration, Berg am Laim being a case in point, are also planning to strengthen their virtual presence.

The knowledge gathered from over thirty years of work and research into live remembrance forms the foundation of this book. The special history of the Rosenfeld family gives insights from different perspectives: from the inside and the outside, from Germany and from exile, the Jewish and the non-Jewish position in relation to marginalisation and persecution. It was

[159] Kellerhoff, In München wachsen Stolpersteine. [160] See www.memoryloops.net

Else Behrend-Rosenfeld's exceptional personal attributes that shaped her resolute view of her fellow human beings who managed to remain human, even when trapped inside a highly dangerous system, and who deployed their own freedom to take action. Else's account serves as a physical representation akin to raising a statue to friendship – the friendship of outstanding men and women. Else's and Siegfried's diaries also stand in so many ways as testimony to a great love which endured beyond the agony of seven terrible years of being forced to live apart. Above all, it is Else's own inner strength, moral courage and faith in herself and others, even in the shadow of death, that serve to touch the heart of any reader, and spur us all on, even in our own troubled times. All of these mark Else Behrend-Rosenfeld out as an exemplary figurehead and role model – a true source of unending inspiration to each and every one of us.

The Diaries of Else Behrend-Rosenfeld and Siegfried Rosenfeld, including Else's Letters to Eva Schmidt

15. One of the few photographs of the Kindertransport out of Munich: Beate Siegel (*right*) travelled with Hanni Sterneck and others on 27 June 1939 from Munich Main Station.

1939

Else's Diary

Isartal, 28 August 1939

Dearest

We've been apart for three days now and the telegram I was waiting for so anxiously with news of your safe arrival in London finally came half an hour ago. Now that I know you've reached safety and are near the children, I'll content myself with hearing from you only from time to time. I won't be able to write that often and will have to leave the most important matters unsaid. That is why I've decided to write down everything that's on my mind during this period of separation – a situation that I hope will not last too long.

I can't push away the images of the last few days; they play over and over in my head like a moving picture, the changing scenes flashing before my eyes. On Wednesday night I took twenty children by train from Munich to Frankfurt, where Jewish children from across the whole Reich were to assemble for onward transportation. The carriage was almost empty. Three compartments had reserved notices on the door, all under the name of 'Meyer, Travel Agent', in order to avoid other passengers suspecting the presence of Jewish children gathered to leave Germany for a new home in England, whether permanent or temporary. The parents' farewells were as calm and dignified as ever, and the children behaved impeccably too.[1]

The youngest were six years old, the oldest fifteen. Once the train set off, I was able to get the little ones bedded down on the bench seats and it wasn't long before their gentle, regular breathing told me they were fast asleep.

In the next compartment the older lads were chatting, making plans for the future, their voices full of hope and excitement now that the pressure in their daily lives had eased. Yes, the children had felt it, too. Three of the older girls swapped their new addresses so they could keep in touch. Hanni, a charming, dark-haired girl whose parents were singers, known and loved in Munich, was already writing a note home so as to feel close. I made sure to keep moving between compartments until the voices gradually died down, even among the older ones, and they were all asleep at last.

I stepped out into the corridor and thought about our own children and how they had done all this without us several months before. Suddenly I heard loud and unsteady footsteps and saw a big burly man standing at the door of one of our compartments, with the little ones fast asleep inside. I was straight there.

'Excuse me, these compartments are reserved,' I told him.

'Out of my way!' he said. 'I want to see these Jewish brats for myself.'

He was drunk, that much was clear, but I knew I had somehow to stop him disturbing my young charges. Fortunately, more footsteps thudded along the corridor just then, and – what a relief! – it was the conductor, who managed to get the man out of our carriage and back to his own. When the conductor returned, he told me how angry he was at the man's behaviour and language, explaining exactly where I could find him or his colleague if I needed any further assistance.

The rest of the journey[2] passed without incident and we arrived in Frankfurt bang on time. After breakfast in the station café, I was able to entrust the younger children to the care of a woman from the local religious community, while I set off with the older ones for a gentle stroll around the Old Town. The children's next train was to take them to the Dutch border and wasn't due to leave until after midday. We were all to assemble again at eleven in a specified meeting place within the station, by which time more children would have arrived from other places in Germany.

It was a fine morning, the sun was shining and the picturesque buildings around the Römerberg square were truly looking their best. In spite of the long overnight journey, the youngsters were all eyes and ears, and I was so pleased to have the chance to show them a few sights and answer their questions as best I could.[3] We took a breather in some gardens by the River Main and were treated to singing and dancing by ten-year-old Rosi, a little girl who'd joined our train at Nuremberg.

'Rosi, you'll tire yourself out. Won't you come and sit down?' I suggested.

She shook her head vehemently, and her chestnut ringlets bounced in sympathy as her brown eyes flashed. 'I can't stay still because I'm so glad to be getting out of Germany! No more getting spat on, no more getting called names by the kids back home in Franconia.[4] D'you know, they even threw stones at me? That doesn't happen in England. I'm just so happy!'

On hearing this, Hanni, the child I mentioned before who was particularly close to her own family, said, 'But wasn't it hard to say goodbye to your mother and father?'

Rosi shook her head again. 'My father's dead. Storm troopers beat him so badly last year – it was 10 November – that he never got better. Since then my mother's been so unhappy that nothing can cheer her up, absolutely nothing, but she's promised she'll follow me over really soon.' Rosi carried on with her singing and dancing.

'Please, Miss, we've still got some German money,' spoke up Walter, a very solemn fifteen-year-old. 'May we go and buy biscuits and chocolate? I saw a shop round the back there, there are a few, an' they all say "No Jews" on the window, but I'm fair-haired and haven't got a nose on me – no one round here will know any different.'

I was quite willing to let him go, together with one of the older girls, so now there was excited whispering as the children placed their orders. The pair were soon back with the goodies. As the group crowded round me, a beaming Hanni handed me a packet of especially nice biscuits, looking slightly bashful as she did so. 'Because you're so kind to us, Miss.'

Once we were back at the station, everything went off smoothly. The children from Bavaria were first on the list. Their papers were inspected, then handed to the woman who was to accompany them on the next part of their journey. We all stood on the platform and waited while the children found their places in the reserved carriage. Up until now, they hadn't quite realised that this meant goodbye, not only to me but also to everything they'd known before. Now at last, they knew it was time to travel into the unknown and leave behind far more than the terrible experiences of which Rosi had spoken. But even so they all bravely held back the tears as their train moved off.

I was in a rush myself now. My train back to Munich was departing shortly, and I knew I had to go back quite a long way down this platform to access the one I needed. On the way, I noticed people crowding round a news hoarding: *German suffering in Poland – horrific new evidence*. This was regular daily news back then – but how much more threatening and provocative it sounds now. It gave me a jolt. This would mean war. All the faces around me betrayed the same fear. It was as if a load had been dropped on these people's shoulders. They looked anxious with it and fearful.

I reminded myself I was in a hurry. *Home! Get home!* I ran for my train and clambered aboard, just in the nick of time. I saw very little on the journey as my tiredness got the better of me, and slept nearly all the way back to Munich Hauptbahnhof.

As soon as I woke, the doubts flooded in. What would become of us now? Would our residence permits have arrived, as promised by the Quakers in England? Were visas still being issued and would we get all the formalities completed in time?

The secretary from the Jewish Gemeinde in Munich, a small friendly woman, met me at the station as usual. I had swiftly written up the report that she had to pass on the following morning to the senior welfare worker in charge of the evacuation of children. I still had an hour to spare before catching the postbus out to Isartal, so I decided to get something to eat.

Emmy K[ohn]. joined me. 'I'm afraid only your husband's permit has come through so far.'[5]

I was horrified. Would I manage somehow to persuade you to leave without me? I sensed then that mine wouldn't come in time, but I had to find a way of getting you to take this last, this only opportunity to escape the terrible fate that will befall German Jews in this war. I had to plead with you to go for the sake of the children, still so young, even though I knew they'd be able to take care of themselves if they really had to. Right now, you were in far greater danger than they were. Silent and preoccupied, I wasn't much of a lunch companion that day, but Emmy knew exactly what was worrying me. She came with me all the way to the postbus. I was relieved there was no one I knew on board, so I could use the time quietly to collect my thoughts. How could we ever have imagined our permits would turn up at exactly the same time? You, after all, as a man, need what they call a permit of guarantee, because you're not allowed to work over there, whereas I would be free to take on domestic employment to support myself and contribute to your keep. These domestic service visas must, of course, be prepared somewhere quite separate from permits of guarantee, and it would have been pure chance for them to arrive at the same time. All this might even have seemed quite unimportant were the ominous axe of war not threatening to cleave us apart, shutting out all possibility of freedom.

Just then, the postbus was passing through the outskirts of the village we loved, so peaceful in the evening sunshine. There was the farmhouse by the bus stop, and there you were, ready to welcome me home, like you always did, whenever I came back from town. We didn't say much during the short walk home. I know only that I begged you to prepare for all eventualities, to go to town the following morning to obtain your visa. You promised to give it some thought. And at last we arrived back at the rickety gate leading to the little garden wilderness that we loved so much and our funny little wooden house with its enormous chimney. A lamp glowed in the living-room window and our dear friend Tilla, with us for a few days then, was standing on the veranda ready to greet me.

The next morning we were woken by a loud knocking at the door. You ran to see who was there and came back with a telegram from Peter, our son.

> Leave as soon as possible. Father may need to travel alone.

Seeing this, I could breathe more easily. Here were the words that would persuade you to leave without me. At first you refused. You reminded me that we had promised never to be parted. How could I have forgotten that? But we could never have foreseen what was happening now. It wasn't ourselves we had to think of, I implored you, but our two children – Peter, barely eighteen and not settled, needed help to get out of farm school and into an agricultural post. And there was Hanna, aged sixteen, quite happy with her domestic service apprenticeship but now unable to carry on as her household was to be disbanded. You were still hesitant about leaving, when Tilla spoke up.

'Sir, I promise you with all my heart that I'll stay with your dear wife and not leave her until she can follow you.'

That was it. From that moment it was a case of all hands on deck to get you ready to leave that same evening. You headed back into town to obtain your visa, withdraw money and carry out the formalities at the foreign exchange counter and with the police. You'd promised us you'd be back home for two o'clock.

At home, Tilla and I launched into a frenzy of activity. I dashed over to see our friend and neighbour in the big house to tell her of your decision. She offered immediate help, inviting us in for a meal for which we were all grateful.

Next I went to our coal merchant, who helped by driving us to the nearest market town in the small car that he keeps for just this sort of eventuality, in our case to see the customs inspector and have him check over your luggage and stamp it with the official seal. We then asked if he might drive us to Munich Hauptbahnhof and he undertook to collect us in good time.

After that we set to with washing, ironing, packing, as well as making lists of everything that was to be stored.

In the midst of all this activity in came our artist friend to tell us she'd heard from her sister that the two young English women lodging at her home had received a telephone call from their consulate, instructing them to leave for England that very evening. For me this was a sign that speed was paramount.

16. Siegfried Rosenfeld at the rented house in Icking, about 1936.

Everything went according to plan. You came back in good time with reports of how the last of the visas had just been dispensed and the consular staff were packing up to leave. We had telephoned the customs inspector in advance. We already knew him from the last time we'd packed up all our goods and chattels, as well as from our elder daughter's emigration to Argentina. His car was outside the door at four thirty. You barely had time to say a swift goodbye to Tilla and our neighbour, who'd come over with her youngest in her arms, her little girl with curly fair hair and laughing blue eyes.

It was just as well that everything had to be done so rapidly, otherwise your farewells to all these kind people, to our home and garden, to the countryside we loved so much with its sparkling river and ring of blue mountains, would have hurt all the more. It still felt like summer as we sped along the fast road on this hot August day, although ominous white thunderclouds towered above us on our way to Munich and we could hear the distant rumble of thunder as the storm edged in our direction. Stopping directly in front of the station, we were immediately caught in a downpour and struggled to get to the ticket hall without getting soaked through.

Our porter spotted immediately who he was dealing with here. It was hard to imagine just how many suitcases he must be in the habit of transporting for Jews leaving this land of servitude for freer foreign nations. While you were busy at the baggage counter, he asked me, 'Is the gentleman travelling alone?' I couldn't speak, just gave a mute nod. You were back with us by now, ready to tip the porter. As he tucked the money away, he came out with something that took us both by surprise. 'Lordy, lordy, sir, keep your chin up now and don't fret about the little lady. Me, I'm porter number 45 an' I live at number 12, North Street, an' your wife can come to me an' my old lady if she has any trouble at all. She'll be safe and sound with us. We can help out, that's for sure.' Then he shook you by the hand, and me the same, and I can't tell you how comforted we were by this display of ordinary decent humanity. My dear Munich porter, I'm unlikely ever to go in search of you, but I'll be sure to think of you when I'm in difficulty and will gain so much consolation from the kindness of a stranger.

We reached the platform and you got on the train bound for Holland, so packed there wasn't a seat to be had. There was no time for anything more than a swift embrace and a few words of farewell before the gigantic iron beast set off with its human cargo. I stood there for ages, watching it pull further and further away, my heart bursting with good wishes for your safe arrival. Then I turned away to make for home, alone, all alone.

QR-Code 13: Siegfried's departure for England

The good-hearted Herr P[ischeltsrieder] was waiting in his car for me outside the station. The storm had finally passed, leaving only the dullness of rain. Once tucked inside the car, my tears flowed: no need to put on a brave face now. When it was time for Herr P[ischeltsrieder] to say goodbye, he looked close to breaking down, too, but made do instead with a stream of invective against the evil forces working against us, all delivered in the choicest Bavarian turns of phrase. On arrival at our garden gate, he helped me out of the vehicle and bade me farewell, saying, 'Listen, ma'am, anything you need, just you be sure to come to me, and in the winter I'll see that you always have enough wood and coal for your fire, because that's what I'm here for.'

The following day I discussed with Tilla how we might best organise running the house together. How good that she's here and has time available. The children she'd previously been taking care of have now started school, so she's been looking for a new position. We hope that in due course she'll find work around here, but there's no great hurry for that. We've decided to suggest to our landlord in Munich, who's a decent sort of fellow, that from now on Tilla should be the main name on our rental contract.

From 1 September I'm due to make myself fully available once again to the Jewish Gemeinde in Munich[6] as a welfare worker, just as I did back in those harsh days of November 1938 until early March this year, when I had to close down our household and prepare the children's belongings for their own journey. I've maintained contact with the organisation by regularly taking on special assignments, such as accompanying the Kindertransport from Munich to Frankfurt.

Tilla has elected to manage our little household. We've discussed various changes to make the place more homely. Up until now you and I have tended to view living here as a temporary arrangement, not really thinking it worthwhile decorating the place to our own liking. We'll somehow have to make it habitable for winter, because actually it was only ever built for summer use.

The day after you left I called on people in the village to pass on your farewells and it did me good to feel their sympathy for us and our fate.

The advent of ration cards for food is causing quite a stir here. Frau L[orenz], the wife of our grocer, moans about all the extra work and says anyone who had their doubts about the war is now proven right. Nonetheless, the rations are perfectly sufficient and everything has been well organised.

Farewell for today, my dear. I've been chattering away to you for ages. I'm heading into town tomorrow to register for work starting 1 September and will discuss with Herr Rat [Alfred Neumeyer], the head of the Jewish Gemeinde, exactly when he wants me to begin.

Letter from Else to Eva Schmidt[7]

Isartal, 2 September 1939

My dearest Eva

A thousand thanks from me for your two kind letters. First, to your immediate question about my funds. For the time being I don't know whether I'll get the full pension or even any portion of it . . . My warmest thanks to you and Elisabeth, and if I really don't receive anything then it'll be the two of you I'll turn to before anyone else. However, I hope very much not to need to make any demands on you.

Just think – yesterday two more letters arrived from Fritz[8] . . . mostly about spending time with Hanna, who was with him all day on Sunday, as the letter relates in great detail. They both write optimistically about seeing me soon. Hanna's precise words were: 'I'll see you in a fortnight – until then, keep smiling!' A nice card came from Peter, too, telling me he'll be visiting Fritz in the next few days, all things being equal. At least I know all three of them are well and thrilled to be living near one another. This might have to be the only satisfaction I can draw from the situation for quite some time.

Starting on Monday, I'll be working in M[unich] again in my old job and that's the best possible thing I can do . . . Tilla will most probably stay on with me . . . We're ready to take on whatever comes to pass and will respond to any demands of the moment. I'll be eternally grateful for the way this has all turned out, and that my three are in relative safety and can get to one another with ease. Please do stop worrying about me. I feel at times like a schoolgirl, ready for the next task and determined to do it to the best of my ability.

Else's Diary

Isartal, 2 September 1939

As I waited with our neighbour yesterday for the usual early train to take me to the city and him to the hospital on the outskirts, where he's a doctor, the stationmaster's loudspeaker suddenly crackled into life. The small platform was quite crowded at that time of day. One moment everyone was chatting as usual, while groups of schoolchildren laughed and joked, the next an unsettling silence descended. The words that followed had been expected for some time but actually hearing them now sent a chill through all of us.

We are at war. German troops have crossed the border into Poland.

The colour drained from Dr B[achmann]'s face and his jaw tightened, but he remained composed, saying, 'So, we're at war again. I wonder how long it'll go on for this time.' We exchanged a firm handshake before continuing to our respective destinations.

QR-Code 14: The outbreak of war, 1939

I reported to the foreign exchange desk as instructed but was then told to wait. The man said the Führer was about to speak and that all staff had assembled in the reception area. I could hear every word from my bench in the corridor. After the customary torrent of hatred, the essence of his speech was to tell the German people that Russia was not with the enemy but a benevolent neutral friend on our side. Enduring the tone of this man's voice was harder than ever for me on this day, as was the storm of applause and cheering from his followers, none of which sounded remotely human.

I'd been summoned to discuss the detail of your pension payments and how much could come to me. The official was perfectly courteous when explaining that only a proportion of your pension would be paid to me and that this would be monthly, according to my outgoings, and by arrangement with the property administrator you had already selected. Later I could see that the fixed sum of 250 Reichsmark per month was indeed generous.[9] It will allow me to keep Tilla, even if she has no income of her own, as well as do the voluntary work I love so much for the Jewish Gemeinde. It's not yet fully clear what those duties will be, but Herr Rat is of the opinion that the circumstances in which we now find ourselves will give rise to additional work, and he is glad to have me available on standby. Initially I'll work as an advisor in welfare assistance in order to ease the pressure on the women already there.

The Gemeinde itself is in turmoil. In every room there's talk of the likely effect of the war on our Jewish people. The know-alls give a slight shrug and advise us simply not to draw attention to ourselves, while the worriers headed by young Fritz A[braham], still a rather disagreeable person, predict darkly that all Jews will be shot dead, starting with the men.

Herr Rat, in his customary kind and calm manner, has a quiet word with me. 'We can be grateful for our work and must take satisfaction from it. Let us put all our efforts into relieving the oppressed and the suffering as far as we can. God knows, there's enough of them. Our welfare work, once the smallest part of our organisation in terms of spread and responsibilities has been developing fast and by all criteria is now in lead position.'

I'm so pleased to be reporting to him and to have the opportunity to take on this work.

I'll be catching the postbus at seven every morning, then in the evening plan to get the one that leaves around six. On Saturdays and Sundays I'll be free. This kind of routine suits me just fine, as you can imagine!

It's glorious summer weather here at the moment. I'm enjoying sitting in the garden, our neighbours' children playing all around me. The whole place exudes peace, and it's a struggle to believe that we are in fact at war. There's none of the exuberance we saw in 1914, not a trace, and even the first reports of victory are leaving people silent and unmoved.

Tilla's gone on a cycling tour to make the best of the good weather. I didn't feel like going away at the moment, as it does me so much good to have time alone with my thoughts of you and the children, with all those darting impressions of good days and bad. It's an endlessly rich trove of memories that never disappoints, a world of recollections to sift through now that the three of you are all so far away. I've never been one to dwell on the past, nor do I let myself live with pointlessly high expectations of what the future might bring. I can only endure this period in my life if I can make the present worth living through a combination of work, companionship and empathy with the suffering and joy of other human beings. This will keep me motivated and capable of making a worthwhile contribution. But I do still need time in my own company to call up my personal memories. Tilla completely understands, which demonstrates to me that she has similar needs, and this will greatly benefit our co-existence.

*In the original German version of Else's diaries (*Leben in zwei Welten*, pp. 56–89) she looks back to Berlin and their lives before 1933, when Siegfried worked at the Prussian state Ministry of Justice and dealt with pleas for clemency and she, once Gustl, Peter and Hanna were old enough, was a welfare worker in a women's prison in Berlin. She tells of Siegfried being forced to*

17. Else Rosenfeld holding Sylvia, the youngest daughter of her neighbour Maina Bachmann, 1939.

retire and the family moving to Bavaria, first to Schönau near Berchtesgaden, then to Bayerisch Gmain near Bad Reichenhall. Her account includes examples of early forms of persecution, such as Peter and Hanna having stones hurled at them by classmates whose teacher had actually provoked their actions, and then the local mayor asking the family to leave their community. In

Bayerisch Gmain they took a flat in the house of one Frau Winterberg, a lady who came across as warm and friendly but who turned out to be a schemer and highly dangerous informant. In statements made by Frau Winterberg it was alleged that Siegfried had spoken out against Hitler and the regime. This resulted in his imprisonment and it was only through good fortune and excellent legal representation that he was released. He was actually arrested in June 1934 and then freed in the middle of August. The family then moved to Icking in the valley of the River Isar, the Isartal.

Isartal, 6 September 1939

Yesterday our neighbour invited us over. She had visitors, among them Herr and Frau P[ringsheim], and music was the main topic of conversation. Tilla and I lamented the fact that we had no opportunity currently to hear good music. Herr P[ringsheim] suggested that he himself, together with his son and the neighbours' older children, might look out some easier pieces and then perform them for the rest of us. Everyone found this a delightful idea and a date was agreed for their first rehearsal. Once we had said our goodbyes, Tilla and I were tempted to linger outside for a stroll, it was such a beautiful evening. We went for a long walk together, savouring the charms of a landscape of which you and I had grown so fond during our time here.

It's true to say, however, that the years spent here [in Icking] were not entirely without mishap, and indeed there were a fair few moments when the otherwise agreeable rhythms of life were disrupted. I need only think of the hideous notices placed everywhere, shouting out: 'Jews are not welcome here'. The Nuremberg Laws left us feeling wretched, too, as we had to let Hedwig go, our loyal domestic help who had been such a part of the family. She had been with us when you were arrested and returned to us as soon as we'd found a permanent home. Saying goodbye to her was so hard.

Next we had to turn our thoughts to finding suitable further training for the children, meaning that at Easter 1937 all three left home. Our eldest, Gustel, left for Argentina to marry her childhood sweetheart.[10] Peter and Hanna went off to Gross Breesen where there was an agricultural training farm for German Jews, he to learn about farming and she to learn about other daily duties on a smallholding. Seeing them all go was so harrowing,

18. Happy times, Siegfried Rosenfeld in Icking, *circa* 1938.

but we soon heard from each of them that they felt they were in the right place, and the two younger ones couldn't have chosen a better form of training. Gustel's letters were full of good cheer and encouragement as she put plans in place for all of us to join her in Argentina. By autumn 1938 the time was looking right, so we booked our crossing on one of the Monte ships, run by the Hamburg-Süd shipping company, for 31 October. Then came some unexpected changes to the migration rules for entering Argentina, news which put paid to all our plans. Shortly before this happened, Tilla had been with us for her continuing recovery and received a visit from our new neighbour, Dr B[achmann]. He was very taken with our house and its location and asked whether our landlord would be wanting to sell once we had left. We undertook to ask our landlord on Dr B[achmann]'s behalf and the matter was resolved with surprising speed. Dr B[achmann] wanted to move in during the early part of the following year and so we were in a position to stay there until then.

Then came 10 November 1938. We got up that morning in all innocence. There was a ring at the doorbell just as we were sitting down to breakfast, all four of us again now, as we had brought Peter and Hanna back from Gross Breesen because of our emigration plans as well as the rumours of war. It was our mayor at the door, the dear man's brow perspiring with embarrassment.

'The Party's District Leader has telephoned. You must be gone in three hours at the very most.'

We both stood there motionless for a moment, but then I managed to say something. 'But where are we supposed to go?' I knew I sounded helpless.

'I don't honestly know,' he replied, equally at a loss. 'I hope it's not for long. Maybe it's to do with that murder in Paris, that Herr vom Rath fellow. Now don't you worry yourselves about all your bits and bobs here. You can be sure to find it all as you left it. Just take enough for a few days, how about that?' Then he was off again.

We told the children. Breakfast was left as good as untouched. Hanna, our youngest, and I set about packing enough for the four of us in two small suitcases, while you went through your papers and correspondence and then Peter helped you burn anything you didn't need to keep. I took the books we had borrowed from the Bavarian state library in to our neighbour's apartment on the top floor. She was away but had given me her key. We settled on Munich as our next destination. In the circumstances a large city felt safer than a small town. We imagined we'd simply find temporary accommodation in a guest house somewhere as we knew no one in Munich other than my dear Herr Neumeyer, a very senior lawyer and chair of the Jewish Community, and his wife, whose son had also been in Gross Breesen for a time. Through them we had met others in the same building, an artist and his wife, Franz and Helene Hecht, who had visited us in the summer and so we'd all got to know one another quite well. And, of course, we knew the lady who owned the large grocery store by the cathedral in Munich, and we really appreciated being able to get all our groceries, preserves and coffee there.

Our train was due to leave around eleven, so we dropped off our key and that of our upstairs neighbour with the mayor. 'Now you be sure to telephone me from Munich before you come back, and be sure to tell me if you need anything. Just remember that I'll do everything I can to have you back with us here as soon as possible!' We all said our goodbyes.

When we climbed aboard the Isartalbahn,[11] we found ourselves in the same compartment as the head of the nearby Jewish college of housekeeping, along with all her teachers and trainees. They'd had to leave just like us, the young ladies carting all their own luggage. We discussed whether they should immediately travel on beyond Munich or seek out some temporary accommodation with fellow students until such time as they could inform their parents of their return. The teachers, however, were convinced their institution would be shut down and that there'd be no return.[12] All of them planned to go either straight to the Jewish Gemeinde office in Lindwurmstrasse or to Herr Rat's home address in order to get further instructions. On arrival of our train at the Isartalbahnhof in Munich, we said fond goodbyes and wished one another well. We were soon to discover how much we needed those good wishes.

We knew of a little guest house near Odeonsplatz as we'd once visited friends staying there, so we set off there by tram. Not so far from the railway station, however, we started to notice how many shops had shattered windows and quickly realised they were all Jewish businesses.[13] It sent a shiver through me in spite of the unseasonably warm autumn day. At the guest house we were told very kindly that everything was booked up. There was another close by, where the owner was previously known to us. I went to this one on my own while the rest of you waited nearby. This woman told me that all guest house owners and hoteliers were under threat of punishment if they took in any Jews. By now it was two in the afternoon. To save time we decided to work on this separately. You decided to take Peter with you and go to the Hechts, while I said I'd take Hanna and try Frau Schwarz, the woman with the grocery shop. We arranged to meet outside her house at half past three.

The Schwarz household was in turmoil. Seventy-year-old Herr Schwarz had been threatened that very morning in his own home by armed Storm Troopers. They had forbidden him and any member of his family from going to their business that day. No one knew what would happen next. Frau Schwarz and her son welcomed us in, and it was from them that I learned that Jewish businesses across the entire Reich had been attacked, their windows smashed and goods either looted or destroyed. The main synagogue in Munich had been demolished a while back, supposedly for technical reasons to do with the building, so it escaped the fires and destruction to which synagogues across the land now fell victim.[14] In spite of the fear and anxiety over the future now felt by every Jew, Frau Schwarz and her family gave us a warm welcome with food and the offer of a bed for the night for myself and Hanna. They said they'd find a corner for us even though they were expecting their married daughter and her husband to arrive from Cologne that same day. I accepted gratefully, hoping desperately that you and Peter would be offered a bed for the night by the Hechts. But when we met up as arranged, you told me the bad news. Helene Hecht had asked you to leave again. She'd explained it like this.

19. Munich department store Heinrich Uhlfelder after the Reich-wide Night of the Pogrom, 10 November 1938.

'I've heard from Herr Rat that every Jewish home is being visited by the SA or the Gestapo[15] and that men are being arrested all over the place. They haven't come to us yet and we mustn't let them find and arrest you and Peter.'

What were we to do? We just walked the crowded streets and kept on seeing groups of people standing outside Jewish shops, either to examine the destruction or to finish off the job where a window had been missed. The crowds were very orderly and you couldn't tell from people's faces what they were really thinking. I heard a bit of gloating here and there, but some words of disgust, too. But what was this all of a sudden?

'Quick, come on!' some young lad was shouting to his pal. 'There's another Jew getting arrested over there!'

Seeing a man being led towards a police vehicle by several officers, I pulled you all away. The four of us carried on walking the streets, me feeling as though I'd stumbled into the witches' Sabbath. A garish poster on a newspaper stall heralded in huge red lettering the publication of a new novel entitled *Those who are hunted* – that was us. So were we about to fall into their hands too? That's how my mind was working. *But no*, I said to myself, *that's not going to happen. You and Peter, you're not going to be arrested; there's got to be some way out.* I then remembered a dressmaker I knew – her husband was from the Baltics, and they weren't Nazis, either of them. Maybe they would take you and Peter in tonight and then we'd have to see about tomorrow. We telephoned her, but no reply. Half an hour later, we called again. This time her son answered, saying his mother would be home around seven. A whole hour to go. We walked on through the streets, found further ravaged shopfronts with people staring silently at the devastation, saw more arrests going on, and there seemed no end to this hour of waiting. At last it was time to make our way to Frau B's address. The clock struck seven. I rang the bell and she herself opened the door. My heart was pounding so hard that I was certain she'd hear it. Would she be brave enough for this? Trembling from head to toe, I stammered out my request and waited anxiously for her reply.

'Bring your menfolk here,' she said quite calmly. 'I'll be happy to keep them until at least tomorrow.'

I don't recall how I managed to express my gratitude before hurrying away to find you both and then, my despair diminished somewhat, setting off with Hanna for the Schwarz house. I was overwhelmed with exhaustion as we finally sat down for supper. Their son ate with us but left soon afterwards to get back to his own home, knowing his wife would be worrying about him. She telephoned about an hour after he'd left, asking if he was still there. The colour drained from Frau Schwarz's face. There could be only one explanation. He must have been arrested on the street and then, like everyone else who was picked up, taken to the concentration camp at Dachau.

The window of the room she'd so generously made available to me and Hanna looked out on to the Frauenkirche. I couldn't bring myself to go to bed and so stood at the window looking at the two domed towers of the cathedral, very much the symbol of Munich. What on earth was going to happen? Could we protect you and Peter from Dachau? He wouldn't be the first seventeen-year-old to be arrested, after all. Whatever was to happen, we had to bear it. At last I lay down on the bed to rest my weary limbs and try to regain my strength even though sleep was out of the question. I heard Frau Schwarz's daughter and son-in-law arrive and was comforted in the knowledge she had the pair of them there to support her. I told myself that if we got out of this safely, we would do anything and everything to emigrate, no matter where. And if it wasn't to be Argentina, then we'd just have to find somewhere else.

Morning came at last. The newspaper reported that acts of revenge on Jews for the murder of Herr von Rath had taken place all over the Reich and that the police had been unable to stop any of this from happening. When we left after breakfast, thanking our kind hosts, we saw white posters stuck prominently all over walls and pillars ordering people to keep the peace. Any individual taking action would be dealt with most severely although clearly the Jews must atone for the villainous murder.

I breathed a little more easily when I found you and Peter safe and well at Frau B's home, but she told us she didn't dare give you a second night of shelter. She explained how she'd been out to buy milk and had heard that local Nazi officials were going round every block asking about hidden Jews.[16] She said we could stay with her until the afternoon but needed to find alternative accommodation after that. But where? I telephoned our mayor to ask if we could now return. He said we couldn't, that we needed to stay away for a good few days in a row before he could hope to bring us back. In my desperation I rang Helene Hecht again. She herself answered.

'Five minutes after your husband and Peter left, the Gestapo came and took my husband. I don't think there's any danger of them coming back. It would be best if you all come here at nightfall. There's plenty of room.'

I was so sorry that Franz Hecht had been arrested and yet also so relieved that there was somewhere for us to stay. The Hechts lived on Keplerstrasse in a building on the corner, just beyond the city centre. Their flat was on the top floor with a lovely large attic and a view over little settlements with gardens, meadows and fields and then on towards the Alps.

Helene Hecht remained warm and composed in spite of the pain she must have been feeling regarding her husband and soulmate. Our being there was a welcome distraction for her. Alone with her elderly aunt, her mother's sister, she'd have had little respite from the gloom, but the mere presence of our children lifted the sombre mood in the flat, bringing light and life to the place. Right from the start it was agreed that you and Peter would not leave the house, and I was so pleased to have Helene's support in this. We stayed with her for twelve days, a period which strengthened our bond of friendship more than would ever have been likely under normal circumstances, not even over many years. It was now obvious to her that a speedy exit from the country was required, something the two of them had never previously imagined would be necessary. Through his work as an artist, Franz had gathered a few good friends in England, one of them a close relative of Sir Winston Churchill and also bearing the Churchill surname.[17] Somehow it didn't seem appropriate, however, to make contact from Germany with a man whose name was now widely reviled. Eventually we came up with the idea of sending this man a telegram, but using only his rather unusual first name, and asking if he could arrange an immigration permit for the two of them, Helene and Franz. I took the telegram to the despatch office myself, and just two days later we had a response to say that he would do everything in his power to bring the Hechts over. He'd signed off with great forethought as Lord Ivor.

In the first few days following 10 November I found that every excursion beyond our four walls required considerable effort. Each time the house door closed behind me, I felt the need to brace myself against the horrors of the outside world. Almost every shop in the city boasted a huge sign saying, *No admittance for Jews*, as did public buildings, cafés and bars. I was immediately able to recognise every Jewish woman, every Jewish girl (for all the men had been taken to Dachau and the few who'd managed to avoid the clutches of the Party and the Gestapo were now in hiding) and not because of the usual well-known racial characteristics, in reality possessed only by some, but because of the blank expression that each wore like a mask, eyes dull, staring straight ahead as if looking through something and yet not directly at anyone.

If the Party's notices had the aim of making it impossible for Jews to buy anything and to leave them unable to satisfy the most basic needs of everyday life, then it failed and had almost the opposite effect. Friends and neighbours, and in many cases shop owners with Jewish customers, hurried to take home enough, often more than enough, of anything they could lay hands on and not only in a few isolated cases but rather as a general rule. During this period Helene often joked about what a good thing it was that she had the four of us there, or else she wouldn't have known what to do with the many blessings that were brought to her. On the second or third day after our arrival at the Hechts I travelled to Isartal to pick up the books we'd borrowed from the state library as I wanted to be sure to return them safely. The newspapers had just made it known that on top of going to the theatre, concerts, cinemas and public performances, the use of public reading rooms and the borrowing of books from all state and city libraries was now also banned.

Back in Isartal I found everything in order, but when I called on the mayor he advised us to wait before coming home and said again that he

20. 'No admittance for Jews': notice outside a Munich library, 1938.

would tell us when the time was right. I consequently didn't spend too long in the house, but headed straight back to the city and the state library. Here I found the same notice: *No admittance for Jews*. Inwardly more than apprehensive, I entered the building. As I handed in my reader's card, the member of staff hesitated and then said, 'May I ask you to wait a moment? Herr Doktor X[18] would like to talk to you.'

Very surprised, I followed him into one of the administrative offices where Herr Doktor X greeted me politely and offered me a seat.

'You've no doubt read in the newspaper that a ban has been imposed on Jews borrowing library books,' he said.[19]

I replied in the affirmative.

'Over the last few years, your husband has been a keen borrower of our books. I assume he needs these for his academic research and that the ban would affect him most severely. May I ask you a few questions? Is your husband fully Jewish?'

I replied once more in the affirmative.

'And you, madam? Please don't see this as an indiscretion on my part – you will soon see why I am posing such questions.'

I replied that I would normally be considered a Mischling but that my marriage had meant this had been revoked.

'That does not matter to us,' he said. 'For us you are a Mischling and this group is permitted to borrow books. We need, however, to have a reason for your borrowing academic works.'

I responded straight away. 'There is a reason. I studied history to doctoral level. I hope this is enough to justify my interest in academic reading.'

'Of course, madam, and you will now understand why I had to ask you those questions. A new reader's card in your own name will be prepared for you straight away. Who you pass the books on to in your own family is not a matter for us. And to collect and return the books you can send anyone, including, of course, your husband. We hope soon to be able to remove that nasty sign from the entrance but even if that cannot be done, it is of no relevance for anyone sent here on your account. One more thing: should you or your husband ever be treated here with anything less than common courtesy, I want you to inform me straight away. Under no circumstances will we tolerate that here, of that we are certain.'

I could scarcely believe that I was being treated as equal to an 'Aryan'. The experiences of the last few days, the newspapers dripping hatred from every page, the confiscation of wealth as 'atonement' for the murder in Paris, the arrests and associated activities, the Aryanisation of Jewish businesses, all this had combined to drive home our pariah status. I stammered out my thanks, fighting to control my emotions. I would have loved to have been able to tell him how much it would mean for you not to have to break off your research, to be able to carry on without hindrance. I haven't forgotten how pleased you were when I told you the news, and I've recorded all this in great detail here because it shows that even government officials don't necessarily endorse all these measures and, where they can, try to alleviate their effect even if they don't dare reject them in public. The popular view that the acts of violence against Jews during 1938 were a spontaneous boiling over of the people's rage was misplaced speculation. A new approach was about to be adopted. Every decree regarding Jews was issued directly through specific newspapers and channels, described as 'secret', with the result that the wider population actually knew very little of the restrictions and rules now being enforced.

With the exception of the Jewish children's home and one rather unprepossessing home for the elderly, the Storm Troopers had had two old people's homes and the administrative offices of the Jewish Community cleared in their entirety.[20] The staff of the latter had now gathered in

Herr Neumeyer's home, in the same building as the Hechts' apartment, in order to talk everything over and see how they could start work again without delay. Between them, however, they were unable to muster enough manpower and were on the lookout for fresh volunteers. I put myself forward immediately. The first job was to track down the old folk who had been hounded out of their home by the SA and whose location was now unknown. Enquiries needed to be made among the relatives and any acquaintances. It took a lot of work and searching but in the end they were all found, many of them now in worse health because of what they'd just gone through.

'When the SA turned up at the home on Kaulbachstrasse and told us we had to get out of the house right there and then,' said an old lady of eighty-three whom I eventually located at a friend's house following a long search, 'I went up to an SA man and asked him where I was supposed to go as I had no family nearby. D'you know what he said? "Starnberg Lake's big enough for the lot of you." So I wandered the streets for a while until I ran into Frau NN and she took me in.'

This lady had had to leave all her belongings at the home. A lot of things went missing when the order came to clear the Kaulbachstrasse place. The second home, the one in Mathildenstrasse, after long negotiations was eventually handed back in early December, and was freshly decorated and made habitable once more. This time round, residents had to make do with less – whereas each had previously had their own room, now it was two or three beds in each one. One of my tasks was to help the head of accommodation in getting the old folk moved back in and settled. It wasn't easy telling them that the lack of space meant they had to be separated from some of their possessions, but they were still so shaken after the experience of being driven out that they were glad to have somewhere they could call home and to get back to a well-ordered life.

The Jewish Gemeinde found possible office accommodation in an old Jewish cigarette factory in Lindwurmstrasse, tucked away in a rear courtyard. Due to the construction of the U-Bahn system the whole street had been ripped up, resulting in a chaos that seemed to me symbolic of what was happening to our own community. But we had to straighten up, grit our teeth and get on with the work. The ugly factory building was transformed, with partition walls creating offices and a lick of bright paint giving everything a more welcoming appearance – anything to ease people's distress. All Jewish men working in department stores along with a range of other businesses had lost their jobs and were not permitted any other employment.

21. Eva Schmidt (1897–1988), a teacher in Weimar, was Else's closest friend and helped her throughout the persecution. Photo: E. Koch, date unknown.

Almost without exception they had been taken to Dachau. But their wives and children still had to go on paying their rent and finding food. They, too, needed help and advice in these radically different conditions that had come about with such speed. All this meant plenty of work for us, overwhelming at times, in caring for the old folk as well as manning the welfare office.

When I stepped down at the beginning of March, circumstances had improved to such an extent that I felt at ease about doing this, all the more so as I had found a suitable replacement and inducted her into the post myself.

Letters from Else to Eva Schmidt

Isartal, 4 March 1939

Dear Eva

In haste today so I'll keep it brief – we're in the middle of this dreadful clearing out as well as selling off one thing after another. Thank goodness we have such heavenly spring sunshine to brighten everything. First of all, we're moving to Dr T's [Tilla's] weekend cottage not so far from here. It's very basic but really pretty, and best of all sits in that beautiful landscape that we love more and more . . . Our plans have not progressed at all, and in fact new obstacles keep cropping up for the children regarding both England and the USA. Our last and only hope seems to be Argentina, and if that comes to nought, what on earth are we to do? But don't you worry yourself: we will take our chances and hold our heads up high.

Isartal, 18 April 1939

My dearest Eva

Warmest thanks for your recent card and letter with all your news. At last I have something good to report! Yesterday Peter received his permit and is getting his English visa today. He'll be leaving within the next ten days. I can just picture your face as you share in our joy and relief that this has happened at last. You're the first person to hear the good news and rightly so – in our eyes such a dear and loyal friend has the absolute right to be the first to hear the liberating news. I'm writing to Hanna, too. I owe her a letter and will do that straight after this. It looks as though Peter won't be going to the school that Hilde Lion founded over there but to a big agricultural training camp, and we think that's much better. For all these arrangements and longed for progress we owe enormous thanks to Curt Bondy, Käthe Liepmann and the Quakers.

Isartal, 8 June 1939

My dearest Eva

I fear I've been far too slow in replying to your last letter, but it's hard to write when there's nothing positive to say, no steps forward, only steps backwards, or a complete standstill to report.

I don't remember whether I've already told you that the Argentinian consulate declined. That happened just before Hanna's departure. It didn't hit us as hard as you might have expected because our hopes were then all pinned on Cuba, but that's gone now since Cuba firmly closed its doors. What remains, we really don't know. We assume that Gustel and Heinz won't be prepared to make do with this rejection . . . But at least we all feel better able to cope now that the children are out of it and in a good place.

Else's Diary

Isartal, Sunday 10 September 1939

As soon as I arrived at work on Friday, Herr Rat called me in. 'I've had a telephone call from the leader of the Jewish Community in Karlsruhe. He tells me that from today onwards we're going to receive a large number of Jewish people from all over Baden. They've been ordered to leave their homes because of their proximity to the French border. Several hundred will need shelter with members of our own community here in Munich. Our own housing department can deal with all this, but we need someone to take on the extra welfare work, liaise with hosts and new arrivals, look after people in a more personal way and be available to offer help and advice. Will you take this on? That would be my preference if the Gestapo think I'm to take on sole responsibility for the seamless integration of these returning emigrants, as they are officially known.'[21] I agreed without even pausing to think about it and Herr Rat continued, 'We'll keep a lookout for an office for you, and you'll have a secretary. Emmy K[ohn] has shown interest in the job, and you know her from your work with the Kindertransport, don't you? Are you happy with all that?' Again, I agreed without hesitation.

A small office was soon found and the two of us settled in. We set up a card index system and at midday the first of the returning emigrants arrived. Our housing department had been in operation since the early part of the year, which now proved a blessing. It had been opened at the instigation of the Office for Aryanisation, a unit founded by the SA and located in Widenmayerstrasse,[22] because the removal of Jewish families from their homes had already begun and their flats and houses were seen as useful for other purposes.[23] It had fallen to our housing department to find shelter for those families and to this end a detailed register had been drawn up, listing all Jewish homes with an accurate listing of the number and size of the rooms and the number of residents. Each person was granted the right to one room but whatever remained had to be made available. This list now came in useful for us. Most Jews in Munich had large flats and so rooms for the new arrivals were found without too much difficulty. We all felt sorry for these folk who'd had to leave home so suddenly and without proper time to prepare themselves for this journey into the unknown. Emmy and I had our hands full. The youngest children were put up in the children's home until suitable accommodation was found for whole families, while the old or sick had to be accompanied to their new quarters, their many questions answered and requests for clothing and other essentials dealt with as swiftly as possible. By late afternoon around sixty arrivals all had somewhere to stay, with any latecomers temporarily placed in other homes on our books.

Next came the matter of feeding everyone. I arranged with our catering section that up to one hundred additional midday meals could be provided at our centre every day, while the apprentices' hostel could offer another twenty. All that wouldn't be enough – we needed to find an additional dining facility. Our small home in Wagnerstrasse, Schwabing, has a kitchen that was previously used for cookery lessons for the older Volksschule pupils although not much goes on there now. Volunteer catering staff have been recruited in no time and the new kitchen will be in service from tomorrow, providing a substantial and nourishing midday meal for up to sixty people. In the same home we'll be setting up emergency quarters, just a basic straw mattress for anyone not immediately placed with a family. About seventy people arrived yesterday and even more are expected tomorrow. The Ludwigshafen Jewish Gemeinde has informed us that their people are being evacuated from the Rhineland and that some of them will be coming to us.

Working with Emmy K[ohn] is absolutely marvellous– I can't imagine anyone better suited to this role, and she's so incredibly pleasant with it. Right from the start we agreed that we would never adopt the brusque approach of some of the other welfare staff, for while a certain briskness is sometimes necessary, we really want our charges to be met with kindness. Only today, however, did we have an example of a very direct approach being more appropriate. One Jewish man with an Aryan-Protestant wife had been found accommodation with a strictly orthodox family. This wife had no idea about Jewish rules on food. This had led to serious clashes and both sides came to me, each enraged by the conduct of the other. It was quite evident that new accommodation would have to be found, but I had to make it very clear to both of the parties concerned that differences like this were best resolved without accusations being hurled back and forth on either side. Following this, the housing department was asked to take such matters into account in future allocations.

On finishing work yesterday as well as the day before, Emmy and I both said how worn out we felt but also pleased with what we'd managed to achieve in such a short time. And we have a plan in case any further new arrivals come today, Sunday. They'll be taken first of all to one of our homes, where we know there are enough straw mattresses to go round, and then tomorrow to their proper accommodation. Today, the two of us can relax, knowing that everything is ready and in place, and recuperate a little before what is likely to be a very intensive period over the coming weeks.

Isartal, Sunday 24 September 1939

It's a fortnight since I last even glanced at my diary, let alone wrote anything in it! There seem never to be enough hours in the day to get all the work done, and then last Sunday I had to go into town. Meanwhile we've had around three hundred and fifty returning emigrants arrive in Munich, although that influx should now be stopping. I truly hope that's the case so we can get on with the existing welfare work. Up until now all we've been able to do is make sure that each one has accommodation, food and basic clothing.

The Munich Quakers have helped us such a lot with the clothing issue, and it's been a real pleasure for me to have formed a closer acquaintance with Frau Annemarie C[ohen] – you'll remember we both got to know her when we were trying so hard to get the children's departure organised. She and her husband lead the Quaker community here, and we felt ourselves strongly drawn to them the first time we ever met.[24]

By far the majority of such returners come here with one small suitcase or just a few things they can carry on their person. Unlike the 'Aryan' population, we don't get any clothing ration stamps,[25] so our people can buy neither clothing nor linen and this is where the Quakers are so helpful. The war

22. Annemarie and Rudolf Cohen, 1930s.

against Poland is over, Hitler's offer of peace with England and France has not been accepted, as was expected, so the real war starts now. What horrors is this going to bring us? And for how long?

Tilla and I listened to Hitler's speech on 19 September as we sat in a café together to mark her birthday, and its content shocked me deeply.

> *'We shall never capitulate, whether the war lasts three years, four years or, yes, even five years.'*

I simply cannot bring myself to believe that this can continue that long and know how it would sap me of any strength to carry on. At the moment I'm taking each day as it comes and simply picking up whatever task presents itself to me, never allowing anything to tear me from the belief that one day I'll be reunited with you and with the children.

Isartal, Sunday 5 November 1939

We have had to set up a new department at the Jewish Gemeinde office. All Jews in Munich are to receive their food ration cards from us, every card being marked with 'J' for Jew. It has now also been decreed that Jews may buy food from specific shops only. Each individual will be assigned to one grocery and one butcher's shop and another for milk and bread, and these shops will in turn be given a list of those Jews who will be buying from them. The grocery is taking on the supply of potatoes and other vegetables. Any Jew setting foot in a shop not listed will be severely punished as this is henceforth strictly forbidden. This is more than harsh as many of our people now have quite some distance to walk to reach their allocated shops.[26] The Jewish Community has been charged with ensuring that these new rules are followed. Goods in short supply such as fresh fruit, along with special rations accessible to the rest of the population such as rice, coffee beans, legumes and so on, are simply not available to Jews, nor are they permitted to have them delivered.

When it was time for the distribution of the food ration cards, everyone in the Jewish Community offices pitched in to help get them prepared and handed out as quickly as possible. There was a great deal to be worked out and correctly listed, including precisely how many people were even entitled to a card and then informing them how to collect it and which shops they could use. This new ruling applies only to those who live within the city boundaries and Munich is required to document every detail so it can continue to justify its title as 'Capital of the Movement'.[27] I'm still able to obtain my own food ration cards outside the city, and without any of these restrictions or indicators to single me out.

These measures are quite obviously intended to ensure that Jews remain acutely aware of their pariah status and to render their lives even more difficult from day to day. Their overall ability to adapt to such changes, however, leaves me full of wonder and admiration. On the outside at least, the incessant needling and harassment are simply not having the required effect. Our people seem calmly to accept that which cannot be changed and to resign themselves to the inevitable. Although not yet visible, the walls of the ghetto are steadily forming around us. We are forced to organise more and more ourselves and to meet our human and cultural needs from within our own circles. Other German cities with a larger Jewish community are better off than we are here in Munich. They each have their own Jewish cultural associations which organise concerts, plays, films and lectures of all kinds. None of that is permitted here. We lack all intellectual distractions and artistic pursuits now that every wireless has been confiscated, the full impact of which should not be underestimated.[28] Outwardly I may present as quite sanguine in face of harassment but for a soul such as mine, the real sense of mortification lurks within. The distress at feeling ostracised leaves a festering wound that in most people slowly poisons the mind and spirit.

One of our welfare colleagues was up in Berlin during this period and reported little or no such harassment going on there. Granted that the Jews in Berlin saw the burning down of their synagogues and the destruction of their shops on 10 November 1938 as well as a wave of arrests and that all this left them in a profound state of shock, but time has moved on. They now lead relatively normal lives, virtually without hindrance, and seem lulled into a dangerous sense of security under this so-called centralisation of all Jewish Gemeinden across the Reich.

Frau Dr R[enner], our member of staff who travelled there, feels that the authorities are observing our ever-increasing difficulties like someone who watches from safe harbour while a ship battles the waves and tries not to go down. Certain that fresh blows will continue to rain down on us, we stand prepared and will grit our teeth and get through it. For most other people, any further blows would seem like bolts of lightning from out of the blue.

Our influx from Baden and the Rhineland have settled in well. Their children attend our schools and make friends easily with the Munich children, while a friendly atmosphere largely reigns in the shared accommodation, sometimes admittedly needing intervention from Emmy or on my part, albeit often belated. The catering facilities we've put in place are working well, providing simple but well-cooked and nourishing meals that keep folks' bellies full. And we're gradually finding bits and pieces to keep them all occupied. The women mend and sew for their own families as well as plenty of others, especially for the larger family groups, and they also help out with the catering at our homes, while the men mostly run errands or perform various odd jobs. All returners have now been found accommodation with families and only a small number of children have been left in the children's home, either because they are in some way difficult to deal with or are physically handicapped.

I am in constant written contact with Jewish Gemeinde offices back in people's home districts, partly to get more detailed information on some of them, and partly to ensure that their home communities continue to look after their interests. In addition I am required by the Gestapo to produce at least twice a week an accurate list of names in order to keep them up to date with the number of returners and their addresses here. This is constantly subject to change because the man in charge of the Widenmayerstrasse office, Hauptsturmführer Wegner, under the jurisdiction of the Gauleiter, is always asking for yet more Jewish flats to be cleared and leaves it entirely to our housing department to find alternative accommodation for all those who then have to be billeted at very short notice – all of which needs his authorisation.

Living conditions here are growing increasingly overcrowded. A whole string of houses with Jewish owners have now been declared 'Jewish houses'.[29] Careful measurements are taken before the total area is divided up and no one is now permitted a whole room to him- or herself. Anything deemed a larger room must be shared with others. This naturally affects my returners and causes a lot of running around, persuasion and negotiation among everyone concerned.

These 'Jewish houses' are the beginning of the ghetto. It's quite obvious how all this is enabling the authorities to keep a close eye on people's movements, while also preventing contact between 'Aryans' and Jews. The hardest hit are the poor, of course. Somewhat surprisingly, any individual with enough money is permitted to rent a room in one of the Munich guest houses for any alien until that person, or the Party, finds something more acceptable – which usually takes a long time. Our housing department has a huge list of such guest houses willing to provide Jews with accommodation as well as meals, something greatly welcomed because it means our people are then spared the now difficult and time-consuming task of shopping for food.

1940

Letters from Else to Eva Schmidt

Isartal, 2 February 1940

Dear Eva

And now something much nicer to tell you about. At long last a letter from Fritz, which came on Saturday. It's dated 7 January and tells about his moving into the same place as Peter two days earlier, and how pleased he is about it. They're sharing a room in the home of a farming family who feed the pair of them as well. They sound like pleasant, well-bred people who welcome their house guests at their table for every meal. Peter is very happy with his job, and is now in charge of an up-to-the-minute dairy shed with ninety cattle and fifty calves, and two cowhands working alongside him.

Isartal, 2 March 1940

My dearest Eva

I've now had a reply to the telegram I sent to Argentina, saying that there's a delay in despatching my entry permit and that I should not in any circumstances expect it before the end of March. This time round I really had been counting on receiving it much sooner, something I know I absolutely should not do, and so the news left me quite low, but 'I've pulled meself together now', as the Bavarians would say, and am just carrying on with the waiting . . .

A letter came from Fritz yesterday, dated 29 January – he's in a constant state of nervousness and expectation, too.

Else's Diary

Isartal, Sunday 3 March 1940

After several months taken up entirely with work, I'm at last able to open my diary once more. Whenever life and work are running reasonably smoothly, I'm far less moved to write anything down and think this is entirely understandable. It may look as though I don't take an interest, because

I don't refer here to all the political and military events directly or indirectly affecting us and our fate, but I hardly need explain that this is absolutely not the case. The fact is that I have neither time nor the energy to go into it all in writing, and you're going through an awful lot, too, albeit on the other side of things, whereas everything I do commit to paper is in order to describe what's happening in the life you're unable to share with me. Today, however, I need to put in writing everything preoccupying my thoughts and to do so with the greatest of urgency.

On Monday we received shocking news from Berlin and the Reich Association of Jews in Germany[1] that on 22 February all the Jews in Stettin and most of Pomerania had been rounded up and taken away without warning, in all around a thousand souls in just a few hours – men, women, children, the elderly. Destination: unknown, probably Poland, where the so-called Generalgouvernement is in charge these days.[2] Is this the start of widespread deportation across the whole Reich, or just the work of one overly zealous Nazi Gauleiter? We have no idea, but personally I tend towards the former hypothesis.[3]

Yesterday young Rabbi Fink[elscherer][4] came to see Herr Rat. You remember him, I'm sure, from when the children took religious instruction from him. Anyway, he was very worked up because he – or rather his parents – had received the first direct news regarding the deportations. Fink[elscherer]'s own brother was a Rabbi in Stettin and had been taken away with his young wife. On the way he'd somehow managed to send a note to his parents. During the night of 12 February, they had been loaded on to a cattle truck in the freezing cold, each with the single suitcase they'd been allowed to pack hastily and then take to the station. Their suitcases were then taken off them, and they were told they'd be put in a special wagon travelling with them. His note said that they were in good health and that it looked as if they were heading for the area around the Polish city of Lublin. He added that he'd write again as soon as he could and that he and his wife were pleased to be with folk from their own community. You could tell he'd had to write in great haste and under pressure, wanting to reassure his parents and brother.

I keep picturing the scene of the deportation: herded on to the icy cattle truck with no proper winter clothes and no human comforts, presumably travelling night and day towards an unknown fate. What was to happen to these people once in Poland? Were they destined for particular jobs? And what had happened to all their elderly folk? And what on earth, finally, is the point of continuing with these questions? We can only wait for further news – that's if they're allowed to write.

Isartal, Sunday 17 March 1940

In the meantime more news has come in. The thousand or so people on that transport have been billeted in three small places in the district of Lublin, around six hundred of them in Piaski, including the young Rabbi and his wife. The old and the sick, numbering around a hundred, were sent to Glusk, some to Belzyce. The journey lasted three days and nights in what must have been indescribable conditions. Many died on the way, mostly from frostbite, and many are still suffering after being exposed to such low temperatures. Once at their three destinations, they were all provided with accommodation with local Jewish residents who, by our standards, live in primitive conditions of the most dreadful poverty. The new arrivals have nothing more than what they took on to the cattle truck, either on their person or in a small backpack or holdall. As of today they have not been reunited with their luggage and, reading between the lines, it's clear they don't expect to see it again. They consequently lack even the basic essentials, including medicines or medical equipment, and have only minimal food of poor quality and wholly inadequate clothing. The local Jewish community is clearly less than delighted to have this additional burden of new arrivals and understand neither their language nor their customs and traditions. What can we do? For the time being all the Fink[elscherer]s could do was send their son a few packages, each weighing a kilo, requesting immediate confirmation of safe arrival. As soon as that comes through, we'll start despatching more and will keep a written log of everything that is sent.

On Wednesday I went to the Quakers as I have done every week for the past several months. Annemarie and I now have a very close working relationship. At the outset she promised her support, and this has proved of the utmost importance to us.

Isartal, Sunday 24 March 1940

Arrival of parcels is now confirmed![5] Various things have gone missing, however, such as all the medicines we sent, as well as fat and sausage, and a good thick woollen coat. So we've learned a sad lesson. Next time we'll take all medicines out of their original packaging and rewrap them as simply as possible, giving each new package a number. What the number refers to will have to be communicated by separate letter. Anything new will have to be altered in some way so it looks used, clothing in particular. Via the young Rabbi from Stettin we have been able to get names and addresses of certain communities who can be trusted to distribute the goods fairly, and where there is the greatest need. We have requested a list of items needed most urgently. Annemarie, our Quaker colleague, and I had already made our own list of items that seemed likely to be most needed.

But then came news from the Reichsvereinigung of Jews in Germany that it was forbidden for the religious community to send anything to deportees. What a blow, but we quickly found a way round it. We're gathering things 'privately', so Emmy K[ohn] and I are sifting through possible items in our office, wrapping them and sending them off as if from private individuals, and wherever possible from different post offices. We knew everything had to be weighed so we got hold of a sturdy and really accurate kitchen scale. Each morning we find such a bright display of goods waiting for us that the office has been renamed 'the Polish Herti', after the old department store. It's truly wonderful to see what has been collected. I sent our list around all the different departments here and then all our staff told their friends and family about what was needed.

The trickiest thing has been storage. Both of us here have cleared the tops of our desks and we've freed up a cupboard. Next to that we've put a big chest for all the clothes and can take that down to the clothing store each time it's full. Quite a group of older gentlemen have put themselves forward to take the packages to the different post offices. One of them has made an especially kind offer and wants to donate all the paper and string we need, and this is not the trifle it might sound, given what we'll be sending off once we're in full swing.

Yes, of course, I know this is all only a drop in the ocean but we want to see it running successfully here before we seek to mobilise people in other communities.

One thing that seemed a major hindrance to me at first is now working to my advantage. Since the beginning of February the postbus service on our route has been discontinued. The only routes surviving are those with no railway connection. For me this has meant rising at half past four every day, a full hour earlier than before. The good thing is that this means I'm in the office by half past seven and can get a good run at all this extra work.

By the way, some of our returning emigrants are in the process of going back home, principally those from Karlsruhe and Offenburg. For the people from Freiburg, the Rhineland and smaller places in Baden, there's still no clarity about going back, but they, too, are hoping soon to be granted permission.

Isartal, Sunday 31 March 1940

The first letters from those deported to Stettin started to come in this week. For me the best and most objective report came from the young wife of the Rabbi in Piaski but reports from Glusk and Belzyce bring plenty of valuable information, too. And all of them convey such enormous gratitude for the fact that we want to help them, that we even want this contact with our fellow creatures. All those who've decided to do everything humanly possible to help these poor souls now find their resolve strengthened yet further. Our chair, Herr Rat, falls into that category, as does his wife, who also gives me a huge amount of practical support. Annemarie, our Quaker contact, Emmy K[ohn] and I myself are also greatly motivated by the news. Naturally I replied straight away to anyone including an address in order to demonstrate empathy with as many as possible of those suffering so much. In addition, I have asked for more names and addresses from among staff and their friends in order to start setting up individual links in the style of a godparenting scheme.

There is more I have been discussing with Herr and Frau Rat. In the next few days a returning emigrant, a lady of eighty-six, will need someone to accompany her back to Offenburg. Her son and his wife went back there a fortnight ago and wrote to say that they'd found a good place for her to live, a room in the home of someone they knew, with meals included. I'll be escorting the lady back to Offenburg and will take the opportunity to establish personal contact with the head and staff of each Jewish Gemeinde in Karlsruhe, Offenburg and Freiburg – colleagues with whom we have already had a lively and productive exchange of letters. Meeting face to face means I can more easily raise a number of important questions returning emigrants may want to voice. But also I want to get more support for the Stettin folk in particular by arranging plenty of useful parcels for them. I'm sure that Karlsruhe has an especially well-off community that could do plenty of good, and they have so often expressed their thanks to our Jewish Community in Munich for the care they received from our members that I feel I can now turn to them with my own requests for support.

To our delight we are now getting regular confirmation that parcels are arriving safely.[6] Since we started to make our chosen contents look 'used' or to repackage them, and to tuck things such as sausage and fats in among unbranded Migetti-type pastries[7] or unripe spelt, take medicines and glucose out of their special packaging and put them instead inside ordinary paper bags, add darns or patches to any new clothing, always separate out boots each to their own package, scratch enamel plates and cups and scrawl over them with wax crayon – since we've been doing all that hardly anything gets taken.

Now we're actually even sending money. Anyone in possession of a passport is permitted to send 10 Reichsmark per month, which in Polish currency is equivalent to 20 zloty. We already have quite a few people willing to send money to Poland against possession of a passport. Anyone not in a position to do so will get the money from me direct as we're now collecting a pleasing amount of cash. I want to pass on all this experience to Karlsruhe, as well as taking with me the letters from Karlsruhe for them to read.

In Berlin it seems far more difficult to send parcels off to Poland. I hope so much that we'll be in a position to go on giving this minimal help for a good long time and without obstacles being put in our way.[8]

I can't get the contents of those letters from Poland out of my head. I know from my own experience that we can all put up with the most basic of living conditions, but to exist in filthy squalor, herded in with people for whom such muck and grime is quite normal and who see no need to make the effort to keep things clean and orderly, indeed who view the task of cleaning with some derision, and to have to live like this with no help and no end in sight, well, that must be so very hard. And yet the women who send these letters are uncomplaining and describe their circumstances with real objectivity, asking for help not for themselves but for the old, the sick, the children. They make a real effort to show understanding of the Polish Jews with whom they have been quartered without anyone asking them if this was acceptable accommodation, and who now see these new arrivals as intruders. These Polish Jews view them not so much as an oppressed group from within their own race and faith, but rather as despicable, impious outsiders bringing in customs and traditions they don't understand. To crown it all, each side can barely communicate with the other.

Frau Fink[elscherer] is asking for a Polish–German and a Yiddish–German dictionary.

There's a shocking mortality rate among deportees who are elderly or sickly. Of the hundred billeted in Glusk twenty-five have now died, not even counting those who didn't survive the journey, and many more will be lost if packages of medicine, tonics and food can no longer be sent. The thought of attempting to assuage the plight of a thousand human beings with the despatch of two-kilo packages leaves us desperate. We know it doesn't help to show impatience, but you'll understand that looking back over all this suffering leaves the bitterest of tastes. I know Annemarie feels the same and that these poor people are constantly in her thoughts as she turns over and over in her mind how we could do something more radical to help them.

Letter from Else to Eva Schmidt

Isartal, 14 April 1940

My dear Eva

Three days ago an air letter arrived from Gustel telling us they'd had a terrible shock at the beginning of March. A government crisis had resulted in a change of administration at the immigration authority and her application for the entry permit had been rejected. The reason given was that we had two other children who could send for me and keep us both. Luckily the very active secretary to the Catholic relief action committee immediately picked this up and arranged for a new application to be submitted and the necessary documents swiftly produced and assembled all over again. But it was 18 March before everything was despatched. The secretary handed in the papers herself, together with a letter of recommendation from the Bishop of Buenos Aires. They all hoped that permission would be granted but didn't know how long it might take.

I must have suspected something already, as all this reminded me of when I was ill and felt constantly the uncertainty of everything, with it all receding into the far distance. That must be why the letter somehow barely affected me . . .

But I was completely bowled over at the news of the death of Ernst Heilmann.[9] I heard it direct from his wife and still can't take in the cruelty and absurdity of it all. How on earth can his family bear it and not feel embittered?

In your letter before last you asked if you could help us get hold of medicines. Wait just a little, if you would, as we've enough at the moment but this may change. The way things are just now it's hard to make out what's going on. Everything is particularly difficult and sometimes I feel so utterly unsettled that I can't think straight or make plans. That'll have to change . . .

Starting tomorrow there's plenty of new work for me as I'm now involved in running our homes, two of which are known to be a challenge and not in the state they should be.

Else's Diary

Isartal, Sunday 14 April 1940

I came back from my trip three days ago and am more than satisfied with what was achieved. I enjoyed meeting my returning emigrants in Karlsruhe and Offenburg and the talks with the community leaders and welfare staff were, I think, valuable on all fronts. And last but not least, my publicising the plight of the Stettin deportees will, I hope, reap rewards. Letters from over there increased prior to my departure and made a powerful impression on everyone I showed them to. Something I learned during my prison work has been reinforced, namely that people are only able to feel sympathy – I'm not talking about empathy here, which is on altogether a different plane – when they themselves or their nearest and dearest have been through a similar experience.

The people from Karlsruhe, of course, knew about the deportation of the folk from Stettin, and will at first have felt shock and a passing sympathy for those affected, but all too soon their own everyday preoccupations and concerns will have overshadowed it all and caused it to fade in their minds. The letters, however, immediately arouse interest as anyone reading them can picture the circumstances all too well. The poor people having to endure and suffer these dreadful conditions suddenly become real flesh and blood beings like ourselves rather than sketchy, unknown figures. On top of all that, Rabbi Fink[elscherer]'s wife is from Baden, from Offenburg itself, and many of those who read her letters in that district remembered her as a girl.

In all three of the communities I went to – I visited Freiburg, too, albeit only for a few hours – there is now an eagerness to send parcels and to learn from our experience. Furthermore, they will report to me on how their own efforts are progressing.

To finish up I spent several days in Baden-Baden where Herr and Frau Rat were spending Easter. The amount of work done through the winter and all the disruption that went with it had really taken it out of me and I must say how much I welcomed spending a period of quiet with these two. You'll remember that they run our own Jewish Community and are in every way a shining example of how to live one's life better. We had time to discuss all those things that remain unresolved during the normal working day, when there is never time enough.

So this was really the first opportunity I'd had to immerse myself in the charms of springtime in that truly blessed spot on our earth and feel overwhelmed by its beauty. As if by magic, everything was in full bloom all at once: lilac, chestnuts, fruit trees full of blossom and magnolia. Do you recall those lines by Gottfried Keller?

> My eyes drink of the beauty cupped in my eyelids,
> When they behold the abundance of the world!

I know you'll believe me when I say that I haven't let the beauty of the scene here make me forget all the pain and suffering of the war and its misery, but these few days away have renewed my strength, given me greater courage to carry on with our good work and consoled me with the dream of our being reunited one day.

Meanwhile, dear Emmy K[ohn], supported by a number of volunteers, has been sending off more relief parcels and ensuring no interruption to our service.

The latest letters ask for baby linen and nappies because two babies are due to be born in Piaski. One wonders how mothers and newborns can even be cared for and hope to thrive under such circumstances. We've managed to assemble two sets of baby equipment as well as tonics for the mothers, powdered milk and baby powder. We were only sorry that we couldn't wrap it all up prettily.

Among the most recent letters came one from a seventy-year-old lady in Stettin, very affluent indeed, who has done a great deal of voluntary work on our behalf. She was deported with her daughter and son-in-law. It's clear from what she wrote how very hard it is not to feel utter despair, and for this reason she has set a lot of store by her voluntary work as it serves as a distraction from her own suffering. She will be someone with whom I stay in regular postal contact.

Even people in mixed marriages felt at risk of deportation. A letter to us from the 'Aryan' wife of a Jewish dentist in Stettin described vividly how difficult it had been to secure a communal kitchen and any rooms that could remotely be used as a makeshift sickbay. I also receive letters daily from deportees who in near despair are writing off to every address they can think of to ask for money and parcels. Many go about it by paying excessive compliments to the recipients while others indulge in exaggerated depictions of their suffering in order to garner sympathy for themselves or their families.

Siegfried's Diary

Burcote, Abingdon, England, 14 April 1940[10]

Seven months into the war and now we hear that every German destroyer remaining in a Norwegian port has been sunk. I have little, if any, compassion left for Germany. If I have ever excused the silent obedience that fails to acknowledge individual responsibility, any such thoughts faded during the early weeks of the war from the moment the people were first armed. The sight of so much blind subservience dispels any respect I might still have had for people who actually bear scant regard for their fatherland and its fate. These people no longer feel any love for their own nation, or at least so little that their slavish compliance cannot now command respect.

Exiles like me may be viewed as pariahs, but we have been unleashed from our country by virtue of the fact that the German people have no love for it. Germany deserves to come to a sticky end and to learn its lesson. The only question is what form those lessons should take in order to give the populace a sense of their own personal agency in future, and a fresh ability to think, feel and act with responsibility.

That is a task that I would like to work on with others if the opportunity arose. Among the German population are individuals with strengths to be valued – good friends, but who, when all is said and done, still bear shared culpability for allowing the last seven or eight years to slip by them and their country, with little or no resistance. They may be few in number, but they in turn have friends, relatives, brothers, fathers and sons who share that culpability.

Am I being too harsh? I don't think so. When I was still living in Germany, the people stood unarmed and defenceless before the guns and cudgels of Hitler's personal militia. But with the outbreak of war and its immediate impact on the people, matters took on a very different complexion. During the early months of the war I was too full of trust and long-nurtured hope, counting on there finally being some show of resistance from the generals in charge of the country's own military. They all bear equal responsibility by virtue of their own inaction. Winter drew on. No resistance to be seen. No resistance to be heard. And then along came this rash and unthinking undertaking by a country with little sea power, engaging in a battle with far superior maritime forces. It was mad and utterly irresponsible, and still there was no resistance.

Burcote, 19 April 1940

It's a fortnight since Germany invaded Denmark and Norway, and this undertaking now looks like nothing more than reckless toying with Germany's very existence. Given the size of Germany's small fleet, every measure was taken during the 1914–18 war to avoid provoking England's far superior naval forces, even though circumstances were considerably more favourable back then. [. . .] This new undertaking will now heap upon Germany the hatred of every small nation, a hatred that will take root and flourish far beyond the time this war finally comes to an end.

And people expect me to say, 'Poor Germany?'

When and how will Germany put itself at the service of Europe once more? How can she be trained to do this and how long will it be until she takes this upon herself without any risk of some new and disastrous development? How can this even be attempted? Everything hinges on that question.

Burcote, 12 May 1940

Oxford is basking in the magnificence of spring. Lilac and apple blossom bring warmth and colour to its ancient quadrangles and distinguished gardens.

It's Saturday and the traffic is quite heavy, and in particular I notice military trucks with women in uniform at the wheel. Certain things strike me as typically English, such as the way the newspaper vendor can leave his stand quite unattended! Where you come out of the post office, two minutes from the busy central crossroads at Carfax, there's a stand stacked with the *Oxford Times*, with the chap nowhere to be seen. Passers-by leave the necessary coin as they collect their reading matter. I'd say there were already ten pennies lying there. I stood there for a while, just to watch, and still the vendor was nowhere in sight. And yet Oxford has a population of around one hundred thousand.

I had noticed similar things back in London where a telephone directory can languish unattached inside a telephone box and a pen similarly at liberty in the post office. It's the same out here in more rural public telephone kiosks. And then there's the London bus, where people think nothing of leaving luggage unattended near the driver or the exit. Even more striking is the way the tills are positioned far apart, such as in a Lyons' Corner House, the space between potentially allowing someone to slip through unnoticed.

Standards of behaviour are determined by morality and manners, which explains the lower incidence of theft and the noticeable lack of external security measures. There are plenty of detached homes with large windows at ground-floor level but with no iron railings to protect them, while gardens are easily accessed along paths with no protection (in comparison with those of Tempelhof in Berlin) leading to washing lines, almost always in use. [. . .]

Hitler invaded Holland and Belgium three days ago. That kind of invasion – done at night, easy victories over small, weak states – puts any decent soldier, any decent people, to shame.

Burcote, 21 May 1940

The conduct of the war is becoming increasingly alarming. The Germans have already advanced on Brussels and are pushing on north-west towards St Quentin and the French coast. There has been continuous heavy fighting for ten days now.

Staying calm is not easy. Any contact with Else is more difficult now that Gertrud Henning (in Denmark) and Richard Roeder have met their end.

If only we could hear something positive from Argentina, ideally before Italy joins the war, or else this route out will be closed for Else as well.

I so much want to concentrate on my personal research. I'm finding that I can draw on material I've already assembled but hadn't previously seen a use for. Shorter, highly detailed accounts based on attempts by individual countries, but ultimately also their failures, to create an overview of the Middle Ages and thereafter.[11] [. . .]

A few days ago – it was a Sunday – I was out with Peter in the fields [. . .] There were a number of pigsties in one part of the field, with breeding sows and their young in simple wooden huts with an open run so the animals could be outdoors in the open air. Valuable assets of this type are left outside, around fifteen to twenty minutes away from the farm itself with no one to watch over them, and the same goes for the henhouse. And all the while, a bare couple of minutes away, lies the busy Oxford Road, one of the main routes into London.

Else's Diary

Isartal, Sunday, 9 June 1940

The stacks of letters received from Poland grow ever higher, and I'm gradually forming an impression of the lives our folk from Stettin (for simplicity I always refer to them thus although there are also people from Stralsund and other such places) are leading in the small towns they're billeted in. We're also now sending books for the grown-ups, teaching materials, exercise books, coloured pencils and toys for the little ones.

Annemarie and I then started to think how important it is for the adults to have some useful jobs to do. So we got hold of some patterns to help them make their own slippers – light ones for the summer, good and warm for the winter – and despatched instructions, fabric cut-outs, thread and needles, together with felt and twine for the soles. It's the kind of work the men can take part in, too. With them in mind we also sent off plenty of knives for carving wood and a few sets of instructions for creating all manner of spoons. The women receive from us a constant supply of crochet hooks, thread, knitting needles, wool, patterns and leftover textiles so they can make things for the children. And there's always plenty of darning to be done, so we never forget the right yarns for that.

During the last fortnight or so, Emmy K[ohn] and I have gone round all the second-hand clothing dealers in Munich to buy up summer dresses for the women and girls, light jackets and trousers for the men and lads. Compared with what we can collect from private individuals, we managed a really good haul!

We have long lists of names with precise descriptions of age and appearance, but we'll soon have to change our systems for dealing with this. In our recent letters we asked for each town to nominate one person to be the recipient of our parcels and then for that person to be responsible for distributing the contents. It takes us far too long to make up so many different parcels to match individual requirements, whereas a centralised system can ensure that items are handed out more fairly and in line with what people actually need. That's not to say that we can't still despatch parcels to meet the request of a particular person, in which case we inform the distribution team at the other end. This different approach means we can take the time to ensure that the weight allowance is used to the full and, more than anything, we can work that much faster.

Comical situations arise, too. Yesterday Herr Rat came into our office and found me busily scribbling on the surfaces of a stack of enamel plates, while Emmy was wearing a lady's shoe on each hand so she could scrub the new soles all the more effectively on sandpaper to make them look worn. All three of us burst out laughing at the scene.

If the Gestapo superintendent who oversees our community suddenly turns up, though, it's rather trickier. The moment his car enters our courtyard, the caretaker telephones my office to say, 'Visitor!' That's when the clothes, shoes, medicines, foodstuffs, insect powder, cutlery, little spirit stoves, wrapping paper, string and weighing scales all vanish into the cupboard and desk drawers as if by magic. By the time the superintendent, a young man in his twenties, reaches our corridor I'm busy dictating while Emmy K[ohn] types, usually the lists required by the Gestapo or a report on matters concerning the returning emigrants, and we don't even look up from our diligent endeavours when he enters the room.

We're now sending off money on a regular basis, too. Each month we have about twenty passes made available to us and so are able to send off roughly 400 zloty against these. The cash is sent directly to our trusted contacts across the three towns, people we have come to know through our exchanges of correspondence and who can be relied upon to take care of any local purchases or plan distribution of funds at their end.

Siegfried's Diary

Burcote, Sunday, 4 June 1940

A cable from Hertha tells me that Else has finally received a visa for Argentina. This means that our sustained efforts over the best part of two years have finally borne fruit and, with the passage already paid for, hope of departure in a fortnight's time! The consulate in Munich will no doubt first need to receive the permit by airmail before issuing the visa itself. And so for me the way ahead at last becomes clear, as it probably also does for Peter and Hanna, and we can set aside our enquiry about joining the Santo Domingo resettlement programme.[12]

Burcote, 11 June 1940

Italy has now joined the war. Argentina rejected Else's application a fortnight ago so her final hopes of leaving the country are dashed.[13] First came the end of peace and now we await the end of the war: both of these determine our fate. I can do nothing more to protect Else. Will she be strong enough to protect herself? Will her friends be able to protect her? For years we found our salvation in the mountains, and that's where she'll be forced to seek it again. Our hope of being reunited after the war will have to remain just that – a hope.

This news means that the war will be more protracted, with even greater uncertainty than before as to its outcome – although it may also mean the final liberation of Europe from dictatorship and Fascism, so long as Russia isn't part of the picture.

It requires a great deal of effort to summon the mental fortitude to carry on with my own writing. I've managed twenty-six pages of typescript thus far. Working like this gives me tremendous satisfaction, more than I'd ever imagined. Having a tangible outcome at the end of the day makes it so fulfilling.

Burcote, 22 June 1940

France fell three days ago: a disaster for Europe. This represents a fundamental turning point in the war and a victory chalked up to Germany. The battle for England is intensifying [...] Our personal fate now looks even worse, as any prospect of the family being reunited slips further out of reach. The war is likely to drag on into 1941 and perhaps beyond. Whatever I thought and wrote on 3 June is no longer valid.

Else's Diary

Isartal, Sunday, 28 July 1940

I'm taking a few days' leave next week. I'm off to the hills where Hanna, an old friend from student days,[14] has for years rented a holiday place with her husband and family. They've invited me to join them and I'm very much looking forward to seeing them as well as having some rest and relaxation. Emmy K[ohn] is covering my absence as there can be no interruption to the

23. Excursion in difficult times. Hanna Schadendorf (*left*) next to Else, and behind them Kurt Schadendorf, 1940.

despatch of packages. We're now sending only to certain names we've been given as these people are known to be trusted committee members. We've started adding costume jewellery to the packages, such as necklaces strung with wooden or glass beads, brooches made of ivory or glass, anything bright and colourful, since we found out that the non-Jewish population over there in Poland love this kind of thing and it gives our own people something to barter with in exchange for essential foodstuffs.

We've done something else of significance this week. With the help of Annemarie, our Quaker colleague, we've compiled a list of essentials for people to take in the event of further deportations – something which I have no doubt will take place, whereas others optimistically prefer to see the despatch of the folk from Stettin as a unique occurrence. We recommend that people get hold of a small stove with the necessary fuel, along with cheap, lightweight cutlery, a cup and a bowl, and have all this ready in a rucksack that they keep close to hand. We also tell them to wear at least two layers of clothing and to make up a sleeping bag following the pattern we can provide, or if not, then to have ready a couple of blankets and a small pillow, and to roll this up with nightclothes and slippers inside and then secure it with a suitable strap. A lot of our people were eager to have this list and we sent copies to the Berlin Reichsvereinigung of Jews in Germany, along with our other communities.

I had arranged with Herr Rat to slightly extend my period of leave so as to visit the chair and welfare staff within each Jewish Community in Dresden, Berlin, Frankfurt am Main, Mannheim and Stuttgart, to help each of them set up a subcommittee with the purpose of sending similar parcels to ours to the deported Pomeranians. I'm taking with me food and medicines to demonstrate what is needed as well as a stack of letters that speak for themselves and a list of essential items. We consider it essential to publicise this now as winter isn't far off and we won't be able to meet the needs of all the deportees on our own.

In the last few days I've received a detailed letter from the 'Aryan' wife of the dentist from Stettin. I had sent her a little gift, something we often do now, in the case of this lady a colour print of Spitzweg's painting *The Poor Poet*. It portrays a miserable attic with the poet himself in a corner using an old mattress as a seat, his back propped against the wall while he writes with one hand and holds an open umbrella over his head with the other, shielding himself from the rain dripping through the building's lamentable roof. Frau Bauchwitz has written back rather drily, saying it looks fit for royalty by comparison with her own fleapit of a room.

Both she and Frau Fink[elscherer] have written that after the worrying weight loss suffered by everyone during the first few months of their changed circumstances, it seems as though people have grown strangely used to this horribly primitive way of life. Death rates and the incidence of serious illness were shockingly high at first but have now fallen significantly. There certainly remain a high proportion of bowel and stomach complaints but these are mostly not serious and probably related to the hot weather they are currently experiencing. It seems an incontrovertible fact that human beings can adapt to almost anything and put up with far more than would generally be thought possible.

Siegfried's Diary

11 July 1940

Interned on 25 June 1940 at eight in the morning.[15] Taken first to the barracks near Oxford with Dr Ernst Cohen and around one hundred and twenty others. In the sports hall I met up with quite a few people I knew [. . .].

Three days later, Thursday 2 July, we were sent to Southampton – four buses for one hundred and sixty-six of us. There, we were billeted in a school. Lectures on philosophy by Heinemann and Eysler. *On the Origins of Naturalism* by Olden, then on Friday an English course. And so on and so forth.[16]

10 July. Taken by rail to B[ury] near Manchester. A ruined factory building (Warth Mills), with four hundred and eighty people in one hall. Barbed wire. Books, manuscripts, and pocket books confiscated. No newspapers. Bibles, Beethoven sonatas taken off us, along with every tiniest scrap of paper, every last cigarette. [. . .] Quaker visit on 20 July from Mrs Bligh and Dora Wesley,[17] bringing today a letter from Hanna and her address. On 9 July Peter arrived in the evening from Seaton; he's been interned since 4 July. A ray of light in this darkness. Others are pleased for me. [. . .]

Douglas, Isle of Man, 28 July 1940

Since 16/17 July we have been living in boarding houses in Douglas, Isle of Man. Thirty men, some women too. 17 July: the beauty of the distant sea and the sight of white gulls flying through the blue, sun-warmed air contrast all too sharply with this harsh lack of freedom. Men at the end of their tether, men left devastated at their abrupt separation from homes they've tried so hard to save, cut off from the outside world in all respects, robbed of personal books, writings, notes, and suddenly left in that filthy place, Warth Mills.

There was a beautiful concert today. It moved many to tears when they thought of their loved ones. Peter is still stuck in Warth Mills – no news for two weeks now, nor from Else and Hanna, so I pour out my heart, all my fears and longing to Hertha.

The majority here are men over fifty-five, eaten up by anxiety and bitterness from everything they've experienced over the last seven years. Anything anybody says is met with dissent, everyone is everybody else's enemy, and all too ready to criticise and blame. This is a mass cry of confusion and despair. There is no relief from newspapers, and very little post. We read vehement criticism of the Home Office and the War Office in the *New Statesman* (20 July).

Douglas, Isle of Man, 29 August 1940

There was an announcement a few days ago that all those over sixty-four were to be released with immediate effect – about ninety men in all. Over the last four weeks our post has been handed out in the canteen, there have been a few organised walks and the camp management has made obvious efforts to improve the conditions here. We hold a big farewell every morning to those leaving, with a chorus of voices by the barbed wire in front of HQ. And a hall has been made available up above the canteen for lectures and concerts. We take our own chairs. [. . .]

Yesterday fifteen married men bearing bunches of flowers went to see their wives held at another camp. The younger chaps played on the lawn, tug-of-war. There's gymnastics in the morning, and bridge to round off the day.

A couple of days ago I got back my notebooks, dictionary and three folders of my own bits and pieces.

Douglas, Isle of Man, 20 September 1940

A strange recurring sight: man with chair on his way to a lecture on the lawn or in the hall. Twice a week I go to hear Dr Stadler on the Middle Ages, or to Dr Sohn-Rethel's study group, or to hear Dr Rosenfeld as war correspondent, or Dr Unger on philosophy. Yesterday a lecture on Eastern European and Western European Judaism attempted to find common ground on

Zionism and the question of Palestine, although it seemed to exclude the huge number of Jews from Eastern Europe now settled in America, as well as those who never got there. By contrast the lecture given by Dr Friedrich on the prehistory of North America showed remarkable depth, as did Dr Rausche on Punishment and the Social Structure, exploring the connection between prison policy and the population movement that is migration.

At the moment I'm writing mostly to Hedi and Else, or Hertha and Else, and long to see Else's familiar hand on anything coming via the US. The two most recent missives came from Marta Rosenbaum and from Else, dated 15 June and 22 June, and took three months to arrive.[18]

Douglas, Isle of Man, 25 September 1940

Three months in internment now. It's as though life itself is closing in during this typically variable time of year, with the onset of autumn and winter close on its tail. And here, a group of people thrown together here without any discernible rhyme or reason, are starting to become a burden unto themselves.

But Peter's release on 23 September has been such relief that I find it less difficult to think ahead to my own release, which until now has been no more than a dark fleck on the distant horizon. It means so much to me that Peter can return to the farm work he loves and earn his keep. That will also be of help to me, once I'm out.

Here are a few more images of life in this place. I want to capture in my mind's eye the man with the chair, walking to a lecture on the lawn or in the hall, by day and of an evening, as well as the group marching every morning at seven right up to the barbed wire to accompany those being released that day, complete with singing or the strains of an accordion. On Monday we bade farewell to our music lecturer, Prof Kastner, with a rendition of 'Ode to Joy', then also to Prof Eysler, carrying with such infinite care the oil painting he completed here, and then there was the Rabbi, accompanied by a Jewish song.

I've just been listening to the former SPD representative in government, Wittelshöfer,[19] giving recollections of his time in office. Yesterday at nine we had Dr Rosenfeld's usual evening briefing on the state of the war (he was a journalist for the *Wiener Arbeiterzeitung*).

Meanwhile distressing news. A ship carrying almost one hundred evacuated children has been torpedoed and sunk in the Atlantic.[20] Of the adults also on board this means the loss of Dr Rudolf Olden, the man we last saw a fortnight ago on the steps of the HQ here, looking ahead to the future, the familiar scarf round his neck and a new position awaiting him in the US. This was a man almost destroyed by internment and in the end finished off by Hitler.

Our worst moments here derive from the uncertainty facing each one of us. When will we regain our freedom and return to our families?

Quite a few are wondering whether enlisting for the Pioneer Corps would provide a way out.[21] A difficult scenario for anyone under fifty, given that this war looks increasingly similar to the last one. A year of glittering prizes for Germany in preparation for a new year that I hope will put the seal on rather a different state of affairs.

Else's Diary

Isartal, Sunday, 27 October 1940

We've always feared this and now it's happened – another wave of deportations.[22] It's hard to take it in, it's all so shocking. This time it's on a far greater scale than the first time around. All Jews from Baden and the Rhineland, along with an entire region of Württemberg, were deported on 22 October, it seems, making a total of five thousand people.

They've been sent not to Poland but to a camp in unoccupied France, that's all we know. And the Jews who previously lived in France in Alsace are thought to be there too. Annemarie came by this alarming news via a friend in Mannheim, a woman I've stayed with during my trips to other communities: a so-called 'Aryan' lady who helps the Jewish people there whenever she can, just as Annemarie helps us here in Munich. When it came to packing up and organising transport, she was of great assistance to her local Jewish community and even accompanied them to the railway station, describing vividly how it took all her self-control not to jump on to the train with them to demonstrate the close kinship she felt with these unfortunates. Only the thought of her own husband and child stopped her. At least those in mixed marriages were spared on this occasion. The chair of the Jewish Gemeinde in Mannheim, a doctor with an 'Aryan' wife, could not find it in his heart to stay behind and went into voluntary exile with his community, leaving behind his wife. She's delicate, apparently, and wouldn't have withstood the ordeal of deportation. Just think what comfort and reassurance such an act must have brought his community, something they'd be quite justified in describing as heroic.

Gripped by fear, all we can do now is wait for news. I know so many of these people from my returning emigrant groups. In the last few weeks we've succeeded in pushing through a request originally opposed by the Nazi authorities, namely to permit a number of Baden Jews from smaller towns such as Breisach to be allowed home. Such joy in their faces when they said farewell and such gratitude in their letters telling of their arrival home! Sadly their enjoyment was to be short-lived. Those who didn't rush to return find themselves better off, and we're asking the Gestapo to grant them permanent residency in Munich.

There was a heartbreaking incident in my office the day before yesterday. A woman from one of the smaller towns in Baden had to take her husband to hospital in Mannheim a fortnight ago and he was due to be discharged on 23 October. Naturally she was planning to be there to bring him home. In the interim she went to visit her brother in Stuttgart and when she got back to Mannheim on 23 October as planned, she discovered he'd been taken away. She pleaded with every possible authority to be allowed to follow him but met with refusal at every turn. We were her last hope. In her desperation she fell to her knees and begged me to do anything in my power to allow her to join her husband and other relatives. We'll do everything we can, of course, but I don't hold out much hope. I have a lot to do with the local Gestapo inspector here, a decent and proper sort of man, and he promised me he'd telephone his colleague in Mannheim. I should be finding out tomorrow. (Note added: 30 October 1940: It's all turned out all right in the end and Frau K is being allowed to follow her husband.)

Isartal, Sunday, 10 November 1940

In the meantime we've had news, both directly and indirectly, of the Baden folk who were deported. They're now in the Département Bas-Pyrénées in Camp de Gurs, a camp of wooden shacks hastily put up during the Spanish Civil War for all the people streaming over the border into France. The French government had declared itself willing to take into unoccupied France the three to four thousand Jews normally resident in Alsace and Lorraine. In addition they were then sent, without any further discussion or agreement, some five thousand Jews from Baden and the Rhineland. They'd not prepared for anything like this number of people and so the food and accommodation did not remotely match the need, as evidenced by all the letters we then received, urgently requesting food. Most of the letters stressed the great humanity shown by the French towards those who'd been deported. Straight away we set to with making up parcels to despatch more relief, calling for support on those who'd previously billeted evacuees for us. Our friend in Mannheim mobilised many of her own friends and is likewise sending off as much as she can.

The Reichsvereinigung proposed a day of fasting in recognition of this appalling treatment of our people, and we were keen to take part. To our horror Herr Rat then told us yesterday that Otto Hirsch, the man who instigated the day of fasting, had been arrested and taken to a concentration camp. (News of his death reached us a few months later.) His proposal was viewed as an act of sabotage over a directive from the authorities.[23]

We're packing and despatching packages to Poland and to France as fast as we can. How much longer we'll be allowed to do this, well, we just don't know. In spite of all the difficulties and privations in the Camp de Gurs, I still get the impression that the poor folk there are having less of a hard time of it than those over in Poland. One thing that's clear from the correspondence is that the French guards treat the inmates with humanity at least and help them wherever they can, whereas the mental torments suffered in Poland under German occupation get worse by the day.

Siegfried's Diary

Oxford, 13 November 1940

A long gap since I last wrote. I came out of internment on 29 September. Overnight accommodation in Oxford, registered with the police as required, then a night on the sofa in the dining room of rather an elegant hotel.

I've found temporary lodgings [. . .] followed by probably something better and for longer at Collinwood Road – that'll be from 18 November.

I've finally got over my earlier fear of life in an era shaped by war. I'm working in the Bodleian Library[24] every day now, although beset by time

ACHTUNG.

Deutschen Fluechtlingen wird dringendst geraten, aeusserst vorsichtig in ihren Gespraechen zu sein.

In Ihrem eigenen Interesse empfehlen wir Ihnen dringend, keine Arbeitsangebote irgendwelcher Art anzunehmen, ohne vorher die Erlaubnis der englischen Regierung eingeholt zu haben.

SIE SIND GAESTE GROSSBRITANNIENS.

Hoeflichkeit und gutes Betragen werden Ihnen ueberall herzliche Aufnahme und Sympathie zusichern.

Sprechen Sie nicht laut auf der Strasse, besonders nicht am Abend.

Nehmen Sie Ruecksicht auf die Bequemlichkeit anderer Leute und vermeiden Sie, deren Eigentum und Moebel zu beschaedigen.

Vergessen Sie nie, dass England's Urteil ueber die deutschen Fluechtlinge von IHREM Verhalten abhaengt.

Attention

German refugees are advised in the strongest possible terms to take the utmost care whenever in conversation.

In your own interests you are asked not to accept employment of any kind without prior permission of the government.

You are guests of the British government

Courtesy and good conduct on your part will ensure a warm welcome and understanding.

Do not talk loudly on the street and especially not in the evening.

Give due consideration to others and avoid any damage to their property and furnishings.

Do not forget that England's opinion of German refugees is dependent on YOUR behaviour.

24. 'Rules of Conduct for Germans Migrating to England', 1940.

pressures, mostly because of *The Jew and His Neighbour* by Parkes [. . .].[25] Parkes and his publisher have given me translation rights (in today's post), although I'm not a translator by profession.[26] It's a huge task with two hundred pages of type. Much of it doesn't really correspond to my own views and I'll be adding plenty of notes. And at the moment who's likely to have any understanding of all this, or see any relevance? 'To encourage a better Germany in the time to come?' Any 'better Germany' is still fast asleep and chained down. All the same, it must be awoken and encouraged, supported, provided with good books. It has slept through so much. We need to shout out: *Wake up, Germany!* Am I being overly optimistic – looking through rose-tinted spectacles perhaps?

Letter from Else to Eva Schmidt

Isartal, 30 November 1940

Listen, I've received another letter direct from my Fritz. It's dated 27 October and in it he tells me all about his life in O[xford]. He's very well indeed, he says, and already has a little group of acquaintances with whom he spends Sundays, and sometimes a weekday evening. At least once a week he also sees Peter on our boy's day off. I'm so surprised the letter ever got here, and with his full address on it at that!

Otherwise, no news here, only lots of work to be done. But wait – perhaps there is a bit of news. Just listen to this! Our greatly respected and well-loved chairman has suddenly managed to secure an entry permit to Argentina, all organised by his son, and so he and his wife will be leaving in January.

This will be such a loss to us here and however delighted we are for the pair of them, it will leave a gap that simply can't be filled. He called me in straight away and told me he had formed the distinct impression that the local consul refused entry to Fritz and me on account of Fritz's background in public service. That's comes as a real blow, but there's nothing to be done about it. It was several days before I could really take in what had happened.

Siegfried's Diary

Oxford, December 1940

[. . .] At last the forms have arrived to sign up for our passage to Santo Domingo, as set in motion by Curt Bondy. Hertha marked the cable as 'urgent'. With two characters like this on my side, well, everything else gets pushed to the back of the queue! And I really do want to try and get a place. If only my Else could go there as well.

On 11 December I wrote to Hertha saying I wanted to go. Today a letter came from Else, dated 3 October, via Hedi with her own letter of 25 October. Else describes an evening of music at the Pringsheims with the Bachmann children (Markus, Almuth, along with Pringsheim father and son). It sounded glorious and is a wonderful scene for me to picture from where I sit.

Oxford, 22 December 1940

I'm spending weekdays in the Radcliffe Camera, the beautiful rotunda library near the Bodleian. Its stairs echo the curve of the building, and when I'm climbing these steps, worn smooth over the years, I like to picture the many distinguished and bewigged gentlemen who have gone before me. The stock of Anglo–American material here is far too impressive to ignore in favour of my own research! [. . .]

Yesterday a letter came from Else, dated 19 October – a long time in its arrival. Soothing in its tone and so calming for me, in spite of the year and three months of separation already behind us and doubtless as much ahead, if not more.

If I were ten years younger, this life would definitely be less hard to bear. Thank goodness I have the children here with me. I saw Hanna in London, Hammersmith to be precise, for an hour and a half on 13 December. I had to go to Woburn House regarding the Santo Domingo programme, as well as the Swiss Embassy to verify my signature for the life certificate to attest that I remain hale and hearty and sound in limb. Hanna tells me she's lost some belongings in one of the air raids. Hitler manages to get to us even here. But he won't succeed. Britain has more staying power and stronger nerves. As far as England is concerned, the war has only been going for four months so far, while Germany's early successes gave it the impression that the whole thing was already in the bag over six months ago. Maybe England's air power can bring about the necessary turnaround without any land battle of doubtful value having to take place on the Continent (in southern Austria, Turkey or Egypt possibly) or even on English soil. What is alarming is the likely success of the U-boats if their impact is not dealt with forthwith.

My second winter here is an even clearer demonstration than the first of how hardy these people are when it comes to the cold! A modest fire suffices in the hearth, or else they consider coal to have been wasted. They will queue patiently and in silence for the bus. This will come along, the conductor will say 'full up', and they'll obediently carry on waiting, without saying a word. There's a similar degree of patience in the shops and on the pavement, where prams are given priority. This is not simply a matter of temperament, of stoicism, or instilled self-control. It's because they don't suffer from that innate sense of inferiority that asserts itself only through shouting and screeching out orders. Here there is calm self-assertion and self-awareness, characteristics allowed to develop and thrive over centuries of peaceful economic and political development.

1941

Else's Diary

Isartal, Sunday, 26 January 1941

We gathered in the prayer room a week ago for a simple ceremony of farewell. This was for Herr and Frau Rat [Neumeyer] prior to their departure for Argentina and the Jewish colony of Avigdor where their son is already settled.[1] I'm happy for the two of them but we'll feel very alone without these two wise and generous people at our head. They too found it hard to say goodbye. In his farewell speech, Herr Rat said this:

> One day when we're old and grey, sitting under trees we haven't yet set eyes on, gazing out over fields that our son has worked so hard to cultivate in our new homeland, our memories will still retain the wonder and hardship of these years that have bound us together, and we will think of all those who worked here so tirelessly and under such harsh conditions.

They would very much have liked to take me with them, not least because they know how dearly I still hope to be reunited with Gustel, our eldest, not to mention all our other relatives over there in Argentina, since the war continues to prevent me from joining you all in England.

Our new chair is the chap who's been running our Welfare Department for some time now. His name is Stahl and he's good to work with.[2] Our only concern is whether he'll be quite up to the job of steering our little ship through the crashing waves to some safe haven that may not even exist.

Siegfried's Diary

Oxford, 15 February 1941

We are now well into a new year and spring is not far off, with signs of new life showing in University Park (in the part known as Mesopotamia), while nearly every front garden on the Banbury Road has anemones, snowdrops, and some blue flowers I've not seen before. It's remarkable how evergreens such as cedar, fir and rhododendron, as well as such an array of mature shrubs, can bring warmth and colour to an otherwise bleak winter scene.

Even the grass seems more verdant here in winter than at home, but as I write that word, 'home', my pen trembles and I have to break off for a moment.

How can this go on? This outrageous disregard for the sovereignty of others, this vindictiveness towards national borders, this constant blackmailing of smaller nations who, if they dare to resist, are afforded only the most limited of freedoms. Three months ago violence was used to drive out German Jews from Baden, Hessen and the Rhineland and despatch them for internment in the south of France. And then there have been attacks on civilians on English streets, while ships have been torpedoed without warning and no thought for their crew, air strikes have targeted civilians on transport ships, and so on and so forth . . .

The occupation of Italy by the German army places the latter in a defensive position, exposed to the full might of England's naval and air forces. And still there is no end in sight and one cannot see how any good can come of it all. This latest move does, however, herald a bloodbath on a scale not seen during the first year and a half of the conflict.

Yesterday, after a month of apparent silence, two letters came from Else via Lisbon, both written in January. They make me so happy even though I can glean from the contents that several of our letters to one another have gone missing over the last year. The Neumeyers, who helped Else so much, have now left for that longed for destination that could so easily have been hers. It looks as though Else has heard nothing regarding the Santo Domingo resettlement programme, now running for three months. It all sounds highly organised – Hertha has sent the annual report along with the documentation in support of our application. It's a huge undertaking with all sorts of support from highly competent people. Peter and Hanna have been admitted to the programme and have now formally applied for their exit permits and visas through the necessary committee.

Else's Diary

Isartal, Sunday, 16 March 1941

Increasing numbers of Jews from Munich are now being forced out of their homes and finding them alternative accommodation is getting more and more difficult. What has particularly shocked us is the way even the nominated 'Jewish houses' are suddenly needing to be cleared when it suits the arbitrary whims of the Gauleiter's deputy in Widenmayerstrasse. A recent example is one such building in Goethestrasse, suddenly cleared of all residents. One of our own staff lived there – just one room, while all the others were rented out. In the nick of time she found herself an alternative in a guest house, 'Aryan' of course, in Landwehrstrasse.

All the signs point to a worsening of the situation. Not long ago a crowd of young Jewish males were, on the orders of the Gauleiter's deputy, quietly despatched by Oberstürmführer Muggler [Mugler][3] to Tegernsee to dismantle the wooden huts once hastily erected to billet Austrians, secretly members of the SA, when they illegally flooded over the border. These Jewish lads were then made to reassemble them miles away in Milbertshofen, an industrial suburb of Munich. We presume this will be a place to house Jews from Munich, creating a new ghetto.[4]

In addition to all this, all Jewish men up to the age of sixty were taken from Milbertshofen and set to work in various different factories and now the same is being done with the women, starting with those under fifty years of age. The younger women are being deployed in making armaments, while the older ones are given lighter work.

Isartal, Sunday, 27 April 1941

Yesterday a telegram came from Käthe, my sister in Argentina, telling me that my *Llamada*, that's the entry permit, had been cabled to the Argentine Consulate in Munich.[5] At the same time I received a note from the Consulate asking me to attend a meeting there tomorrow! Is this really true? Can I really leave? Is this constant pressure going to be lifted? Will I truly have direct contact with you three again and complete freedom to write to all of you, and more than anything to you, my dear? But I don't dare think this way! I've had my hopes up in the past and had to bear the disappointment. My papers are ready, my passport's in order, I can be ready to depart just like that. Let's hope it happens.

Siegfried's Diary

Oxford, 4 May 1941

The children would perhaps have had a faster track to an independent existence in Santo Domingo than would be possible in Argentina. Nonetheless reuniting the family is paramount in these harsh times, especially while Peter and Hanna are so young still, and with my age making me so reliant on them both. [...] And most importantly, the climate in Argentina is better for Else's health than that in Domingo.

I cabled the content of my telegram straight to Lisbon because Else may well arrive there sometime over the coming fortnight. Even my fear that Latin America may become a refuge for Nazis on the run will have to take a back seat for the moment. Nowhere is safe. All I can hope is that the war will end in 1942 and in England's favour.

We continentals have always set our sights on territorial gains and losses. Such matters have held little interest for the inhabitants of these islands, however, rarely featuring in England's history when seen as a whole. Advances and withdrawals of this nature are only of interest to the Nazis themselves as a means to an end, namely to ensure a ready supply of food and raw materials in the event of a long drawn-out war.

Winning or losing depends on the outcome of the Battle of the Atlantic, any land war in defence of British territory, and on the war in the air. The current severity of the U-boat attacks will tail off once the US is jointly watching over the Atlantic, of that I have complete confidence. [...]

Over the last five weeks my work on *Die Zeitung* has taken more time and given me further things for my reading pile. Sebastian Haffner, for example, in his *Offensive against Germany*, along with other similar publications.[6]

Else's Diary

Isartal, Sunday, 4 May 1941

On Monday confirmation came from the Consulate that I should be receiving my visa and could make the final arrangements with getting things organised. So that same day I went to the medical officer in Wolfratshausen for my medical certificate, and he gave me the necessary immunisations and provided me with the appropriate document to prove it.

With this joyous news in the air I was better able to celebrate my fiftieth birthday on Thursday and did so with the many good friends here. Missing from the party were my neighbours, the Pr[ingsheim] family and our wonderful grocer, who had earlier asked Tilla why she was buying so many special things. Since your own departure I had experienced no similar thrill over an impending journey as I did about this one but it was not to last.

In the office the next day I was met with so many gifts and warm greetings – 1 May was a public holiday, of course – but then Tilla telephoned to say that a letter had come from the Argentine Embassy. I asked her to open it and read it

25. Else Rosenfeld, date unknown.

aloud. My visa confirmation was being revoked due to new instructions from Argentina. Deeply distressed, I rushed over to the embassy in person only to be told by the secretary that additional written information was required from my relatives. I immediately sent a telegram to my sister Käthe in Argentina to tell her of this change through from Buenos Aires. I'm still hoping this turns into no more than a slight delay. The information asked for will all be in order – there is simply no valid reason to refuse me a visa. At times, though, I have had more than a few suspicions with reference to this particular consul – you and I are both aware of his poor reputation – as he is quite open regarding his antisemitic views and is doing everything he can to delay or obstruct the whole issue of my visa. The fact that we Jews have been treated like pariahs by an entire series of consulates across the Reich shows this man is no exception, but I refuse to give up hope yet!

Siegfried's Diary

Oxford, 18 May 1941

Two weeks ago a telegram came saying that Else now has her visa for Argentina. Since then I've spent every waking moment waiting for further news, but so far in vain. Peter's also in a state of waiting. He came to see me as usual last Friday. [. . .] Something quite astonishing happened a week ago. Rudolf Hess landed in England.[7] The effect of this incident, the landing of Rudolf Hess on English soil, provides yet another opportunity to reiterate the differences between the English outlook and the 'continental'.

At first he was greeted with nothing but suspicion until the context gradually became all too clear, namely that he had travelled alone. He had fled in the belief that his life was in danger or, alternatively, that German success was now in doubt.

Nothing in particular happened during the first few days, and the interpretation given by German radio sounded both clumsy and mendacious.

This whole incident constituted a severe blow aimed directly at Hitler, with the express intention of further weakening a country already divided, the man's flight being a clear indicator of his purpose. I along with many others saw this as the salient interpretation of the whole affair.

England, however, dealt with it all very differently. He was not allowed radio time, not used as a tool of propaganda against the Nazis, but instead treated with the utmost disdain and dubbed an absolute rogue, his complicity with every Nazi crime well and truly spelled out to the last letter.

I myself look at it another way and think of how one might treat a man who has been attacked by a band of robbers and locked up. One night one of the thieves offers to set him free, something that surely anyone would accept even if the liberator is a thief and a murderer.

But no, England says the very idea of a noble robber is the stuff of pure fantasy. The *Daily Mirror* publishes a cartoon drawing of Hess leaning over the body of a child killed in an air raid, saying, 'Will you be my friend?' Well, what a question! In Hess I see only the enemy of my enemy, and that is England's enemy, too, and the commonality of the primary enemy affords any rationale necessary for making the most capital out of this incident.

For England, however, an outraged notion of morality is of greater significance, where there is 'no common ground' to be found. The man is merely viewed as quite as monstrous as the rest of them, even after his split from Hitler and his very public act of faith in England, the land to which he fled. His military and political knowledge will inevitably be put under the microscope for analysis by the experts. To some degree it's right that this kind of information should be held secret, or Germany could attempt to benefit from the opportunity to deny or defend its activities. Leaving the Germans in the dark as to what has been revealed would more usefully feed their unease, not to mention ratcheting up concern as to precisely how many

26. Cartoon from the *Daily Mirror* on Rudolf Hess's landing on British soil. Hess addresses a child, killed in an air raid: 'Will you be my friend?'

secrets we might now have out in the open. A dog won't bother with a piece of dry bread.

And so we can see how contempt for the enemy, as personified in this one Nazi deserter, can become a state-sanctioned murder weapon.

Oxford, 8 June 1941

Sunday, one of the rare warm days in this chilly spring. Beautiful blossom and fragrance from the whitethorn and the laburnum. I walked right to the outskirts of the city. People can live so comfortably here, mostly in houses, large and small, all nestling in their own gardens. The gardens look far better tended than the houses, I have to say! Out of a total population of around 100,000, I'd say that 99,000 live in homes like this, ranging from just a couple of rooms to half a dozen or so. True, they don't have basements and attics like we do in Germany, and all lack anything beyond a straightforward fireplace for heating, but they're so much nicer than our tenanted apartment blocks, crammed with hundreds of families.

Passers-by show no signs of fear or war weariness, absolutely none of that. I'm constantly surprised at how cheerful people are, old and young alike. The gravity of the war really only became apparent – well, apart from the air raids, that is – in January 1941 when rations decreased, and yet everyone took that on the chin too. The women chat away in the food queues, perfectly patient and without any squabbling. Someone seems always to be singing or whistling somewhere and even the elderly, both men and women, cycle around as if out hunting for their favourite biscuit! It is vital for this sweet-toothed nation to have something with their cup of tea. These are contented people who clearly feel smiled upon, which is why the true gravity of the situation is only just sinking in. Aside from the air raids, as I say. This is probably more apparent in Oxford than anywhere else. Two thousand students here, and usually double that number. A lot of affluent folk all in one place.

Oxford, 23 June 1941

As of yesterday the war has taken a shocking turn against Russia and Hitler is pushing hard in that direction.[8] Russia's true inner grit will now gradually reveal itself, and we shall see how deeply the people are faithful to the Soviet system and whether its varying stance towards Nazi Germany has been fully understood or simply driven them mad.

And what about the German workforce for whom Russia represents their last hope – how on earth will they accept this volte-face when back in August 1939 there was an alliance struck with Russia? I'm thinking here of the older German soldiers and men of advancing years employed in the war effort: how will they take it? Won't the German army lose a lot of its men to this new Front? And in practice how much real resistance will there be to Russia?

Germany's objective here is clearly to access a new source of bread to feed the people as well as fuel to feed the war machinery. These are the preconditions necessary for maintaining a lengthy conflict, and without them they will struggle even to get through the coming winter of 1941/42. A distraction of such proportions on the eastern front is excellent news for England and America, allowing them – as it surely will – to recoup time and strength. The Nazis will know this, that's for certain, and the fact that they're carrying on regardless demonstrates their utter desperation to procure these basic commodities.

Else's Diary

Isartal, Saturday, 28 June 1941

Everything's happening in a rush. The wooden huts in Milbertshofen are ready – rows of basic bunk beds lined up military-style. There are wash-rooms, a kitchen, canteen and dining areas and the camp has received its first admissions – all single men to begin with. It has capacity for around eight hundred.

On 21 June – last Saturday – I received a summons to report on Monday 23 June to Hauptsturmführer Wegner at the office in Widenmayerstrasse. This man is the Gauleiter's deputy. The handwriting on the summons was of some note, the capital letters being a good five centimetres in height! Instinct told me that this document could only mean something very unpleasant.

I arrived bang on the appointed hour and found a line of other people, none of whom were known to me. After about an hour a voice called out.

'Jew Behrend!'

I stepped into a room and saw several men. The one facing me was of unimpressive stature but had fury written all over his face. He bawled at me.

'You are Jew Behrend?'

'I am.'

'Where d'you live?'

'Isartal.'

'Who owns the house you're living in?'

I gave him the owner's name and added that I was the subtenant.

'That is not what I asked!' he raged, spraying spittle as he spoke. After the briefest of pauses and with outstretched arm, he pointed at the door. 'Out!'

I left the room and one of the staff told me to wait. A further hour passed, with Wegner's voice and that of another man providing background bawling. Then a large man hurried towards me, a sealed envelope in his hand.

'Go to the employment office on Wednesday and take this letter with you.'

'But I'm already in work,' I replied evenly.

'That's of no interest to us!' he shouted. 'You'll now be given appropriate work.' With that he left and I went on to our own place of work.

It was still a mystery to me as to why these two men were quite so incensed. The second of the two had turned out to be Obersturmführer Muggler [Mugler] who, prior to his role with the Party, had operated a swing boat in Regensburg. When I described the scene to Stahl, our head, he grimaced and said, 'At the moment they're after any Jew living outside the city – something they consider rank treachery and to be punished at all costs. There's no point in my trying to intervene, nor would it help if Hellinger [Hechinger][9] did so in his capacity as deputy chair – Hellinger's [Hechinger's] backed up by the Gestapo, so I fear it would just make the situation even worse for you. We'll have to wait and see what the employment office decides about the letter.'

I was there spot on time but then had to wait alongside so many other women with their own letters from Widenmayerstrasse that it took a great deal of patience to stick it out until referred to an official, who opened with, 'What on earth did you do to make the Gauleiter's deputy quite this furious?'

I replied that it could only be because I was living beyond the confines of the city, something which had never actually been prohibited.

'You're probably right,' she replied. 'It says here: "Inform Jew Behrend she is to move immediately into the city's Jewish quarter and report without delay for work at the Lohhof flax mill."[10] There's nothing I can do about it.'

I put it to her that I needed time to find a bed in the city, give up my lodgings in Isartal and pack. I asked if she might give me a couple of days for that. She nodded. 'I can see you need a short period of grace, but you must report early for work on 1 July. Come back the day after tomorrow and pick up your document of referral.' I thanked her for her gesture of goodwill and went.

I know about Lohhof, of course, but up to now it's only been the younger women and girls who've been sent there. Mill work itself is well known for being arduous, and if you're out in the fields with the sun beating down on you, that's notoriously tough. The location isn't helpful either. Lohhof railway station is the one beyond Schleissheim, so you have to take the train and then walk, making it a total of hour and a quarter to an hour and a half to reach the site, and then the same back.

When I returned to the office our deputy actually suggested that I get a medical certificate stating that I'm just not physically suited to factory work. I gave this a great deal of thought. As a result of a birth defect my left arm has always been shorter than my right and has restricted movement, but after long reflection I decided not to give the opinionated gentleman of Widenmayerstrasse any new grounds for anger, nor to jeopardise my emigration to Argentina. I therefore resolved to get on with the work.

The main thing now is to find myself new accommodation. It turns out there's a corner free in Herr Stahl's flat – one of our staff has a room there which was designated for two. But maybe I'll still be able to find a little bedsit, however small, and then I can live on my own.

On Thursday I was over at our old people's home in Kaulbachstrasse as I once again have a supervisory overview of all our old folks' homes. Because the Gestapo is the lead organisation, it controls the finances of the Reichsvereinigung and of every Jewish Gemeinde in Germany and has ordered a reduction in staff. That unfortunately hit the previous lady in charge of all the homes so it fell to me to take over this work I'm so passionate about just as she once did from me. I started on 1 May.

I had the opportunity to tell Frau Tuchmann my own news. With the greatest of warmth she offered me the second room in her small attic flat, as at the moment only her fourteen-year-old daughter was there with her. She urged me to stay as long as I needed while looking for something suitable. In addition I would be permitted to take all my meals at the old folks' home, something I was especially grateful for, given the ten-hour working day and long journey there and back from the new site. I'm moving to her flat this very evening, then tomorrow and the day after I'll make the necessary arrangements at the office and start work at Lohhof early on Wednesday.

Letters from Else to Eva Schmidt

Isartal, 15 June 1941

My dear Eva

Thank you so much for your note. I would very much like the hot-water bottle you mention, please – that could be so useful here. Whether I can actually take it with me, I don't know yet, but I'll make sure it's returned to you or, if you don't need it, I'll leave it for Tilla as she doesn't have one.

There's a hard week behind me now, which felt like a huge mountain looming over me, but all turned out to be far less difficult than I'd feared. I'm so glad it's behind me. I'll tell you more when you're here.

Still nothing from Argentina, no letter either.

27. Else Rosenfeld in Icking, 1941.

Isartal, 27 June 1941

My dearest Eva

My warmest thanks for the little parcel. It's taken a while but arrived yesterday.

It's also been a long while since I found it this hard to write about something but I must – I'll keep it short and to the point. I've got to leave here and move into the city on 1 July. I'll be staying in one of our homes to begin with. On 2 July I start the new work that's been allocated to me. I know it's outdoors and not too hard, I hope. It's quite a long journey to get there, so I'll have to set off early and will get home relatively late.

If you go to see Tilla and she's agreeable, you can leave it with her, and then you'll hear the whole story. By then we'll both know more. Do write to Tilla, won't you? She'd write to you herself except that she's terribly busy at the moment. I'm in good spirits, so please don't worry about me.

Farewell for now and please accept my fondest greetings,

Yours ever, E.

Else's Diary

Isartal, Sunday, 6 July 1941

The first few days in the factory have left me dog-tired. I can't tell you how much I'd like to stretch out flat on my back on the grass in our garden, all the better to feast my eyes on the blue sky over Isartal and breathe in the fragrance of our flowers. Still, I don't know when I'll next get time to write and want to keep you up to date with what's going on, so here I am.

I left everything in good order at the office and the homes will carry on without me. As far as the despatch of packages goes, Emmy K[ohn] is taking on a large part and the rest will be done by Annemarie, our Quaker friend, along with her troop of helpers. The one thing I want to keep going myself is my own correspondence with the folk sent to those three locations in Lublin. They're like old friends to me now and I want to maintain that contact for as long as remotely possible.

On Tuesday I received a telephone call from an official at the central telegram office. 'Am I speaking to Frau Doktor Behrend?' he asked.

I confirmed.

'Have you recently sent a cable to Argentina?'

I confirmed once again.

'Do you have a relative there by the name of Gustel?'

'That's right – my daughter.'

'Where does she live?'

'In S . . . s, Province of Córdoba.'

'In that case I can now explain why I'm asking you these questions,' said the man on the phone. 'I have here in front of me a telegram from S . . . s, signed by a certain Gustel. Unfortunately the address has scrambled en route, and all I can make out is "Mother, Munich". Well, I'm delighted to say I have now identified the pertinent mother in Munich, and will send the telegram on to you straight away.'

I thanked him. The telegram was to let me know that efforts were still underway to get me over there as soon as possible.

I've fallen on my feet with my new lodgings and am deeply touched by the way Frau Tuchmann is looking after me. As warden in the home, she is outstanding – she clearly loves the elderly people in her care and does everything she can for them. They are all very attached to her. It has become much more difficult to run the place since staff have had to be released for factory work and the food supply is now less plentiful. They're far worse off now in terms of quality and quantity of food than when they had individual ration cards.

Anyway, Wednesday was my first day at Lohhof. I had to leave the house just after six and found quite a crowd of young girls at the station, all bound for the same flax mill. We reached the station for Lohhof soon after seven and then had a ten-minute walk to the factory itself. The buildings stood on a sprawling site and the whole place had a desolate air of neglect. With the document from the employment office in my hand, I was first sent to the factory office.

'Get into your work clothes and report to Supervisor X.'

A gesture of dismissal accompanied the instruction. My Jewish Community colleagues had found me a work dress, a large straw hat and some sandals in our own clothes store. At the factory, however, the changing room was scruffy and uncared for, each of us sharing an army-style cupboard with another worker. At the door stood a supervisor telling us to get changed and to do it fast. I turned to him and asked for Herr X, the man I'd been told would assign me my tasks.

'You're looking at him,' he snapped back. 'How old are you?'

'Fifty.'

'Makes me wonder what the employment office is playing at, sending people of that age,' he muttered

I just smiled at him and said I couldn't offer an explanation.

'You can do sorting for the bundling machine.'

For what seemed a long five minutes we walked along a beaten track over a large and featureless expanse with heaps of flax stacked high as a house at irregular intervals on each side, along with various open barns, most of them also full of flax. As we came into more open country, I saw a group of eight people standing at two tables, sorting piles of flax ready to be secured with hemp rope by the bundling machine. The supervisor simply told the women at one table to show me what to do and went off.

I like my work colleagues a lot and there's a good comradely atmosphere. On the machine itself is a Frenchman, a prisoner of war, and there are other men whose job it is to keep us supplied with flax from the heaps I'd just seen. It's strictly forbidden for us to speak to the French, but the temptation to do so is enormous, particularly as we're alone with them out there at these two tables, each with a bundling machine beside it, and from where we're standing we have sight of the whole factory area. We were all chatting away with one of the French flax carriers when one of his group hissed, '*Attention! Le Chapeau Gris!*' Someone swiftly explained for my benefit that the three overseers have nicknames according to the colour of their hat. Two of them, namely Grey Hat and White Hat are known to be extremely unpleasant indeed, while the third, Green Hat, is a good-natured, reasonable sort of chap with far less to say for himself than the others.

The work's not hard for anyone with two strong arms. The flax pile has to be gone through very thoroughly and each individual stem checked for strength. If it breaks, it's discarded on the waste heap. We have to make sure of forming piles of equal size for the different types of flax and check that the end of each stem has a smooth, rounded surface. The French chaps make jokes about the amount of waste. It seems those heaps have been there a long time as they're full of mould and give off a disgusting stench. Even the dust we get covered in smells bad. The worst part of the work, however, is constantly standing in the burning heat. On the first few days I got terrible sunburn on my arms and the back of my neck in spite of carefully rubbing oil into my skin, and it's still tender even now.

At lunchtime we get a forty-five–minute break which I spend with my colleagues in the shade of one of the heaps we're currently working to reduce. One of us goes off to the sentry box by the main gate to fetch beer bottles full of the most heavenly chilled skimmed milk provided to us by the guard's wife. The heat and dust leave us with a desperate thirst not easily quenched by milk alone but at least it relieves it a little. This break is always over far too soon but it's an opportunity to get to know my colleagues better.

There's the wife of a bank director, and I like her for her even temper and friendly, helpful nature. Next to her is a lady popularly known as Little Aunt Julie, actually Fräulein H. [Irma Holzer], about forty-five years of age and with such a dry sense of humour that she often has us all in stitches.

Another entertainer is Little Erna, her nickname derived from the collection of stories of the same name set in Hamburg, and, boy, she certainly knew how to tell 'em! She's also a devout Christian. Her father died when she was very small, and her mother then married again, this time a major and 'Aryan'. Little Erna grew very fond of him. When her mother's health failed, she took on all the housekeeping. She had had no connection at all with Jewish people or anything that had happened to them in recent years until Obersturmführer Muggler [Mugler] summoned her two months ago and sent her to work at Lohhof.

Something similar happened to other colleagues here, Frau Brand [Frieda Brandl], a Mischling, but whose parents had registered her as a member of the Jewish Community in spite of her indifference to all religion and her complete lack of knowledge of the Jewish faith. She is another nice, friendly person, early thirties I'd say, like Little Erna. Those two are good friends.

Then there's our youngest, always referred to here as 'Baby',[11] who also had little or nothing to do with Jewish people and the Jewish faith. Her father, half-Jewish, a gifted doctor, was for many years head of a sanatorium in Ebenhausen but has since died. Her mother, fully Jewish, lives with her. The parents and daughter were all baptised. She looks completely 'Aryan', with blonde hair and blue eyes and has nothing of the so-called typical Jewish features. These are, however, discernible in the last member of our group, Frau Irma, widow of a Jewish dentist who died a year ago.

I'm concerned as to how long I'll be able to do this kind of work with my left arm the way it is. When I'm straightening out and smoothing down the bundles of flax, which aren't exactly light to handle, I'm relying equally on the strength of both arms because the work can't be done with just one. It's only been three and a half days and but that old familiar nerve pain is making itself felt as always if I overdo things.

I was invited for coffee yesterday afternoon with our Chair, Herr Stahl, and his lovely wife. The two of them were keen first of all to hear about Lohhof and then he went on to tell me that the Widenmayerstrasse office are planning a second camp for Jews because Milbertshofen is becoming too crowded. He also explained that the Catholic nursing sisters of the Order of St Vincent de Paul are based at their convent at Berg am Laim, another Munich suburb, but also have a residential home for the elderly members of their order as well as for any sisters in poor health. The latter is a relatively new addition, built only three years ago in the convent grounds, and Widenmayerstrasse is apparently now thinking of taking over two floors in order to create additional accommodation for Jews. A decision will be made soon as to whether this plan can become reality and, if so, the necessary laundry facilities will need to be installed, and kitchen and canteen areas set up in the basement. The Party, he told us, intends to accommodate about three hundred and fifty Jewish people on the two floors.[12]

'We're going to need someone to take on the housekeeping and care of the women,' he concluded, 'and I would like that person to be you.'

I replied that this was work I would very much like to do and certainly felt capable of, but couldn't see how Hauptsturmführer Wegner or Obersturmführer Muggler [Mugler] would ever agree.

'I don't know how we'll manage it, no, but I remain hopeful. Meanwhile, just be at the ready and stop that factory work before you do serious damage to your arm.'

I promised but actually I want to stick it out a little longer at the flax mill, simply to show goodwill.

Munich, Sunday, 27 July 1941

I left my job in Lohhof three days ago. On Thursday I was suffering such terrible nerve pain in my bad arm that I was forced to give up. With us at the time was 'Le Chapeau Vert'. We were working that day in one of the open barns with the usual machine, as was often the case, to clear the space taken up by last year's flax mountains in order to fit in the new harvest that was quite literally waiting at the gates. I reported my problem to the supervisor, and he gave a good-humoured reply in his local dialect, 'Well then now, you pack it in with work right away and get yourself off to that there doctor. I can see you're not feeling right.'

That same afternoon I was seen by our Jewish doctor who deals with workplace certification. I assume I'll also have to report in the next few days to a similar type of doctor but at the medical insurance place, as he'll be the one to make the final decision as to what's to become of me.

Our little band of workers are very supportive of my stopping but really sad too. We have all got on so well together, including our French friends who we've helped as much as possible with food, especially bread. They've told us so much about their homeland, showed us family photographs and were united in the belief that the Allies would win the war in spite of German successes to date. We were lucky enough to have had 'Le Chapeau Vert' as our supervisor and his lack of ability in the French language gave rise to some humorous exchanges. I think the French had probably picked up quite a bit of German along the way, but they still appeared not to understand him, most especially as he generally spoke pure Bavarian.

Lucien, a colleague from southern France, one day asked me as he fed the bundling machine, '*Madame, que veut dire "Dagoumer"?*'

I couldn't think what it might be and just shrugged. But he pursued the matter, saying, '*Mais "Le Chapeau Vert" dit cela souvent.*'

Another colleague, the one we always called Baby, overheard and burst out laughing, saying, 'Oh, I know what he means! "Le Chapeau Vert" is always calling him over and then says "*Da kumm her*" – you know, like "Come 'ere".'

We explained it all to him and enjoyed a good laugh together.

Then there was the day 'Le Chapeau Vert' caught one of the Frenchmen fast asleep on a mountain of flax and came to ask the rest of us, 'Hey, how do I say "*Du oiter Schlawiner*", you idle rascal, in French?' But none of us had enough French to convey this play on words where the Bavarian for 'rascal' sounds similar to the normal German for 'sleep'.

In the meantime the camp at Berg am Laim has become a reality and the first residents moved in eight days ago on the orders of the Obersturmführer in spite of no kitchen or other facilities being fully ready. There are about twenty people there in all and the temporary arrangement is for the nuns to provide them with coffee in the mornings, a hearty stew at midday and then soup in the evening. Anything else they have to buy with their own food ration cards. The camp is expected to accommodate those who are no longer fit for work, whether old or sick, while the younger ones are sent off to the wooden huts of Milbertshofen. Our chair, Herr Stahl, is now definitely hopeful of my being offered the housekeeping post at Berg am Laim once the doctor confirms I am to be released from the factory work at Lohhof.

There are changes there, too. Any Jewish girl aged between fifteen and eighteen is now expected not just to work there but also to live on site in the newly erected wooden hut run by a Jewish friend of Anne-Marie, a woman who had previously managed small-scale accommodation for the elderly in her own home. When she had to vacate her own place, her residents moved to us, while she herself became head of the new Jewish work camp at Lohhof. Our colleague Baby is to be her right hand. There are also women from Poland and Ukraine working there now, but living in a separate wooden hut. Any remaining workers classified as 'Aryan', along with the French prisoners of war, have now gone. Lohhof is to be run with Jewish workers only, all overseen by Herr G[rabower], previously a senior official in the Reich finance ministry in Berlin and until recently working at Milbertshofen.

I nearly forgot to tell you what I was earning at the factory. For a ten-hour day I was paid 11 marks 70 pfennig per week. I've not been receiving the 250 Reichsmark per month from your pension for over a year now, so it's a bit of luck that I do have access to 200 Reichsmark from our brother-in-law's account, blocked by the authorities as far as he's concerned because he's been living in America.

Munich, Sunday, 3 August 1941

I've now been formally declared medically unfit for factory work so the Lohhof job was only for three weeks in the end. On the basis of this certification the Gauleiter's deputy gave Herr Stahl permission to assign me to Berg am Laim as head of housekeeping with responsibility for the welfare of female inmates.[13] I'm starting the new position tomorrow and taking up residence there as well. Yesterday I went with Hellinger [Hechinger] to look over the new home for the first time and to introduce myself to the managers who'll be my new colleagues. There are three of them, among them Herr Alb[recht],[14] a senior schoolmaster in his mid-fifties and very typical of his profession with all the usual strengths and weaknesses. The other two were at school with Hellinger [Hechinger], both around the age of forty, both originally in business. One of them, Heilbronner by name,[15] is an extremely nice, quiet man, but clever, really shrewd with it. The other is Abel[es],[16] a lively individual with good practical and technical skills, is the enthusiastic type who takes an obvious delight in work. I knew immediately that we'd all get on well.

The place now goes by the name officially chosen by the Party, the Residential Facility for Jews at Berg am Laim, and is open. It's a nice building with a good modern interior. We have half the basement, as well as the whole ground floor and first floor; the nuns retain the second floor and the

28. Now a memorial, the entrance to the internment camp, north wing of the convent of the Barmherzige Schwestern. Photo: Werner Götz, 1980.

other half of the basement for themselves. Getting around the building is straightforward via the wide staircases and broad corridors. All the floors are covered in green linoleum. There's a beautiful terrace on every level with views across fields and gardens towards the Bavarian Alps. Together with the lavatories and bathrooms, all the rooms in the basement are decorated in pale green with white tiling, while all the other rooms are in the same green, also with lino on the floors. Can this really be for us? Certainly, the rooms are going to be horribly cramped once any furniture and belongings go in. Each occupant gets a narrow military-style locker and a narrow plank bed, all arranged like bunks. That's just like at Milbertshofen, although there they've got those unprepossessing stark wooden huts to contend with.

'Do you think we'll be left here for some time?' I asked doubtfully.

'There's no telling,' replied Hellinger [Hechinger]. 'We might as well get settled in as though it were for a while, though.'

Next I was allowed to select my own room, right in the middle section of the first floor, which has been designated for the women. I can't assume it'll always be for me and me alone but instead of the usual six beds in the other rooms, there'll only be four in mine, leaving space for my desk, the one Frau

Tuchmann is giving me, and my lovely old chest of drawers containing all sorts that will be useful in a place like this. Each floor has a row of rooms measuring four metres by two and a half, but there are also larger ones to accommodate twelve, sixteen or eighteen. On the ground floor is a substantial room previously used for prayers and meetings by the nuns – thirty-six people will now be billeted in there. All in all the place is scheduled to take three hundred and twenty.

Every room bears the name of a saint, and in my case it's St Theresa who'll give me sanctuary behind the white-painted door picked out in green. My large window looks out on to the courtyard of the convent, part of the garden and the nave of the fine baroque church,[17] as well as giving me a good view of the sky. I love this room already and the calming atmosphere of this peaceful place safely enclosed by a surrounding wall.

Alb[recht] chose the porter's lodge for himself, which he'll have to share with one other, while Heilbronner and Abel[es] have elected to live and sleep in the office. The previous residents moved out of their own accord – mostly younger people working in one of the factories in Munich, along with a number of elderly women no longer up to factory work but who will now work here. There are also a few souls who were transferred here by the Hauptsturmführer as punishment. We are not being assigned any staff other than a volunteer cook, Fräulein Lind[auer], who lives out.[18] She has been in charge of the kitchen at our small home in Wagnerstrasse, the one we set up originally for the returners and the many Jewish people living in Schwabing to provide them all with a hot meal in the middle of the day. With so many dwellings being vacated, however, fewer and fewer people have been eating there so we felt we could take her on here with a clear conscience, handing her previous work over to one of her helpers.

Letter from Else to Eva Schmidt

Berg am Laim, 7 August 1941

My dearest Eva

At long last I'm allowing myself time to write so I can thank you properly for your kind note and the nightdress you've mended so beautifully! You're so far away again, but it was wonderful to have you close by in the area we both know and love so well. Thank you for everything, my dear. I needed your presence more than ever this time – I do so wish I could do more giving and less taking these days.

I'm sitting at my charming little desk that seems just made for this corner by the window here. You can picture the room, I know – I couldn't have got a better fit if I'd measured it up myself! The room looks so pretty, and I do hope I can have it all to myself for a little longer. I'm on my feet from early 'til late, and in the evenings there are lengthy meetings with my 'triumvirate', as I think of them, so it does me endless good to have some time to myself afterwards. It's all going well with my chaps though and the people living here are so kind. They seem to read my mind in terms of what needs doing here – one of them even offering to wash, iron and darn my underclothes for me! That might need a bit of guidance, I expect.

The cooking range was finally delivered today although it won't be properly installed for a fortnight. At least this gives me time for other aspects of preparation. This afternoon I'm going over to two of our old folks' homes (Klenzestrasse and Mathildenstrasse) to see what I can have by way of crockery and pans. The food the convent gives us is very good, and there's plenty of it, and it's wonderful that we don't have to hand in any ration stamps for it. So we're quite well off for the time being. I'm even sleeping well. Herr Heilbronner showed me how you can make these beds a bit softer through clever use of the two blankets and now I sleep better than in Kaulbachstrasse.

Do write soon. I think of you lots (whenever I can make enough time . . . !)

Else's Diary

Berg am Laim, Sunday, 10 August 1941

Moving out of my existing accommodation and into the new place could not have gone more smoothly, and all the more so with the kind help of both Heilbronner and Abel[es]. During the process they told me how hard it was proving to form a satisfactory working relationship with Alb[recht], the schoolmaster, and that in fact they'd both wondered whether it might be better for them to give up the work entirely, but had then decided to wait and see whether I might help improve matters.

I've come to see that one of my most pressing tasks is to mediate between these two practical types, and the philosophising theorist who approaches everything with a thoroughness that verges on the pedantic. For the moment, the straightforward housekeeping presents no difficulties as cleaning of rooms and dishwashing are carried out with no trouble by the women who have not been assigned to factory work. The four of us divide our duties as follows: the schoolmaster deals with anything to do with the authorities, i.e. registering residents with the local police, telephone calls with the community offices when the subject matter is other than the rest of us would normally undertake. In addition he takes on the care of all male residents and arbitrates between them in the case of disputes. Heilbronner is in charge of finances. The home is supposed to be self-sufficient on the strength of the fees for board and lodging paid by residents, although these are still to be determined. He also oversees the budget when it comes to the purchase of food and materials, while Abel[es] manages everything related to technical and manual work, as well as repair jobs. We plan to take it in turns to carry out checks on the communal rooms in terms of cleanliness and tidiness, while all significant changes and observations will be discussed by us as a group.

It's wonderful not to have to provide food and drink for the residents who have just moved in. Every morning at seven thirty the convent kitchen sends us a huge pot of milky coffee and then at midday and a regular time in the evening food is carried over, after which an enormous bucket of hot water appears for washing the dishes. In any case when new residents move in, they bring their own cups, plates and cutlery, and often all manner of other things besides, because most of them have had to close up their own homes.

The Party orders forbid any association between our residents and the nuns. Only the schoolmaster, Alb[recht], and I have express permission to have any contact with them, in his case because our own lack of telephone means he has to conduct all such matters in the main building, and in my case because I have to go over there several times a day to talk about the number of meals required. It's still possible, though, for Heilbronner and Abel[es] sometimes to have contact with the Mother Superior or her 'builder', as they like to call the building superintendent here, be it regarding use of the telephone or a query related to their individual areas of responsibility.

Yesterday the convent assured us that we'd be allocated our own storage space for potatoes, something that I'd been quite worried about resolving. We've also been told we may use the bit of lawn in front of our building to set up an area for drying our clothes – just those personal items that the women will soon be able to wash for themselves in the new laundry room. The Party is to tell us which laundry service to use for the main wash.

Then tomorrow Heilbronner, Abel[es] and I need to draw up a six-month provisional budget, not an easy matter because nothing is fixed yet, although my past work at the old folks' home gave me some experience and it's not to be binding, fortunately, just an outline to get us started.

As a result of one of my ideas, it was decided not to go for so-called communal catering but to request a food ration card for each individual resident. We knew this would create a great deal of extra administrative bother for us, me in particular, but doing things this way meant we would at least know precisely how much we had to work with. As well as being told which laundry to use, we have also been allocated certain food shops to go to, specifically which grocery shop, then one for butter, milk and eggs, and a butcher. All three are on the workers' housing estate only five minutes from here.

Heilbronner and I are going over there tomorrow in order to discuss everything with the owners of the shops in question. We plan to set up a little indoor market here for our residents as they themselves are not allowed to enter the local food shops. This will give them the chance to cash in a proportion of their own food ration cards and buy what they want on our own premises. The best person to run this was an obvious choice: Herr Klein,[19] one of our older residents, formerly a salesman by profession, and a quiet and reliable man known to Heilbronner. And thus another element in the completion of our residential facility was added.

The kitchen is a particularly large and airy room. We're still waiting for the large cooking range to be sited right in the middle of the space and then in each corner on the window side of the room there's a sink. Have I told you already that we have central heating? I'm such a chilly mortal that it's a real consolation, and all the more so as the convent will take charge of looking after the heating system and the coal supply, as it also serves the nuns' own floors. Also in the kitchen is a huge boiler that will be heated by the cooking range as there's no gas in Berg am Laim, and nor is there a big electric stove or any power for such a thing.

I'm sure you can tell, my beloved, how much I would have enjoyed this kind of work if it had come my way under different circumstances. I can at least tell myself that here we are putting in place all the conditions necessary for a model field hospital.

I haven't mentioned the flower garden, have I? The convent has made part of it available to our residents! We've asked the accommodation office to tell all new arrivals to bring deckchairs with them and any other garden furniture. The next group of residents arrive on 15 August. The difficult job of allocating new arrivals to their rooms is something we want to work on together – we're very keen to place people with someone they'll get on with. The four of us are in full agreement on one fundamental question – although I still have ample opportunity to practise my mediation skills – which is this:

we do not want to see the military-style rule followed at Milbertshofen brought here. Maybe the harsh conditions and higher number of residents oblige them to run things differently there. Our home, however, is to be run with kindness, patience and understanding of the individual, with firm and energetic intervention only where necessary.

Heilbronner was quite right when he said to me: 'Let nobody ever say of us that we were the Party's henchmen. It's true that we accept from them our responsibility for cleanliness, quiet and good order, but our obligation is far more to our people, easing the burden placed upon their shoulders.'

We were united in our agreement with his words.

Berg am Laim, Sunday, 17 August 1941

We've reached a satisfactory arrangement with the three shopkeepers that Heilbronner and I visited early last week. The butcher and the man for butter, milk and eggs are particularly agreeable. Far less so, however, is our general groceries and greengrocer fellow. There's a hint of the National Socialist about him, along with a marked lack of vim and vigour when it comes to business. We'll find some way of working with him, however, that's for sure, and there seems nothing intrinsically malicious about the chap. Our requirements will mean plenty of additional revenue for all three businesses as up to now they've been reliant on customers from the small settlement nearby. They all expressed concern over the extra work involved in stamping so many individual food ration cards, so we offered to take this on for them and it was with relief that they each handed us a stamp to represent their business. One can safely assume that the Party would not have agreed to this arrangement if it had come to their attention!

The convent boasts extensive vegetable gardens cultivated by one of the nuns. When I was in conversation with her a few days ago, she promised to let us have vegetables and tomatoes, even fresh fruit, whatever she could find. This will be such a wonderful help! She also told me how the convent buys all sorts of cabbage and root vegetables and stores these in clamps over the winter months. If we were interested, she said, she could ensure that extra quantities were bought in and stored for us, another proposal we're pleased to accept and make good use of, as you can imagine!

Whenever we're working outdoors, this wonderful summer weather makes us feel as though we're on holiday. Eating a meal on the lower terrace, looking out over the garden, is a joy in itself because here we can feel free of the constant pressures of life in the city centre. Not that we can forget who

29. The Barmherzige Schwestern novitiate was from 1941 to 1943 the Residential Facility for Jews at Berg am Laim. Photo: 1960s.

we are, cursed for whatever reason, threatened by the unknown, but the beautiful garden and church, the reassuring kindness in the smiling faces of the nuns when they pass by, our knowing that they neither hate nor despise us but view us with sisterly affection, all these combine to ease our load.

Let me tell you about some of the remarkable people here. First, there's the Mother Superior, a highly intelligent woman who empathises with our situation and is actually delighted that we've been installed here rather than some Party-related organisation. Then there's the senior nun in charge of the office by the front gate and thus the telephone, an elderly lady whose face radiates wisdom, purity and goodness. I could list so many more of whom we are especially fond but will otherwise mention only the nun who organises the kitchen, so efficient and friendly, always ready to lend me a hand and offer the benefit of her experience, and the nun in charge of the garden, whose sparkling eyes and weather-beaten face do so much to convey the joy she takes in her work.

The day before yesterday fifteen or so new people arrived. The biggest problem at the moment is trying to persuade incomers not to bring too many things with them! We've worked out that each person can keep three normal-sized suitcases here, one under the bed and the other two in their narrow locker in the corridor. A couple of bedside tables, a chest of drawers and a chair or two also tend to find their way into each bedroom. Every item of furniture that comes into the home comes under community ownership and use, however – which is not easy for everyone to understand or accept. The latest arrivals have mostly come here of their own volition, creating what you might call an elite of willing souls on whom we can rely, something that makes our own work a whole lot easier. This will be so useful when this facility is running at full capacity. At the moment only small numbers are being admitted at any one time as the kitchen and canteen areas are not ready, and we don't want to put undue strain on the convent's own kitchen. Just imagine, the Mother Superior has informed me that they want neither payment nor ration cards in return for all this. We have, however, explained to our residents that we'll be snipping off and putting by a certain number of ration stamps in order to build up a little reserve. According to our calculations, this should be enough to keep us going until the middle of September!

Berg am Laim, Sunday, 21 September 1941

I've been sitting here a while, staring at my diary, pen in hand, and I just don't know where or how to start! Chronological order would be best, I suppose. Well, we at last brought the kitchen into service on 15 September. We have one of those big new cooking ranges, rather like the type you'd find in a professional hotel kitchen. In addition we now have two huge cooking pots, one of which has a capacity of one hundred and twenty-five litres, the other one hundred and eighty. The smaller one will be for making soup, the other for cooking vegetables and casserole dishes. The cooking range isn't drawing quite as it should yet but that's often the case with a new one. Our residents are so pleased to have the kitchen at last and Fräulein Lind[auer] knows what she's doing all right! Our people here now number fifty-five but we're reckoning on a big increase over this coming week. By around three weeks' time, this place will be full. But we're prepared.

It's been more than a slap in the face for us – and for all the Jewish people in the Reich – to learn of the new decree that every Jew must now publicly display on the left side of his or her chest the Star of David as a distinguishing mark of race.[20] Made of artificial yellow silk, the star bears the word 'Jew' in large letters that are made to resemble the Hebrew script. With effect from Friday 19 September, the day before yesterday in other words, nobody is allowed out of the house without one. We had to cut out the stars ourselves from broad swatches of cloth and then hem each one individually to stop the poor-quality cloth from fraying. And to cap it all, we each had to pay 10 pfennig for our 'decoration'.

I'm sure you're wondering how other people have reacted on seeing this? Most people act as though they can't even see the star but there are isolated incidents on the tram when someone will give a satisfied glance, as if to say that at least they can now identify exactly who belongs to the 'Jewish rabble'. We encountered, and still do, far more expressions of revulsion and sympathy than anything else. The worst thing is that schoolchildren as young as six are being made to wear them. Two seven-year-old boys were badly beaten by two 'Aryans' of their own age. An elderly man saw what was happening, chased the attackers away, cursing them as they fled the scene, then escorted one of the weeping victims all the way home. A soldier gave an elderly resident of ours enough food ration cards for a week, and on the tram a gentleman made a deep and deliberately ostentatious bow before giving up his seat to one of our women left standing on her way to work. Our kindly butcher and butter supplier said they'd be ensuring tip-top deliveries for us and expressed their anger and contempt at this humiliating treatment we are now getting. Once again we saw our people walking through the streets, their faces blank, their eyes not fixing on anything, many with heads bowed, although many with their heads held high, and I was one of these. It seems to me that in Munich at least, those in power will find it hard to achieve their aim of every Jew being condemned by the rest of the population. But it's only been three days so far, and too soon to make a final judgement.

Letter from Else Rosenfeld to Eva Schmidt

Berg am Laim, 21 September 1941

My dearest Eva

It's been on my mind that I haven't written, and I know full well that you worry if you don't hear from me regularly. There really is no cause for alarm – the only thing I lack is time! Everyone here is well, and we're so grateful that fate has washed us up on this particular shore.

Since Wednesday we've been able to cook for ourselves. I still feel I can't spread myself thinly enough, what with all the new arrivals each day. There are now 82 of us here and that'll rise to 100 by the first day of October,

I know. More people require more time and more energy. Still, we have an excellent cook (not an easy person, though!) and everyone is happy with the food here, which is the main thing.

Just a few days ago the longed-for letter came from my Fritz. It's a lovely letter, full of questions about my new work and new accommodation. He and the children are well, and he's contributing occasional pieces to a magazine, something that brings in a bit of money and a whole lot of satisfaction. [...]

Farewell, my dearest and most loyal friend. My regards to Elisabeth, and fondest wishes from me to you,

Else

Siegfried's Diary

Oxford, 29 September 1941

These last three months of conflict between Germany and Russia have been an ample demonstration of the latter's enormous strength, an inner might that shows it to be the only nation capable of challenging Hitler's Germany. [...]

It's a paradox that the nervous strain I've been under since the start of the war, my desperate separation from Else and the subsequent misery of living in isolation have all brought me to a place like this that exposes me to the benefit of a host of different views and fresh experiences of this country's own distinctive culture. It demands a new kind of personal growth, a close relationship with the people of this nation and, above all, an excellent grasp of the language. Without that, any close contact is impossible and I could remain isolated.

This is where the younger generation are so fortunate, and where a gap opens up between young and old. I see this in Peter and Hanna, so mature in their resolve and ability to build lives for themselves here, fully integrated as part of society. They've dropped all contact with the older generation who have moved here, and that's perfectly understandable, for they are the ones who will never completely fit in like natives. It's natural for them to favour the company of local Brits now. [...]

Telegram from Hertha today:

> *Providing transit visa Cuba, later USA, can you send Else funds for passage Lisbon Quaker Office*

I reply to her:

> *Transfer of cash at present impossible. Who can order Argentine funds for passage from Ybarra Company Bilbao?*

In Bilbao two hundred dollars have been duly deposited by Hertha or Käthe for Else's crossing to B. Aires, except that the Munich Consul has now refused her a visa. So it's all off. I have appealed to Cardinal Faulhaber via the Neumeyers and prompted intervention with the Consulate.[21]

Else's Diary

Berg am Laim, Sunday, 26 October 1941

I've been reading through my last diary entry and can fully confirm that I'm quite justified in saying that the people beyond these walls act as though they can't see our stars, and are going out of their way to treat us with the utmost kindness in public and even more so in private. Rarely do we hear any disdainful or hateful remarks directed at us. Sadly I suspect that this public reaction is what's given rise to the latest and most hostile decree so far from the authorities: Jews are no longer to step outside their homes, not even for a Sunday stroll, and are not allowed on public transport unless their journey to work is longer than a seven-kilometre round trip, in which case they may use the tram. This is now Reich law. Here in Munich, however, the Gauleiter and his deputy don't appear too bothered about the precise details of Reich law. Jews in Munich aren't allowed to use the tram even for long journeys into work!

In the meantime all men up to the age of seventy-five and all women up to seventy have been assigned to labour in the factories. Only those not up to manufacturing tasks are let off and set to work in the camps instead. Even old people's homes are affected by the scope of this dispersal. Most people have long journeys, often two hours there and back, to their place of employment. Many businesses have turned to the Gauleiter's deputy and explained that productivity will fall if people arrived at work tired out by the journey, but no notice was taken whatsoever. In the end the employment office came up with a solution: the railway! It's hardly a main-line service but there are a number of small stations in and around the periphery of the city, and from these it's generally a shortish walk to the various places of work. Every Jewish employee has therefore been issued with a travel permit, prepared by the employment office and then signed and officially stamped by the local police in each district. The only reason I have described all this to you in such detail is to show you what a 'Reich law' really is: a sheet of paper that can be blown together by any local Party heavyweight.

With only a handful of spaces left, this home of ours is now close to capacity, and I have a great deal of work on my hands. Finally we are seeing the benefits of having set up our volunteer structure to support our function as management. When so many human beings are brought together under one roof after experiencing distress and humiliation, as well as being separated from their nearest and dearest and then forced into exhausting manual work, it's entirely natural for altercations and difficulties to arise. We have nonetheless always managed to restore peace and unity with unwavering calm, patience and kindness. It's one of the schoolmaster's main areas of responsibility and he's proved extremely good at tackling conflict.

I'm almost finished with organising the women but it's hard to find enough of them to carry out all the cleaning and cooking required so as to avoid overloading any one person in particular.

There have been two inspections so far, one carried out by Obersturmführer Muggler [Mugler] early in September, when he expressed great satisfaction, and another a couple of days ago this time also with Hauptsturmführer Wegner in attendance, whom I hadn't clapped eyes on since my last visit to Widenmayerstrasse. He hadn't yet seen the place since it came into service, and as he passed through the building was quite evidently on the lookout for any tiniest detail that might furnish him with the excuse for a whole tirade of criticism. Sadly for him, it was all tip-top! It would have been so much harder to give a good impression in an old building that had seen better days. He found not one single thing to query.

On the first floor at the far end of a corridor, we've set up a bit of a sewing room with several sewing machines, but this is only ever used during the afternoons. In the mornings we need all hands on deck for cleaning and cooking. Gleeful that he had finally discovered something to complain about, the Hauptsturmführer announced that henceforth the sewing room is also to be used in the mornings in spite of the explanation we'd just given him as to why this is not practical. Oh well, he had to have his way, so we decided that whenever an inspection is due, around half a dozen of the women will rush to the room and settle down as if they've been there for several hours, busy darning clothes and working on the humming machines. It's a sad day when deceit and lies are the only way to get by.

As the two inspectors were leaving the building, the Hauptsturmführer did his usual thing of not looking any of us in the eye, hissing on his way out:

30. SA Sturmführer and deputy head of the Office for Aryanisation, Franz Mugler, with his daughter, date unknown.

'The home was in good order today, but woe betide those of you in charge if I or any of my staff should ever find anything amiss!' And with that he vanished, without a single word of farewell – as per usual.

The matter of costs has now been settled. Initially the Gauleiter's deputy was asking for one Reichsmark per day from each and every inmate simply for the privilege of living here. We then heard from the 'builder' that the convent would receive only 20 pfennig of this amount while the remainder would go straight to the Party to cover our use of the plank beds and lockers. By our own calculations, a 2.5-meter room occupied by six people would bring in a rent of 180 Reichsmark per month if this demand were to be met in full. The majority of our residents simply would not be in a position to pay this level of rent on top of food, heating and lighting costs. We ended up having to get the Jewish Gemeinde involved, although they no longer have a free hand with allocating their own funds. Nonetheless, our concerns were then passed on to the Reichsvereinigung and a judgment requested from the overseeing authority, the Reichssicherheitshauptamt.[22]

The decision handed down to us is this: every resident is to pay 50 pfennig a day for living in the home here. Even this ruling represents what you might call a nice little earner of 30 pfennig per person going to the Party. All our rent is to be presented at Widenmayerstrasse every Friday, together with the menu for the coming week, the responsibility for which falls to me.

The new travel decree has challenging implications for our home, all the more so for those who are advanced in years. It means a lot of shifting people around because journeys to work from the camp at Milbertshofen take a terribly long time, while Berg am Laim has its own little railway stop. All this means that most of our elderly and infirm have had to relocate to Milbertshofen, while any workers living there have had to come to us instead. I felt so sorry for our old folk when this happened. It was so hard for them moving in with us in the first place, and then they all managed to settle in so well that it wasn't easy to say goodbye. On top of all this they truly feared the impending winter even more than going to Milbertshofen. I found it so hard to see them off. Many of them were such good workers in our home and garden that it's a real headache working out how best to reallocate their tasks to the others here.

I was particularly afraid that one of those to be transferred to Milbertshofen would be a man I've been wanting to tell you about – a certain Professor Cossmann[23] who lived in Ebenhausen until mid-September but has been with us ever since. He's over seventy, of medium height and very lean, with a wonderfully spiritual face. In the first few days he was barely noticeable, very quiet, keeping himself to himself. A deeply pious man, he's a Catholic with eyes that radiate only goodness and wisdom. He doesn't complain and never has about this sudden and radical change in his life and finds calming words for everyone, even those who feel discouraged, disgruntled and depressed. Even with us barely seeing or hearing him about the place, we four at the helm all sense his reassuring influence at work, and he is held in the highest regard. As far as the trivia of daily life goes, he comes across as somewhat helpless and everybody lends a hand without him needing to ask, at which he gives a slightly sheepish smile of thanks.

He and I will readily acknowledge that we sit in different camps politically but nonetheless there is a strong mutual bond. I have tremendous respect for him and see him as a friend with whom I can freely discuss subjects of grave import, such as the humane treatment of our fellows on this earth. He immediately understands whatever I'm trying to get across, and I'm so glad that he's here. I do worry about his delicate health though.

Not so long ago, one of his room-mates told me such a charming story about him – everyone refers to him as Professor, by the way. Anyway, we had to move him and the five others sharing his room because their rather generous quarters were to be set up as a workroom instead. We gave the men two days' notice in advance of the changeover to give them plenty of time to organise their belongings and shift them to their new quarters. On the afternoon of the last day, the Professor went to ask the others if they had already transferred their things, and if not, could they please do so as soon as possible? Most were already finished, but one man was just on the point of packing up.

'Why are you so bothered about us all getting it done, Professor?'

He gave his sweetest smile in reply, saying, 'Well, once all of you are out of there, then I can get started because I'll know that whatever's left behind is mine!'

Letter from Else to Eva Schmidt

Berg am Laim, 13 November 1941

My dear Eva

Just a brief note to stop you worrying! I'm still here but seventy-five of our people are due to leave us today or tomorrow, for a very long time and perhaps for good.[24] It's all rather open-ended. I've known about this since Friday of last week, and then on Saturday the list of names came through, and I had to tell the women. It's hard to take in everything that's happened over the course of one short day, but when I think that over the last three months we've created a community of people here who've stuck together through all this hardship and will carry on helping one another, that really does seem wonderful and something of great importance.

Farewell for now, my dear, and I'll write again as soon as I can. I send you a thousand warm wishes.

Your E

Else's Diary

Berg am Laim, Sunday, 16 November 1941

I've been sitting at my desk for a while now but the last ten days have left me in deep shock and I'm struggling to put pen to paper. It's hard to find the right words, but I'll do my best to describe all the things that have thrown me, along with everyone else here, in such utter turmoil.

It's my practice to keep my office door open to all residents for an hour each day, and on the evening of 5 November a chap turned up, asking if I knew there was a plan for the mass transportation of Jews from Munich. I replied quite truthfully that I knew nothing of this whatsoever, and my own sense of shock moved me to add somewhat angrily that we shouldn't let our imaginations run away with us as there was already quite enough going on here with all the actual problems we were facing at the time. I asked him to remain calm and not to spread this dreadful rumour any further. He gave his solemn word, but the next day the schoolmaster told me he'd been asked by another of our residents if there was any truth in that same rumour.

Then on 7 November a telephone call came from the Gemeinde asking the three of us – that's the schoolmaster, Heilbronner and I – to attend a meeting at the Lindwurmstrasse office on the following day in order to discuss matters concerning the home. Abel[es] would have to stay behind as an inspection was in the offing and we couldn't all be absent at the same time. On arrival, we found the managers of all the other homes present, as well as the head of housing for the entire district and both co-chairs of the Jewish Community.

Stahl, our director, spoke briefly in complete seriousness, and the impact of his devastating announcement is still with me. He informed us that around a thousand Jews were to be deported from central Munich in the coming week. The precise selection of these poor souls was yet to be finalised. The Gestapo had ordered that we be informed in readiness and yet we were to be sworn to silence until the list of names was issued. We were all left numb at this news, our faces drained of all colour, and I saw once again those same blank expressions on the faces of the people around me as on the streets of Munich in November 1938.

QR Code 15: The first deportation, 1941

On this occasion, our questions tumbled out, each of us wanting to know how many would be on the list from our own homes. The schoolmaster, Heilbronner and I exchanged horrified glances when we were told that eighty-five of our residents would be affected. We heard that our

Committee had managed to secure agreement that young children would not be separated from their parents, nor women from their husbands, but they had not succeeded in getting a similar agreement for siblings. Only those under sixty, sixty-five at the most, were to be deported. This was all that was known thus far. We were once again reminded of the strict order to remain silent, and told in no uncertain terms that the Gestapo had threatened severe reprisals for anyone who disobeyed. Only Abel[es], as a member of our management team, was to be informed.

The silence on our way home was broken only once, and that was by schoolmaster Alb[recht]. 'You do realise that our own names could be on that deportation list?'

Heilbronner and I had both fleetingly thought along the same lines, but right then it was of little import as to whether or not we were on it because a further decree had left us even more downcast. With immediate effect any emigration was now forbidden to all Jews of sixty or under. For me this meant the final dashing of the hope that had danced so tantalisingly before me, as only three days earlier I had at last received the telegram confirming my visa for Cuba. All that now paled into insignificance, however, with the shattering announcement of this new round of deportations.

Then something struck me. I remembered that Thekla Land[mann], one of our own residents and a woman whose quick-wittedness and cheery disposition I had always valued so greatly, had also now received her visa for Cuba and had in fact been due to leave the very next day. She was a widow of about forty, with her only daughter now settled in North America, so it would be a truly dreadful blow for her to have come so close to achieving the hard-won goal she'd longed for with all her heart and for it now to come to nothing. And here was I, not allowed to tell her because we had been sworn to silence. She would most probably be called to see her lawyer shortly before the time scheduled for her departure, and he would be the one to have to break the bad news.

By now we were back at the home and Alb[recht] opened the gate in the wall to the grounds of the convent. I took a deep breath and pulled myself together in the full expectation of enquiring looks and direct questions, hoping not to give away the strong emotions now coursing through me. It was late, just before nine, but those of us in management roles at all the homes had special dispensation to be outside the gates until ten, even though Reich law had stated since the earliest days of the war that Jews were not permitted to leave their homes between eight in the evening and six in the morning. Special exceptions were only made for such people as shift workers.

The large hallway on the ground floor was full of life, as always at this time of day when everyone was at home. Today, in particular, people were on edge as they waited for our return, hoping to be told something reassuring following the meeting we had attended, such as the groundlessness of the many rumours now circulating. As anticipated, each of us was immediately surrounded by groups clamouring for information, but we had agreed to fend them off by reporting that the meeting had merely concerned internal matters of home management. On hearing this concise and unsatisfactory reply, the disbelief and disappointment was clear on every face.

Brader came over, the man who'd asked me three days earlier about the rumour, saying with a light laugh, 'Well, thank goodness it was only about managerial issues – that's a load off my mind! Right then, Frau Doktor Behrend, it's time for that card game we've been promising ourselves, now we can put our worries at rest.'

I read his thoughts and agreed straight away. As soon as we were sitting opposite one another at one of the tables in the day room, out of earshot of the other residents, he said to me in low tones, 'I can tell you've heard the worst but are probably not allowed to say. If people see you sitting here over a quiet game of cards with me, they'll calm down soon enough.'

Can you imagine how grateful I was to this dear man and my utter relief? I played dreadfully badly but that was of no consequence. The game gradually turned into a proper diversion of sorts, and the sight of the two of us sitting there playing cards and chatting had a beneficial effect on everyone else. A little later I went to the office, where Heilbronner had made it his business to inform Abel[es].

Abel[es] turned to me and said, 'I'll be on that list, you wait and see, and if Gertrud Lind[auer]'s name is there too, then I've no objection.' Gertrud Lind[auer] is our cook and his fiancée. He went on, 'I'm convinced that the plan is to deport us in batches and I'd rather be among the first to go than to remain waiting for the news to hit me. I just hope we get the full list soon.'

I shared his wish that the list be revealed as soon as possible.

Sure enough at noon the following Sunday a messenger arrived bearing the individual deportation orders. As the management team, we four shut ourselves in the office and went through the names on the list. Abel[es]'s name was right at the top, immediately followed by that of Gertrud Lind[auer] and then eighty-three more, including Brader and Thekla Land[mann]. So I really was going to be the one to send them plunging from hope into despair and then on into the abyss, while the impending catastrophe hovered over the rest of us.

Abel[es] was the first to speak. With something approaching calm and good cheer, he managed to say, 'So I guessed right then. Well, I'm glad I know now and that they're letting Gertrud and me leave together.'

The three of us to remain struggled to keep our composure but knew we had to put on a brave face for the remaining eighty-three on the list, all of whom had the right to know as rapidly as possible what was being imposed upon them. Swiftly we read through the specific instructions that had been sent. On Tuesday and Wednesday those concerned were to be sent from our home at Berg am Laim to the Milbertshofen transit camp. Each person was to be provided with enough food rations for three days and was permitted fifty kilos of luggage. This had to be spread over one suitcase, one rucksack or one travel bag per person. Each was allowed a bedroll. No one at all was now to leave the home until the departure time for the transit camp. We decided that the schoolmaster would have the task of telling the men their fate, while I would tell the women.

Abel[es] wanted to be the one to tell Gertrud Lind[auer]. She was still busy in the kitchen, and he asked if we could allow her to spend those last days living with us at the home and wanted to be the one to offer this to her as it would surely be better than being collected from the boarding house in which she was otherwise staying. I agreed, of course, and said that Gertrud could sleep in my room. We had decided to keep some spare capacity in my quarters until all other rooms were fully occupied.

It was then time to start our difficult task. Only now does it occur to me that the psychology behind each individual's reaction to the shocking news could have been of great interest to an outside observer, but at the time I felt far too low in spirits even to consider such a thing. Writing this now simply brings it all back to me.

Thekla Land[mann] was one of the first women I called in. All colour drained from her face and lips but her courage was admirable. My affection and regard for her only increased all the more. There were plenty of other women who took the news with equal dignity and calm. Only three lost control, weeping, crying out and complaining that God and the whole world had brought about their misery. I was trying to soothe one of these women – yet another occasion when I felt the inadequacy of language alone to demonstrate sympathy and empathy towards our fellow creatures – when our own doctor came to lend a hand. This was Frau Doktor Weiß [Schwarz],[25] already on site for her usual surgery and fully aware of the situation. Together we managed to help this lady cease her screaming and shouting.

Next I called in Fräulein Schüle who shared a room with her partially paralysed sister and her sickly sister-in-law, both of whom she cared for with a devotion that was truly touching. Frau Doktor Weiß [Schwarz] and I were united in our agreement that it was unthinkable for these three to be separated by the deportation of the one healthy sister while the two others were left alone and helpless. Fräulein Schüle virtually collapsed when we gave her the letter and told her she had to leave. Frau Doktor Weiß [Schwarz] promised her she would try to use her professional position with the Gestapo to free the poor woman from this order while at the same time urging her not to assume she'd succeed. I'll tell you straight away that the good doctor failed in her attempt, and nor did she succeed in persuading anyone else to step into the woman's shoes. The Gestapo flatly refused to make any changes to the plan.

Frau Doktor Weiß [Schwarz] is a courageous and energetic person and a capable physician, renowned for her willingness to help, but now that we sat facing one another in my room, we both felt utterly miserable about the situation in which we all found ourselves. We couldn't afford to give in to our feelings, however, as there was still so much to be done. The doctor wanted first of all to visit the Schüle sisters to calm and reassure them as best she could. Meanwhile I hurried downstairs to gather all those women not on the deportation list to ask for their help with the various preparations now to be made.

On the way I crossed paths with Gertrud Lind[auer], who held me in a silent embrace.

'You're spending a few days here with us, I think,' I said to her.

She nodded, and I saw what a relief it was to her that we were alone.

Thank goodness it was Sunday. This meant that nearly all of our women were here at home and could be swiftly assembled in the day room. Keeping it brief and to the point, I informed them of the situation and asked them to help me do everything possible to ease the burden on those facing deportation. I needed someone with immediate effect to take over Gertrud Lind[auer]'s duties as cook until a long-term replacement could be found. Frau Nehm stepped forward without hesitation. This sixty-five-year-old resident had always helped out in the kitchen here and was a very good worker in spite of a serious health issue that meant she had been excused from factory work. I then asked a number of women to make themselves available to run errands in town, something the potential deportees were no longer permitted to do. Others would now be expected to help with packing.

31. Dr Magdalena Schwarz, doctor, date unknown.

It was fortunate that I still had to hand the guidance on preparing a deportation pack from when we helped the Jews from Baden and the Rhineland, so I had it posted up on the blackboard. The remaining women were to make small bags for provisions using scraps of linen and any other washable remnants. Everyone was so willing to help that it was cheering to be reminded that here we'd created a community capable of facing each new test with such strength.

Everyone immediately set to work. I hurried off to the stockroom to check on food supplies and to see what we were short of. On the way to the canteen, where every resident could use their coupons to buy food, I saw Heilbronner who called over to me that one of our number had suggested we all go without meat for one meal over the following week in order to generate a larger ration of sausage for the provision bags.

The head of the canteen, Herr Klein, and I then talked over what to allocate to those who were departing. Each person was to receive a two-pound loaf, a packet of crispbread, a pack of biscuits, half a pound of cube sugar, half a pound of jam, two hundred and fifty grams of sausage and a hundred and twenty-five grams of butter. Herr Klein undertook to have everything available by Monday afternoon.

It helped that there was so much to do. After I had given each female deportee the terrible news, I had felt drained of all energy but put that behind me now that I was busy going from room to room, first to the men to advise them on what to pack and then looking in on the women doing the sewing. It was a huge task to stitch enough bags for the provisions, and then there was darning and mending aplenty for those leaving us, so I decided to work alongside them all that night in order to get everything done. We sat working in the day room until three o'clock in the morning.

Gertrud Lind[auer] then joined me in my own room, where we had prepared one of the plank beds for her, although sleep was quite out of the question. Thekla Land[mann] came in, too, and the three of us talked at length in spite of the hour. Like others being forced to leave, they expressed a touching degree of gratitude for the helping hand we were seeking to offer, which only reinforced the strong sense of attachment we all felt for one another.

So what else is there to tell you about? We've worked throughout this evening sorting through the provisions and then packing them into neat parcels. One unexpected but very welcome addition has come from the nuns, two of whom called in to see me.[26] They brought with them two large sacks, one full of real cocoa, something it hasn't been possible to buy for ages, not even with the right stamps, and the other full of high-quality loose sugar. They told us they had been asked to give us these things on behalf of the Mother Superior and all the nuns as a token of their fellow feeling for us all. They had also been asked to pass on to us that a special rogation service was to be held the next day for all those departing, and that they felt a strong sisterly bond with us. This was not the first occasion on which we had experienced such kindness from the nuns, not to mention their readiness to help in any way they could. They had shown many times before that we could count on their support, and this always gave us the boost we needed to do things that would otherwise have seemed quite beyond us.

I think a fair number of us were in full agreement with the schoolmaster Alb[recht] when he stated, 'I was outraged at first that Jews like us should be sent to a convent. Ever since earliest childhood I was brought up to have a strong aversion against stepping into a Christian church. It was a genuine

32. The rococo church of St Michael, Berg am Laim, behind which, in the north wing of the convent, was the internment camp.

struggle for me when we first came here to hold any kind of discussion with the Mother Superior or one of the nuns, but there's been a gradual change within me. I've seen with my own eyes the natural, simple dedication with which they set about their work. I've sensed their sympathy with our plight, their empathy regarding what we've endured and their eagerness to bring us relief and practical assistance. At first I was taken aback at their obvious goodness and kindness. My almost grudging feeling of respect has grown into affection and the recognition that I, an Orthodox Jew, was caught up in prejudice and invalid presumptions. I often now enter their church in the knowledge that their God is our God, and it now seems irrelevant where we offer our prayers to Him. I have never before felt such a powerful wish to bow in reverence as I do before them.'

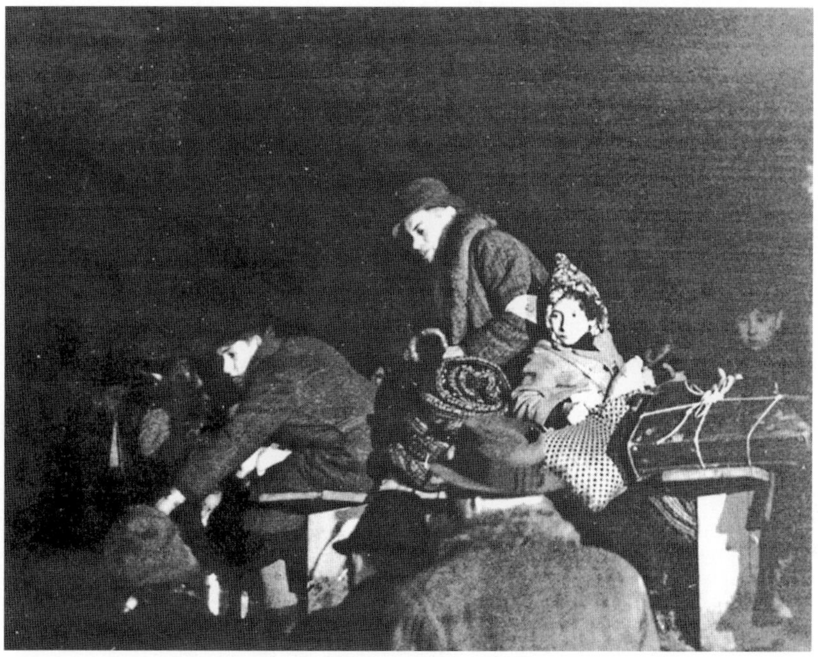

33. Deportation to Kaunas (Kowno) from the Milbertshofen camp. Police photograph dated 20 November 1941.

I was so glad to hear an admission of this kind for I knew that many of our residents had experienced similar awakenings. Not in my case, though, as you and I had already experienced support and kindness from devout Catholics. What was clear to me all over again, however, is the importance of recognising how any barrier created by religious dogma can actually fall away in the face of adversity to be replaced by human ties every bit as strong as those between siblings. 'Pure humanity heals all human affliction.' Goethe's unforgettable line shone like a beacon throughout those difficult days.

Our mutual sense of familiarity and belonging made the farewells more bearable over the few days spent at the transit camp, as demonstrated by the letters we later received. All the greater, then, was the gaping hole left behind for those of us remaining, a hole that could never be filled, not even by the many new arrivals who then flooded in.[27]

34. Gestapo and security police accompanied the deportations from Milbertshofen. Police photograph of the deportation to Kaunas (Kowno) dated 20 November 1941.

Letter from Else to Eva Schmidt

Berg am Laim, 16 November 1941

Dearest Eva

My heartfelt thanks for the kindest of letters from you. Your words have done me so much good. Last week compares only with the worst of past times, like when you visited BL [Berg am Laim], or those other events of three years ago. Our people have conducted themselves superbly, and we have succeeded in creating a real community here in just a bare few months, a community that has demonstrated its fortitude and resilience, something truly uplifting to behold in the face of such harsh challenges. To be honest, I'd rather have left along with our first batch of core troops as for me that would have been easier than staying here and facing up to the far more difficult task now being assigned to me.

My dear, listen to this – on one of the most difficult days yet, what came but a letter from my dear Fritz, so calm, loving and detailed in its content that it brought me great solace. He's so concerned about me – if only I could give him reassurance that everything is all right. I'm absolutely certain, however, that this whole operation will continue and that we will all have to leave in the end, the only unknown being the timing. I really don't know that I can ask you to make the journey over the weekend, into such an unknown state of affairs here. It's far too much of a strain, one you really should not put yourself through. I must close now, as new residents are arriving daily, almost all of them elderly and in poor health.

My warmest wishes to you, a thousand times over.

Your E

Siegfried's Diary

Oxford, 18 November 1941

I've had a deal of trouble with my health over the last few weeks. Else's hope of Cuba seems to have fallen by the wayside due to lack of funds (1,800 dollars), while the visa for Argentina has been refused yet again.

My darling Else's situation now looks far more difficult and dangerous, while I sit here powerless to help her. It chokes me to think of her distress and possible deportation to even greater misery. [. . .] Every fibre in my body longs for an end to this terrible war, in anything between six and ten months, in accordance with Stalin's own aims.

[. . .] My historical research demands a personal tranquillity and degree of concentration that I'm simply not capable of summoning at present. At the moment I'm looking at something very topical: the idea of a Federal Union in Europe in tandem with the development of an organisation for English agricultural workers. I'd like to make something of that and have been able to establish contact with Fox, Secretary to the Federal Union, via Frau Dr Rosenau.

Oxford, 1 December 1941

Else's letter dated 31 October leaves me in no doubt that she's going to have to stay in Germany right through to the bitter end. Fate could not be more cruel to us.

One last hope – a sudden end to hostilities. And then those who have decimated Germany will be struck down so fast that it will put a stop to their shouting of sham political slogans and every one of their followers will lose faith and fall away.

Meanwhile here am I in the warmth of my room, working in freedom among people who are living their lives without being treated like slaves. I take no pleasure in being in so much better a position than my darling wife. How did it ever come to this? I accept all the blame. I was too slow in planning our own departure once the children had left. I don't know why I didn't do it straight away. The guilt will never leave me.[28]

'The dream of Cuba has vanished,' Else wrote. The grief behind those words. Nothing can console me. I face an absolute void.

Oxford, 16 December 1941

I've just come from a small gathering of the Oxford branch of the Federal Union, where eight others (seven Englishmen and one other émigré) were discussing forthcoming meetings. I am proud to wear their distinctive badge, demonstrating so clearly that I am part of this free country. The Federal Union is the one and only practical, non-Utopian idea for the post-war period. [...]

Over the past few weeks we had been on tenterhooks for the imminent fall of Moscow. It seemed as good as in the bag and had been widely trumpeted. A setback on this scale must have felt utterly disastrous for soldiers who have grown accustomed to seeing themselves as invincible. It will have hit them harder than any other army. One hundred divisions are said to be on the retreat. The thought of this huge defeat for Germany has left me almost overcome with joy. With Japan's entry into the war, America will now be armed to the teeth and ready and victory will be ensured, if perhaps a little slower to come than we'd hoped.[29]

My thoughts are constantly with Else as I wonder over and over what is happening to her, but no answer comes. Her last letter, dated 15 November, made clear how insecure her position has become. Please, please let her be spared deportation to Poland. I was hesitant in sending off my own last missive to her, but she too is having to face up to some of the grimmest things imaginable.

A noteworthy parallel at this point. In 1917 German victory over Russia freed the country from the grip of the Tsar. Will a Russian victory over Germany in 1941 likewise free National Socialist Germany from the talons of Hitler and his cronies?

1942

Letter from Else to Eva Schmidt

Berg am Laim, 2 January 1942

My dear, kind Eva

I've spent the whole of the last three days at Annemarie's with her family. This change of scene is doing me a power of good. On Monday I want – well, part of me wants, that is – to get back to work and I'm glad I feel ready. I've had a real nervous breakdown, something I never thought could happen to me. I've had fantastic care here with the whole household somehow competing for who could be nicest to me!

I'm so happy and grateful to be able to sense your presence with me too, my beloved friend.

Else's Diary

Berg am Laim, Sunday, 4 January 1942

My health isn't so good at the moment. The dizzy spells that started in November are now occurring more often and the most stultifying weariness frequently leaves me quite unable to get out of bed. I've been losing weight for some months now.

Among the new arrivals who came in the wake of the deportations in November was a woman who was not only the widow of a doctor but an ex-nurse in her own right. Sister Irma [Heilbronner], as we called her, nursed a few of us and took wonderful care of me. She's no youngster – early sixties, in fact – but nonetheless capable and tireless. We got on famously from the moment we met. When I was at my lowest ebb she took on a lot of my duties for me.

Yesterday, however, she was forced to leave us because Hauptsturmführer Wegner ordered her transfer to Milbertshofen on disciplinary grounds. She was summoned to appear before him on the morning of 24 December, no less. I hadn't been well during this normally festive period and so didn't find out until afterwards what had been going on. Shortly before she'd been sent to us, on a day when she'd been called in to our Jewish Community office, she'd had to make her way out to her own flat on the outer edge of

Schwabing. It would have taken her a couple of hours on foot so she'd jumped on the tram – a means of transport that was, of course, forbidden to Jews. She travelled on the platform at the rear of the carriage in an effort to conceal her Star of David. As passengers jostled against one another in the increasingly crowded tram, a member of the SA standing close by spotted the yellow of the star. He immediately ordered the conductor to note down her particulars and report her to the Party.

This happened early in November, so she spent the next few days anxiously awaiting a summons to Widenmayerstrasse but nothing happened, and during that time she was sent to us and started work. She had almost forgotten the whole incident when the summons came for her to appear before Wegner on 24 December. Arriving on time, Irma found him practically foaming with rage about what he clearly considered the most heinous offence. She stayed calm in spite of all the coarse language he was throwing at her and no doubt her composure enraged him even further. All of a sudden he was standing horribly close, right in front of her, and she could feel his breath in her face as he bawled out, 'I'll teach you lot to disobey! Get yourself to Milbertshofen on 2 January. The Berg am Laim home is far too comfortable for creatures like you. Now get out of my sight!'

Numb with shock, she stumbled from the room and somehow got herself down the stairs and out of the building, only to stop and gaze long and hard at the River Isar, fighting the urge to throw herself into its icy waters in search of oblivion and eternal peace. Somehow she got her feelings back under control and slowly made her way home to Berg am Laim, by which time she was sufficiently recovered to come to my room, calm as calm could be, to tell me her trip to Widenmayerstrasse had been concerning a financial matter. On Friday she went off to work as a nurse at Milbertshofen, as cool, calm and collected as ever. Our farewell was painful, particularly on my side.

Our Professor, too, has suffered ill health, so much so that he had to be taken to our hospital facility. He's improved a little already but it'll be quite a while before he can return to us. His gentle presence in our home is sorely missed, his kindly smile each time I pass by on my rounds, and I know many others feel the same way.

New arrivals are due this coming week and we've made up all remaining beds, including those in my own room. I must confess it's going to be hard to lose the few quiet hours I have alone here at night. I've already chosen my room-mates, though. There's Frau Dillenius, a refined, quiet lady, widowed, who's always come across as very pleasant. Then there's Frau Altschüler, rather brisk and a little moody but highly intelligent, married to a bank director with horrendous injuries from his service in the last war, who can only walk with the aid of two sticks.[1] He was given a bed in the Professor's room and the two quickly became friends. His wife always stays close by his side. When Herr Altschüler was forced to leave his employment, the couple rented a house in the countryside near Walchensee, only to be removed from there by the Party in November. My third room-mate is to be Frau Schönberg, currently in one of our medical facilities with heart trouble. Her husband, now seventy, built the Deutsches Museum in Munich but now works at a cement plant. At least he's been put in the office where he can draw up plans. He cuts a small and modest figure and accepts everything with considerable ease, as is so often the case with people who have previously held senior positions and achieved great things.

I really shouldn't make it sound as though we only have the quiet and the distinguished in our midst. On the contrary, for here as in the outside world there are plenty of disagreeable people – the ones who always moan and complain, who get angry about everything and make life difficult for anyone who comes near them. We have to spend a fair portion of our time quashing rumours and that's among the men quite as much as the women, not to mention sorting out disagreements and calming tempers. But with the Sword of Damocles constantly hanging over us all in the form of possible punishment transfers to Milbertshofen or worse at the hands of the Party, most people pull themselves together fairly rapidly after any outburst. In my view it's simply a waste of time reporting in detail on troublemakers or particular individuals behind the endless flare-ups.

Siegfried's Diary

Oxford, 12 January 1942

Still no news from or about Else. Suppose the worst really has happened? Suppose she herself has now suffered the fate of so many others and been transported to Poland, to the chill wasteland of some camp where every life is at stake? I cannot shake off these terrible imaginings. I feel that I have brought only misfortune to the two women to whom I have been closest in my life.[2] Gertrud had three years of happiness with me but with someone else might perhaps have lived for thirty more. Else's life has been more than soured by my embroiling her in the whole Jewish plight. Beyond all shade of doubt, the joining of our two lives has led inexorably to this current situation. Can that ever be excused? [. . .]

Nonetheless, the Federal Union and the eight points I've already forwarded to Fox are still managing to keep me occupied from day to day.

I have also now been in contact with Dr Breslauer, a member of the board at the Association of Jewish Refugees (AJR).[3] He's recommending me for a position on the new committee looking at post-war issues. Working on highly practical matters of this nature is an excellent tonic where I myself am concerned, while also adhering closely to the wider theoretical issues to be addressed, namely:

How can the survival of the Jewish people over 2,000 years of the diaspora best be explained via the application of reason? (And not in line with Mann's somewhat transcendental conjecture).

Can a wide dispersal to every known corner of the globe be seen to reduce the risk of decline, especially when hand in hand with the reduced political power of any one small nation?

Does a barter economy justly require social mobility and economic movement of capital for the majority of the population of a city, when weighted in favour of the poor, combined with a Christian-style renunciation of self-interest?

Do the following serve to strengthen both the bonds of faith and personal character, namely a sense of being unfairly singled out as adherents of a particular religion when hammered home via political and legal discrimination, unjust accusations of apostasy and blood libel, etc., and even heighten an individual's loyalty towards the said religion, its literature and commandments?

Do the day-to-day personal needs of individuals regarding how they earn their crust and their consequent standard of living inevitably foster a broad range of intellectual talent? (Certain people can become indispensable to the prevailing powers and the acquisition of income becomes their single best weapon in the daily struggle of life, along with the usual advantages of accumulated wealth and the ability to sway political outcomes for their own benefit, ultimately bringing the downfall of society and the wider economy.)

Oxford, 2 February 1942

A letter has come at last from my beloved Else, dated 5 January 1942, with no news of any change to her own circumstances but talking of a picture of Peter that she's received via Gustel! Strangely, the fact of there being no change feels like some small improvement in itself, particularly as we're already halfway through the winter. May this be the last such season for the war in Europe.

After a wretched six months of the most colossal effort and human sacrifice in fighting this futile battle which daily drains supplies and takes lives in deep snow and freezing temperatures as low as minus forty, I struggle to believe that the German army is regaining the upper hand and renewing its spirit of attack to force the Russians back into their place as underdog.

Powerful though Germany's attacking spirit may be, it rapidly loses vitality when in a defensive position. With the English, however, it's the other way round. Their strength comes to the fore when under attack. [...]

At a recent gathering of the Federal Union we held a very lively political debate. Written questions had been invited and were discussed for a good hour and a half, our advisory panel giving clear, concise answers from the front.

Sample question: Will the formation of a Federal Union prevent future conflict within the area?

ANSWER: Future hostilities can only be less likely.

Q: How does the Federal Union differ from the League of Nations?

Q: Can only democracies join?

A. Absolutely.

Organ music opened and closed the meeting. There was then a silver collection, which brought in a few pounds in support. We had charged an entry fee of two shillings and six, and there were between six hundred and eight hundred people attending! A meeting held in such harmony is evidence of the confidence of the English and their political maturity, or rather their political serenity.

Oxford, 19 February 1942

Else's letter came yesterday, dated 22 January. Fortunately there's no worsening of the situation over there and another chance of leaving the country. She's had Tilla with her for a fortnight and been corresponding with friends.

My beloved's fortitude is admirable, but I do hope that it's not all simply a show on my behalf. Her work is intensive and time-consuming and must at least spur her on and help fill the days. If only the war in Europe would end this year. The killing cannot carry on, month after month. Exhaustion and collapse set in more speedily for the attacker than the defender who is at least gradually ridding his country of the enemy.

This summer, autumn at the latest, must surely bring some decisive turn of events, praying that nothing unforeseen occurs in the meantime. Can nothing help me glimpse some way out of this transient existence, so we are free to come together again as a family? Anywhere at all in the world.

I'm very preoccupied just now with how things will look in the period following the war. Through Dr Alexander, and as part of my work with the sub-group of the Association of Jewish Refugees, I've been able to map out something of a programme. Settlements of mixed groups in European and non-European countries. Individual migration to be an exception rather than the rule, and only in very particular circumstances, or when requested by a whole family.

Oxford, 18 March 1942

I set off to London for a meeting of the Board of the Association of Jewish Refugees. A report from Adler-Rudel, with Schoyer in the chair, and, Breslauer, the lawyer.[4] Next in line were Prof Brodetzky and Dr Alexander (from Krefeld), Chair of the Committee looking into matters of post-war reparation. I then gave a summary of the points I'd submitted previously, referring to the inseparable link between reparation, the reconstructing of settlements, and of lives now bereft of means, and yet the sheer impossibility of reparation on an individual basis.

Letters from Else to Eva Schmidt

Berg am Laim, 26 February 1942

My dearest Eva

I'm sure you've been expecting to hear from me – your lovely long letter and cards definitely deserved faster replies than this, but I just haven't been able to get on with things. Each day I've intended to write and then have been so worn out by the evening that I just couldn't. And I no longer have my room to myself now but have had to start sharing with three other women, one of whom has actually been in hospital for some time. During the day the other two are out working, both excellent people, but when I get to my room in the evening around half past nine or ten, it's hard no longer having this space all to myself. Otherwise I'm well, except that I tire more easily than before my illness.

Eva, I've had more news from Fritz. He seems to be fretting about me a lot, which concerns me greatly. In each letter I try to stop him worrying so much but to no avail.

Here it's a case of constant arrivals and linen changes, but we hope this will stop next week as by then we'll be full, and then we'll finally find time for all the other jobs that need doing around the place.

Berg am Laim, 24 March 1942

My dearest Eva

Heartfelt thanks from me to you for your lovely letter and card, the latter so colourful and cheering, and now displayed here on my desk. Thank you also for offering us a supply of garlic but we've plenty here and it wouldn't be worth the trouble of your sending us any.

It's a pity our veranda has now been set up for other uses as the only day room we now have is upstairs, and you can imagine how much in demand that is, what with so many people here currently.

The snow has almost gone apart from a few patches on the northerly side and the weather feels quite springlike, but I'm not really taking any of this in.

Here at the home, all signs suggest yet more change being imminent. We must face this with quiet stoicism and, my dear, I promise you I'm doing precisely that. There'd be no point in you coming here now, as no visits are permitted for the time being. In any case, rest assured that I'll tell you as soon as I know anything definite. Living in a state of perpetual uncertainty is the hardest thing to bear but has to be endured.

I'm eternally grateful that I am at least recovered and fit for work once more, although a few kilos lighter – and that can only be a good thing! – and thus ready for whatever may come next.

All my best,

Your E

Berg am Laim, 29 March 1942

Now it's time, I've just been informed I have to leave. Many many of us will go together. We don't know when or where. I'm very calm, in good cheer and determined to pull through. I can take very little with me. Give my best to Hanna and Kurt and the children. I can't write to them any more. And you, my dear friend, every good wish, I know that wherever I am, you're always near me, and I'm so glad of that.

Farewell, I embrace you!

Your E.

Else's Diary

Berg am Laim, Sunday, 12 April 1942

It's been a long time since I even opened my diary, there's been so much to do. We're really missing Abel[es] with his practical mind and clever hands, always so quick to carry out repairs or make something for us. More than anyone I miss Gertrud Lind[auer] and the way I could rely on her in the kitchen.

And we've never had any word whatsoever from all those who were deported.[5]

A nineteen-year-old lad was sent me to fill Gertrud's post – his name is Siegbert, and he'd been working in the old people's home run by Frau Tuchmann. For his age he's very capable, and trustworthy with it, but I still have to take care of quite a few things myself, even with Frau Nehm alongside him and in overall charge.

Oh well, there's little point my going into all that in great detail; I wanted only to mention it. There's something far more important to report now.

Rumours of a new round of deportations began to circulate during the final week of March. Like bees disturbed in their hive, the place was positively humming with conjecture about the likely scale and purpose of any such operation, feared by us all.

On 28 March, as he did on every Saturday afternoon, one of the Committee members was with us to spend time with his elderly mother. I took the opportunity of asking him whether a new mass of deportations was in the offing. He said yes, adding that neither he nor the other Committee members knew any further details and that the list of names had not yet been presented to them. It was expected later that day.

Quite late that evening, our caretaker knocked on my door and asked to see me for a moment. His wife's 'Aryan', and they have seven children all raised in their mother's Catholic faith. The man's a real character, a tireless worker, small and plump with such an open and friendly face, a bawdy joke or two never far from his lips. Now he was standing in front of me, an uncharacteristically solemn expression on his face.

'I've just been over at the Gemeinde,' he said. 'An old mate of mine works there, and just as I was leaving, Herr Stahl, the director, came over and asked me to tell you they've now received the deportation list. You'll get it officially around noon tomorrow.' His voice broke. 'Frau Doktor, you and the rest of the management of the home are down on the list. All in all, seventy-five residents are due to leave together. You'll be sure to tell our dear schoolmaster and Herr Heilbronner, won't you? It's bad enough having to tell you, but Director Stahl thought you'd rather know straight away so you can prepare yourselves.'

His broad, honest face showed an anguish I'd never before seen in him. I thanked him for coming out of his way to let me know. He himself was at least in a mixed marriage, so he wasn't forced to wear the Star of David and was permitted to use the tram and live normally with his family. He usually has Saturday afternoons and Sundays off but had promised on this occasion to come in regardless.

There'd be a lot of additional work again if these lists were to be out in practice.

Next I hurried down to the office where Heilbronner was still at his desk and told him what I'd just heard. There was a short pause before he gave any response and when he did, he spoke slowly.

'It's strange, but it's almost a relief to be part of it this time, not simply having to break the dreadful news to other people, and then having to calm and soothe them.'

'I feel exactly the same,' I said to him, 'and I'm so very glad to be leaving at the same time as you.'

He came over and held out his hand and I reciprocated his warm gesture.

'I hardly need say how pleased I am that we can move on together to whatever awaits us. Right this minute, however, we need to fetch Herr Alb[recht]. Like us, he's entitled to hear the news straight away. Please just wait while I fetch him.'

He was back almost immediately, Alb[recht] in his wake. I related everything that Hermann, the caretaker, had told me.

Alb[recht] gave a start, then swiftly got a grip and let out a deep sigh, followed by the words, 'We knew it would happen sooner or later. It's good we'll be leaving together.'

We agreed to maintain silence in front of our residents until the written confirmation came through, then went off to our own quarters. It came as a relief to find both of my room-mates fast asleep. I'd have found it very hard to be forced into any inconsequential chatter.

Sitting down quietly at my desk with the lamp dimmed, I tried to gather my thoughts and seek some clarity. The worst thing about this news was that any contact with you and the children would now be impossible. Our correspondence had by necessity been infrequent and sketchy, but our sister-in-law in Lisbon had at least been able to facilitate the posting and receipt of letters, providing us all with a sense of connection and some measure of happiness in our respective situations. Now I was forced to write to her about being moved to the transit camp, from whence I would be undertaking a far longer journey but with no forwarding address.

And what would become of the home we'd established here at Berg am Laim? I'll admit I'd grown fond of the place and never more so than at that moment, where the three of us in charge were set to leave. But there was no point in getting caught up in such thoughts. *Get yourself to bed*, I told myself, *if only to get a little rest* – proper sleep was out of the question, but recuperation was essential. There were tough days ahead and I needed to be prepared.

The individual deportation orders, as they were called, arrived on the Sunday afternoon. Breaking the news was somehow easier this time round because at the very least we could now say, 'We'll be going with you, and it's not just us – we're pretty sure that every single Jew from Munich and indeed across the whole Reich will be deported. It's almost better this way, don't you think, given that we're being spared a long and agonising wait for whatever comes next?'

There was no weeping or screaming. Pale, silent and composed, each woman took the letter offered her. What upset me most was that the Altschülers were also on the deportation list. How on earth was this dear man with such horrendous injuries from his service during the last war to cope with the strain of the transit camp and then the journey, never mind what was to follow?

There was another thing that rendered this situation particularly heart-rending. As a couple they'd been childless but had taken in a little boy and later adopted him. Both were desperately attached to him, as was he to them. Since he was an 'Aryan' child, other people had already created a lot of difficulty for the couple, so they had chosen to have him educated at one of the large boarding schools in the countryside outside Munich, where they were still able to see him now and then. This latest separation from their boy, now aged fifteen, had hit them harder than anything else. Nonetheless they continued to conduct themselves with great dignity and restraint.

There was no need to sit up all night to get us kitted out on this occasion. As a precaution, I'd had a large stack of food bags stitched in readiness and prompted everyone to keep the belongings they'd be taking on standby – this time a mere thirty kilos' worth. We'd made sleeping bags, and for anyone with no blankets but a duvet, we fashioned an additional cover by removing some of the feathery down from the duvet, spreading it out thin and stitching it into a further quilt of sorts. The bedrolls needed some sort of carry strap and anyone without a leather one of their own was given one for that purpose from our stock. All this assistance was provided by Annemarie's Quaker helpers, together with women who'd travelled out from the city centre to do whatever they could for us.

Those having to stay behind were even more distressed than those having to leave. The rumour circulating was that the home would in future be run by members of the SS. We'd heard nothing to justify this but if there was any truth in it, then it really was better to be moving on. While something equally terrible might just as easily happen in Poland, it somehow seemed less awful for it to happen there and not within the walls of this home we've all grown so fond of and where we've always fostered an atmosphere of gentleness and kindness.

I handed the keys to the food store and all the cupboards to Gertrud Lind [auer]'s successor, Frau Nehm. She and the young lad were now running the kitchen together and maintaining a meticulous logbook with information on all the quantities needed each week for anything and everything.

At the same time as I was occupied in the kitchen, Heilbronner was busy inducting an old colleague, Adlatus Löwenberger, a gentleman of seventy and in very poor health. He had been a wholesaler in the food sector and had always proved not only extremely helpful but also outstanding at organisation. He had, for example, created an extremely practical and time-saving device in the form of a small filing system for the food ration cards. Heilbronner now stressed to him how vital it was to pay the community's rent on time every Friday and with it to supply an accurate register of current residents to the Gauleiter's deputy at the Widenmayerstrasse office. The register had to be delivered by messenger.

The departure for the transit camp at Milbertshofen was set for Wednesday, 1 April. On the evening before this, we came together in the dining hall for a service of worship that without question will stay with us all forever. We said a few prayers and then someone read out Psalm 94. When the service came to a close all the residents filed past the three of us – that's myself, Alb[recht] and Heilbronner – and shook each of us by the hand.

Many a resident attempted to stammer out a phrase or two of appreciation and unity but most couldn't even begin to speak, so overpowering were their emotions and tears. I had to swallow hard to stop myself from breaking down when I saw all those familiar faces, so contorted with grief. My hand ached from the strength of those handshakes. Up in our room Frau Altschüler was comforting Frau Dillenius who was not to be deported and had to stay.

One task remained. I was in possession of a quantity of the drug Veronal, enough to permit three people quietly to take their own lives, so the doctor had told me. I sewed a third into the hem of my old grey coat and the remaining two-thirds I passed to Frau Altschüler for her to stitch inside clothing for herself and her husband. He himself was unaware of this, but I realised what a relief it must be for her to know that they'd have this option if the situation became more than they could bear. Simply knowing that they had the means to determine their own fate would give them strength and some comfort.

I then handed my diary to Frau Dillenius and asked her to send it to Tilla in Isartal once I'd left so that the dear girl could keep it safely there.

During the night, near sleepless for all of us, my thoughts turned repeatedly to you and the children. With every passing year of separation the gulf that forced itself between us has grown wider and wider and at this point appeared to stretch into eternity. The agony of being apart mingled with the desperate longing to see you all overcame me that night like no other. I struggled to remain in control and it was early morning before I fell into a restless sleep.

When I awoke, I saw the tear-streaked face of Frau Dillenius leaning towards me before she set off for her job at the factory. Without saying a word I embraced her, then immediately turned my face away so as not to prolong the pain of farewell any more than necessary.

I watched the sun come up then went to my desk, this time simply to gaze out of the window at the view I'd grown to love so much. A number of scenes presented themselves to my particularly appreciative gaze on this beautiful morning. I saw the swifts that always swished and called around the two church towers on summer evenings, the sedate procession of nuns in their black gowns and winged white head coverings as they walked down the straight paths in the green of the convent gardens. I will always associate these images now with the tranquillity of eventide.

Shortly before our service the previous evening, I had taken my leave of the convent nuns. I started with the Mother Superior, such a quiet person but also so intelligent, then went to visit my beloved senior nun, well known to me from her regular duty at the front gate and supervision of the telephone used by both of us. Everyone held her in the highest regard. Next came the kitchen nun, who'd so often helped us out with supplies when we were stuck. And here was the garden nun with the sunburned open face, and the laughter lines crinkling around her twinkling eyes that bore witness to her constant good humour. Our shared passion for houseplants and cut flowers, always in generous supply from her to adorn my little room, meant that I felt a special bond with this fine woman.

If I had to give a summary of my time there, I'd describe it as an abundance of work, suffering and joys, both great and small. And in the end I could permit myself the thought that each one of us had done our duty. We could leave with our consciences clear. Once again I felt how much easier it is to live among those suffering injustice than among those who mete it out.[6] We would face this harsh and unknown destiny with our heads held high, our dignity and self-esteem intact. I want neither to sound as though I'm speaking with the arrogance of the Pharisees nor to forget my belief that humility and modesty are among those virtues to which we should most aspire. The hour of contemplation had done me good, and I now felt able to turn to the obligations of the coming day.

Our simple breakfast brought us all together as usual. Then it was a case of fetching the luggage from my room and adding it to the stack already by the front door. One last look at number 38. Thank you, St Theresa, guardian of my room.

We heard the distinctive sound of car tyres as a large vehicle with a luggage trailer now swung into the courtyard. *Quick, downstairs!* We said our good-byes once more, but swiftly this time. My two colleagues and I had agreed to go on the first run. The vehicle would need to make three journeys to take all seventy-five of us over to the transit camp. With me were the Altschülers and Heilbronner, as we all wanted to stay together for as long as we possibly could. We moved off, the convent gate opened, and those remaining behind waved as they wept, while a handful of curious passers-by stood outside on the street and watched us drive away. And then we were gone.

The familiar city streets slipped by as I kept thinking: *This is the last time.* It occurred to me that I'd never actually seen the transit camp where so many people known to us were now living. Through the window I now saw only long bleak roads lined on one side by factories and on the other by a single wall until all of a sudden there was a gate. It opened, our vehicle turned in and came to a halt in a stark square surrounded on all four sides by

35. Arrival at the Milbertshofen camp. Police photograph dated 1941.

wooden huts. These were of a very rough construction, built without proper foundations. Not a single tree or other form of greenery anywhere to be seen. I thought how much harder it would be to live there than in our own beautiful place with its uplifting gardens, but this was no time for such musings – we were commanded simply to get out and line up. Each of us was then given something along the lines of a cloakroom ticket, green with a number printed on it in black. Heilbronner was 273, I got 274, and the subsequent consecutive numbers went to the Altschülers. An instruction was bawled out to march in single file for inspection by the Gestapo in one of the huts.[7]

Behind a makeshift barrier sat a man, who snapped at me, 'Empty your handbag.'

I tipped out the contents on the table in front of him. First he snatched up my identity card and put it in the pile he'd been making.

'Where are the rest of your papers? Birth and marriage certificates, emigration documents?'

'I've destroyed them,' I replied.

'What made you do that?' he said, annoyed.

'They all seemed quite superfluous to deportation,' I said quietly. The truth was that I'd left them behind in safe hands as I knew they'd only be destroyed here.

He then snatched the few photos I had with me, all of you and the children, and in one angry movement ripped them in half and tossed the pieces behind him. Disgust and rage flooded through me, but I knew there was no point in showing how much his opening gesture had hurt me. He opened my purse. It contained only a few coins.

'Where's all your money?' he asked, his tone harsh.

'I have none left,' I replied. As I reached forward to put the few remaining items back in my bag, he batted my hand away.

'That's it, move on. Next!' he shouted.

I passed through to the adjoining room.

'The key to your suitcase!' demanded another official.

I pointed behind me, saying, 'It's there, on the table.'

'Move on!' he yelled at me. 'Women to the right.'

I entered a room where two women were sitting behind a table.

'Open your food bag and bedroll,' said one. They inspected both. To protect my camel rug and my quilt, I'd wrapped them up in an old woollen blanket. 'You're allowed only two blankets,' stated the older of the two women, not unkindly. I pushed my old woollen rug to the side. Nothing else was queried. With some difficulty I tucked the now separated rugs under my arm, together with the few things that had been wrapped inside them, and left the hut.

Waiting for me outside were a few lads from our own home for apprentices, sent over by our Gemeinde on days such as these to help out at Milbertshofen. Rain was now falling. Two of the boys helped me carry my things. They led me to another hut, above its door the number 7. I looked around for the Altschülers and Heilbronner, but couldn't see them so asked the boys what they knew.

The taller one said, 'They'll be in different huts from you. Married couples are housed in separate huts from single men and women – although you can meet up with them at the door of their hut,' he added, trying to be kind, and then showed me into a room already occupied by a large number of women. Grey paper sacks filled with wood shavings were set out all over the floor, each one 80 centimetres in width and 1.8 metres in length.

One of the younger women broke away from her group to introduce herself to me. 'I'm the room senior, you might say. There's capacity for fifty women to live in here. Everyone gets half of one sack to lie down or just sit on. It's going to be really packed.' She heaved a sigh. 'We've been here since yesterday evening,' she added, naming the small Bavarian community she'd come from.

Just then a former resident of our home recognised me and came over. 'Do join us,' she said kindly, drawing me towards one of the windows. 'There's space for you on my sack.'

I was relieved to follow her, set down my food bag and blankets, then gave myself a moment to look more closely at my surroundings. The sacks were already mucky with dirt trodden in from outside as people arrived, and it was quite evident who'd just arrived and who'd already been here a while. The latter were unkempt and dirt from the sacks had transferred on to their clothing. But I couldn't go on standing like this – there was no proper seating at all, and in any case, the room was so tightly packed there wouldn't have been space for anything such thing – so I sank down on to my half of the sack, letting out a sigh as I did so.

Our room filled up rapidly. I counted around forty women and the babble of voices in such confined surroundings became too much for me. The rain had stopped, and I wanted to get out and away from the din and the lack of fresh air. Once outside I found Heilbronner surrounded by a large group of our former inmates. He called over to me, 'Good that you're here, Frau Doktor! Our people have just said we should do something to ensure that those of us from Berg am Laim make the onward journey together.'

I thought for a moment and said, 'Well, it's best then that we approach whoever is in charge of the actual transportation.' One of our group asked if we knew who this was. 'It'll be whoever's in charge of the huts here. I happen to know that the Gestapo have done the same as us with regard to allocating people to transport – the person in charge here is leaving, too. I'll seek him out and ask if he can arrange for us all to travel together.'

The sun had now broken through and enticed most of the others outside. But wait, who was that over there? It was none other than Baby from my time at the Lohhof flax mill, closely followed by Little Erna and Frau Brand [Brandl], two other good chums from my time at Lohhof. I remembered straight away that the latter two were not fully Jewish. I said hello to all three, turning then to those two in particular with a questioning look.

'Surely you're not among those leaving?' I asked them.

'We don't know yet for sure,' replied Little Erna. 'Frau Brand [Brandl] and I were told we'd be held back as substitutes in case any of the target number of seven hundred and seventy-eight deportees were, for some reason, excluded from leaving.'

Then Baby spoke of her own situation. 'As a Mischling I've prepared myself to leave in spite of the Aryanisation petition still pending. My mother's sixty-three and on the "fully Jewish" list, and if they won't release her, then I'm certainly not going to abandon her, and my Aryanisation petition can go hang. Quite apart from that, I've been a supervisor at the Lohhof labour camp since November and nearly all the girls from there are on the list to leave. I'd rather go with them than later on with a load of strangers.'

Yes, here was that same feeling of togetherness that we'd all felt at Berg am Laim too. I gave Baby a nod of encouragement to show that I fully understood her decision.

Having talked as we strolled, we had now arrived at a hut on the fringes of the camp. A few of its inmates were standing outside, people I recognised as our own. We exchanged greetings, and an elderly lady among them spoke to me.

'If there's anything you need for the journey, something you don't have or that's been taken from you, please let us know. We want so much to help a little and this may be the only way we can.'

I thanked her and promised to keep her kind offer in mind.

'There's really nothing you have need of?' This question came from another woman, the widow of a previously well-known artist.

I remembered the small heap of things I'd tipped out of my handbag and been forced to leave behind on arrival and recalled my fountain pen. With some hesitation I indicated that I might like another one.

Upon hearing this, the woman asked me to wait a moment or, if I wished, to go into the hut with her while she fetched me one. I followed her, curious to see what it was like inside. Well, listen to this! Although small and nothing compared to our lovely facility at Berg am Laim, the place was clean, homely and well furnished. I thanked her most warmly for the gift of the fountain pen and found several other old acquaintances to greet before leaving the hut.

'Things aren't so bad for us,' one of the old ladies said to me. 'At least we weren't asked to vacate our hut the way a lot of others had to for the duration of the transit camps, what with so many deportees needing to be accommodated.'

And now here was another former inmate from Berg am Laim, asking if I'd had any lunch. I said no. 'Then you need to get back to your own hut,' he urged me. 'You'll definitely all be taken for your meal shortly. It'll be what we've all just had.'

I hurried off back to number 7 and found our room senior lining everyone up in pairs to make our way to the dining hut. I got in line and off we went. We received our food in a hut near the main gate, which we'd been driven through on arrival. The place was packed to the gunnels but others shifted along a bit to make space for us. I met up with the Altschülers, sat myself down and asked how everything was going for them so far? It seemed the guards had been very hard on Herr Altschüler at the entry inspection, taking all sorts of things from his backpack and bedroll, including the leather strap that held the latter together. I promised I'd get hold of another strap or belt of some sort from one of the permanent residents.

The food then arrived. It was a basic one-pot meal comprising white cabbage and potatoes, served out by youngsters, everything nicely prepared and organised, no small feat when you consider that as well as the usual eight hundred inmates, there were suddenly as many again to be fed.

In the afternoon all members of my hut were despatched to the kitchen to peel potatoes and prepare other vegetables. Yet more old faces to greet again here, too! That evening came potato soup with a hunk of bread, and then it was time to be marched back to our quarters. No one was ever allowed to linger outside. Finally we were sent off in batches to the washrooms.

Just as we were coming back, we noticed a small bus arriving. It was raining heavily once more, soaking the passengers, their bedrolls and luggage as they stepped down from the vehicle. Soon afterwards a dozen or so new arrivals were brought to our hut, meaning we had now reached a total of fifty. It worried me how crowded the place was becoming as the new people found themselves any last remaining spots on the bedsacks. They told us they were from Augsburg. We lent them some of our blankets and hung their wet ones to dry from the military lockers lining the long sides of the room. This did nothing, of course, to improve the dank air in the overcrowded quarters and blackout regulations meant that no windows were to be opened. We stretched out on our sacks for the night as far as we were able. A young woman, not someone previously known to me, was complaining to her neighbours about the body search she'd been subjected to. Gradually the voices fell silent and the only sounds were the snores and snuffles of the few who'd actually fallen asleep, as by far the majority of us lay awake all night.

On Thursday I went with my two former colleagues from Berg am Laim to speak to the man in charge of the camp and transportation about our wish to travel onward together in groups of our own choosing. He replied that this would definitely be possible and explained that each vehicle would be taking fifty passengers.

'And what kind of vehicle is this exactly?' I asked him.

'An old French thing,' he explained. 'It's dreadfully cramped, absolutely filthy, a real museum piece to be honest, but at least it has seats and is considerably better than a cattle truck.'

The schoolmaster then asked about our luggage.

Reiling gave a shrug. 'It's all supposed to get loaded on to a goods truck but whether that gets hitched on to our train is another matter. I think it's probably unlikely.' He went on to tell me that I was expected to take charge of welfare matters during the journey in conjunction with Sister Irma, who would give practical care as required.

'Oh, will Sister Irma be there too? I'm so pleased. When can I see her to say hello?'

With a smile he checked the list on his desk and told me where to find her, then continued. 'Just before you came in, Frau Tuchmann was asking after you. I gave her the number of your hut.'

We said goodbye to him, but then he added, 'The final departure will take place on Friday to Saturday night at around four in the morning. A full run-through has been ordered for tomorrow afternoon; more information will follow for everyone.'

I went to seek out Sister Irma and found her outside her hut. We were so pleased to see one another again even though there were few grounds for joy, given our situation. We were to learn precisely what duties would be expected of us while on the move following tomorrow's practice.

On return to my own hut, I ran into Frau Tuchmann, the lady who had previously run our old folks' home in Kaulbachstrasse and who had shown me so much kindness during my spell at Lohhof. She gave me an emotional hug.

'My first comfort is that we're going together, but my second is that I speak Polish and hope so much to be able to help all of you.'

That night something occurred to me. Might we be heading somewhere around Lublin, a place I felt I knew already from the many reports we'd had from our friends from Stettin? Under such circumstances as these, nothing was certain, but just suppose I was to be granted the privilege of coming face to face with all those dear people with whom I'd exchanged so many letters that they felt like old friends? To meet them all in person would be some form of relief.

Early on Friday – the Friday before Easter – we were all at breakfast when the announcement was made about the practice. We were all to assemble in the square at three thirty as if heading off on a real march, grouped hut by hut and carrying hand luggage only. We would then be informed of everything we needed to know for the real march. Everyone's blood ran cold.

This was now deadly serious, and the finality of what we were living through was suddenly glaringly obvious. I wouldn't allow myself to give in to such thoughts, however. Our hut was suddenly a hive of activity as we all tried to get our luggage and bedrolls fit for the march. My own things didn't take long to pack, so I could at least respond quickly to the many requests for help coming my way. A young girl and I helped one woman put on as many layers of clothing as our combined perspiring efforts could muster, and despite the gravity of the situation we couldn't help but laugh at the end result when the woman stood before us resembling nothing more than an overstuffed sausage, quite fit to burst.

Only yesterday afternoon I had managed to procure the required strap for Herr Altschüler's bedroll, but now everyone seemed to need something when it came to packing up. I did whatever I could, rushing from one hut to another to try and find what folk needed, soothing the anxious one minute and helping to fasten a bedroll the next. The morning passed so quickly that it was soon time for the midday meal. Everyone got their food down even faster than usual, then any slowcoaches were given a hand with any last-minute packing, and finally the room senior called us all to line up in groups of four outside the hut.

So there we were, at three thirty sharp – around eight hundred of us standing with our belongings in the square. Not far from us I noticed the Party bigwigs standing in front of the admin hut: Hauptsturmführer Wegner, Obersturmführer Muggler [Mugler], Schroth [Schrott], the senior official, and various others I didn't know. They were all laughing and chatting as if awaiting some kind of performance to gratify their sadistic instincts, although Dr Weiß [Schwarz], our medical doctor, was also there and she gave a friendly nod in my direction.

Now Reiling, the leader for this transport, climbed on to a table and began to speak. He informed us of his responsibility to ensure that the march to the railway station, due to take place early the next morning at four, went off in an orderly fashion, and this could only happen if everyone knew their place. He then went on to say that he wanted people to have the opportunity to choose which leader to travel with on the train. To this end he would now read out the names of the fifteen leaders and their deputies and we were then to muster in groups of fifty around each leader in order to travel in the same railway carriage.

One of these leaders was Heilbronner, with me as his deputy. In no time at all, most of the folk from Berg am Laim had clustered around us. Heilbronner counted off fifty and got us lined up in groups of four. From the chaos that had broken out following Reiling's initial announcement, fifteen groups of twenty-five people each had nonetheless soon formed up. I stood more or less in the centre of our group, with the Altschülers in front of me.

QR Code 16: Reprieve at the eleventh hour

The unseasonal heat was quite oppressive, humid almost, strange for a day so early in April. Beads of sweat gathered on my forehead and my arms and legs were trembling. The luggage I was carrying was far too heavy; it was too much for me, even over a short distance.

Her face full of concern, Dr Weiß [Schwarz] came over and asked, 'Are you feeling unwell?'

I was literally gritting my teeth but managed to mumble, 'I've got too much. My luggage is too heavy.'

Straight away she said, 'Put everything down. It's far worse to have to stand in the burning sun than to walk a long way in a normal temperature.'

I found the energy from somewhere and pulled myself together. I couldn't afford to look sloppy. One look at the group standing around the SA leader, still laughing and chatting, and that was quite enough to give me all the strength I needed.

Reiling then started to address us all once more. We were asked to make a mental note of where we were standing, together with who was next to us and who in front, so that in the early morning darkness the march could happen in a quick and orderly fashion. He told us we'd have a twenty-minute walk to the railroad track itself, where our train would be waiting, and then on reaching our destination we would have to cover several kilometres on foot and should be ready to carry our own luggage. Each of us was asked to check that we could actually carry our things as it would be far better to leave behind anything too heavy than to discard a bedroll or suitcase en route.

At that precise moment I could see Herr Altschüler about to collapse under the strain of his backpack. I was just reaching out to help him take it off when the woman next to me gave me a prod, saying, 'Frau Doktor, your name's being called.'

I looked around in surprise as I'd been so preoccupied with Herr Altschüler that I hadn't heard a thing. Yes, there it was again, Reiling's voice, calling out, 'Frau Doktor Behrend! Over to the Gestapo hut.'

Moving away from my group, I was joined by a female member of staff from the Jewish Community office whose name had been called out after mine. A Gestapo inspector I'd met before through my work with returning emigrants came over to us.

'You two are to stay here!' he shouted.

Fräulein Penz immediately retorted, 'I'm not staying if my fiancé has to leave. Herr Stahl, our director, promised he wouldn't force me to stay if my husband-to-be wasn't permitted to stay behind too.'

I added quietly, 'I want to go with the others as well.'

The inspector looked past us to someone coming up from behind. 'These two don't seem to want to stay behind, Herr Stahl,' he told our chairman, then shrugged, saying, 'and there was I, thinking I was the bearer of glad tidings. You decide what to do with them.'[8]

Fräulein Penz, even more agitated now, turned on Herr Stahl. 'Have you forgotten what you promised me?' she said, her tone almost menacing.

In an attempt to calm her, Stahl nodded, replying quietly, 'No, I have not forgotten and stand by my promise, however difficult that may make matters. It is most unfortunate that in spite of all my efforts I have not succeeded in securing your fiancé's release. It's up to you whether you stay or leave.'

'I'm going with him,' she said immediately and with a calm dignity. She was dismissed.

Stahl then turned to me. 'You, however, must stay here, Frau Doktor – you have no such overriding reason for leaving with the others.'

It took all my strength to remain composed as I said to him, 'I've burnt all my boats to get this far and the only way is forward now, so please let me go with them, Herr Direktor.'

He gave a firm shake of his head. 'I have urgent need of you here and am delighted that the Party and the Gestapo have agreed to release you.'

'Well, the matter's all settled then and you're staying here,' announced the inspector, flicking a hand in my direction. He turned away, and then back again as if something else had occurred to him. 'If you stay behind, we'll be missing a person on the tally of deportees. It has to be seven hundred and seventy-eight, so I'll need someone else as a substitute.'

My heart pounded as I realised this could mean Little Erna, or Frau Brand [Brandl] or some other poor Mischling, having to take my place when they were counting on their freedom. I heard footsteps approaching briskly towards us.

'I'm Jew H.,' the man said by introduction, standing to attention as he did so. 'I'm here with the authorisation of the Bückeburg Gestapo. My parents are here for deportation and I'm volunteering to leave with them.'

With a smile the inspector turned towards me, saying, 'Then we have our substitute.' And with that he vanished into the hut, Stahl following on behind.

I stood stock-still. My poor brain was quite unable to take in this sudden about-turn. Enraged, the whole thing reminded me of cattle being loaded on to trucks and sent off. Slowly I crept back to the starting point for the march. Reiling had just dismissed everyone and the group of bigwigs had melted away. I heard much later that they hadn't got their money's worth that afternoon. They'd been counting on people weeping and wailing, begging them on bended knee, but there'd been nothing of the kind.

On the contrary, when Baby was called forward to hear of her release due to her pending Aryanisation application, she simply asked, 'So can my mother stay behind if I do?'

The Hauptsturmführer said no. 'Your mother has to leave, come what may.'

'Well then, it's only right if I go too.'

The Hauptsturmführer turned away in fury. Did it perhaps cross his mind at that moment that they, these big shots in the Party and the people who gave the orders, were morally in a far more wretched position than this whole defenceless crowd of Jews who were destined to suffer the worst? I don't know the answer, but it's possible that people like him and his accomplices are just quite unable to register their feelings in any normal way. In any case they were annoyed and dissatisfied with the way the operation had gone, and so thought it better to quit the scene. Only later did I become aware of all that.

When I got back to the place we were to march off from, still completely confused and dazed by what had happened, the crowd was scattering and a group formed a circle around me.

Heilbronner called out, saying, 'What did they want from you?'

Close to him I saw Sister Irma and Frau Tuchmann, former residents of our home, all waiting on tenterhooks for my reply.

My voice had no expression left as I managed to stammer out the words, 'I have to stay here.'

This utterance of mine, audible to all, was like the first trickle of a dam about to burst. The months of pent-up emotion overflowed and tears poured down everyone's faces as the waves of torment surged and broke.

Then we heard it: 'Everyone back to the huts!'

Heilbronner, normally such a calm fellow, let his tears fall freely as he fought his way through the crowd to reach me. His arms went around me. 'Goodbye, my dear. I did so much want to share with you the burdens that our future clearly holds for us.'

Overwhelmed with it all, I was quite unable to speak but he knew what I was going through. Then the rest of them came to me one by one, most in silent farewell, everything in their hearts written plainly on their faces. I saw in those eyes all the pain they had managed to quell thus far, as well as their fondness for me and sadness at the enforced separation. Without any exaggeration I can truly describe this as the most difficult hour of my life – and despite all the suffering I had already experienced.

As per orders they all then dispersed, and suddenly alone, I found my way slowly to a bench outside the dining hut. A young man happened to emerge from the door and was about to pass me. The look on his face and his whole demeanour shocked me to the very core. It was eighteen-year-old Werner [Walter Geismar], one of the Jewish Mischlings due to be released. He and his father were residents of our home, while his 'Aryan' mother had been left behind in their flat. I called out to him and he turned to look at me, visibly distraught, and suddenly far older than his years.

'What's wrong?' I asked him.

'Let me be on my way, Frau Doktor,' he burst out. 'I can't stand it any longer – I can't go on.'

So I spoke to him sharply. 'Stop right there! I'm not letting you go until you tell me exactly what's happened.'

The words came tumbling out so fast it was hard to understand what he was saying. When Reiling read his name out from the list of those to be set free, the Hauptsturmführer had apparently waved him over.

'Don't go thinking you can just go back to Berg am Laim and your old job,' he'd snarled at the lad. 'You'll be at Widenmayerstrasse with me. I'll teach you manners, just you wait and see.' With a mocking laugh, he then added, 'Now you know what's waiting for you!' And with that he'd sent the poor lad off, quite beside himself with fear.

This was all just too much for the young man, his nerves already stretched to the limit by the events of the last few days. 'I'm going to do away with myself before that bastard can carry out his threat.'

I was horrified. Here was someone ready to take the most extreme step of all. 'You'll do no such thing,' I said to him quietly, taking hold of his arm. 'Please don't think only of yourself. Do you really want your parents to hear that their son was spared deportation but then took his own life because of some idle threat that may never even be carried out? Come on, my lad, we can't let them see you weak like this! I won't let you go until you've shaken on a promise that you won't go any further with this preposterous idea, which I can only put down to your current inner distress.'

On hearing this, he broke down and wept. I let him shed his tears as I knew it would release the anxiety tormenting him, then gently laid my hand on his shoulder. 'So what do you say, Werner [Walter]?' I said.

'If you promise that my parents will never know what I just said, then I'll shake hands on my promise not to harm myself.'

I kept my voice low and replied, 'Your parents will never hear a word.'

Full of gratitude, he stared back at me and took my hand in a grip so firm that it hurt. I let him go on his way.

This whole episode had somehow released me from the stress of the preceding hour but when I saw Stahl heading across the square towards me, I found myself seething again at the sudden turn of events and my anger boiled over. 'Couldn't you have dreamt up this plan for me a tiny bit sooner? D'you think it was easy to prepare myself mentally and physically for being deported, get everything ready in practical terms, and then suddenly to fall in with these new instructions of, "Oh, by the way, we're looking at the matter a little differently now and you're staying right here"?'

Quietly he interrupted my flow, saying, 'I'll explain it all once we're home – please be patient. Then, if you still feel the same way, you have every right to complain.' He gave a slight smile.

'And where am I supposed to go now?' I asked him, still quite agitated.

'You're coming back with me. My wife wants me to say how absolutely delighted she'll be to see you. My cousin's down on the list to leave so her bed in Fräulein Friedenthal's room is now free and being made ready for you. Once we're home, we can all sit down and have a proper talk when you've had a chance to catch up with some rest.' He gave me a friendly nod and started heading through into the admin hut.

I called him back. 'I don't know where my things are – what's happened to my suitcase?'

'I've had your hand luggage brought to this shed over here, but as for the case, well, I'll need to ask the Gestapo about that.' And then he really did go. I slumped on to a bench and waited to see what would happen next.

After a while Stahl re-emerged, now accompanied by one of our doctors, Spahn [Spanier], who spoke to me kindly.

'You go on ahead to my car which is waiting at the gate. We'll be with you shortly.'

I went as instructed but was stopped at the gate by the Gestapo guard. 'Where are you going? You don't have permission to leave.'

'I don't actually want to leave. I'm being forced to,' I snapped back at him.

The man just stared at me, shaking his head in disbelief, clearly thinking I wasn't completely with it, which I wasn't, that's for sure. But then Stahl and Spahn [Spanier] came into sight, gave the guard the order and I was finally permitted to go through. Stahl helped me into the car which was parked not far from the gate. It struck me as strange that Stahl and our doctors were allowed a motor vehicle and didn't have to use the tram like everybody else. The pair of them climbed in with me, the driver loaded my luggage on board and off we set.

What had been an oppressively humid afternoon had now turned into a fine spring evening, the clear sky tinged with an enchanting green shimmer as I settled back into my generously upholstered seat. Was all of this really happening to me? After days spent in the cramped, noisy, filthy conditions of the camp huts, was I really and truly sitting in this motor car, gently purring its way through the city? It felt like some kind of miracle. I could see how spring was making its presence felt and began to recognise streets I'd previously said farewell to as my fellow unfortunates and I gazed out from the bus travelling in the opposite direction only a couple of days earlier – although it felt more like years. Everything seemed unreal as if I were caught in a dream.

We finally reached Goethestrasse and stopped outside the building where Stahl lived. As we got out of the car I saw Frau Stahl, ready and waiting for us at the door, her hands outstretched in greeting. There were only two steps up to their flat from street level and soon I was in the hallway being helped out of my coat and ushered through to wash and freshen up before being led into the only room of their flat they'd been permitted to retain. It was a lovely room, cosily furnished, and the table they so warmly invited me to sit at had been nicely laid for an evening meal with napkins and all the right cutlery and glassware. I still thought I was dreaming and that I'd soon be waking up in that terrible hut with all the attendant absence of fresh air and presence of far too many people.

But this was real all right, and all the discomfort was behind me now. Once we'd finished supper, other residents of the building came in to say hello, some of whom I knew, and to ask what had been happening over the last couple of days. Every one of them had a friend or relative who'd been affected. At first I thought I couldn't bring myself to talk about it, but in response to their many questions all of a sudden I couldn't stop and wanted to describe everything in the greatest of detail. It was half past midnight before I'd finally poured it all out.

'Right, that's enough for today,' said Stahl, getting to his feet. 'Let's find something to help you sleep.'

I was soon in a full-size bed, freshly made and comfortable, and fell into a near dreamless sleep only to wake on the dot of four. *They're setting off for the train now*, I thought. In my mind's eye I tried to follow them all, as the rain pattered softly on the windowpane. After a while I fell asleep once more and woke soon after eight, not sure of where I was. Yesterday's events gradually flooded back and then the good news hit me: I'd be allowed to hear from you and the children at last! I wanted to write to Alice in Lisbon straight away in order to retract as fast as possible my previous news about being taken to the transit camp. The joy now stirring within me was swiftly quashed at the thought of that train and all those dear friends being taken further and further away from us.

Let me close now with a poem someone recently taught me, as I feel it offers a better reflection of what I have gone through over the last few days than any long description of mine could ever do. It's called *Deportation*, writer unknown, but we are all reciting it to one another so as to pass it on.

Here it is:

Today I saw a thousand faces, every one distraught
Today I saw a thousand Jews, destined for nought,
The condemned marched on in the grey morning light
And their old lives faded out of sight

They passed through the gates and knew: no return,
All liberty and happiness now left behind.
Where are they taking you? Where does this path end?
One thing they know: a place with barbed wire.

All that awaits is misery, anguish, hardship,
Poverty, hunger, thirst, and death for the many.
I looked into their eyes with the love of a brother,
Expecting only sorrow in the face of such adversity,

But instead of despair their eyes glowed with determination,
Steadfast and strong, emotion reined in.
I saw their love of life, saw courage and hope,
And many a face wore a firm smile.

Deeply moved, I saw the spirit in these folk,
A people chosen to suffer, and always suffering,
Yet rising above wretchedness and misery,
Above drudgery and loathing, with such fortitude.

Today I saw a thousand faces, every one distraught
And saw in the grey of morning a beam of eternal light.

On Saturday morning Herr Stahl and I had the opportunity to sit down and have a quiet talk with no interruptions. He told me that he and the Committee had received the list of deportees a week ago. They had seen with horror the names of the entire management of Berg am Laim, as well as their deputy chair, Hellinger [Hechinger], and Fräulein Penz, the latter having worked at the Jewish Community office for twenty years and possessing a unique knowledge of the files and the archive. He went on to explain how he had then immediately telephoned the Berlin office of the Reichsvereinigung of Jews in Germany to raise the matter with the decision-makers at the Gestapo and was called back on the Thursday to be informed that three people could be released and that he was to say who seemed the most important, whereupon he had named Hellinger [Hechinger], Fräulein Penz and me. At that stage, however, he was not yet empowered to release us.

He was informed that the final decision would arrive on Friday afternoon, again by telephone, and told me that was how it had then all transpired. At the same time it was communicated from Berlin that the Gestapo post at the transit camp itself was authorised to release the three people named. I apologised for the way I had rounded on him the previous day, but he brushed this off with a smile.

‘I understood your feelings entirely – who knows what I’d have done in your position? But I wanted to bring up the question of your suitcase. Don’t count on getting it back. You should make an application to the Gestapo about it as a matter of course but I doubt it'll come to anything.' His tone changed now. 'Nor do I reckon our friends in the transport will ever see their luggage again.'

I nodded. 'And what am I to do now? Should I go back to Berg am Laim?'

'Yes. I wouldn't know who better to ask, although you'll have to run it single-handed. I know that places an enormous burden on your shoulders, but my hope is that Löwenberger will be able to lend you a hand, along with others sent to live at the home. They can support you with duties such as office work, bookkeeping and so on. Will you give it a go?' He gave me a kind and friendly look.

'All right then,' I replied, 'I'll give it a go. I just hope I can manage it all.'

He tried then to lighten the atmosphere by putting on a pathetic tone. 'Well, that lightens my heavy old heart a little bit. Now, off you go to our clothes store and get yourself whatever you need. Give yourself a couple of days' rest before going back to the home. Just hearing that you're coming back will keep the place going until then.'

'But I want to go straight back there tomorrow,' I said beseechingly. 'Fair enough that I benefit from a little recovery time today, but no more than that.'

He reflected a while before saying, 'Very well then. You can travel back by car tomorrow but accompanied by a nurse. It won't work without her because if I'm not there the car can only be used for transporting the sick and I can't come out tomorrow. One need only look at you to see that you're not well. I beg you to start off gently: we all need every ounce of strength we've got.' Rising to his feet, he then bid me farewell.

I walked now along the streets I used so often to hurry along from my office to Lindwurmstrasse but this time as if in a trance. And then suddenly there was dear Emmy K[ohn] with whom I had worked for so long. She leapt up from her seat at the switchboard the moment she saw me. The old privilege of not working on a Sunday had long since fallen away thanks to the folk at Widenmayerstrasse.

Emmy rushed towards me with tears in her eyes, vigorously shaking me by the hand. 'Let me fetch the others! They'll all want to see you!'

And here they all were, each expressing their joy in their own way, and I realised I was seen as someone who'd been destined for the hangman, the noose firmly around my neck until at the precise moment of its tightening, when the call came to halt the proceedings and the hangman enabled me to slip free. I had a similar reception when I went to the clothing store to request fresh underclothes and a dress. I would receive everything I needed once we'd heard for sure that I'd not be getting my suitcase back.

In the afternoon my loyal friends Tilla and Annemarie came to see me, and we had a couple of lovely tranquil hours together.

Easter Sunday – the Day of Resurrection! And wasn't I experiencing something like this myself? When I thought of how I'd had to leave everything that was dear to me and step into the abyss of deportation with my companions, why was I suddenly pulled back with my foot already poised to leap into the darkness? Did this now signify some special mission and purpose in life for me? I was sure of it, and knew I intended to fulfil both with every ounce of strength I could muster. The memory of all those who'd left on the first transport in November and those now on the second would help me shoulder this burden, I knew that for sure.

My mind occupied with such thoughts, I set off with the usual nurse on the journey back to Berg am Laim. At last we were turning into the little road, and I saw the wall of the convent and the gate opening for us. We stopped at the main gate and there was the familiar honest face of Hermann, our caretaker, as he held out his hand to help me from the vehicle. He was about to say something but I gestured for him not to.

'Not just yet,' I said to him. 'Tell all our residents, please, that I need a couple of hours to myself. In the afternoon I'll discuss priorities with Herr Löwenberger, then this evening at eight I'll be in the dining room to give everyone a detailed account of the last few days.'

Returning was harder than I'd imagined. My feet felt heavy on the steps that I otherwise took at a good pace, but then finally I reached my own room. *St Theresa, take me up into your peace once more.* In the doorway I stopped dead, greeted by a whole sea of flowers! Gently I closed the door and headed straight over to the chest of drawers and the writing desk to take a closer look at the display. Nestling among the floral gifts were immaculately folded small bundles of clothing. All the self-control I'd been exercising with such great effort now evaporated, and the tears began to fall. I lay down on the bed and felt the tension and anguish of the preceding week start to drain away.

The bell signalled mealtime but I didn't feel like going down and had no appetite. Then came a gentle knock on my door and it opened before I could even say 'Come in'.

There was Frau Nehm, as cool and capable as ever, bearing a large tray. 'You're just going to have to put up with a bit of special treatment today – with the approval of all the residents! I can't tell you how glad I am that you're back.'

Barely had I thanked her than she'd whisked back out of the room, leaving me with a cup of delicious broth and my favourite, omelette spread with jam! I couldn't possibly not eat what she'd brought me so kindly. Very slowly I tasted a small mouthful. It was delicious and confirmed for me how utterly essential familiar comforts are to a person in times of distress.

I had just eaten up when there was another knock on the door. Frau Dillenius came in and flung her arms around me. I knew we were both thinking of our absent third member, Frau Altschüler, but we managed to pull ourselves together and I started by asking who had brought all the flowers and other things. The heavenly white azalea was from the convent, the pink one from all the women here, the red from the men and the remaining flowers and gifts each bore little cards saying who they were from. Before Frau Dillenius went away again, she returned my diary to me.

When I entered the dining hall at eight that evening, all the residents were already assembled. I passed on the good wishes of all those who had already left as well as their cards and letters. It was time then for me to report in detail on what had happened. You know how often I've had to speak in public, or stand up and canvass for the welfare of those at risk, and that I've frequently been exposed to the starkly differing life experiences of those under my care back in the female prison – but *never* before have I addressed a group like my audience on that Easter Sunday, their attention so completely focused on me, their concern almost palpable as they hung on my every word.

On concluding my account of events, I went on to explain that I now had to run the home single-handed and knew I'd taken on something huge that would only be manageable with the support of every single one of them. I told them I'd have to turn to each of them when it came to getting the practical work done and knew what I was asking was a lot, given that some of them were working ten-hour days in the factories. I reassured them that I would try to organise the maintenance and domestic chores in such a way that each resident would only be called upon once a week, or even once a fortnight, for a couple of hours in the evening. I would only be able to run the place if everybody went along with this, I told them.

This prompted one woman in particular to signal that she wanted to say something. She'd often been a great help in the past and now said that all the female residents had asked her to say that each one of them was at the ready to take on whatever special tasks I deemed necessary, adding that there was enormous gladness over my return and that I could rely on the backing of every woman there.

I hadn't expected a reaction quite of this kind but was overjoyed. I knew there'd be all the usual problems in running the place but if I could continue to rely on this general state of goodwill, then this was the best possible basis on which to proceed.

Herr Löwenberger, with whom I had already discussed various matters that afternoon, now rose to his feet and commented that on this occasion the women had outflanked the men! I was very pleased about that part ... But he also added that he'd been asked to speak on behalf of all the men and confirm their agreement with my proposals and to thank me warmly for my readiness in taking on this difficult task.

I thanked everyone and brought the meeting to a close. But before I could leave the room, I had to wait and let many of the residents shake me by the hand and express how thrilled they were at my return.

The night is almost over and in only an hour from now Frau Dillenius will be getting up for work, but I felt compelled to pour my soul out on to the page as this always makes me feel I can share with you some small measure of what occupies my mind and my heart.

Letter from Else to Eva Schmidt

Berg am Laim, 8 April 1942

My dearest Eva

It'll only be a few lines today, I'm afraid, as I don't feel up to writing at any great length. My thoughts and my feelings are all over the place, and then on top of that I barely get a moment's peace. I've had to take on running this place literally single-handed and even with so many good folk positively vying with one another as to whom is the most pleased that I'm back, none of that diminishes the fact that it's a colossal task and an even greater responsibility.

It was like a scene straight out of a novel when the call came for me to stay behind – the way the order came at precisely the moment we were practising the start of the march, along with all our luggage. I'd been designated as one of the group leaders for the train and was just at that moment lending a hand to poor Ludwig Altschüler, severely hampered physically at the best of times but all the more so now with the backpack, when my name rang out and I was summoned. I didn't want to stay behind. I tried my hardest to leave with the rest of the group but I failed.

Someone's just calling me here so I'd better go, but only after sending you my fondest, warmest greetings for your birthday! It's harder than ever today to find the right words to express all my love and appreciation, dearest girl, so all I can say is to please read between the lines.

And I still have nothing to send you and would love so much to have some little gift to offer, but all my things have gone. My suitcase was already loaded for departure, you see, and impossible to get back, and the practice for the march to the station the following day was all over so fast that I gave anything I had left to those leaving and in need.

So please accept instead my humble thanks for all your recent letters and not least the coffee, which helped restore my spirits when they were nearly at their lowest ebb. And do please write again soon, I beg of you!

My very best wishes to you, your dear mother, and Hilde and Grete too.

As ever, your E.

Siegfried's Diary

Oxford, 13 April 1942

I have been daring enough to risk making an attempt at drafting an outline of Jewish post-war objectives and had a detailed response from Dr Bienenfeld,[9] which is now being circulated among committee members. This will lead me at the very least to some positive collaboration with the venture, not out of any personal ambition on my own behalf but rather concern for the next generation and indeed the generation after that. At its core lies the problem of mass migration, an objective assessment of the aims of the organisation and how to fund it, as well as its spiritual, cultural and religious aspects. It's becoming increasingly clear to me that religious momentum, however divisive, may also have a much needed unifying effect, although its many nuances are highly variable and subjective.

The day before yesterday I attended a service of blessing for Bertram H. What a stale and stuffy experience that was, with the women all squashed up together, the tuneless voice of the prayer leader, the 'cry to heaven' that seemed to carry with it every bit of medieval misery, kissing the Torah, the whole excess of the liturgy. Nonetheless ours remains the oldest spiritual community on earth, now scattered to all corners. The Jewish community's last undertaking in Europe was a call to re-energise the economy through modern capitalist systems, in which many had an extensive track record through years of experience in the financial sector. But now those same people have become dispensable, and other groups equally capable. [. . .]

If Jews were allowed to continue bolstering the global economy by underpinning capitalism in the USA as well as in England, then a new role can also be found for the remaining millions of our people – or they will simply vanish and fade away. Might this new role include the creation of large new settlements, beyond the confines of Palestine itself, via the development of model cultural states or enclaves within South America, Africa, Australia, or even Alaska?

Oxford, 8 May 1942

At the end of March, deportation stared Else in the face. My dearest was lined up with others only to be summoned and ordered back to run the home single-handed. I try my hardest to imagine how this must have affected her but struggle fully to do so. Did it feel like a blessing in the very nick of time? Yet think what it must have done to her!

When, oh when, will this all end?

Yesterday Peter and I went to a meeting at the Town Hall. Labour MP, Manny Shinwell,[10] critical of what he saw as the tub-thumping style of Churchill's government, called for help on Russia's second front. Wasn't England already contending on several further fronts (in the Indian Ocean, Libya and the Mediterranean?). It's hard to write about this with any real confidence.

Oxford, 17 May 1942

Yesterday I revisited the splendid New Theatre, this time to see *Macbeth*. We had initially wanted to go on Tuesday but then Peter felt more like the cinema so I went to this final performance on my own. My ticket was only nine pence. I was eager to let the theatre work its magic on me this time too and definitely felt a heightened appreciation of the stage, just as when I saw *The Merchant of Venice*.

Even in this tragedy with so many murders, so well suited to its time, there were still plenty of comic scenes for light relief. After Duncan has been murdered and messengers are knocking at the castle gate, the watchman takes all the time in the world putting on his trousers, and after a triple murder this has the effect of releasing the tension. The performances were extremely good. But there was something very English for me about the lack of presence in the royal scenes, which would have had far greater emphasis in Germany. As always I found myself quite moved by the national anthem and the way the audience showed such respect when it is played. Even in the theatre the English act as a unified people.

As expected the spring offensive has begun. If only Russia's superiority could show itself straight away! That would mean the war ending this summer. I can't believe that the German army would accept many more months of indecision going back and forth over their heads. Hitler's insistence on decisive action shows that.

Else's Diary

Berg am Laim, Sunday, 24 May 1942

I can't believe it's almost summer. The days seem to fly. We receive regular news from our residents who were deported, who really did go to Piaski, but haven't managed to trace a single person from our group from Stettin, whose whereabouts are currently unknown. The only things we're allowed to despatch now are letter packages of up to one kilo in weight.

Heilbronner puts a brave face on things in his letters, doing his best to describe the situation in which he and his wife now find themselves, even managing the odd joke here and there. Together with other men deemed fit enough to do so, he's building roads in harsh conditions and without sufficient nutrition. Their luggage never turned up. The application I made to track down my own belongings was immediately rejected as was the request I made on behalf of Werner [Walter]. He and his father are living with us again as his old employer, a man who really values his work, called him back in the moment he could.[11]

On the Tuesday after Easter I received a visit from Schroth [Schrott], formerly a travelling cigar salesman but now a high-up official at Widenmayerstrasse. He proceeded to explain that I should consider it a particular honour that the Party is in full agreement with my taking sole charge at Berg am Laim, adding that a man would normally be the obvious choice for the job. I was told in no uncertain terms that I would be fully responsible for anything and everything that was to happen in the facility and would be called to account for any carelessness or sloppiness.

He went on to inform me of the latest decrees recently brought into force. Henceforth there would be a guard on our gate to check all those arriving and leaving. To this end we would have to introduce a logbook, to be made available at any inspection. Any 'Aryan' was to be forbidden entry. Guards must make this abundantly clear. Only the 'Aryan' wives of our Jewish residents were to be permitted Saturday afternoon and Sunday visits within the facility. It was for me to determine and communicate details of visiting hours. In addition I was required to hold a weekly roll call in order to communicate essential information to inmates. In future, residents were to be forbidden any excursion to the city beyond going to work or on exceptional grounds, such as attending a dental appointment, for which I could issue a special exit permit.

I refrained from commenting on these instructions with all their increasingly onerous restrictions being imposed on us. Constant gate duty was a burden for the men, as well, but it didn't help to complain about it. It had to be organised, and it was. It was surprising how many of our folk needed to attend dental appointments and receive treatment over the next few weeks, though! It took quite a lot of time and effort to get some of them to understand that overly frequent trips to the dentist could result in the withdrawal of our one remaining opportunity.

The Professor has been back with us for three weeks now. He may look frail but there's real strength within. We were so pleased to see one another again. And for me it means I now have someone here with whom I can discuss the questions and problems that preoccupy me and weigh heavily on my mind. He can always see a good way through and gives sound advice. I see him as the 'good spirit' of our home.

What really hit me hard was the decree that no 'Aryan' could enter our home. Soon after Schroth's [Schrott's] departure, I was called to the telephone, where Mother Superior Agatha noticed how subdued I was and, in her caring way, asked me what was wrong.

'It's so hard that my friend from Isartal and my Quaker friend, Annemarie, can no longer come and see me,' I admitted to her. 'And you know that I'm not allowed out and wouldn't dare conceal my Star of David even if I did.'

She looked at me kindly, saying, 'Don't let that get you down. Your friends can come in through our own gate and into our meeting room. I'll contact you using the house telephone so you know when to come over. You're called to the telephone so often here that no one will notice the difference.'

I was deeply touched and thanked her, adding, 'It's terrible that we have to use lies to help ourselves.' I let out a deep sigh.

Agatha looked at me, her face grave. 'Please take to heart my conviction that these will not be counted as lies, which is why I have no fear of uttering them. We all lack other means of facing these injustices and defending ourselves against them, so let us do exactly as discussed.'

What on earth would I do without help like this? I can't even begin to list all the things these good people undertake on our account, and they do so as if it were the most natural thing in the world, without the slightest fuss or bother. Whenever I feel that I just can't carry on giving my time to such endless tasks as smoothing over petty quarrels between folk, all it takes is one look at our nuns as they glide serenely by and my despondent state melts away. Nonetheless, I do still question at times my ability to bear this burden for much longer.

Berg am Laim, Sunday, 14 June 1942

But for a few spaces our home is almost full once more. Among the new arrivals are two with wonderful musical talent, one of whom, Lisel Beer [Baerlein], plays the violin beautifully. She was in the middle of her training at the Conservatoire when Widenmayerstrasse despatched her to factory work. Her violin has come here with her, as have her parents. The girl is in fact a Mischling and this is why she's been allowed the freedom to indulge her passion for music. It's strange that her mother, an 'Aryan', has been permitted to join her Jewish husband and daughter here in our facility, but things like this often happen and leave us puzzling over the inexplicable. The other newly arrived musician is Herr Walder [Waldner], a gifted pianist. So now we have the pleasure of listening to music together, as we've had a good cellist in residence for some time, and can therefore now listen to a proper trio on a Saturday!

QR Code 17: Cultural life in the ghetto

We've all fallen into spending the rest of Saturday evening together after my weekly roll call, and sometimes I give a little talk on some topic of interest. This might be about my work with female prisoners or something to do with education, or whatever else is preoccupying me at the time. It's a way of providing a distraction from the worry and strain we live with each day and allows us a brief respite from the ongoing pressures of our existence.

Last Sunday was beautifully warm and most residents were out enjoying the garden when the Obersturmführer suddenly turned up at four o'clock to carry out a spot inspection. He was in affable mood and this always unnerves me far more than when he's being curt with everyone. He called to me from some way off, lapsing into his standard broad Bavarian. 'Well, this is a bit of all right, what you've got here – wish I had it as good as this! Let's take a nice turn around the garden.' He fell in step beside me and made a beeline for a married couple sitting in the sunshine.

The man leapt to his feet, stood stiffly to attention and gave his name, then gestured towards the lady sitting next to him. 'This is my wife, an Aryan. She's here to see me today.'

'Right you are,' replied the Obersturmführer. 'Well, let's take a shufti at your identification papers.' He turned to the woman who was quite taken aback by what was going on here.

Being Munich born and bred, however, she wasn't one to be easily intimidated. 'Oh, you want a look at my identification papers, do you? Well, why not show me yours before asking to see mine?'

She spoke without paying the slightest heed to her husband or me as we made desperate but covert shushing gestures to try and stop her from making things worse.

Her husband stuttered out nervously, 'Forgive us, Herr Obersturmführer, my wife simply doesn't realise who you are.'

No longer playing the affable, Muggler [Mugler] bellowed back, 'If she didn't know me before, well, she'll certainly know me now!' He turned the full force of his temper back on her. 'So have you got identification on your person or haven't you?'

'No, I'aven't,' she snapped back at him.

'We're in the third year of this blooming war and you're telling me you think you can go swanning around with no papers?' He was furious with her but then turned to me and flattened his usual vernacular towards a bit of formality. 'This evening you are to hold an extra roll call. Tell everyone that the guard on your gate is required to see every single person's pass. Nobody is to be admitted without one.'[12]

He stomped off to the next closest couple. This 'Aryan' wife had no pass either but at least she managed to stay calm. And the next one did have the correct papers with her, thank goodness.

I was worried as to how the following couple might behave, though. The wife was 'Aryan', had often created trouble before and was not someone to stick to the rules. The guard had often had to call me on account of her trying to come and see her husband outside visiting times, but I couldn't ever give in on this or it would have represented a loss of control. On those occasions she'd make a huge scene, ranting and raving to such an extent that it was always a real struggle to get rid of her. The husband was a thoroughly disagreeable individual to boot, constantly moaning about something or other – one of those people who can never get on with his room-mates. Both he and his wife were deeply disliked. When asked about her identification document, all she said was, 'Whether I have my papers or not, it's damn all to do with you. Me, I'm an Aryan, so don't think you can go treating me like you do the poor Jews.'

Thus far the Obersturmführer had managed to contain his seething rage but this time it boiled over. 'So you reckon I can't get you for anything just because you're an Aryan! A fine Aryan you are, to have gone and married a Jew! Don't you go getting any fancy ideas about yourself! It's high time you found out the hard way whether I can get you for anything or not, mind.' Then he started to yell instructions at me. 'This woman's staying put, right here – lock her up in a room somewhere for a week, and that's my last word on the subject.'

The woman turned pale. She was about to come out with some retort, but I gestured for her to show restraint. The Obersturmführer was still holding forth so I hissed at her, 'Be quiet!' Then I hurried off in the wake of the raging man. Fortunately he'd stopped asking to see people's papers at least.

'The kitchen and service areas – I want to see them now!' he barked at me. I heaved a sigh of relief, as I knew everything there was in good order. Maybe that would put him in a better mood.

What on earth was I to do with this dreadful woman? To detain her in our home was simply too grotesque and absurd a prospect even to contemplate. *Perhaps if I wait a bit*, I thought to myself, *something else will stop it from happening*. I was right. The kitchen was immaculately clean and the beautifully kept dining rooms and service areas were faultless, and the more he saw the better his mood became. Just as he reached the door to leave, I said to him in as light a tone as I could muster and as if I'd only just thought of it, 'So we'll just let Frau N N go now, won't we?'

'Well, she's had a good fright so let her take that away with her, shall we? But if she gives you the slightest cause for annoyance, I'll have her locked up on your behalf for a whole week.' And with that he gave a gracious nod in my direction and disappeared.

The rock weighing so heavily on my heart had somehow lightened. I rushed off to see the couple in question and found her subdued but still waiting to hear the final verdict. She gave a loud sigh of relief when I told her she could go, although I made it crystal clear that I would not be tolerating any further lack of good manners on her part.

Siegfried's Diary

Oxford, 29 June 1942

Since 22 June I have been employed in the Dairy section at the Oxford branch of the Co-op after hearing by chance through Frl. Lotti that there might be a vacancy.

I've really had to concentrate on learning how to add up in pounds, shillings and pence and doing the carry forward, making sure that everything tallies properly. The nature of the work suits me overall but my knowledge of English still presents huge difficulties. But I'm going to make a big effort with it and want to earn enough to pay for a few basics, such as shoe repairs and laundry. It'll reduce the strain on Peter and enable him to save more money himself.

In spite of Else's reassurances, my anxiety over her never leaves me. The danger she may be facing feels even worse now that Germany's position in the war has deteriorated. At the moment the attack on Egypt has brought some success in North Africa but the Russian front is under serious threat. There is no suggestion that the war will be over in 1942. And yet nobody can know for sure.

Else's Diary

Berg am Laim, Sunday, 5 July 1942

The deportations are once more underway. At the start of the week our entire medical facility was moved out, including the doctor in charge, the matron, most of the nurses and every last one of the patients.

I heard via a phone call from Stahl when he rang to fix up a meeting but then went on to pass on the news. This time round the deportations were not to Poland but to Theresienstadt in Reichsgau Sudetenland. The Reichsvereinigung had informed him that a huge ghetto was being set up there, and those destined for this place were predominantly people over sixty-five, those left severely disabled after the last war, Jewish 'Mischlinge', and Jews honoured with bravery medals or the Iron Cross 1st Class, also in the last war. Others to be sent there included some of the Jewish

Community's most capable members, then also Jews who for one reason or another enjoyed the protection of influential 'Aryans'. It looked as if they wanted to set up some sort of 'elite ghetto' which could perhaps admit people from other countries too. He said he wasn't sure how true that part of it was but it was better than being sent direct to Poland and killed. We were no longer in any doubt of that outcome. We'd heard nothing from our Piaski deportees in a fortnight. All hopes of ever seeing them again once the war had ended had evaporated into thin air.[13]

It's one thing simply to record this and quite another to imagine the distress, suffering and fear we were all feeling. Mere words are quite inadequate for the task. People of a sensitive disposition may be able to feel something of the horror once they understand what is actually being carried out within our society. Only those who are living through this hell can ever feel the true extent of it all.

Yesterday I received a new list with the names of those to be deported on Tuesday. Thirty-five from Berg am Laim will be going to Theresienstadt, among them quite a few who have done such valuable work in our home as well as a man severely wounded in the last war – his wife was dumbstruck when I broke the news to her.

The worst news from Stahl was that there will now be one transport every week.[14] How on earth is our community, already suffering so much, to endure the constant fear and incessant turmoil? Over the last few weeks we've managed to create a modicum of tranquillity in this place. True, our lives here can never be free of care, but that immediate fear of life-threatening deportation had somehow seemed to shrink into the background just a little. It has done us all good to have a bit of summer weather and to feel we can dare enjoy the garden on a warm evening. But with this terrible phantom now perpetually hovering over each of us and at such close quarters, I don't know how we're expected to manage our daily work or any vestige of normal life. It's assumed that the deportations to Poland will start up again, that there'll be no waiting until the old folk have been evacuated.

In the thick of all this, I still need to apply myself to running the home and ensuring that the essentials are carried out. We've had to organise an additional sickroom as our own medical facility is no longer available to us. One of the Jewish doctors, still authorised to practise, should be moving into our home here, and the two Jewish nurses who were left behind will now be helping us also. All this means new work aplenty on my account and yet what we had before was already too much. I can't afford to lose my nerve, though. I've noticed again and again how much the mood of the others depends on mine.

I had to stop writing just then as a female resident asked to talk to me. The conversation was short but its content has left me unable to sleep and demands that I commit it to paper. Frau Schulmann is one of those due to leave us on Tuesday for Theresienstadt. She has no close relatives surviving and is quite alone in this world. I'd often sensed that she was simply limping through from one day to the next, and with the greatest effort and difficulty. She told me now how she had wanted to end her life on first arriving with us but been dissuaded by a friend. Then she noticed how much better she felt in our home, where she got on with the others, grew fond of me and all in all had been surprised to realise how this place had cast its spell on her. In spite of her age and poor health, factors which had ruled her out for factory work, her contribution to our home had brought her a great deal of pleasure and satisfaction.

And now she was expected to leave. Yes, she said, she knew what I was perhaps thinking, that Theresienstadt isn't the worst place to be sent, but she explained how she simply didn't have the strength to start all over again and once more go through such fundamental change in her life. And her close friend, the woman who'd previously kept her from the final act of self-harm, had since been deported to the East. She said she didn't want to turn her back on life without telling me but begged me not to attempt to talk her out of her decision as she had made up her mind. I was to try to understand her, she said. Both physically and mentally she felt too fragile to cope with any new demands and knew she'd be a burden on her companions and didn't want that. She related that she was utterly exhausted and rejoicing in the thought of eternal sleep. *You'll grant me that, won't you?* I heard her ask me. The woman explained that she hadn't wanted to leave this world without first having thanked me. I gently batted away her kind remarks, but she insisted that I allow her a few words of gratitude, explaining the strength of her need to talk to me.

I can't write any more now. Naturally, I didn't take it upon myself to try and dissuade her. She spoke of this decision with such calm determination that I did not feel empowered to try and present any counter-arguments to the balanced rationale with which she had presented me. Any such words from me would merely have come across as idle chatter.

Her room-mates all routinely get up and leave very early in the mornings, so they won't suspect a thing if she's still asleep when they slip out of the room. Over the course of the morning I'll go in search of her and then notify our Dr Kupfer.[15] I consider him sufficiently intuitive not to try and bring her back. This is the first suicide in our home. Prior to this, I had always felt proud there had been none to record.

I can't begin to describe the pain I'm feeling in my heart over this. What next lies on the horizon?

Letters from Else to Eva Schmidt

Berg am Laim, 11 July 1942

My dearest Eva

I'm writing so you know I'm still here and that everything has arrived safely. Dreadful things are afoot. This past week has been one of the worst of my life, and I'm so glad the previous fortnight was at least different. I wasn't able to see Tilla or Annemarie, and that's now out of the question too. The entire workforce here is leaving on Monday. I'm at a complete loss as to what may happen after that.

The thing that had never happened here before, well, it's now happened several times, which is leaving me quite drained.

My finger has almost healed, so at least I can do all my usual jobs. That is how it has to be.

Farewell, my dearest, my good friend, and I'm so happy you're taking a rest. Don't work yourself too hard! Take time to recuperate.

With fondest wishes

Yours ever

Else

Berg am Laim, 18 July 1942

Dear Eva

Heartfelt thanks for the beautiful cushions! They'll be passed on today with precise instructions as to their use – Tilla will have plenty to tell you, just think![16]

It's hard to say why my mood has changed so much. I can only explain it with reference to everything that's been happening here over the last few weeks, which feel more like years, to be quite honest. Tell Tilla that in Berlin she can seek help from my brother-in-law, Georg F. [Fischer] in Tplhof [Tempelhof]. It could be he can help track down my identification pass, the one with the photograph on it.

Still, no time for more now. One hundred and fifty people are waiting on me to cook the next meal – again.

Farewell, my dearest friend, and oh, if only you were all here to lend me a hand! For you and Tilla, most loyal of friends, my fondest greetings.

Your E.

Else's Diary

Berg am Laim, Sunday, 26 July 1942

My life has turned into a living hell, and it's as much as I can do to drag myself through each day. The list of people to be deported arrives on the Friday of every single week. This isn't just about older people being sent to Theresienstadt now – the deportations to Poland are still going on.

Last week Frau Dillenius left us, as did our pianist, Herr Waldner. Both were despatched to Poland, while our violinist, Lisel Beer [Baerlein], and our cellist went to Theresienstadt. Stahl and his wife were sent along with them – Stahl, a man once honoured with the Iron Cross 1st Class. These two asked if they might spend their last day in my company before they were taken away to the transit camp at Milbertshofen, which meant I could help them pack and proffer some few words of comfort. The strength of the bonds forged when people work and endure suffering alongside one another truly came home to me that day. Our farewells were more heart-rending than any of us could find words to express.

Even the Schönbergs were to be on this transport. I found myself wondering how her heart could possibly withstand the strain, while he, a seventy-year-old engineer and the architectural brains behind the Deutsches Museum in Munich, was admirable in his composure. Bidding me goodbye, he said, 'I'm far less distressed at this moment than when it looked as though you'd be going too. We really can't thank you enough for all you've done for every single one of us.'

What I had most been fearing since Frau Schulmann took her own life has indeed now come to pass. A further eight of our residents, all heading for deportation, have quietly chosen to end it all.[17] In the wake of a suicide, the police homicide commission always send an officer to investigate the case before releasing the body for burial. On his last visit he made rather a misjudged attempt at humour. 'You're my best customer, Frau Doktor!' I rather think this was his own way of coping with the steady increase in suicides, something that affected him in a way it wouldn't have done under normal circumstances.

After a long gap, one of your letters reached me three weeks ago by way of Lisbon. Reading between the lines I could see you were trying to sow the seeds in my mind of my attempting to escape. I have to say this had never previously occurred to me but I gave it plenty of thought before rejecting the whole idea. This was a critical time for the home and I couldn't possibly leave now. For me to flee would be tantamount to desertion, quite apart from all the planning it would entail. No, I simply cannot leave while the running of this place lies in my hands. But at the same time, my dearest, I do never lose sight of my responsibility and duty towards you and the children, even though the prospect of our being reunited seems to slip further and further into the distance.

I know there are a fair few here toying with the idea of escape but only four have tried to date.[18] The first was a young man listed for deportation to the east. He'd been a member of the Freikorps Epp in the days of the old Räte Republic so we all assumed he'd been helped by his former comrades. We never heard from him again. The other three, a mother and her two daughters, vanished a fortnight ago. They left me a letter saying they planned to go to a wood near the city and take their own lives. I arranged for a missing persons notice through the local police, who promised to inform me when they'd been found. They never were though, so I allow myself to believe that they maybe crossed the border into Switzerland or are living in hiding with relatives.

For me the idea of a life on the run is abhorrent, existing in constant terror of being found out. That kind of leap in the dark would have to be into some neutral country or other, and I'd still need enormous determination to do even that. For the moment I have neither the time nor the will to expend any energy on such thoughts.

Those still left at the children's home have now taken refuge with us and they number twelve children aged between two and thirteen, all but two of them without parents or any other close family.[19] They were being looked after at Milbertshofen for a while, but that seems to be being emptied out even faster than our place here, so the children moved in with us a fortnight ago. We made the large communal room ready for them, which was previously inhabited by thirty-six men. It was a relief to me that Widenmayerstrasse was willing to authorise the conversion of this room for their use, together with two ladies living in to look after them. For all the sad reasons we know, our home is not that full and it was easy to find alternative accommodation for the few men who remain. Their old room has turned out to be ideal for the children now that we've used a few large cupboards to divide it off into three areas. There's one for the youngest with the nursery beds and other furniture that arrived with them, then the middle section is for school-age children, and the last is for the ladies caring for them all. I've known these two women for a long time and hold them in high regard. Since they came to us, I've often sat down with them for half an hour

36. At the Berg am Laim residential home, 1942: (*back row, from left*) Charlotte Koch, Hanni Schmidt, Clara Schwalb, Judith Hirsch and Ilse Nussbaum; (*front row, from left*) Rolf Heufeld, Werner Grube, Bernhardt Schmidt and Ernst Grube.

or so at the end of the evening and it's good to feel how well they understand our predicament here. As for the children, well, they bring more than a ray of sunshine into our otherwise gloomy and joyless existence!

It wasn't long, naturally, before Obersturmführer Muggler [Mugler] and Schroth [Schrott] hove into view to carry out an inspection. They showed great interest in our newly set-up sickbay and nursery area. As soon as we entered the latter, the two little ones ran towards him – two-year-old Dina and three-year-old Schorsch, the only two to have their mothers here at the home with them, although they were currently out at work, of course, at one of the factories. Beaming with excitement, Dina held up her little doll for the Obersturmführer to admire, only for him to push it away so roughly that the terrified child burst into tears. I was furious but managed to bite my tongue. Fortunately the other children fell silent and Fräulein Jacob swooped Dina up in her arms to console her.

The 'bigwigs' seemed satisfied with the way the two new rooms had been set up and found nothing to niggle about, even though I'd made certain to tell them beforehand that the kitchen wasn't quite in its usual pristine condition. So many of the women who'd helped me in the past had been deported in the last round, and I hadn't been able to replace them yet. Somehow these two didn't query a thing.

QR Code 18: Attacks on Jews

Just as we were on our way to the main gate, with me thinking thank goodness, that's another inspection out of the way, the Obersturmführer's lady friend called out to him from the waiting car, saying that she'd seen a female inmate wearing the Star of David go into the church, and asking if that was allowed. I cut in swiftly to explain that we also had Catholic inmates who were regular churchgoers, but the Obersturmführer had already done an about-turn and was marching off towards the church. Suspecting the worst, I went after him and his crony. There in the church sat two women, one of them ours, yes, and one not known to me, so deep in conversation that they only spotted the Obersturmführer once he was standing directly in front of them. With an ominous gesture he beckoned towards the doors leading out into the convent garden, right where we'd stopped to await developments. We quickly realised that the unknown woman was in fact the former housekeeper of Frau Stern[efeld], the lady who was our resident. It wasn't clear how the women had come to meet here, and fortunately nobody asked. The Obersturmführer, now beside himself with rage, raised his arm and brought his hand down hard across Frau Stern[efeld]'s face and then carried on slapping her over and over. For a moment I stood frozen in shock but then quickly positioned myself between the two of them without any thought to the consequences. Muggler [Mugler] paused and glared at me so furiously I thought it would be my turn next, but that didn't happen.

QR Code 19: Inhumanity and abuse of power

Instead he huffed and puffed at me, saying, 'You're to send this woman to see me at Widenmayerstrasse first thing tomorrow morning. She's not getting away with this.'

'I'm afraid I won't be able to do that,' I retorted. 'Frau Stern[efeld] is due to be deported early on Tuesday and is no longer permitted to leave the residential home.'

By now both of the women had vanished.

'Ah, I see, she's being deported,' muttered the Obersturmführer, looking slightly mollified at the prospect.

But then he turned back to me. 'You're to tell the Mother Superior that from now on these rear doors are to be kept bolted.'

Whereupon he finally did return to his car, Schroth [Schrott] following silently in his wake. I heaved a huge sigh of relief when the car finally slid away, and went to seek out Frau Stern[efeld]. She was in tears, with her face horribly swollen, so I took her to our nurse for a decent cold compress. It was quite some time before I stopped shaking.

Munich, Friday, 7 August 1942

I've been staying with Frau Dr Weiß [Schwarz} for the last three days. I'd been feeling so below par that on Tuesday she simply telephoned the Party and the Gestapo and with her customary forthright style told them I was to leave the home immediately and that was that. My heart won't stop racing and the good doctor is giving me regular injections.

Right before this, I'd ended up cooking for the entire home all on my own because Frau Nehm and Siegbert, our young cook, had both been deported.

Only when Frau Dr Weiß [Schwarz] declared me unfit for work did the Obersturmführer send over help, in the form of a young cook from Milbertshofen. And it was Frau Dr Weiß [Schwarz] who also pushed for me to be given leave of absence in her own home. Just before she came to collect me, I had a visit from Schroth [Schrott] informing me that I was to be relieved of my role as head of the residential facility. He went on to explain that the Milbertshofen camp was as good as empty with almost all inmates forcibly despatched, the only ones left being men born of mixed marriages and destined now for Berg am Laim, not for deportation. The man in charge at Milbertshofen, himself in a mixed marriage and thus protected, was consequently to take over at Berg am Laim. For me this means only one thing: I'll be part of the next round of deportations going to Poland.

The final few days in the home were harrowing. Cases of suicide increased and the relentless frequency of deportations left fewer and fewer people to keep our place going. I could barely sleep and really now felt at the end of my tether in every respect. Even the dear Professor had finally been deported.

And yet here I am, sitting in this cosy room with all the windows flung open so I can better relish all the colours of the garden. But inside I'm in complete turmoil and my thoughts are all over the place. What on earth am I to do? As soon as Schroth [Schrott] announced they were taking the leadership of the home away from me, my immediate thought was that I could now flee with a clear conscience. Frau Dr Weiß [Schwarz] has implored me to do so. She'd already told Tilla that I was at her home and so my good friend came to see me the day before yesterday. Timidly I aired my new thoughts, whereupon she offered her assistance. The three of us then had a long conversation about how it might be organised and made to happen. Our first idea was that I could hide with someone I knew in Munich but we decided not to pursue that.

'If only you could just cross straight over the border and into Switzerland,' Tilla said, with a longing that sounded truly heartfelt.

'That's what I'd like most of all,' I said.

'Listen, I've just thought of something!' she went on. 'Tomorrow I'm leaving early to go and visit your friend Eva [Schmidt] on Lake Constance. She's on holiday there by the lake. I'll get her to help me find out if there's some way to get you across the border from there. If that doesn't work, we'll come back and we can all put our heads together again.'

You know who we're talking about here, I'm sure – my dear old friend from student days. She's now a secondary school teacher in central Germany. She's always been very attached to us and since you've been away she's really looked after me and never fails to visit when she's on vacation from school. We're very active correspondents even though my side of it often has to be couched in language more akin to a telegram.

'Well, if you have no luck there,' broke in Dr Weiß [Schwarz], 'then I reckon Berlin's the best possible place to consider. Isn't there anyone who might take you in over there?'

The dear faces of all my friends in Berlin flashed through my mind's eye, but I found myself wondering how I could possibly burden anyone with this. Wait, I had a cousin [sister] there. She lived with her 'Aryan' husband in a small house on the outskirts of the city. They lived on their own, didn't socialise and were reasonably well off, a situation that meant little danger. I shared these thoughts rapidly with my eager listeners.

'Marvellous,' said Tilla decisively. 'So if we don't get anywhere down in Lake Constance, I'll send Eva to keep you company while I go on to Berlin to ask your cousin Erna [sister Eva] and her husband if they'll take you in.'

I couldn't speak for emotion and hoped she could see that. She left early the day before yesterday. What on earth will she and Eva really be able to do on my account? I spend a lot of time trying to rest but sleep eludes me. I'm being really spoiled here, though, and that's a treat I'm too weak at the moment to resist. I'd love to get stronger and in better shape. I weigh only ninety pounds these days.

I'd got this far with my diary when I was called to the telephone. It was the inspector from the Gestapo.

'I have to ask you to return to the home tomorrow or early the next morning at the latest. On Wednesday of next week the last deportation for the time being will depart from Bavaria for Theresienstadt. Twenty-five are to go from Munich. The facility of Milbertshofen is closing, hence we must use Berg am Laim as a muster point. We can't do this without you. We promise that you can immediately resume your leave of absence following the deportation. Widenmayerstrasse is in full agreement with this. The Milbertshofen people will come to Berg am Laim on Friday and you'll be free again from Saturday onwards.'

So, it's time to go back, time to gather the last of my strength. Dr Weiß [Schwarz] was furious when I told her about the telephone call, but I reassured her. I know that I have to see this through, and I know I can do it.

Berlin, Tuesday, 18 August 1942

It's not easy to relate everything in the right order, but I'll do my best.

In the end, I returned to the home on Saturday 8 August. I could have stayed with Frau Dr Weiß [Schwarz] until the Sunday but couldn't rest, and it was better for me to leave sooner so as to have plenty of time to prepare for the deportation.[20]

First of all we had to free up a room to accommodate twenty-five people. I decided to use the big room on the ground floor, right opposite the entrance. With windows overlooking the garden and French windows giving direct access to the outside, it was one of the finest rooms in the home and had served us well as a day room when we all first arrived. Our caretaker, Hermann, once again proved himself a tireless and first-rate worker, setting up all the plank beds and laying out mattresses. Since the succession of deportations we'd accumulated quite a stock of both of these basic items, now really coming into its own.

Once we'd completed these preparations I found myself thinking how different, dare I say homely, it all looked in comparison with those terrible makeshift mattresses stuffed with wood shavings that we'd had to put up with back at Milbertshofen, although I'll admit what we were doing here was much easier, caring for twenty-five and not eight hundred.

But we hadn't quite finished. A small room was to be provided for the Gestapo, while two further rooms were required for segregated male and female searches and then a fourth for storing luggage once it had been checked. Doubtless these rooms would require some level of furnishing as well.

Of our own residents a total of six were included on this occasion, among them yet another elderly man left disabled by the last war and his wife. The man could not walk without help. It was so touching to see his wife attend to him constantly while herself always remaining kind and cheerful. And all the more remarkable when you think that her only daughter had already been deported at the age of sixteen along with other workers from Lohhof.

Come Monday lunchtime everything was ready, and our Chairman came to check what we'd done. He explained that those departing would arrive early on Tuesday and soon after that Gestapo officials would come to carry out the usual formalities. The bus would depart at half past seven on Wednesday morning for Regensburg, where the full transport was to be assembled.

On Tuesday those destined for this particular wave of deportations arrived on time, their faces registering relief and surprise at finding such relatively agreeable surroundings for the final twenty-four hours in their home city. Once again I came across someone I knew within the group, a young man who'd been the caretaker at one of our old folks' homes. His name was Roch, a capable and energetic fellow, and being a Mischling he was to be sent to Theresienstadt not Poland. I nominated him as room senior, a role he was more than willing to take on.

Soon afterwards we were informed that the Gestapo officials had arrived – four men and two women. I showed them the rooms we had set up for them but this was met with little interest. Instead they asked to see the garden area allocated to us by the nuns and definitely liked the look of that!

'Have some deck chairs brought out here for us! And your caretaker can bring us a keg of beer.'

Their orders left me more than a little taken aback. What a strange world. Here we had twenty-five people waiting to be searched before leaving behind all that was dear to them while six officials chose to lounge around in the garden, chattering and laughing without a care in the world, without sparing a single thought for their victims, only their own comfort. Hermann carted the keg over to them and it wasn't long before we heard the clinking of glasses and the usual sounds of merriment, interrupted every now and then by shrill female laughter. The two women were young, pretty and well dressed, but I didn't like the look of them one bit. Their brazen enjoyment of the company of men of this ilk, coupled with such totally inappropriate behaviour, only added to my dislike of them both and of their presence in our home.

They didn't get on with their work until eleven, by which time the men had polished off the beer. The men then showed the usual lack of compassion and, as I could have predicted, the women dealt with our people disgracefully too. Even Frau Rosen, wife of the severely disabled war veteran, emerged from the female search room with red eyes and tear-stained cheeks.

She said to me, 'I had to let them do a complete body search, and it wouldn't have been half so bad if they'd only refrained from using the vilest language while doing it. They didn't address me properly, just barked out instructions over my head and talked to each other about me, deliberately saying things to hurt my feelings. I was so angry with myself for crying in front of them. They even took some of my things – extra underwear I'd put on, as well as a spare dress I'd pulled on over the top of everything else.'

I comforted her as best I could and hurried off to my storeroom to see if there was anything that might remotely make up for what they'd taken. But I found nothing that would do and so asked one of the women to make a few enquiries in the hope something would materialise.

Then I made haste to get back to the officials, as I was expected to stay near them as well as keeping watch over those due to leave. After three hours the whole horrible business to which the twenty-five had had to subject themselves was finally over. One of the Gestapo officials came to tell me they'd finished and proceeded to reel off rules of conduct to me.

'You are responsible for every one of these twenty-five people. You are to keep each one in your sight at all times, or if not, place them under lock and key. You are personally charged with escorting them to meals and then accompanying them back. Have you arranged food for them?'

I confirmed that this was the case.

'You'll have to provide for one more,' he said. 'We're picking up Cossmann en route tomorrow, because he tried to escape deportation by running off. But we've nabbed him!'

I froze at hearing his triumphant shout of laughter. He'd used the same surname as that of the Professor, who I happened to know had a brother – it had to be him, poor fellow. Somewhat later I heard from Frau Dr Weiß [Schwarz] that he'd been lying low with friends for several weeks, but a resident in the same building had somehow got wind of an extra presence and reported it to the Gestapo. They'd found him during their search of the property.[21]

Once the group of Gestapo officials had roared off in their car and the convent gate had closed behind them, I took the party due to leave in the morning downstairs to eat. I'd discussed it all previously with my helpers, and we were all keen to make everything as nice as we possibly could for these people. We'd therefore got out the best crockery and even I was surprised at how attractive the table looked. My helpers had truly excelled themselves. Everything was cooked to a turn and beautifully presented, lifting the mood for these poor people after all they'd endured over the last few hours. With such dreadful experiences behind them, they were quite cheered to learn that there was a terrace right outside their room, complete with deckchairs so they could at least enjoy some sunshine and fresh air during the afternoon.

I tried also to console them about their belongings that had been confiscated, things they were already missing. I told them they'd get back whatever we were able to recover. The rest of the day passed off without incident and the evening meal was exactly the distraction that all twenty-five were sorely in need of. I suggested an early night all round as the day had not been without its trials. Doubtless more would lie ahead.

Breakfast the next day was set for half past six to enable everyone to get ready without being rushed and the bus was due at half past seven. I planned to wake everyone at half past five. I was up at four to get the stove going and to lay the table. Many of our residents, most of them now deported, had originally brought in with them their own beautiful crockery, which now combined with an embroidered cloth to make for a welcoming sight. We even had fresh flowers on the table as I'd gone to the gardening nun the evening before and been permitted to cut whatever I felt might help. By agreement with the other residents I had used flour coupons for white bread which I then toasted up ready to be buttered and spread with the various jams I'd managed to get hold of for the occasion. The greatest joy seemed to stem from the variety of hot drinks we had on offer. Just imagine, we'd had a donation of proper ground coffee, and then for those wanting something different there was real tea or cocoa. Luxury beyond words in these times. My young chef, Dieter, arrived at five and we worked together to prepare it all.

The few residents not due to go out to work on this day were to have their breakfast only once the twenty-five had departed on the special bus. Everything went without a hitch and the breakfast almost took on the atmosphere of a family gathering, so bonded were people by everything that had taken place over the last twenty-four hours. There was even a speech to mark the occasion.

Roch, the room senior, rose to his feet. 'Let us take as a good omen this shared start to the day, our courage fortified for the unknown that lies ahead. Even in difficult times we will always remember how you people here have tried to brighten the final hours in our homeland, and that will remain a beacon of comfort and hope in our hearts.'

Just before the appointed time of departure, everyone stood to bid me farewell. One dear old lady put her arms around me and whispered, 'Since you're young enough to be my daughter, please allow me to leave you with a blessing. The only way I can show my gratitude is through my promise to pray for you. I feel sure things will turn out right for you.'

Our Chairman turned up, wanting to see for himself how things were managed, and was surprised at our group's apparent composure as they boarded the bus.

Around midday I was called to the gatekeeper's office on the agreed pretext of a telephone call. There stood my dear friend Eva.

'We had no luck on Lake Constance,' she said, after our quick greeting, 'but Tilla's just phoned from Berlin. Erna [Eva Fischer] and her husband have said they'll take you in straight away. Tilla's back first thing tomorrow and will come and find you at some point during the day. She'll bring you a travel ticket. It's time for you to make your mind up and go.'

'Impossible before first thing on Saturday,' I told her, 'but after that, yes, I'll do it.'

I couldn't quite believe what I was saying.

Eva continued. 'I need to go home this evening. Pack a few things in a suitcase and bring it to me in the nuns' office here. I'm sure you'll find some excuse. I'll take it and then head off to the station. I'll get myself a ticket for Berlin via my own destination, then hand in the case and send the luggage ticket to your cousin [sister] by registered post.'

It all seemed quite straightforward.

'One last thing,' said Eva. 'It's best if you take the five past eight on Saturday morning. I'll try and get on at Jena and travel with you as far as Halle. I'll feel more settled if I've seen you and spoken to you actually on the train.'

'I'm still in shock,' I whispered to her. 'I can't believe I'm really leaving. Oh goodness, I'd best be getting back though.' The time had slipped by, I now realised in horror. 'Farewell, my dearest friend. And thank you, thank you for everything.'

With that I tore myself away and went to tell Sister Theodora that I'd be bringing a suitcase over a little later, something to do with one of the deportees. I said that my friend would be collecting it and arranging to take it to someone known to the deportee for safe storage. The nun gave a discreet nod. It wasn't the first time she'd heard something along those lines and had always been ready to help without asking any tricky questions.

When Tilla came the following day, she praised my cousin [sister] and her husband to the skies for the way they had agreed to take me in. I was so glad to hear all this. Mind you, they had set a number of conditions. I had to swear not to leave the house and not to contact any of my old friends and acquaintances. Naturally I was fully prepared to agree to this as they were the ones taking the risk and so had the right to set the rules.

Tilla handed me my ticket. 'I've already seen Frau Dr Weiß [Schwarz]. She wants you to put the rest of your things in the furniture van coming over from Milbertshofen tomorrow. It's bringing folk from the camp along with their belongings. The carrier will take your case to her house, something that won't seem the slightest bit out of the ordinary as you are after all spending your leave there. She doesn't think there'd be any difficulty in her then sending the case on later to Erna [Eva Fischer] in Berlin. On Saturday morning simply take with you whatever you can easily carry yourself. Everyone needs to think you're just going off back home with Dr Weiß [Schwarz]. She'll go through it with you tomorrow evening during your appointment in her regular surgery hour. Right, I must get going now. Try not to show any upset over your farewells. I won't rest until I know from Eva that your journey's gone according to plan. I've done so many trips this week, to and from Lake Constance and up and down from Berlin, and the police and Gestapo were doing identity checks all over the place. They actually checked me twice over on the return journey to Berlin. What worries me most of all is how you're going to negotiate all that. Make sure you have a very good excuse for not having your papers.' Her face was anxious as we embraced and clasped hands, and then she was gone.

I drifted slowly back through the garden. Was I really about to undertake this journey? I still couldn't quite believe it. What if it all went wrong? The very thought sent a chill right through my bones. I pictured all the questioning on board the train about my papers. If I couldn't somehow conjure up the right answers, all would be lost. Thoughts of this nature tormented me right through until Friday evening. I scarcely registered carrying out my remaining duties at the home, only to be plagued by nightmares during my few short hours of sleep that night.

Early on Friday morning I was called for.

'Schroth [Schrott] and our Chair are here,' Hermann told me. 'Schroth's [Schrott's] in a real mood – won't even come in.'

I sped down to the ground floor where I found the two men standing at the door. Schroth [Schrott] looked absolutely livid and snarled at me, 'Get your things on. You're under arrest.'

You have to understand this wasn't entirely an unfamiliar scenario, as so many inspections started off in this manner. With my nerves already on edge, I decided to give him something to think about.

'Fine. Go ahead and arrest me then, sir. At least I'd finally get a bit of peace and quiet.'

Schroth [Schrott] stared at me in astonishment. I didn't normally speak to him in such tones.

'You don't even know the case against you,' he said, slightly less enraged all of a sudden. 'I hear you've bought meat in town with no stamps.'

Secretly, I was relieved. I knew I'd never done anything so foolish and could in any case guess precisely where this latest nonsense came from.

'I imagine our butcher's been complaining that we've not asked him for any meat over the last fortnight,' came my measured response. 'I can prove to you that our meat stamps have been used for sausage and meat loaf direct from the authorised processor because the butcher's offering was so pathetic we couldn't make a decent meal out of it.'

'You'll have to prove that!' shrieked Schroth [Schrott].

'I can do that straight away,' I replied swiftly. 'Would you like to come to the office?'

'No, you can bring the evidence out here to me!' he snarled.

I promptly presented him with the last fortnight's receipts, clearly showing that I'd used food stamps for sausage and meat loaf.

Then something quite odd occurred. Schroth [Schrott] must have been absolutely convinced that he had caught me out this time and would emerge triumphant. I can only assume that his high hopes plummeted so hard and fast that all he could do was turn on his heel and march off without a word. In amazement we watched him leave and then turned to stare at one another. Our Chair mopped his brow.[22]

'Well, thank God for that,' he said. 'I was really fearful for you this time.'

He then told me how some of the people from Milbertshofen would be arriving around midday, with the remainder in the evening, along with the furniture van that was bringing their things.

'And you're on leave from early tomorrow. I wish you all the rest and recuperation you need.'

Time seemed to stand still that day, in spite of there being so much to do. Although some of the folk from Milbertshofen came as expected, Herr Metz [Mezger] was unfortunately not among them. He was designated to take over from me at the home, and I had hoped to make good use of the afternoon for a detailed handover so that he could take up the reins with confidence. Alternatively, this was maybe a good thing – a sign that I should abandon this daring idea of taking flight, something which now looked more and more hazardous, and simply be brave and go to dear Dr Weiß [Schwarz] for a break. That thought was more than tempting. All the necessary scheming had drained me more than I can say and the thought of her pretty little house on the edge of Munich's *Englischer Garten* was just heavenly. I pictured myself resting there and not needing to think through all the complications and obstacles to be encountered on the route to Berlin! Tilla and Eva would be cross with me, the dear souls that they are, and Dr Weiß [Schwarz] too perhaps, but none of this could change the fact that I no longer had the mental stamina to take on the risk.

That afternoon I was walking back from the nuns' domain and through the convent garden after taking some telephone calls, when I heard someone approach behind me. It wasn't our usual nun from the gate office but her deputy.

'Frau Doktor Behrend, our Sister Theodora requests that you come back about half past six this evening. She knows you're going on leave early in the morning and wants to say goodbye to you in person.'

I promised to be there.

Later that afternoon the furniture van arrived with the remaining Milbertshofen inmates, together with their possessions. Herr Metz [Mezger] was the first to emerge and came straight over to me.

'If we could just unload and put our things away first, then you and I can talk over the essentials this evening.'

That was fine with me. Now I'd decided not to make a run for it, it didn't bother me how far into the evening I had to work. At half past six I went over to the convent and found Sister Theodora in her usual place, the gatekeeper's office. She came towards me, hands outstretched.

QR Code 20: Encouragement and consolation

'My dear Frau Doktor Behrend.' She greeted me even more warmly than usual on this occasion. 'I didn't want you to leave without us talking one last time. I don't know what will happen, when or whether we'll ever meet again, but please always remember that our thoughts and prayers are with you wherever you may be. We know what difficult times you have gone through and can't see what lies ahead, but feel confident that your circumstances will change for the better.'

I found myself looking back at her in some confusion, saw her gentle face with its fine lines, her clear intelligent eyes that seemed to know so much of life. Did she know more than I realised? I couldn't quite fathom it, but that didn't really matter. One thing I did know for sure: her words gave me strength, banished my fear and apprehension, and suddenly I regained my old energy, along with the courage to take the risk! Unable to speak, I took her hands in mine, nodded and turned to follow the familiar pathway back to the home. Calmly I carried out some essential tasks and told myself that the kitchen and office would continue to run without me. The caretaker telephoned.

'Frau Dr Weiß [Schwarz] is here as usual. She's waiting for you in the surgery.'

I went upstairs. Her agitation was evident. 'It's best you don't make the journey. The risk is far too high. Your friend Eva has telephoned and told me of all the strict checks going on, and that's on all trains. Don't you think that might be a little too much for you?'

'An hour or so ago, I'd have agreed but nothing will stop me now – I know everything will turn out all right.'

She let out a sigh. 'Well, I hope you're right. One more thing. Are you thinking of leaving a letter, you know, saying you're ending it all?'

'I'd be most reluctant to do that. Do you feel it necessary?'

She shook her head. 'This is how I think it'll go. Everyone here believes you're coming to my home tomorrow, is that right?'

'Yes. Whenever anyone's asked, I've said that with the approval of the Party and the Gestapo I'm spending my leave at your house.'

'Good. That means nobody will be asking about you until Tuesday, when I'm next due here for my surgery hour. I'll then just ask Hermann to send you to see me in the usual room. When he acts all shocked, saying that you'd told him you were to spend some of your annual leave with me, I'll get all worked up and will say something along these lines: she didn't say a word on Friday evening about her holiday starting on Saturday. What on earth can she have been up to?'

At this point she interrupted her own narrative, saying she didn't really need to play out the whole story to me. 'All you really need to know is that I've thought of every last detail and got my story straight. It's all covered, as far as I'm concerned.'

'I know that,' I said to her warmly.

'Right, I'd better head off then. Fortunately no one here is gravely ill at the moment so nobody will involve me today in conversations about your impending time off, thank goodness, or that could interfere with all our best-laid plans.'

She rose to her feet. Farewell. Eva or Tilla will keep me informed.'

And with that she ushered me from the room. I watched her hurry across the courtyard, giving a little nod towards the gate before it was closed behind her.

I felt relieved at the way the conversation had gone.

Then I heard Herr Metz [Mezger]. 'I've brought a basket of wild strawberries with me from Milbertshofen. Must be around five pounds here. We dug through a patch of waste ground behind the huts and made a few beds for cultivation. I couldn't abandon the crops! The chances are we can harvest a similar quantity again in a few days' time and give the children a second treat, as well as anyone who misses out today. Would you like to take them round to all the people who've been out at work today? They're downstairs having their evening meal at the moment, aren't they?'

I was of course delighted to do so. These succulent little berries were hard to find even at the best of times and now belonged only in our dreams, so for this to be my final task in our home was something really special. The delight on everyone's face was obvious. These people, so weary and careworn, brightened at the sight of the basket and were suddenly all smiles and jokes, their otherwise gloomy expressions transformed by so relatively little. Remarkable how a handful of hard to come by wild berries could momentarily dispel the greyness. I took a long last look around the room and left. That was how I wanted to remember them all.

In the office I found Herr Metz [Mezger] deep in conversation with Herr Löwenberger, who was talking him through the books. I joined them. Herr Metz [Mezger] looked quite at ease already in his new surroundings. 'I've just had a bit of a look around the place and feel there's no need for a long meeting this evening. You must be weary and I've had a tiring day too. Herr Löwenberger has given me the plan of work for the coming week as well as the catering list. Everything will carry on as normal for the whole time you're away on leave, and then we can talk on your return about anything that needs sorting out. The main thing now is that you get full rest and a good recovery.'

It was a great relief to be spared any long conversations. And he certainly didn't lack experience, having already run a far larger and more complex establishment than our own. There was no cause for concern.

Since the forced departure of Frau Dillenius I had my room to myself again, and I confess it was a bit of a relief not to have to make small talk or follow any of those same old conversations, some of which can be quite maddening after a while. Most items here would have to be left behind, and many of them in fact had been handed on by others. In any case I had to avoid doing anything that might arouse suspicion that I wasn't coming back. My diary had been stowed away in the suitcase that Eva had despatched to my cousin Erna [sister Eva Fischer] in Berlin, and the bag I used for shopping and carrying my work had been quickly packed. Fatigue overcame me now, and I lay on my bed and instantly fell asleep.

When the alarm sounded in the morning, I felt fresh and rested. That sense of certainty that everything would go well had stayed with me and made my final tasks easy. As part of my plan I had the previous evening mentioned to a few women whose route to work took them by way of the Hauptbahnhof that I would be joining them in the morning. I told them I had a few things to sort out in town before going off to Frau Dr Weiß [Schwarz] for my break.

They waited for me after breakfast so we could set off together for the little station in Berg am Laim. There were quite a few of us, men too. I knew that most of them had to travel on from Munich Hauptbahnhof and would be hurrying for connecting trains, so wouldn't have time to bother looking where I was headed, with the possible exception of Frau Stein, who worked near the station and seemed to have latched on to me. The train was crowded and that suited me well. It made conversation impossible, and people just got off at their stop with a quick nod or a wave of the hand. I had already made light of my departure for what would be nothing more than a short absence of leave, saying I didn't want to go in for any big goodbyes. Frau Stein was still glued to my side, and now said, 'I've got plenty of time this morning, so if it's all right with you I'll come and help with your errands.'

'Please don't be offended if I say no,' I said to her. 'I'm so looking forward to having a little time on my own that I wouldn't be much company for you!'

She smiled. 'Oh, I quite understand! I've often wondered how you put up with answering everybody's questions all the time. I hope you have a really restful stay with Frau Dr Weiß [Schwarz]. We'll all be looking forward to seeing you back with us, rested and refreshed.'

By now we were at the ticket barrier. With a friendly nod she melted into the crowds streaming out of the station. I stopped at the barrier and took a quiet look around me, noticing with relief that no one was paying me the slightest bit of attention as they were all in a rush, and there were no familiar faces to be seen. Slowly I went through the barrier and handed over my ticket for the section of the journey as far as Munich Hauptbahnhof. Keeping my Star of David well hidden, I set off for the ladies' washroom. There was nobody else in there and it was easy to remove my Star, as I had unpicked the stitches the day before and just tacked it back on as a temporary measure. Now I put it right at the bottom of my shopping bag together with my Jewish identity card. Next I headed to the ticket barrier opposite and had my Munich to Berlin ticket clipped. The train was just coming in as I stepped on to the platform. For a moment I wondered whether I should catch a train leaving ten minutes earlier, an extra service they'd put on in view of the expected increase in passengers, but then remembered that Eva would be looking for me on the train we'd agreed she'd be joining at Jena. While every minute spent in Munich was risky, there were quite as many risks on the train itself. All it needed was some person from my old life to end up in the seat opposite mine. It was 15th August, the end of school holidays in Berlin and I'd also have to deal there with running into someone familiar. That risk didn't change whether I took the train as instructed or the earlier one.

So I kept to the plan and stuck with the agreed train, still as good as empty, and found myself a nice comfortable window seat in a non-smoking compartment in the second coach. I settled down to read a novel that I'd picked out from the many books left ownerless back at the home but my mind wasn't on it. Every now and again I looked up to see my compartment gradually filling and to watch the hand of the station clock tick slowly onward. On the inside, I quietly congratulated myself on staying confident in my expectation that I could overcome whatever obstacles were to be put in my way.

It was time at last for the train to depart. My compartment was now full with no familiar faces in view. A platform attendant in the customary red cap raised his baton, and our train creaked into motion. I turned my attention back to my book, a light novel written originally in English but now translated into German. The plot proved to be rather thrilling and full of twists and turns so that I eventually lost track of time. Augsburg, Nürnberg, all the well-known stations flashed by. The train was packed and the corridors crammed as well, making getting in and out increasingly difficult, and still there had been no official check, but I knew that even when it came I'd be more than ready.

By now we were approaching Jena. I tried to ease my way across the compartment to get close to the corridor window, but it was hopeless. How on earth was Eva going to find me on this train with so many carriages, all bursting at the seams? Now we were moving again and I resigned myself to going back to my window seat, but wait – was I seeing things? Wasn't that Eva, standing in the doorway of my compartment and looking around for me? Yes, it was her all right. Somehow she'd spotted me. The anxious look on her face gave way to a smile. Seated next to me was a young sergeant who gallantly rose to his feet to offer his seat to my friend. It was hard for either of us to believe that this was all really happening at last, but the sheer happiness that flooded through me at this magical encounter served only to strengthen my confidence yet further! In hushed tones, Eva told me what a relief it was to see with her own eyes that I was safely on my way so she could return home with some peace of mind. She said that when she got off the train she'd be sending Tilla a note as arranged and that Tilla would in turn pass the message on to Frau Dr Weiß [Schwarz]. We promised to continue writing to one another, and I told Eva she could address her letters directly to my cousin Erna [sister Eva Fischer]. Other than that we didn't say a lot; it was enough simply to sit there together for a while.

At Halle she got off the train and as it pulled away again, I saw her waving, her face relaxed and beaming. Wittenberg and Luckenwalde were now behind us, and the train was drawing close to the suburbs of Berlin.

There had been no checks and I had miraculously been spared the inevitable drama of explaining why I was carrying no identity papers on my person. The brakes screeched as the train drew to a halt at Berlin Anhalter Bahnhof.

The station was filled with August sunshine in spite of the dusting of soot on every window in the building. It was far too light for me to risk walking the streets straight away, so I let the stream of passengers pass me by and discreetly joined the stragglers as far as the steps that led to the main hall and onward to the street. Where should I wait for the sun to go down? More than anything I wanted a good wash and freshen up. It didn't bother me at all that there was a long line of women waiting outside the ladies' washroom. Suddenly I had time on my hands, the strangest sensation after so many months, indeed years, packed day after day with endless work. Gradually the queue moved up and at last it was my turn to go in. I had all the time and space I needed to wash the grime of the journey from my hands and face, but when I came out it was still broad daylight so I decided to stay within the station perimeter and found myself a bench to sit on, then fished out my book.

Twilight began to fall and finally I could set off on the rest of my journey. I had decided to cover it on foot as I had the same old fear of being spotted on the tram or U-Bahn, but then realised how tired I was and ached with every step. It was over an hour before I reached the house where Gustav and Erna [Georg and Eva Fischer] lived. I rang the bell and Erna [Eva] opened the door, then hurriedly ushered me inside where she gave me a warm welcome. Gustav [Georg] wasn't home as he was away on a business trip, so Erna [Eva] was there all alone. I recounted the details of my journey then asked how I might best dispose of my Star of David and my Jewish identity card. Without a moment's hesitation she lit a fire in the kitchen range, and we both watched as the flames licked at and then consumed those two objects that had borne witness to such brutal times, reducing them to a tiny heap of ash. As I write I'm sitting in the pretty room I've been given up on the second floor. From my window I can enjoy the sight of a beautiful robinia tree, the only one in the whole street to have a whole head of gleaming white blossom. I take this as another good omen and look forward to what might lie ahead.

Gustav [Georg] came home at lunchtime today and welcomed me with the same warmth as his wife. We then all sat down to discuss how I should conduct myself here. If Erna's [Eva's] out shopping, I'm not to respond to anyone knocking at the door or ringing the bell but must stay quietly in my own room. I am never to leave the house, may not allow myself to be seen at

37. Eva Schmidt in Cranachstraße, Weimar, around 1940.

the window nor make contact with old friends. All that in itself is perfectly clear, but every time the telephone goes or there's a ring on the doorbell, it makes me jump out of my skin and leaves me in a cold sweat. The nights are even worse. I find it hard to get to sleep and when I do finally drift off, I'm woken by nightmares that leave me in a lather of perspiration. I dream of being back in the home and happy among old friends, but then the truth dawns that in actual fact I'm a fugitive now and can't let anyone catch sight of me. In desperation I search for a credible explanation to enable my return but to no avail. I am bombarded by questions to which I have no answers. Once I'm awake, I stay awake, fearful that sleep will only bring me more of the same terrors.

Else's First Letter to Eva Schmidt from Life Underground

Berlin, 30 August 1942

My dearest Eva

Thank you so much for your lovely letter. It was only on reading it that I realised what a long gap I'd left since the last one and how long you've been waiting for news. Well, you know, so far I've spent the entire time napping and continue to do so! Sleep is the only way to get myself back to rights, it seems. As regards my health, I'm so much better now – excellent even, in comparison with how I was feeling previously.

You need have no worries at all about the care we're getting here. It's all fine and we have everything we need. You can rest easy!

So what about us seeing one another? We're really not that far apart any more, so there's bound to be some opportunity to meet up. I'm so looking forward to that.

Farewell, my dearest friend, and stay well. We all send you our warmest regards, especially E.

Siegfried's Diary

Oxford, 8 September 1942

It's now two months since I started in the Dairy section at the Co-op here in Oxford. I'm not naturally suited to the world of commerce and the daily routine that it requires of me. I leave home at 8 and come back at 7, sometimes even later. The sedentary nature of the work makes me long for a bit of activity out in the fresh air.

The best time of year is now, early autumn, and today is a perfect example. I finished work at 6 and then walked in the grounds of Worcester College with my colleague and good friend, Herr Seidl, who kindly invited me home for soup afterwards. He always bids me to 'Help yourself'. That's how it is for me now. Do everything yourself. And being at work all day makes the domestic side all the more difficult than in my previous life, when I could shape the day to my requirements.[23]

But no complaints now, because look how much better off I am than Else. She sounds so brave in her letters, no doubt concealing far more than she actually lets on. Just imagine what it's like for her to face the unknown, to stare into the abyss. May heaven protect her.

This stage of the war presents the greatest threat to Else, in both physical and mental terms.

There's no end in sight this year, or even before the spring. If the winter sees no great success for Germany and the Russians manage to keep control of their home front, then it's bound to continue for the best part of 1943.

Oxford, 11 October 1942

A letter has come from Alice Rosenberg bearing the news that my Else is now living at the home of Eva Fischer and that her illness has been successfully treated, although she needs to regain her strength – she mentions the need for rest and recuperation, over a few days' leave.

What does this actually mean? Has she been given a few short weeks of freedom from her labours at the home? Will she have to go back there afterwards, and when? What kind of illness is she having to cope with? It must be heavenly for her to be in a private house and not working like a slave as she has been for the last year or so.

Georg is a man in whom I have real faith. He has always shown himself to be a decent chap, ready to do everything possible for Else. But what on earth will happen to her if, after this brief respite, she is forced to carry on with the same burden of work as before? And how did she even manage the journey? That makes me think she must still be reasonably strong. But I worry that all the deprivation will have left her undernourished and underweight. Will she be able to regain her previous state of health? The questions crowd in on me. What horrors has she had to endure? When will all this end? And how?

Letter from Else to Eva Schmidt

Berlin, 12 November 1942

My dearest Eva

Now for the most important news! My doctor has said that I need a change of air at the earliest opportunity, so we're getting my things ready.[24] We've asked T to come over and help with the preparations for my departure. There's no need for any concern whatsoever on your part, but the air round here has never suited me at this time of year, and particularly not at the moment. The last thing I'd want to do is pass you by and so I'm wondering if I might stay a few days with you en route? I'll be sure not to make any demands on you. And I'll be able to bring you up to date with all my news.

Anyway, it'll be good to see a different neck of the woods after so much time living in close proximity to others here. That brings its own problems, and all the more so when one isn't on top form. But it's never like that when staying with you! You do know, don't you, that I wouldn't come if I couldn't square it with my conscience?

Else's Diary

Berlin, 17 November 1942

I've been here for three months now but haven't once felt able to open my diary, let alone write a single word. But I've just given myself a good talking to as today is the birthday of our youngest. My dear hearts, I'm longing for you all more than ever before in this time of separation, so much so that it hurts. I'm thinking of you, my dearest loves, especially you, my little Hanna, and wondering how you're spending your twentieth birthday. You were just a child when you left me, and hard though I try, I can't imagine how you now look, or how you sound when you talk or laugh.

QR Code 21: Emotion and life underground

I've had to go underground and am living illegally. It leaves me so low not to have contact with any of you. At least back in Munich I could send post for you through my sister-in-law in Portugal in the knowledge that she'd be able to send my letters on to you just as she unfailingly passed to me any news from you. But for a long time now letters from abroad can be collected in person only, and with the right papers to hand, so any correspondence via Portugal is out of the question. I just can't allow myself to be crushed by such thoughts and feelings at the moment, however – given the crisis I'm living through that could prove dangerous.

I don't know what's wrong with me. It's as if I've been beaten into submission by a pair of the heaviest, darkest wings, one bearing melancholy and the other despair. Now that I no longer have the weight of my workload to brood over and busy myself with, I find the silence and cramped quarters here strangely hard to bear. Gustav [Georg] is out all day and gets home late from the factory, and Erna [Eva] is out a lot as well because food shopping these days occupies so much of her time. I help her with the house as best I can but sense that I'm not doing things the way she likes it, which leaves me feeling insecure and only seems to add to my clumsiness. The misery and distress suffered by the Jewish people, shared by me to the point of near-suffocation, has followed me here too. Erna [Eva] is forever telling me of the deportation of good friends or more distant acquaintances.

I could withstand all the bad news if I didn't constantly feel my presence here as an almost intolerable burden on Gustav and Erna [Georg and Eva]. It's true that not many people come to the house, so at least there's no sense of immediate danger, but my feelings count for little against their own jittery state, and they simply won't be able to endure my presence in their home for much longer.

But where on earth am I supposed to go instead? Gustav [Georg] has tried, and not without hope of success, to investigate a route to Switzerland for me but the intermediary with whom he was negotiating has since vanished. We don't know whether the fellow suddenly lost his nerve or was himself picked up. All of us were in agreement, however, that I needed some sort of identification papers, and Erna [Eva] managed to procure for me an identity card of the type issued by the police. It belonged previously to an 'Aryan' woman for whom it was accepted as identification in every part of the country. The card was purchased with the last of my own money, along with funds drummed up for me among our friends by Eva and Tilla. It bears the name Leonie Maier and was issued in Düsseldorf. But even if we could easily make the personal details match – she was only four years younger than me – the photograph and part of the official stamp still need adding. An acquaintance of Gustav [Georg] promised to do this but has then seemed to let him down, or else there's some other obstacle. To change your place of residence with no papers, however – well, that seems to me nigh on impossible.

My loyal friend, Eva, has guessed from the changed tone of my last letter how depressed I am and wants to come here as soon as possible. She asks me to be patient for just one more fortnight and then hopes to stay for the weekend. I'm clinging to this prospect like a drowning man clutches at a straw, but I don't know what her visit can possibly hope to change regarding my situation.

Siegfried's Diary

Oxford, 2 December 1942

I know pitifully little about what's happening to Else but gleaned this much from Henny Rewald's[25] letter to Alice Rosenberg. A parcel for Else despatched by Alice, our stalwart mediator, has been delivered to my dearest by

Henny herself. That was in the first half of October. So can I assume from that that she has been at Eva Fischer's ever since? Dare I even presume that she may still be there now, at this moment, as I write these very words? Everyone is afraid of being caught posting items abroad and that goes for Henny and Eva [Fischer] too, as they are bound to consider their own safety as well as that of Else. If all this explains the lack of news, I can live with that. But nothing stops the same question from haunting me day and night: where is my Else?

As the war enters its fourth winter, life becomes ever more miserable. The longer I work at the office, the greater the pressure I am under and yet I must stick it out for however many months they are prepared to keep me. I realise that my poor spoken English puts me at a great disadvantage and cannot tell how long they will tolerate that. I have no complaints about how the other staff treat me. At times I struggle to concentrate on my bookkeeping and can sense that my rather contemplative manner is distinctly at odds with the noisy banter between my young English colleagues, who fool around and even sing while they are working. Everything is taken so lightly here.

Oxford, 3 December 1942

The temperament here is so different, the people so much tougher somehow. (I keep coming back to those similarities between the two wars, namely three years of failure before the tide eventually turned. What a different picture for older Germans, who will recall only too well the collapse of their nation in the fourth year.) To us the general mood would seem to indicate a degree of callousness or lack of feeling in the face of events that would leave our own people downcast and disheartened. Here in Britain it is not indifference, but rather a quiet reassurance and unshakable confidence in a good outcome, together with the backbone developed from leading an empire. This has brought centuries of continued progress and an unswerving conviction that things will turn out for the best. This explains the good cheer seen in young and old alike of a people whose fate is determined in greater part by its character. Therein lies the key to the difference between our two nations. [. . .]

Yesterday I sent off my Post Office savings book to London to have the interest added and recorded. I wish with all my heart this money could be used to bring my dear Else back to us.

Where on earth can she be now?

Oxford, Saturday, 12 December 1942

Over the last ten days or so the press has been reporting the extermination of all those Jews in Hitler's grasp. It's likely that much of this reporting comes from his own propaganda machine but it is a fact that deportation leaves Jews fearing for their lives and justifiably so.

The thought tears me apart. When my mind is churning with possibilities regarding Else's likely fate, that's when the demons come and I can no longer function as I need to. I try to discipline myself not to give in to these fears when I am at work, but I still find myself overwhelmed at times at the thought that she may have been despatched by these brutes. There's little or no prospect of hearing anything definite about her whereabouts and health for now. I picture how my poor darling must be trapped by uncertainty both night and day, not knowing if or when she is to be forced into slave labour to meet a miserable end. No one can rescue my Else, pure and guileless as she is, so untainted by life's darker forces before now. Will I ever see her again? Will she ever see the three of us here? This prolonged ordeal must have left its mark on her – and this is precisely why I must see her.

Jewish gatherings and fasting have been arranged for tomorrow, Sunday. I plan a period of quiet contemplation; no fasting for me, as I don't hold with any form of self-chastisement. But every day and almost every hour, my mind is filled with the image of my innocent wife undergoing interrogation.

Else's Diary

Berlin, 14 December 1942

The day after I wrote my last diary entry, I received a wonderful letter from Tilla with the following news. Two long-standing, dear friends of ours, Maria [Eva Kunkel] and Irma [Irmgard Baer],[26] had written to Isartal asking Tilla if she knew anything of what had happened to me. Tilla has sensed how lonely I am, so she quickly decided to indicate my whereabouts but without giving Erna's [Eva's] married name or address. The others knew of Erna [Eva] as my cousin [sister] from a fair number of earlier birthday visits, so it was enough to refer to her first name and the family relationship.

At first I was really shocked, fearful that Gustav and Erna [Georg and Eva] would be furious that our promise not to reveal my whereabouts had been broken, but this was quickly overcome by the joy of seeing them both again. Erna [Eva] was very understanding and assured me that she'd pacify Gustav [Georg].

38. Eva Kunkel (*left*), a primary school teacher in Berlin, with Else and Siegfried Rosenfeld at Lake Starnberg, 1930s. Eva facilitated Else's contact with Hans Kollmorgen in Berlin.

Two days later, there stood Irma in front of me. Both of us in floods of tears, we simply clung to each other, quite unable to speak. We knew we were both remembering the occasion of our last meeting. It was in early August 1939 in Isartal, when Tilla, you, these two and I had all gone for a long walk together. Since then we'd only been in contact by letter, although the final few months at Berg am Laim had left me neither time nor energy to keep up any private correspondence. It did me so much good to see Irma again. After the initial tears we began to talk, all the questions and stories pouring out, and since then both of these good friends have taken it in turns to come and see me at least once a week.

I'm sure it went against the grain for Gustav [Georg] to know that two new people were in on the secret, but he passed no comment. I'm sure his strong sense of justice meant he saw me as the innocent party in the whole business.

At the end of November Eva [Schmidt] wrote saying she would come on 5 December. That was a Saturday, and she'd arrive in Berlin about half past eight and would stay until Sunday evening. She asked if I could write back to confirm that she could stay overnight with us. Erna [Eva Fischer] was in agreement, saying there was plenty enough room for her. I hadn't liked asking her for yet another favour, particularly as despite my best efforts her dissatisfaction with my housework seemed greater than ever. It was clear to me that I had to leave, which was precisely what I wanted to talk over with Eva.

Gustav's [Georg's] unease and anger had worsened. He was rarely home in the evenings and I overheard Erna [Eva] ask if there was anything wrong. I don't know what in particular had heightened his anxiety to this extent. In the first fortnight of my stay in their home I thought it entirely understandable. We had no knowledge at that time of whether the Party or the Munich Gestapo would come looking for me. I was constantly expecting to hear from Tilla, by some circuitous route, that someone in Isartal had been asking questions about me or that there'd been a house search at her place or that of a neighbour, but nothing of that kind occurred. Frau Doktor Weiß [Schwarz] had told me she was under the impression I was thought no longer to be alive.

When people are so fearful it affects the nerves, and I can quite see why Gustav and Erna [Georg and Eva Fischer] would have been constantly on edge with mental strain. I'm very conscious of how much I owe them both, and it weighs on my mind more than I can say that I never had the right opportunity to express my immense gratitude to them both. I needed to set them free of my presence in their home as fast as possible.

Eva [Schmidt] arrived as planned in the evening of that Saturday. I can't begin to describe how much her visit meant to me. Over the last year she's become, next to Tilla, the person to whom I feel closest and I've never turned to her in vain. These two have lived with me through all the emotions and experiences that have oppressed me or given me cause for elation, and I have shared everything with them to the full. You can imagine what a comfort it was to have Eva sitting opposite me and to be able to tell her everything I'd been thinking and feeling and, more than anything, about the dreadful weight now bearing down on me to such an extent that I felt I could no longer carry on. Eva was of the same opinion that I needed to leave – but where should I go?

I suggested she pay a call on Maria [Eva Kunkel] and Irma on Sunday and talk it over with them. These two have a very extensive circle of friends and acquaintances and would perhaps know of someone who'd be willing to take me in. Eva knew the two women slightly and was keen to grasp this opportunity to discuss the matter with them. Like me, she didn't really hold out much hope but nonetheless when I went to bed that night my heart felt lighter than it had done in weeks.

Eva absolutely insisted on taking herself off somewhere for lunch on the Sunday, and that's when Gustav [Georg] finally exploded, something I had long been expecting and dreading. He said his constant anxiety and concern meant he could no longer sleep at night and that I had to leave at the earliest opportunity. I replied that I would do everything I could to bring this about including steps being taken that very afternoon by Eva herself. I asked him to speak to his acquaintance again about speeding along the Leonie Maier identification document. Anyone taking me in would be in considerably more danger if I still lacked the necessary papers. He promised to do all he could but also made it clear that it would be out of the question for me to stay with them until I had the document in my hands. He said that others must now bear the risk, just as they already had.

I recounted the conversation to Eva the moment she returned from lunch. She set off straight away to see Maria [Eva Kunkel] and Irma to ask if they might agree to take me in with immediate effect. For one thing no one in their building would recognise me as it was so many years since I'd last been a frequent visitor, and for another, I now looked very different indeed. I had lost all my previous plumpness and was now thin as a lathe. Eva had set off at half past one and just two hours later I heard via Erna [Eva Fischer] that I was to come over.

It felt so strange to be outside in the fresh air and among other people once more![27] The last time I had done this it had been summer, in the middle of August, and now all the trees were bare and there was a definite wintry feeling. It did me good to draw in deep breaths of the chill air. The bright lights of the U-Bahn terrified me so I opted for the tram. Up at the front with the driver I wouldn't run the risk of being seen and recognised by old acquaintances. In addition, I was wearing a thick black veil over my face, as if I were in mourning. Reaching the familiar old place in no time and without incident, I encountered no one on the communal staircase. I rang the bell to the apartment and the door opened straight away.

Eva was there with our two friends, as well as another old contact they had invited to join us as a source of advice. You'll remember a student of Eva Kunkel's called Gretchen,[28] I'm sure – she used to come and visit us in Isartal during our first few years there. It was a sign of how much I've altered in appearance that she barely recognised me, which under the current circumstances can only be welcome.

Something had occurred to Gretchen once she'd heard the summary of my own current situation. Not so long ago she'd been employed as secretary to a factory owner, who according to her description sounded a very special individual. He was sixty-seven, a bachelor, and owned a small factory near his apartment on Nollendorfplatz. She described him as the most ardent opponent of the Nazis of anyone she'd ever known and extraordinarily willing to help anyone in need. He treated his staff and workers like a father and they in turn were deeply attached to him. The only reason she'd left her post with him was that she'd been given the opportunity to return to her old job as office manager in a legal office, but said that she still goes back to help 'Uncle Karl' [Hans] every month with the bookkeeping as well as paying him more regular social calls. She told us he'd been looking for some time for a reliable older lady to see to his flat and laundry and wondered if he might take me on. There was plenty of space as the flat had four rooms.

'I'll telephone him straight away and tell him I've found someone to be his housekeeper!' she said eagerly.

The gentleman in question, Herr R. [Kollmorgen], answered the phone on the first ring. Gretchen put forward her idea, and he invited her to bring Frau Maier, as I now had to be known, over to meet him so that we could get the measure of one another. He was a genuine old Berlin gent and loved using the vernacular in its purest form! We set off immediately. It wasn't far so it was no time at all before he was opening the door and ushering us into his front room.

I left it to Gretchen to introduce me and tell him whatever was necessary about me and my state of affairs.

'She's been living with relatives for the last four months and needs to move on. They've become very anxious about the situation and in any case it's best to keep changing location. Frau Maier – or do you want to know her real name?' Herr Herr R. [Kollmorgen] gave a firm shake of the head, so Gretchen continued. 'Very well then – the less you know, the lighter your burden. Frau Maier is happy to carry out your housekeeping, to keep everything in order and do your mending. I remember you saying not so long ago that you were looking for someone to take on this sort of work. You won't, however, have been expecting that someone to want to live in.'

Herr R. [Kollmorgen] interjected at this point. 'That is absolutely no obstacle. We need discuss this no further. Frau Maier, may I now show you my apartment and the room that will be yours, then you'll know what you're taking on and where you'll be living. After that all you need do is tell me is when you want to move in.'

Well, that was the end of all my efforts to remain composed and the tears began to fall.

'Now, now, you poor soul,' came Herr R. [Kollmorgen]'s soothing voice. 'No harm in shedding a few tears, I'll be bound. It'd be a strange cove who didn't understand why you'd be all of aflutter just now, with what's been happening to you. Things'll change for the better in the end, you just mark my words!'

'Thank you, Herr R. [Kollmorgen], thank you so much,' was all I could manage at first, until I eventually came out with, 'but there's something else we need to bring up, something important. I've no food stamps.'

'Now, you're not to call me "Herr" – I'm "Uncle Karl" [Hans] to you, d'you hear? And I'd like to call you Little Maier, Maierchen, if that's all the same to you. The fact you've got no ration cards is neither here nor there to me. Don't you fret one bit! I buy on the black market without a scrap of conscience and get hold of whatever I can. Luckily I've plenty of good contacts. If I'm taking on my very own housekeeper then it's my duty to damn well feed her, eh, Gretchen?'

Gretchen warmly agreed, smiling at him with affection.

'Now, my dears, that's it with all the sentimental tosh! Let me show you around the flat, Maierchen. This room we're in, well, this is really the old drawing room – smoking room, if you will. See this big couch? Well, in an emergency that can serve as a bed, for one if not two, provided they're of the same gender or a married couple, of course.' Next he opened a sliding door. 'And this is the dining room, a real old-fashioned Berlin room with no windows, but you can air it by way of the drawing room if the door's left open a bit. Maierchen, I think you can pretty well see what needs doing here! I'm really not on top of things at home and keep ticking myself off over all this mess and clutter.'

He was not wrong. His beautiful Chippendale furniture was piled high with books, papers, newspapers and little glass phials. We went through into a hall with a huge wooden display case on the right, its shelves heaped higgledy-piggledy with all manner of objects. There'd be plenty for me to do here all right.

Next he opened a door to the left, smiling proudly as he did so. 'This is my holy of holies, Maierchen: my kitchen! I'm a passionate cook actually and I love baking – my favourite activity in any free time I can get. Sadly, the place doesn't look the way a good housewife would want it to.'

I was gazing round in sheer delight. Any woman would love this kitchen! It boasted every modern gadget you could possibly imagine. There was a powered mixer with a separate attachment for whisking egg whites and cream. I also saw a machine for grating raw vegetables, including cabbage, something that would make such wearisome tasks really quite enjoyable. A housewife could want for nothing in a kitchen like this!

All this equipment was displayed in a large, modern kitchen cupboard which in itself enhanced the room. There were enamelled steel cooking pots and pans of every shape and size. Oh, what a pleasure it would be to work in such a place! Uncle Karl [Hans] was watching closely as the different expressions flitted across my features and smiled at my obvious appreciation.

To my further delight he then unlocked a door alongside the kitchen to reveal two large electric refrigerators and a wine store on one side with a huge store cupboard and row upon row of shelving on the other. The latter boasted large glass storage jars full of ground rice, dried pasta and sugar, little glass jars full of all kinds of spices, as well as rows of canned fruit and vegetables. The highest level of shelving was home to soap and cleaning materials, including a whole pyramid of bars of Sunlight soap, good-quality washing powder, and even bath salts and fine soap for the bathroom. In the food cupboard I noticed plenty of cocoa, tea and coffee – all those things that now belonged only in the dreams of ordinary mortals.

'That's right, there are plenty of goodies here, as you can see, but I fear they won't last the war out,' said Uncle Karl [Hans]. 'I do hope that seeing this will help you feel you won't be suffering while living here.'

At the end of the hallway lay Uncle Karl's [Hans'] bedroom, through from the room he had assigned to me. It boasted all the essentials, so a lovely comfortable sofa, a big washstand and a wardrobe. Finally at the end came the bathroom, another precious sight to behold!

'I appreciate it's not ideal my needing to pass through this way, Maierchen, but I'm an early bird and will tiptoe so carefully you won't notice. Sleep as late as you want in the mornings and then you'll have the whole place to yourself!'

We left it such that I'd move in two days later, on the evening of 8 December, and then we bid one another goodbye.

Gretchen and I returned in high spirits to our friends who were still anxiously waiting for news. They were like children listening to a fairy tale. And wasn't it the truth? Wasn't this exactly like some wonderful kind of fantasy, where a complete and utter stranger was prepared to risk offering me food and shelter, and all with the utmost consideration and gentleness as if it were his total pleasure to do so?

Eva then accompanied me back to Erna and Gustav [Eva and Georg Fischer]. For Uncle Karl's [Hans'] sake we had decided to say the barest minimum regarding where I was to go next. When Eva took her leave of me, she admitted that finding such a favourable solution was like shaking off her worst nightmare.

I moved here on Tuesday evening. I can't tell you how this has bucked up my spirits no end! It does me so much good to have the day to myself. I find I can get started properly on what needs to be done, and then in the evenings Uncle Karl [Hans] is unstinting in his praise for the new sense of order and homeliness that is gradually making itself felt. We get on terrifically well and, for me, that sense of making myself useful and no longer being a burden to others is helping to restore my confidence and self-esteem.

'Well now, Maierchen, you look altogether different from when you first moved in, and I'll properly rejoice if you one day even mention having put on a little weight while living here. You're finding the meals bearable, then?'

What could I do but laugh and agree with all my heart? I really do believe I can recover here; the conditions are perfect.

It's gradually become clear to me why I grew quite so dreadfully depressed during those months with Erna and Gustav [Eva and Georg]. Erna [Eva] is a particularly ponderous woman, if truth be told, but also deeply melancholy and terribly withdrawn. She's completely absorbed with running the house, something she does with a conscientiousness that borders on the painful. As a result she has no time for anything else and hardly ever opens a book. She never goes to a concert or to the theatre. She and I are simply too different to develop any real kind of intimacy. Gustav [Georg], on the other hand, is completely taken up with his work and comes home worn out. Any dealings with this couple were not designed to cheer or divert me, all the more so as the silence and sense of isolation I felt in their home only intensified the severity of what I had already gone through. On top of all that, the feeling of being cut off from the rest of the world, of being imprisoned, only served to deepen my depression. Here, everything is quite different. I can move about freely, am no longer a burden and am getting back on my feet with Uncle Karl's [Hans'] generous and humorous way of going about all the normal routines of daily life.

By the way, we've fixed on a version of accounts that should cover all eventualities. If anyone should start to make trouble or ask too many questions, we're going to say that Uncle Karl [Hans] met me one day in the street. Uncle Karl [Hans] is the kind of man people trust implicitly, however odd the story might seem. Our particular narrative is that I've come from Düsseldorf to flee the bombing and arrived in Berlin with the intention of heading to a small private guest house I already knew, not far from Nollendorfplatz in Motzstrasse, but due to the blackout I couldn't find my way. I noticed Uncle Karl [Hans] parking his car nearby and went over to ask him the way to Motzstrasse. He kindly offered to drive me the short distance, we exchanged pleasantries on the way and it was clear to him that I needed somewhere to rest and recuperate. He therefore offered to put me up and, after a moment of hesitation, I gladly accepted. I asked him to waive the usual requirement of police registration as I was so fearful that my little flat in Düsseldorf would otherwise be taken away from me and used to house civilians bombed out of their own homes. To be honest, I doubted whether in an emergency anyone would actually believe this, but we just hoped such a situation would never actually arise. So far as Uncle Karl's [Hans'] friends and neighbours are concerned, I'm an old acquaintance to whom he has offered refuge. People have readily accepted this as his hospitality is legendary, and quite a few times a woman neighbour along with other acquaintances have said what a relief it is to see some signs of homeliness being imposed on his bachelor untidiness. As for me, I have thoroughly been enjoying the company of others again, and all the more so given the interesting and stimulating people here.

Uncle Karl [Hans] and I were further in agreement that Gretchen needed to be taken account of in our little fiction. Consequently, once I'd been here a couple of days, she came over by arrangement and we were formally introduced to one another. She and I fell into conversation and everyone present must have noticed the ease with which two such apparent strangers were talking with one another, and so it was suggested that Uncle Karl [Hans] ask Gretchen to come over more frequently.

Here too, I am to leave the building as little as possible. If I do go outside, I do so in darkness and with the thick mourning veil covering my face. I never use the U-Bahn or the city train because they're too brightly lit but instead take the tram and stand in the gloom on the front or rear platform. Once a week I telephone Erna [Eva Fischer], she previously declared herself willing to facilitate correspondence between myself and Eva. If she says she's looking forward to my visit, then I know she means there's a letter there for me, in which case I go that evening to collect it and also to remind Gustav [Georg] yet again about the identification document he said he'd arrange on my behalf. I'd be so glad to have this for Uncle Karl's [Hans'] sake, as it would offer both of us some measure of protection.

All in all, the world is looking a little less grey for me now that I'm here. It's people like Uncle Karl [Hans] who give us all the courage to carry on.

Siegfried's Diary

Oxford, 24 December 1942

This is my fourth Christmas Eve in England. The last time we spent Christmas as a family was 1938, in the wake of the hounding of Jews and destruction of buildings that November. We invested so much effort in trying to leave during the course of that year but with minimal success.

Today I long to be sure that Else is still staying at her sister's home.

I sense a glimmer of hope in the last letter, dated 20 November 1942, in which she indicates that she is soon to take up a new post. What am I to make of that? I can't ask her anything, and she can't tell me anything for the sake of her own safety, so all I can do is sit on my hands and wonder. [...]

It is now six months since I started this job and the most awkward part is that I still struggle with my English and don't understand much of what is going on around me. I have no proper home and cannot envisage ever finding one. At times my life can feel quite futile.

1943

Else's Diary

Berlin, 12 January 1943

Christmas passed very quietly. Uncle Karl [Hans] never was one for celebrations. He doesn't even mark his own birthday, the date of which is probably known only to a few select friends. As for me, I celebrated it regardless, equally quietly, all alone in the peace of my room.

Two occasions stood out for me that Christmas. First of all, both Tilla and Eva visited, which was an absolute joy for me. It would otherwise have been the first Christmas since you and the children went away that I'd have had to spend without Tilla, because even at Berg am Laim she'd find a way of stealing a bit of time with me in my room on Christmas Eve. Both these dear friends were pleased to see the calm and serene surroundings in which I was now living and visibly gaining in strength.

The significance of this Christmas was also down to a second particular event. Going to Erna [Eva Fischer] to collect Eva's most recent letter, I found that it brought not only good wishes from Annemarie, our Quaker friend, and news of a Christmas parcel to be brought to me by Eva, but also a request from a Quaker in Berlin for my address. This person had been a good friend of ours for years and was asking now for my written address, or better still my telephone number. She elaborated on how she might be of assistance if I needed to find somewhere else to stay or any other kind of support. Speaking obliquely she indicated that she knew much of what had befallen me over the last few months but wanted to see me and talk to me in person. On the strength of this, I made the call from a public telephone on my way back home to Uncle Karl's [Hans']. Frau Hopf[1] expressed delight on hearing from me and stated that she'd come and visit on the following day, 22 December.

She arrived punctually so we were able to make the most of the time and space afforded us within Uncle Karl's [Hans'] flat. I had, of course, secured Uncle Karl's [Hans'] permission to receive a visitor, as I did on any other occasion. She wanted to hear about everything I'd gone through and promised to contact more of her friends on my behalf in case I should ever be in urgent need of new accommodation. As she was leaving she told me she'd be taking a Christmas break near Berlin with her husband and daughter, adding that she'd be meeting up with other friends there, people who might help me, and that she'd be sure to call on me again around mid-January as soon as she was back. I'm glad this friendship has been revived, not only for the high regard in which I hold her as a person but also for her willingness to help and her wide circle of acquaintances. I felt a moral obligation to ensure that I had other accommodation in reserve should anything go wrong. Never again would I let myself be forced into a drastic move with no alternative in place.

Uncle Karl [Hans] seemed a little agitated when he came home last night and wasted no time in telling me why.

Over our supper, he announced, 'I need to talk to you about something, Maierchen. One of my longest-serving employees came to me today asking for advice. This lady lives in Grunewald and the apartment building opposite hers was bombed yesterday. A number of residents were consequently allocated to her apartment, where, as I was already aware, she has for some time been hiding a young Jewish girl. We can't know for how long she'll be expected to shelter her neighbours and as she doesn't know exactly who these people are, she feels it only right and proper for this young girl to go somewhere else for the time being. She enquired as to whether I might know of a safe place, and I immediately offered my own flat. Susi [Susanne Mendel] – that's the name of the girl – is coming here this evening as it's better she drops out of sight from where she is. The general confusion after the bombing made it all right for her to be somewhere she shouldn't be during the day as everyone had their minds set on other matters. If questioned she could simply have said she'd been visiting and couldn't get home after the incident. So, Maierchen, you're going to have a companion – an agreeable one, I trust. It'll all be fine as far as you're concerned, and I really had no choice in the matter.'

I was in full agreement, of course, and put aside a good portion of our evening meal for her, then set about making up the couch in the rather splendid study for this girl who, for the time being, was to join me in my precarious situation.

The doorbell rang shortly afterwards. Uncle Karl [Hans] went to answer and ushered in Susi, who was aged around twenty, of medium height, with light blond hair, blue eyes and a gorgeous complexion. She didn't look Jewish at all. She came across as very shy at first, fighting back the tears, but Uncle Karl's [Hans'] kind and gently humorous manner eased her through the difficult first half hour or so, and then Susi quickly collected herself and regained her natural exuberance. Even on this first day I had plenty of occasion to talk with her in depth as she seemed to trust me from early on. She and her mother had made the decision to go underground – to use the technical term – a few weeks earlier when all the signs were pointing to their imminent deportation. Her mother had found accommodation with a friend and up till now Susi had been staying with Uncle Karl's [Hans'] employee, whose son was around her age and already known to her.

Susi's fiancé is half Jewish and is in Palestine, but she herself is in constant contact with his parents in Berlin. They help her and her mother with food of all sorts, but can't take them in as too many people in the building would recognise them. It's true that her future in-laws aren't themselves directly under threat as the fiancé's mother is 'Aryan', but they have to be extremely careful. Susi made clear from the outset that she wouldn't be needing food from Uncle Karl [Hans] as she and her mother have plenty of contacts. Having two mouths to feed is one thing, but three is quite another, so I think Uncle Karl [Hans] was pleased to hear that. People are constantly making requests of him and whatever he can do to help, he never refuses. In true comradely spirit, dear Susi has already offered me a share of her provisions, and I have thanked her most warmly but added that this can only be if she herself has enough.[2]

Berlin, 24 January 1943

A couple of days ago Frau Hopf, the Quaker lady, was here again and on hearing what she had to say I found myself marvelling all over again at the wondrous ways in which people are helping us.

She'd been in R. together with her daughter and quite a crowd of the girl's young Quaker friends, men and women alike. One evening she had related my story to one of the young women and the two of them had put their heads together regarding emergency accommodation for me. So this young Quaker woman, Hella, had then sent for her boyfriend, Peter, to see if he had any advice on the matter.[3] Frau Hopf had gone on to talk a little more about me – and Peter, on hearing her mention my real name, was immediately all ears! He was delighted to tell Frau Hopf and Hella that he knew me and my family from our years in Isartal.

'Well, this just has to be our old friend Buddeli!'

In his delight and surprise he referred to me by the pet name our own little Peter had innocently given me when he was first learning to talk! You'll have guessed already that this young Quaker man was none other than Peter Merkel [Heilmann].[4]

I can't remember whether I ever wrote to tell you how hard it was at the beginning of my time in Berlin not to allow myself a visit to the home of his mother Lene and his Aunt Kläre, our old friends. This was made all the harder as I was about to learn that Kläre had passed away just before the threatened deportation.

Now she was back, Frau Hopf was eager to convey Peter Merkel's [Heilmann's] good wishes and to say that he would be getting in touch with me at the earliest opportunity. His mother had gone to friends in Freiburg[5] to convalesce following a debilitating disorder of the gall bladder and wouldn't be back until March, but that Peter would tell her all about me once he and I had caught up with news.

You can imagine how much I'm longing for him to visit. Frau Hopf said he'd grown into a splendid young man who, like his mother and older sister, Eva, and with scant regard for their own situation as half 'Aryans', has given sanctuary to a whole series of Jewish people in hiding and done so with exemplary courage and commitment.

But there's yet more to relate – Susi and I are no longer alone here. As of yesterday there are, just think, five of us! Allow me to introduce our new companions. First, the oldest – that's Lotte [Dr Charlotte Bamberg].[6] She's around my age, in her fifties, of medium height, rather stocky, her face lively and clever, with dark hair and eyes; all notably Jewish characteristics, I'd say. Before all this she held exceptionally high office at the Ministry of Commerce, a responsible position to which she was eminently suited, given her academic background in political science, her knowledge of foreign languages and overall ability. In more recent years she learned how to make quilts and eiderdowns while living with relatives and so now applies her exceptional skills to the practical arts as well. On hearing alarming rumours of the impending transportations, she had turned to Uncle Karl [Hans] for advice – she'd come across him several years ago via a mutual friend who's now resident in America. He'd immediately offered her sanctuary in his flat.[7]

The other two are a young married couple. Herbert's around thirty and comes from Jena where he trained as an optometrist and was kept on for as long as the firm was permitted Jewish employees. Back then, these two had turned to Uncle Karl [Hans] as a result of his business connections with Zeiss, asking if he might have work for Herbert. Uncle Karl [Hans] had immediately agreed. Herbert had stayed on until all remaining Jews were removed from private commerce in Berlin as well. Uncle Karl [Hans] values Herbert as a man as well as an optometrist and had stayed in contact with him and his young wife ever since his forced dismissal.

His twenty-three-year-old wife is called Evchen. She's pretty as a picture, wonderfully vivacious and with a naturally cheery nature that's quite infectious. Herbert provides the calm counterpoint to her spirited contributions when in company! Whenever we're all eating together and Lotte throws in one of her drily entertaining remarks making Susi shriek with laughter, Uncle Karl [Hans] casts a long look around the table, smiling benignly as he does so, and any outsider looking in would see a contented household sharing a meal. Having said that, Evchen knows only too well what a perilous situation she, her husband and the rest of us are living in. But we all know that brooding and complaining will neither change nor improve things, and find ourselves in this little community that's somehow liberating and uplifting, all the more so since the five of us get on wonderfully well and have true respect for one another.

There are endless topics for conversation. We are all keen to hear details of each other's story so far, where everyone comes from, what we've all lived through, and our plans for the future. Evchen, for one, worked from the age of seventeen in her Uncle's huge clothing empire and knew that her husband, Herbert, was at high risk as he was of an age to be conscripted. Before they came here, she had made arrangements for their illegal entry into Sweden and it had almost worked out. They'd been allocated two places in a truck that was due to smuggle out twenty people in total, but then Evchen had withdrawn at the last moment. It turned out to have been a lucky move. The truck was intercepted, and it's not hard to guess what happened to those on board. On hearing about this failed attempt, Uncle Karl [Hans] had offered his assistance, asking if I might be in on the plan. She'd agreed whereupon Uncle Karl had put me in touch with her. Before she and Herbert came to us, I had already met them several times.

We all know that such a gathering of people living in secret in the same dwelling represents the utmost danger for each one of us, but especially so for Uncle Karl [Hans], leaving his flat 'empty' all day long as he does. We must all try and find somewhere else to stay and as soon as possible. The only one with any realistic prospect of doing so is Susi, however, firstly because of her connections and secondly because she's in possession of a proof of identity. It's an authentic work pass issued by the Deutsche Arbeitsfront[8] and bearing her photograph, which thereby gives her total freedom of movement. Otherwise there's not one single identity paper between the rest of us at the moment. Lotte had bought herself a false identity card, in the same way as I had, and yet we both still lacked the requisite photograph and official stamp. Each time I've called on Gustav

[Georg] he's indicated that something better was in the offing but his contact has let us down more than once already.

Uncle Karl [Hans] has given up all his comforts to ensure everyone has somewhere to sleep. On this particular Sunday he's shown me his factory and the basic bedroom he's always kept there for when he has to work until late and needs to rest. He's now set it up for use over the duration of our stay.

Tomorrow the rest of us will have to spend the day away from the flat so as not to be spotted by the long-standing cleaning lady, Frau Schmidt. We've talked it through together and decided that she's not to catch sight of any of the four of us, given the great thoroughness with which she cleans the whole place. Granted, she's reliable in her political views – Uncle Karl [Hans] would never tolerate a Nazi supporter in his home – but the fewer people who know of the presence of so many guests in the flat, the better and safer for all concerned, clearly. Early in the morning, any belongings that might reveal our presence here will be stowed safely out of sight in the storeroom to which I hold the key, and which Frau Schmidt only cleans every couple of months.

Susi's going over to her mother, Herbert has an aunt with an 'Aryan' husband, Evchen will look up a girlfriend and Lotte has a contact who previously did odd jobs for her – a willing and energetic fellow who'd do anything for the 'Fräulein Doktor'.

Frau Schmidt always arrives at ten and stays until five. I myself was introduced to her by Uncle Karl [Hans] when I first moved in. My impression is that she is fully in agreement with my being there.

Letter from Else to Eva Schmidt

Berlin, 26 January 1943

My dearest Eva

Very brief as I'm so short of time today. Well, this week I'm lodging with a family and helping to reduce the mountain of mending and darning that's piled up while the wife's been ill.

I've heard from Lilli (Else) and am in constant touch with her. By the way she's asked whether you might see if Tilla could post on the field glasses she left at her place in the summer. They're in a leather case. Would she be so kind as to address it to the landlady and send it by registered post?[9]

Siegfried's Diary

Oxford, 3 February 1943

The last two weeks have brought changes that could still spell an end to the war in Europe this year. Can we now be sure of some better news for Else? I have heard nothing since early December.

The Russian Front is edging west and approaching Rostov – Stalingrad has been cleared of German occupation.

The tenth anniversary of the Nazi takeover has passed with no speech from Hitler. A speechless Hitler? For once conspicuous by his absence? Definitely a wrong move on his part as the gutter press are now spreading rumours of his presumed demise. Oh, the shame this one man heaps on Germany, time and time again.

This kind of deluded adoration, akin to what a child might feel for a favourite teacher, is something known only in Germany, that is for sure. It renders impossible any kind of rational evaluation of the past or sensible planning for the future as it encompasses a complete failure to recognise and acknowledge any level of superiority that is not specifically German greatness! Generation after generation has been brought up with this mentality shaped by legends and lies, with no proper knowledge of the world as it exists in reality, thereby adding fuel to its delusions of grandeur and supremacy and leading to its downfall. The underdog has at last turned on its master, and one of the principal tasks in a new and civilised world will be the re-education of all those who have fed, or succumbed to, this woeful delusion.

Else's Diary

Berlin, 18 February 1943

There are five of us still! With each passing day, the sense of living on a volcano that could erupt at any moment is growing stronger and stronger. Susi is leaving us in a few days' time as she's found somewhere else to live. And we're now worrying about food supplies. At the beginning Herbert, Evchen and Lotte had Jewish ration coupons and could at least get hold of basics like bread, fats, sugar and other staples, although not without taking risks.

But we were unified in our belief that we five needed to get by with food without always relying on Uncle Karl [Hans] for help. Susi has a good contact – how she met him, I've no idea but that's neither here nor there – who works in a large greengrocers in the central market at Alexanderplatz. We all know him simply as Walter.

He came over to see Susi during our first few days together, bringing with him a good quantity of vegetables together with the miracle of a few oranges and lemons! We all chatted for quite some time, and I took a real liking to him. He's pretty much in his best years – a Communist who's already spent four years in a concentration camp for his political beliefs and survived to tell the tale. Married, doting father to a twelve-year-old boy, he found work early on in the war in the fruit and veg place and when the owner was conscripted he stayed on in a position of trust, fitting for a man of such deserving character.

Once he realised the predicament in which Susi and I found ourselves, he said straight away that he'd be able to supply us with enough potatoes and other vegetables, fruit as well on occasion, and would even be able to come up with meat and fish by bartering some of his vegetable supplies. I asked him a couple of gentle questions to check whether this would put him in any danger, but he soon brushed off any concerns.

'My boss lady's a good soul – she's no Nazi and based on what I've told her, without giving away any detail, of course, she quite understands your circumstances. Because I'm staff I can buy stuff at a lower price and no one asks what I'm going to do with it. It's a real pleasure if I can do anything to help you and Susi. I know just how it feels to have those bastards in brown on your tail.'

Walter kept his word even when our numbers grew from two to five. We have more than enough fresh stuff and quite a bit of other food also comes our way, all from Walter. Yesterday evening, however, he had to come and say his goodbyes. He showed us the conscription papers he'd been sent, ordering him to report to Heuberg for military training as a soldier – second class, of course, due to his political history. What a blow that was. We hear so many stories about the way these soldiers are treated and how they are sent to the worst places at the Front. But Walter speaks only of having four years in concentration camp behind him and thus being optimistic that he'll survive the rest of the war. For all of us it felt like saying farewell to a dear friend when we bid him goodbye.

After a recent visit to her in-laws, Susi came back full of news of their tenants. It turned out these were a Slovak couple, a major and his wife belonging to the Diplomatic Corps. This meant they were not subject to the same rationing as ordinary mortals and could use their diplomatic pass to get unlimited quantities of food that could then be used for bartering. They'd managed to come by masses of bed linen in exchange for butter and coffee.

'And now the Major is after a pair of field glasses, preferably Zeiss or Goerz.'

In a flash I recalled that our field glasses were still back in Isartal, although I should really have handed them in a long time ago. Since early summer 1942, Jews had been banned from owning field glasses, opera glasses or cameras, along with certain electrical appliances such as hotplates, immersion heaters, cooking pots and so on, and were required to hand them in without receiving any compensation at all.

I gave Susi the little job of finding out via her in-laws what the Major would offer by way of foodstuffs, preferably butter or some other fat, for a pair of field glasses that had cost one hundred and fifty Reichsmark new in 1914. A couple of days later I heard back via Susi that the Major would very much like these particular field glasses and would give me four and a half pounds of butter and some real coffee in return. I really had no idea if this was a fair exchange, but Herbert and Lotte reckoned I could find it acceptable, and they know about these things.

So I wrote to Tilla but put Susi's 'Aryan' mother-in-law's details as the sender, asking her to despatch the field glasses to that address. When I think now that the Slovak Major paid only 1.80 Reichsmark for the butter, I reckon he got those field glasses very cheaply! But for us any fat at all in our diet is so important, while a set of field glasses would be a luxury and quite superfluous to our needs.

Peter Merkel [Heilmann] still hasn't come. On my most recent visit to my Cousin Erna [sister Eva], she told me she'd heard from Frau Hopf that Peter was actually in hospital. I was deeply shocked and hoped this wasn't another way of saying he'd been arrested. But Frau Hopf made it clear that I shouldn't enquire any further nor phone her, that her hands were tied and that there was nothing further to be done. I may have to wait a long time before I hear anything more.

It was on this visit to my cousin [sister] that I did at last receive the identity card I'd been after for so long. That was another huge disappointment, as the stamp was of such poor quality that even an amateur would spot it was fake – a whole lot of money, in other words, wasted on something that couldn't even be used for its intended purpose. Uncle Karl [Hans] has a reliable contact who confirmed it would be extremely dangerous to attempt any use of this document. This has all left me thoroughly downcast. I see no way ahead at all.

Nonetheless, it does make it a little easier to live through these low periods in the company of like-minded sufferers than to have to do so alone. When I see how plucky and cheerful Evchen is the whole time even though she and Herbert are still looking – in vain thus far – for a route out of Germany, and how hard Lotte tries not to show her anxiety about the apparent hopelessness of her own case, then I find I can pull myself together.

Berlin, 28 February 1943

Yesterday at Erna's [Eva's] I hoped to pick up some news about Peter Merkel [Heilmann] from Frau Hopf, but she hadn't written. On my way home I was seized by that special courage born of desperation and on the spur of the moment went to a public telephone in the U-Bahn station to get in touch with the Merkels [Heilmanns].

They still had the same old familiar telephone number but I tried twice with no success as the line was engaged. A young girl was waiting to use the phone after me, so I let her go ahead and carried on waiting. At first she had as little success with the machine as I'd had. She replaced the receiver, stepped out of the booth and with a smile gave me the handbag I'd left inside by mistake. After my second unsuccessful attempt and the end of her own conversation, she came out once more and this time handed me my umbrella. With great kindness she said, 'Check around more carefully next time, madam! I'm off home now.'

As I tried for a third time to make the call, I noticed I was shaking. This time I got through. A young man answered at the other end.

'It's Buddeli,' I said flatly.

'Hello, Buddeli, Peter here. You must have been wondering where I've been. I know I've not been in touch, but I've been flat out in bed with such a rotten cold – it got me good and proper this one. Don't worry, I've not forgotten you're my first port of call when I'm up and about again.'

My voice noticeably brighter now, I said to him, 'I can't tell you how glad I am to hear your voice. Is it at home you've been so sick then? I'd heard you were in hospital and was frightened that something terrible had happened to you.'

He knew straight away what I meant and gave a gentle laugh. 'No, nothing like that, Buddeli, someone must have got that wrong. I've been here at home the whole time – bit of a caper with my lungs, couldn't shift it, but I'm on the mend now. We didn't write to Mama about how bad I was as she needs to get better herself and she'd only have been worrying without being able to do anything for me. But how are you? That matters more than what's going on with me.'

I replied that I was well, and we left it that I would call him regularly every few days in order to keep abreast of his recovery. He suggested telephoning me but I declined. The five of us had all agreed that we wouldn't take or receive any calls at Uncle Karl's [Hans'].

Stepping out of the public phone booth I noticed how light-headed I felt all of a sudden, but remembered also the girl's friendly warning about not leaving anything behind! So Peter really had been ill, seriously ill, that much was clear from all the time he'd had to spend in bed, something the doctor would not have insisted on had it not been essential. After all, every worker had long since been required not to miss days of work unless it was a case of serious illness. Whatever the facts, he was free and had not been picked up by the Gestapo, something I'd been fearing for weeks. My cousin Erna [sister Eva] must have misunderstood Frau Hopf during their telephone conversation. None of that mattered now. What did matter was the hope that now stirred within me again that with Peter's help, I might still find a way out.

At home, everyone in 'the family' as Uncle Karl [Hans] called the five of us, noticed my excitement and at last I could tell them exactly what had been worrying me and how my hopes were up once more.

'Oh, I'd be so happy for you, Maierchen, if you could find a good place to go to,' said Evchen warmly, placing her hand over mine. 'It's such a miracle that we've all got this far.'

We heard the door and in came Uncle Karl [Hans], greeting us all with great affection. 'I have to say it warms the cockles of my heart to come home and find you all at the table! I thought of something today for when all this shenanigans is finally over. What better way of having some proof of my personal opposition to the Nazis than having my portrait painted with the five of you? It would be such a lovely memory of our time together. But where would I find a suitable artist? That's the real obstacle, I fear.'

We couldn't help but laugh.

'There's no need to have yourself immortalised with us, Papa,' said Evchen in her best and most flattering voice. 'I'm sure we'd all love a picture like that, but maybe one day we can all find a way of repaying you for everything you've done. Now that's something we'd all agree to!'

Uncle Karl [Hans] shrank from all displays of emotion and muttered something in reply, then said cheerfully, 'And don't forget I've come home hungry as a hunter and fancy words won't fill my belly!'

Still laughing happily, Susi and Evchen bustled off into the kitchen.

Berlin, 8 March 1943

Peter Merkel [Heilmann] has just been here. What a tall, handsome young man he is now and, even more importantly, how right-thinking and clever! He's certainly mature beyond his twenty years.

He told me all about his mother and siblings at first, but then talked mostly about his Aunt Kläre's final days. I heard how everything had been made ready for her to depart in secrecy. Peter himself had travelled to Freiburg and made the necessary arrangement through his friends there. But when he went to her home – she'd not been able to live with them for some time as others in the building had been deeply offended at the presence of a Jewish woman – on the morning they'd agreed, ready to accompany her to the station, he found her dead in bed. She'd left a note explaining that she'd taken her own life because she hadn't felt able to summon the strength to go through with an escape into a life on the run. Her note begged Lene and the children – whom she'd adored – to forgive her and let her rest in peace.

'Aunt Kläre never got over Father's death in the concentration camp after years of torment. I'd say the death knell was sounding as early as spring 1940,' explained Peter.

He then spoke about their mother's harsh routine, working half the day in an armaments factory and then taking care of the house and meals for everyone else. His sister Eva holds a demanding post as a laboratory assistant and gets home late and tired. Meanwhile, the younger brother works as a farmhand in Schleswig-Holstein and Brigitte, the baby of the family, is due to finish school at Easter and then has to do a duty year of agricultural work.

'But what about you, Buddeli? Tell me how you are – I want to know everything.'

He looked shocked when I said there were five of us living 'underground' in the flat.

'That won't do, Buddeli, that really won't do long-term. You need to get out of here at the earliest opportunity. I'd love to say to come to us but we've already got two people hiding out with us, and they're staying until Mum comes back. I'm sure we could find room for you in an emergency though.'

I declined. 'That would be no different from here, as there'd be three of us at your place and that's too many. No, I'll stay put here until your people have left and your mother's back, and then if I'm permitted to come to you, I'll be very grateful indeed. I won't want to stay too long, as that'd make things dangerous for you too. I'd much rather just get out of Berlin altogether. Might it be possible for me to go to your friends in Freiburg? Being that close to the Swiss border would be lovely. Do you think I'll get the chance to get to Switzerland eventually?'

Peter gave a nod. 'Rest assured that I'll do everything in my power to help you get over there. That'll take time, however, and at the moment I don't have the contacts. There are people in Freiburg who'd be glad to take you in. Let's talk it over some more once you're at home with us.'

As we said goodbye, he added, 'Listen, if anything happens here, come to us straight away. We'll sort something out.'

Berlin, 24 March 1943

I've been at the Merkels [Heilmanns] since the day before yesterday. Lene let me know she'd be back on the morning of the 22nd and that I should move in on the evening of the same day.

Saying goodbye to the 'family' and Uncle Karl [Hans] wasn't easy. The circumstances we've all been living under create the strongest of bonds and far more quickly than you'd otherwise find. Nonetheless, my departure does mean that those staying on are at less risk and Uncle Karl [Hans] can reclaim his own bedroom. I'll go over and see them all from time to time.

Setting eyes on my old friend Lene again stirred up so many painful memories for the pair of us that we were both reduced to tears. My physical appearance upset her too.

'My dear, you look thoroughly underfed and so much older.'

I did protest a little. 'You're seeing me now that I'm well again – it's a good thing you didn't see me before. I have recovered quite considerably with Uncle Karl [Hans].'

The kindness of everyone was so touching, and I truly felt they were glad I was there. I'll be able to take a lot of the work off Lene's shoulders, and she's grateful for that.

Yesterday evening, when the whole family was gathered together, we discussed my plans. Everyone was in full agreement that I should get out of Berlin and go to Freiburg once I was in possession of a watertight identity card. That was my goal and they all approved. Once again the hopeless card I had already was passed from hand to hand with everyone saying the same – there was no way it would pass muster.

Lene was first to give her opinion. 'If we can't find anything better than this, we'll get you a company identity card with a photograph on it and a vacation pass from the same firm to go along with that. And the third thing you absolutely need is a clothing ration card. You have to present one of those during any period of convalescence after an illness. The duration of your stay has to be marked on it too. The first two things I can get from our firm if you can't get hold of them anywhere else.'

'That won't be necessary,' said Peter, breaking in. 'My girlfriend, Hella, can sort all that out. She's the company secretary where she works and has access to all the right forms. And I'll talk to Belter about the clothing card.'

This nickname had been given to a young Frenchman sent to Germany as a forced labourer at Peter's place of work. In French his proper name sounded like 'Belter'. He enjoyed great popularity with everyone. Belter had fingers in plenty of pies on the black market, more for the sake of a bit of economic sabotage than for any material gain. 'He'll be able to get hold of food stamps for you, I hope, and I'll speak to him about a clothing card first thing in the morning.'

By the way, I must also just tell you that the plan for the field glasses worked out in the end and turned up two and a quarter kilos of butter and a hundred and twenty-five grams of real coffee. The butter will come in instalments only, so one pound per week. I shared out the first two pounds with the 'family' and the rest will be used here.

It's after the event now but I simply must tell you about the worst bombing we've had in Berlin since the war started. It was on 1 March, late in the evening. The alarm sounded at around half past nine. The five of us were all at home, but Uncle Karl [Hans] was working late at the factory, as was usual at the beginning and end of any month.

The first bombs started to fall immediately the alarm sounded. They seemed really close by. Even more frightening than the sound of the bombs was the harsh and constant chatter of the big anti-aircraft guns located centrally at the zoo. Our building wasn't particularly robust, offered no cellar for us to shelter in, shook noticeably and all the windowpanes rattled, but we got all the windows open fast enough to stop them breaking as happened in neighbouring flats. And we could afford some measure of relief at the lack of an air-raid shelter as seeking it out would only have exposed us to the scrutiny of the other residents.

During this one and all the other bombing raids, I noticed how I felt no fear of all the awful booms and crashes, as though I were merely some objective observer with no involvement in the scene. We had decided to stay together in the beautiful main room as it ran from the front to the back of the building and was therefore the best protected. From time to time Herbert and I would dart into the darkened study to peep out on to the street.

It wasn't long before we saw the sky aglow and thick smoke billowing from a building opposite. The glow grew brighter – clearly there was a huge fire somewhere nearby. Through the open window we felt that sinister roar of the warm wind that heralds a serious blaze.

Shouts rang out as people hurried along the street, small flames growing as they licked around their ankles. It was only later that we heard this was phosphorus. People didn't yet know much about its insidious dangers at that time nor about enveloping the fire in wet cloths. Observed from the second storey of our building the scene came across as unreal and ghostly, all the more so with the accompaniment of the ack-ack guns, the cries of the people caught outside and the buzzing aircraft. After about forty minutes it was over and the all clear sounded.

We telephoned Uncle Karl [Hans] and were relieved to hear his voice. He promised to come home immediately and told us that Winterfeldtplatz was on fire and a whole row of houses in Gleditschstrasse had been badly hit. Buildings around Prager Platz had collapsed. Later we heard of even greater damage in many different parts of the city.

This attack gave the people of Berlin a real shock and a hint of what was to come. That evening they scurried along the streets even more frantically than usual to get home before the next alarm. There was a lot of impatient pushing and shoving at tram stops and all the stations, whether for the U-Bahn or regular trains. Faces were more serious, more anxious, grim in fact, and all the normal community spirit had fallen by the wayside.

There's one story in particular that I want to tell you, and it's about the woman who owned that grocery store where Uncle Karl [Hans] shopped for years, buying all manner of things no longer available to ordinary mortals. Well, her home and her shop were both in Gleditschstrasse, although in separate buildings, and both were badly hit. She herself was thought to be missing along with most of the others from her block. The cellar was destroyed so the people were presumed lost.

Two days later they all turned up, exhausted and grimy with soot, having climbed out of a different cellar some streets away. They had feared their own cellar would collapse under the bombardment and so broke through into the neighbouring building and then worked their way from basement to basement. Eventually they had found themselves in what must have been the underground storage area of a food shop. It held enough canned goods and wine to satisfy their hunger and thirst before they made their way up and out of the last cellar on the street, keeping a close lookout as they emerged.

I had never much liked the woman who owned the grocery, and Uncle Karl [Hans] wasn't too keen either, but she recounted this tale in great detail and he then passed it on to all of us.

At Prager Platz almost everything's gone apart from one or two residential buildings. As I went by on the tram I saw a girl hanging out washing on the second-floor balcony of a building that was somehow still intact. Set against the surrounding ruins, it came across as quite grotesque.

Letters from Else to Eva Schmidt

Berlin, 27 March 1943

My dearest

Since Monday I've been giving a bit of neighbourly help to some acquaintances here. It's quite good fun and I'm glad to be able to assist. It's likely that I'll stay here until Easter or soon after, and then I want to accompany Anni[10] to South Germany.

Do write to her when you can. The address is Magdalena Heilmann, Blücherstrasse 65, Entrance on Brachvogelstrasse.

39. Magdalena (Lene) Heilmann (1894–1986), date unknown.

Berlin, 18 April 1943

My dearest

You can imagine quite what a state Annemarie's news has thrown me into. It's truly agonising waiting to hear still if the sanatorium will prove suitable for Anni. Even if she can get to Fr[eiburg], it's still not a proper place of convalescence with all the facilities her weakened condition demands. And you yourself know only too well how difficult it is these days to find a suitable place of rest and recuperation for someone so fragile, particularly given her need of a doctor's care, something which is absolutely essential.

Siegfried's Diary

Oxford, 7 April 1943

A few days ago Arthur Rewald forwarded a letter from Alice in Lisbon. The only news is that Else had written to Alice to inform her of Martin Rosenberg's death on 21 December 1942. This is a sign of life at least, although it relates only to early January 1943. It sounds as though Else is still in Berlin and had written from there to Henny Rewald about Martin's death. Sadly it appears that Henny herself has since died after a long struggle with a nervous disorder. She and her husband were always the lynchpin when it came to facilitating the smooth passage of correspondence via Alice.

I received a card from Alice today, dated 2 February! It has taken a very long time to wend its way to me but brings no further news of Else. So can I still cling to the belief that Else survived those critical last months of 1942 and is living in relative tranquillity? Is she working? Doing what exactly and where? Maybe in Georg Fischer's business? [...]

Picking up again on the progress of the war, the Russian advance to the west has halted with a setback at Kharkov, while in North Africa there has been slow but sure success for the Allies. On top of that there has been increased aerial bombardment of a variety of targets, including Germany (Berlin Tempelhof), France (St Nazaire) as well as Paris itself, Antwerp and Kiel.

Oxford, 1 May 1943 (Else's 52nd birthday)

My love, I have thought of you every waking moment of this day and have only this lifeless notebook to confide in. Oh, how I wish I could let you know that you are always in my thoughts! I hope that you, my dearest, understand that it is only the barrier thrown up by this war that prevents messages getting through to you from me. May you never doubt that you are an unwavering presence in my mind. The last thing Alice told me was that you are well but suffering some sort of distress, and that was perhaps back in around January and February. Does that mean forced labour in a factory, on your feet for hours amid deafening machinery?

So, what else is there to tell? I've had a note from Hanna reminding me that it's Mama's birthday, and she's wondering how on earth you'd be spending it? Your children too, you see, always have you in their thoughts – and not just on this special day, but every day. Peter spoke of you when I saw him just now on his way to the May Day celebrations with those lively and energetic Austrians he knows here. There was a speech from a British trade unionist, followed by a drama performance in which Peter himself took part.

How will this situation find resolution? All I want is to think of you, my love, to focus on hopes of our joyful reunion, and never to forget for one minute that you are enduring far worse than me, both physically and mentally, in constant uncertainty of where on earth the next day might take you.

I don't want to think of my advancing years and am determined to control the excessive emotion that age can sometimes bring. My lack of free time makes any unexpected chore or repair very hard to get done, leading to a certain degree of personal stress and irritation, neither of which are at all helpful when calm is required. I do my best to keep at bay a constant buzz of anxiety over maintaining the bare essentials of daily living – if I can just manage that, it will help my need for inner calm. The job leaves me quite worked up at times, particularly when I make errors, and that's largely still down to my poor level of English. I'm just not cut out for the world of business – hard for an old dog to learn new tricks, you might say! Something more along the lines of my previous occupation would suit me so much better.

I find myself hoping that the war in Tunis will quickly move in the right direction, enough to facilitate a new push into Europe from the north, south or south-east.

I noticed today that the trade union speaker referred to the need for action on a second front.

Else's Diary

Berlin, 18 May 1943

Peter came home triumphant one evening recently, calling out the moment he arrived in the hall.

'Buddeli, guess what I've got!'

'I simply can't imagine,' I said. 'Has Belter got hold of some margarine I can take to the "*famille*"?'

'Yes, you can have that as well if you want me to order it, but what I have here is the clothing card you've been needing so badly! It's a real one even, and wasn't exorbitant. Here you are!'

Lost for words I took it from him. It was tatty – a bit grubby, to be honest. Whoever owned it must have been in dire need of cash for them to sell it. The bearer's name was Martha Schröder, with the date of birth given as 20 October 1906.

'Peter, what a magnificent chap you are!' I shouted with joy, flinging my arms round him. 'And as for Belter, he can get hold of absolutely anything, as far as I can see!'

'I'll have a peck on both cheeks then! One for me and one for him!' He was bursting with delight.

Then Lene called from the living room. 'What's going on out there? The rest of us want to know what you're both so thrilled about!'

There followed a swift explanation. 'But, Peter, listen . . . Buddeli, I don't want to sound rude – but who's going to believe you were born in 1906? That's fifteen years later than the real date!'

'No, we don't expect anyone to go along with that,' explained Peter good-naturedly. 'It's all been thought through. We couldn't have wished for a better number than 1906. Just look at the nought – that easily turns into a nine. And the first nine can be made into an eight. A few measly years of difference between 1891 and 1896, well, that's nothing, and because the name, address and date of birth are in ink that's a little faded, any changes can be made without being noticeable. But most of all, I just love this name – Martha Schröder. Such a nice name, and much better than Leonie Maier, wouldn't you all agree?'

We certainly did.

'It's just the photograph missing now,' said Eva Merkel [Heilmann], 'and then you have everything you need, Buddeli. Well, I've had an idea about that. Shall we talk it over now? My friend's been telling me about two women being 'housed' at her place – they've been trying to get postal identity cards for themselves. I asked something about these and apparently they're as good as any national identity card and valid wherever you might need personal identification. On top of that you usually need a birth certificate but that can sometimes be disregarded if, for example, the man or woman who delivers your post is able to identify the person who wants the postal identity card.

'What we'll therefore do over the next ten to twelve days or so is send Buddeli a couple of registered letters. Buddeli, you'll need to receive them, you know, in person, and when you see our nice postwoman for maybe the third time or so, tell her you'd like to talk to her about what to do in the future. Tell her you'll often be getting registered letters, sometimes with cash remittances, and at the moment it's all quite easy because you're on leave from work and can receive all the post yourself. You can say that your period of leave will be over soon and your working hours are so awkward that the post office is always closed when you're free. Our postwoman is terribly kind and understanding and will be sure to say, 'That's easy to solve – just get a postal identity card and your landlady or anyone trustworthy you care to ask can receive or collect any post on your behalf.'

'Eva, that's a truly magnificent plan!' I said. 'Say no more – we've got this far and I can sort out the rest.'

'Excellent!' Peter chimed in. 'That all looks very workable. Right then, tomorrow I'll send you the first registered letter, and then in five days' time Eva can send you another one. I almost think that should do it if in the meantime Buddeli always takes in the letters herself from this postwoman. A third registered letter over such a short period of time might get noticed, you see. But I think what's really important, Buddeli, is that you always exchange a few words with the postwoman so the lady feels she knows you, and then when you request anything special later about cash remittances she won't be overly taken aback.'

I couldn't get to sleep that night. My mind was full of the grotesque nature of the world in which I was now deeply embroiled, a world of deception and untruths, not to mention the falsification of documents. I found myself longing to extricate myself from this web of lies and get back to a life of living legally and honestly, out in the open. But when on earth might that be?

And there was another side to all this. I knew how indebted I was to all those people who've repeatedly put their own lives at risk by offering me food and shelter and helping me on to the next stage. I swore to myself that if I could get this business of the postal identity card sorted out – which all sounded far too straightforward and simple to be true! – then I'd be out of Berlin in no time and away from so many others sharing my fate, living underground, and most of all the Merkels [Heilmanns], burdened enough as half 'Aryans' without having to deal with me as well, not to mention already marked out for their earlier political views and their courageous involvement with the persecuted and the hounded.

The following morning brought my first opportunity to speak with our genuinely nice postwoman as someone else's post had been delivered to us in error. And then the day after that I received the first registered letter, another easy way of having a bit of a chat. I commented sympathetically on how heavy her postbag looked that day, and she replied how wonderful it was to find someone who understood that her job wasn't that easy. She went on to say that most people just took the post off her and then slammed their doors.

'But you haven't been here that long,' she added.

This was perfect for me. Referring to the address on my clothing card, I said, 'I've just moved here from Rathausstrasse. I took some leave from work in order to get moved. I've got ten days left to get sorted out and settled in, then it's back to work for me.'

'Well, I hope you enjoy the rest of your time off!' she said to me with a nod of recognition and off she went.

Six days later, the second registered letter arrived, this one sent by Eva Merkel [Heilmann]. My conversation with the postwoman went exactly to plan. Yes, she commented, it would indeed be best if I got a postal identity card and then I'd just need a birth certificate on top of that.

'But I haven't got that,' I said, 'and can't get a replacement that quickly either. I'm from Essen in the Rheinland, and what with all the bombing, the police stations there have all been blown up. It's going to be ages before any new certificates can be sorted out and distributed.'

She was so very kind in her reply. 'Don't you worry about that. It's fine not to show a birth certificate if the person who delivers your post knows and can identify the individual concerned. Tomorrow's no good as it's my day off, but if you come to the office the day after – make it around eleven – I'll be there then. Just go to Room X and tell whoever's on duty that you know postwoman N N and someone will call me in.'

I thanked her for her kindness.

So tomorrow at eleven I'm going to the post office. I still can't believe that I'm really going to have this longed-for document in my hands at last!

Siegfried's Diary

Oxford, Monday, 24 May 1943

I have received a letter from Else, dated 29 April! It has come here via Portugal and brought us the greatest joy even though it is still not clear where my dearest is living. She describes herself as being 'in familiar and much-loved surroundings'. In the same letter she writes 'It's wonderful to see the kind of young people the children have grown into.' First of all I thought she might mean the Schadendorfs, but Hanna, who's taking a few days' leave with me here at the moment, is sure it must refer to folk in Icking. That would certainly fit but worries me greatly as so many people know us there that it cannot be without danger. Or has she somehow found permission to reside there?

There is something else in her letter that I want to pick out: 'Still shining somewhere ahead is my – our – guiding star.' Such optimism after all this time apart makes me feel that the reunion I long for so much could actually happen one day. And I gather also that Else is no longer having to do that exhausting job she has hinted at in the past. It sounds more as if she's currently engaged in domestic work in somebody's home, and no longer in Berlin. This must surely mean that all the terrible things she has gone through, all the experiences that will have left their mark, can slowly start to fade from her thoughts as her new life shuffles the old into the shadows and her soul feels less burdened. I often ask myself how many times she must have felt close to death. I can only presume that the air raids over Berlin put an end to her staying on at Eva's house.

For the first time in many months, I can breathe more easily since the arrival of this letter. The stress is easing and I will be able to focus once more on my research as a welcome distraction from these times. If only this war would reach a conclusion. The real salvation would be an end to conflict before the winter sets in, with any last remaining operations confined to Italy.

Else's Diary

Berlin, 24 May 1943

Well now, here's evidence of how essential it is to be able to find new accommodation in an emergency. At this moment I'm sitting on the balcony of some old friends after moving here earlier in the day with the help of a telephone call from Eva Merkel [Heilmann].

But let me tell you everything in the right order.

On 19 May I went to the post office, my heart pounding. You'll remember the place – that great big building on Tempelhof Ufer near Hallesches Tor. I went straight to the room our postwoman had directed me to. The female official there asked what I wanted. I said I was there to request a postal identity card and gave the name of our postwoman, saying she would be able to confirm who I was.

Frau N N was summoned by telephone, appeared immediately and greeted me like an old friend. She confirmed my name as Martha Schröder and gave my address. The official nodded and the postwoman left.

I handed over my new photographs. She affixed one to the card, filled out my personal details, then just below my own photo positioned the stamp bearing the image of the Führer and presented the whole thing to me for my signature. I wrote Martha Schröder with a steady hand.

This service cost fifty pfennig plus the registered postal charge for its delivery to me. This would likely be the next day as the signature of some higher official still had to be obtained. And with that I was dismissed. I still couldn't believe my good fortune.

But sure enough on Friday, our usual and ever punctual postwoman handed me our regular post, together with a registered item – my card. I thanked her for her help and kindness – she had, of course, no idea how much this meant to me – and gave her a little tip to show my appreciation. She declined at first but then gratefully accepted.

Finally I had a properly valid proof of identity. Would it open the door to my freedom? It certainly felt a little closer. Everybody shared my joy, passing the card from hand to hand with the reverence it deserved, while Lene, at my request, immediately sat down to write to the folk in Freiburg to confirm that I'd be arriving with them in about a week's time. She told them all the conditions had now been met and that my arrival date would follow.

I was determined before my departure to pay one last call on Uncle Karl [Hans] and the 'family' which, just as when I'd left, still consisted of Lotte, Herbert and Evchen. I knew that Lotte was still waiting for her own identity card and was deeply pessimistic about its eventual potential for use. I wanted to talk a few things over with Lotte, thinking it might be possible to get her what I now had. In the meantime relationships with the rest of the building had become strained. The frequency of air raids had prompted the porter's wife to ask Uncle Karl [Hans] for the key to his flat while he was at work, so now when the alarm sounded, the 'family' had to vanish without being seen in order to ensure this lady didn't spot them on her rounds.

Up until now everything had gone fine as Uncle Karl [Hans] had taken all possible measures to protect them all. He'd taken one of his employees into his confidence, a thoroughly reliable sort of woman, and a company pass in her name but bearing Evchen's photograph had been prepared, with something similar for Herbert bearing the name and address of one of his male employees. For these purposes Evchen was known as Hildegard Müller and Herbert, Walter Krüger.

If Lotte could now acquire a postal identity card then the greatest risk would be out of the way. It was widely known in the building that Uncle Karl [Hans] had always been more than generous with his hospitality and that his staff saw him as a genuine father figure and were often at his home outside working hours, occasionally staying overnight as well.

I telephoned to say that I'd come on Saturday afternoon.

That spring day was truly dazzling, the light of a type rarely seen in Berlin, and then normally just in May. The trees lining the streets, the hedges and lawns were all a tender green and free of grime, the sky seemed even more expansive than usual as it spanned the city, and even the solemn faces of passers-by seemed a little sunnier.

It may have appeared like that to me on this day of all days because I myself could at last look ahead with greater confidence and a sense of freedom. I don't know for sure, but I felt an awareness of spring on that day in a way that I hadn't since life in Isartal in 1941. I savoured the glorious afternoon and couldn't then face having to push my way on to a packed tram, so covered the route on foot instead. After a thirty-minute walk I was there. Evchen opened the door when she heard the coded ring on the bell that we reserved for close friends.

'How lovely you're here, Maierchen.' She led me through.

In the study Lotte was sitting in a comfortable chair at the table, while Herbert and a young man I didn't recognise were working together on what looked like fixing Uncle Karl's [Hans'] big but long-broken gramophone. The young man was introduced to me as Felix H, a chum of Herbert's and a Jew, also living underground like the rest of us.

I came straight to the point, explaining that I wanted to say my farewells before leaving for Freiburg during the coming week. Then with great pride I showed them my new card and explained how I'd come by it. Everyone was all ears.

'Well, even if you're called Schröder now, you'll always be Maierchen to us, won't you?' said Evchen fondly. I nodded.

'Lotte, now listen, you should talk to Uncle Karl [Hans] about your getting one of these cards in a similar way. This business of your identity card doesn't seem to be progressing – you could left be waiting for an absolute age. I know it would be tricky suddenly to have post sent to you here but there must be some way of fixing that. It's a shame Uncle Karl [Hans] isn't here or we could all have worked it out together.'

She agreed, and I knew already how much it got her down not to have any papers.

'So what kind of pass have you got then, Felix?' asked Evchen.

Leaving the gramophone for a moment he came over to show her. 'I've got this. It says I'm an Italian worker.'

'Do you know enough Italian to put up a good show?' asked Herbert.

'Afraid not.' Felix looked rueful. 'I've picked up a few phrases and am trying to teach myself a bit more but that's not up to much, to be honest. There was an Italian chap at the last place I worked and it was through him that I got my identification card – I used to practise the lingo with him. I'm grateful to have the card though. The postal one is wonderful for women to have, but it's useless for us younger men. All we get asked about is military papers.'

And with that he went back to his work.

There was a ring at the doorbell. This was always a major event and we exchanged nervous glances. No one could hear the doorbell ring without being frightened out of their wits. After a moment Evchen got to her feet.

'It's better to answer it. Someone's heard us talking. We should have been more careful.'

We heard the bolt draw back and close, and then she came back with a great big policeman at her side. Our hearts seemed to stand still. Nobody moved. The man was quite young and wore a green uniform. He raised his arm in the standard salute.

'Is there another exit?' His tone was clipped, military.

'No,' said Evchen.

'Good. Show me around.'

'Please permit me first to telephone the owner of this flat, Herr R. [Kollmorgen],' said Evchen, with great calm and determination. 'We don't all actually live here.'

'That can be done later,' he said brusquely. 'I want to see around the flat first.'

'As you wish,' replied Evchen. She took him through to the adjoining rooms and then out into the hall to see the others.

The rest of us exchanged horrified looks. Lotte, her lips drained and bloodless, turned to me and whispered, 'Should we make a run for it?' I grabbed her hand. It was like ice.

I whispered back, 'No, Lotte, that would be the worst thing we could possibly do. The more normally we can behave, the better. If our two men can just carry on working over there, we'll sit right here, and it can look as though we've just been chatting. Leave the officer to me and Evchen. Don't you worry about it.'

They came back.

'Right, I need to see everyone's identification papers next, please.'

'Of course,' spoke up Evchen, reaching for her bag on the table and taking out the Hildegard Müller pass. 'And maybe I could just add something by way of explanation?' She spoke with such elegance and poise. 'You'll see from my pass that I'm employed by Herr R. [Kollmorgen] He's an unmarried gentleman, and so after my own work I often come here to do some housework and tidying up for him, sometimes a little cooking. He'll be here any minute. He always has so much work on at the factory – that's why he's not back yet.'

The policeman had taken out his notebook and was writing down the name and address for Hildegard Müller. He returned it to her with a courteous little bow.

'Wouldn't you like to sit down?' I asked him. 'It's so awkward trying to write when you're standing up.'

Another little bow, this time in my direction. 'If you will permit me, thank you.' He sat down next to me.

'Walter, have you got your pass on you?' Evchen called over to Herbert. He gave a nod so she went to take it from him and handed it to the visitor, saying, 'Walter Krüger's a colleague of mine. Herr R. [Kollmorgen] asked if he'd come over and mend his broken gramophone.'

Then Herbert chimed in. 'And I've asked another colleague, Giovanni Corti, to lend a hand as he knows a fair bit about machines like these. He's working with us at the firm at the moment.'

The police officer busily made a note of Walter Krüger's personal details and then returned the pass to Evchen.

'Herr Corti, your pass, if you please,' Evchen said to Felix, who took his pass out of his breast pocket without saying a word. His details were all noted down too.

Evchen then gestured towards Lotte, saying, 'And this is my mother, Frau Minna Müller. Herr R. [Kollmorgen] invited my mother and our mutual friend here, Fräulein Schröder, for tea with him.' She turned to me. 'Fräulein Schröder, do you have your pass with you?'

'Of course, I do,' I said. 'It's the postal identity card I've just been issued with.' I handed it to the policeman, who wrote down the number, my name and then asked for my address. I gave him the address from my clothing card, the Rathausstrasse one.

'The one in Steglitz?' he asked.

'No, the city centre,' I replied.

'And finally,' he said, his tone now quite friendly as he tucked away his notebook and pencil in his breast pocket and leaned back in the chair with the look of a man glad to have brought his duties to a successful conclusion, 'I'd like to enlarge upon the reasons for my visit. First of all, I'm pleased to say that everything here is in the best possible order. We have, however, received a denunciation regarding Herr R. [Kollmorgen] to the effect that he's harbouring illegal Jews in his own home. Amazing, isn't it? You'd never believe how many denunciations we have to listen to every day at our station!' He heaved a sigh but was eager to talk. 'And it's our duty to investigate every single one even though most are no more than malicious bothersome slander. So let me waste your time no longer. Please forgive this tiresome interruption. I wish you all a very good evening!' And with this, he rose to his feet, clicked his heels and raised his arm in a parting salute.

Evchen accompanied him to the door, and we heard her voice again in the hallway. On her return, she plopped on to the sofa next to me, saying 'Well, well, well.'

Now that we seemed out of danger I noticed that I was trembling all over. It was a little while before anyone could speak. I gave myself a bit of a shake. Herbert and Felix had come over to join us at the table.

'Right, let's think through what's going to be happening next,' I said. 'He'll head back to the police station and will have to submit a report, either spoken or in writing. This being a Saturday afternoon, nothing will get followed up until Monday, particularly if he sees the denunciation as something just pulled out of the air. Next he'll confirm the address for Hildegard and Minna, that both have lived there a long time, and that the personal details are all as they should be. The same will go for Walter Krüger. It could be that a spot check like this will be enough for them, but they might also want to dig a little deeper –and that's when we could run into trouble. Neither Giovanni Corti nor Martha Schröder live where they said. You'll have to relay all this to Uncle Karl [Hans] as soon as he comes home, and it may even be a good idea for him to go to the police station – they'll know him as he's lived here so long, but that has to be his decision.'

Evchen broke in. 'Can any of you guess where this denunciation came from?'

Our heads turned in unison to look at her, waiting to be enlightened.

'I asked the man when we were in the hall. All in the best interests of Herr R. [Kollmorgen], I said, as I'd need to report back to him. He said he wasn't really permitted to tell me but would do so because he knew Herr R. [Kollmorgen] to be a fine upstanding gentleman and considered this denunciation to be absolutely despicable. It was that grocery woman, the one who got bombed out. The one who had to go through all those basements and who Papa actually allowed to stay here for a few days because he felt so sorry for her! And we did, too – remember how we had to sleep at the factory and hang around all day because of her!' Her eyes flashed. 'Well, I'm glad we know who it was, I can tell you.'

I waited a little before saying, 'It might be a good idea for you all to sleep at the factory again for the time being. I'll stay here for a while. You can't be sure whether he's still waiting outside or whether he's sent a colleague to watch the whole building. I'll keep a good lookout when I do go down and then phone you from the U-Bahn – there's a public telephone there, and I'll say it's Frau Maier, and if the coast is looking clear outside I'll say I'm just getting in touch before my trip to say farewell. If I do get the sense though that the entrance is being watched, I'll say something about not being in touch for a while because I've been ill. Felix should leave as soon as I've called.

'Listen, Evchen, I really admire your presence of mind! You made it all look so easy! And introducing Lotte as your mother – well, that was a stroke of real genius!'

'He didn't even notice that Lotte had no pass,' Evchen said eagerly. 'It was when I was showing him round that I thought it up.' She laughed in sheer delight.

People slowly relaxed after the period of high tension, our tongues loosened and we were once more able to talk.

'I felt sick to my stomach when I saw him standing there in the doorway,' said Lotte.

'Oh, you poor thing,' Evchen said sympathetically. 'You were really in the worst position out of us all, and I'm so glad we were able to help.'

About half an hour later I left the flat, met no one in the stairwell, nor in the main entrance hall. There was a tram stop right outside the front door, and I thought it best to mingle with the various people waiting there. I walked back and forth for a while, scouring both sides of the road, but there was nothing to arouse my suspicion.

I waited another five minutes or so before slowly heading to the U-Bahn station to make the telephone call. Evchen answered and I could feel her relief at the other end when she heard my agreed form of words.

I went home. The first person I saw was Lene, and I recounted the whole sorry tale. She was deeply shocked as were Peter and Eva when I related it all to them a little later in the day.

'Poor old Buddeli,' said Eva Merkel [Heilmann] with real sympathy. 'You were so pleased to get that postal identity card and then this goes and happens.'

Peter looked thoughtful. 'D'you know something, Buddeli? I reckon you should be on your way as soon as possible, and until then go to some friends of ours.'

'Peter's right,' said Lene. 'Pack your things today. Lord knows there's not much to pack, so just take the essentials and early in the morning head over to Fritz K. When you leave the house, one of us can let him know from the public phone box.'

'What do you all think – should I stop off in Central Germany as we'd planned or just head straight to Freiburg?' I couldn't make my mind up on the matter.

Peter answered immediately, saying, 'It'll be fine to stay with your old friend Eva on the way, but make sure then to leave on the Monday.'

'Yes, that sounds right. But could then one of you please send Eva a telegram saying I'm on the way? Just say "Martha coming Monday at . . . ." Put a time in so she'll know to meet me from the train.'

'I'll see to that in the morning,' Eva Merkel [Heilmann] said. 'You'll be at Anhalter Bahnhof on Monday as soon as you leave the friends' place. I'll take your suitcase there in advance, buy you a ticket and reserve a seat for you.'

Incredibly touched by all this, I sat looking at them, marvelling at the way in which they were able to put themselves in my position and offer every help possible as if it were a matter of course.

So that's how I came to be sitting here on Fritz and Gertrud's[11] balcony, in solitary peace and quiet. Fritz has gone to work, and Gertrud's helping her neighbour with the laundry.

We'll be eating together late this afternoon before Fritz takes me to the station.

Siegfried's Diary

Oxford, 29 May 1943

I am overjoyed – another letter from Else, dated 12 May, hot on the heels of the last and composed in her own hand! Reading between the lines, I sense that she's now in a much safer position and is set to stay there for the rest of the war – although her apparent overconfidence does leave me uneasy. I remind myself, however, that I don't know her actual circumstances. Can she really be in Icking or in Elmau, both high-risk locations as far as she is concerned? Well, she does say we needn't worry about her. And at least she doesn't have to lose sleep on our account as much as we do about her!

'I'm hoping for a happy ending,' she writes, which can only mean she believes that Germany will soon suffer defeat, something that I await also and with increasing frustration and impatience. Italy and Germany are under daily bombardment as part of what's referred to as 'softening'. What will this achieve? Nobody knows.

Letter from Else to Eva Schmidt

Freiburg, 30 May 1943

My dear Eva

I'm currently sitting at the top of a wooded hill after a three-hour hike with my host. She's such a nice woman. We've walked from Günterstal encountering only forested slopes along the way and I had to keep pinching myself to be sure it wasn't all a dream. Everything here is indescribable – quite literally!

Sunday afternoon found me looking around the cathedral as well as the square outside and yesterday I was the only person up on the Schlossberg where I enjoyed a whole morning of peaceful solitude.

You must be one of the very few people I know who will fully understand what all of this means to me.

My host family and I are living in complete harmony together and I've even found a friend in their twelve-year-old son, Rolf, a thoroughly nice lad. He's cheerful too, and I know I'll enjoy helping him with his German and English schoolwork.

It was just wonderful that Lena was able to travel down with me. And I've finally received my ration cards that have been sent on by her, right down to the necessary food stamps.

Lunch is on its way and we'll eat on this beautifully situated terrace, surrounded by the mountains of the Black Forest and so many glorious fields and meadows.

Farewell for now, my dearest.

Else's Diary

Freiburg, 8 June 1943

I've been here for ten days now, in this city you've always loved so much, and am constantly asking myself if this is real or a dream. You've so often told me about that first semester you spent here as a student, and how you always found it well-nigh impossible to describe to anyone unfamiliar with the place the effect on you of this landscape, divinely blessed in its serenity and yet not set apart from the city but rather an integral part of it. It must have made quite an impression on the young man previously accustomed only to the grim plains of northern Germany!

Now that I'm here myself, however, I can fully empathise with that sentiment. It's as if all the harshness of the last few years has heightened my awareness of the beauties of nature as well as in other people.

And here, where my host family are the only people who remember me from the old days, I'm free to go walking again and undertake little excursions – such a joy after Berlin and the constant fear of being recognised and picked up by the authorities. But I'm racing ahead here and I really must tell you everything in the right order!

Let's think back to Berlin Anhalter Bahnhof, half an hour before my train to Weimar was due to depart, where Eva Merkel [Heilmann] was waving to me through one of the windows on the train, where she'd already found me a window seat. She handed me a ticket to Erfurt, as we'd decided it would be better to choose a more neutral-sounding destination. I needed to go from Weimar to Erfurt in order to catch the train to Freiburg and would buy the ticket for the last part of the journey in Erfurt itself. I had only a small suitcase which Eva had stowed away in the rack while the rest of my luggage, a very modest amount, was to be sent on afterwards by Peter.

Lene Merkel [Heilmann] came on to the platform to say goodbye. She told me she'd telephoned Uncle Karl [Hans] one last time, and he'd asked her to let me know that everything was all right there and to send me his very best wishes for the journey and that he'd be in touch again soon.[12]

We didn't want to make the farewells too painful and yet I could barely contain my emotion. Recent events had not left me unmarked.

Once the train had set off I was able to compose myself. I've always enjoyed travelling, after all, and from my window the sight of fields and woods in all their spring colours made it easy to push the darkness from my mind and turn my thoughts to the future. It was wonderful to spend time in Weimar with Eva in her little flat, a place I'd never seen with my own eyes, only pictured from her descriptions of it. As twilight came I closed my eyes and tried to sleep. Ever since those daily train rides between Munich and Isartal, sleep had come easily in response to the clickety-clack of the moving train, and now the most elusive thing during my life as a person living beyond the fringes of society, namely a deep and tranquil sleep, came to me just like that. I awoke just before arrival at Weimar, fully refreshed and ready for anything.

Eva was waiting for me on the platform. We had a bit of a distance to walk through the darkened city until we reached her flat on a quiet street, well away from the centre. It was an attic flat in a two-storey house and had a kitchen, living room and bedroom, as well as a tiny box room. I felt immediately at home, but Eva didn't allow me much time to look around as she wanted to know straight away how everything had gone so far, why I'd brought everything forward, whether I had a proper identity pass, and so on and so forth, and expected detailed answers into the bargain. In return she hung on my every word. My postal identity card met with her full approval but she shook her head in bewilderment at my tale of the police visit during my final 'family' visit.

'If I didn't know that story was from your own experience, my dear, I'd think it came straight out of some trashy crime novel.'

I smiled and replied, 'If ever I've hankered after a good crime novel, well, that's one desire well and truly satisfied! It may sound a good yarn but it's a wretched life to live.'

'I don't doubt that for a moment.' Eva looked chastened. 'I truly hope the next chapter will offer you some balm for your soul. We're going to enjoy real peace and quiet together while you're here with me. How long can you stay?'

'I've asked Lene to let the people in Freiburg know that I'll be there on the 28th, so I'll have to leave here on Thursday evening but not too late.'

We sat up chatting until late.

The days flew by and in the twinkling of an eye it was Thursday evening. The air raid sirens went off half an hour before we were due to set off for the station.

Eva tried to keep me calm, saying, 'If it doesn't last too long, you'll still make the connection at Erfurt. And if the worst comes to the worst, I'll send a telegram saying you'll be one day late.'

The all-clear came after forty minutes and we left immediately. The closer we got to the station, the more people we met on the streets. A huge crowd was building outside the station.

'What's happening?' Eva asked a woman standing near us.

'Didn't you hear the bombs go off?' replied the woman, quite agitated. 'The station's been hit. Some of the track's been damaged as well as part of the building. People have been killed.'

A commanding voice now rang out. 'Disperse! Disperse! Only those in possession of a valid ticket may remain!' This came from a police officer.

I asked Eva to get herself home and reassured her that part of the track seemed to be perfectly usable still. I wanted to attempt the journey to Erfurt. The alarm would almost certainly have delayed the onward train to Freiburg, and I'd still get there in time. Eva was unwilling to leave me. The police instructions meanwhile had become even more imperative and people were being herded away. Only passengers with tickets – thank goodness I had mine to Erfurt – were being allowed to stay behind in the station. So we all stood there, awaiting permission to go on to the platform. I heard someone say that the waiting room had been hit, as had one of the platforms, but by far the most bombs had fallen on Jena.

Then there was an announcement about a stopping train to Erfurt from platform two. 'Connecting train to Frankfurt am Main, Freiburg, Konstanz, Basel!'

I edged my way forwards, through the barrier and up some steps to the platform, all in darkness. Something crunched beneath my feet. Broken glass. There was the train, also in darkness – get in, get in, quickly! Inside we felt our way for seats. It filled up fast, then set off.

Once in Erfurt I found out that my connection was due in about thirty minutes. I got myself a ticket to Freiburg and waited on the platform. It was dark here too, but not cold. My train came in and I got in the first decent coach, but it was terribly full with every seat taken, every corridor packed with people and their luggage. I stood in the corridor as best I could. The prospect of a night on my feet was not a good one and on top of that the air was pretty foul, but that was all to be expected. After hours standing at the barrier, those who hadn't secured a seat on a fast train simply had to make do with any space whatsoever on one of the few remaining civilian departures. There was, after all, a war on, and our train was taken up mostly by soldiers.

After a while the nearby compartment door opened and two soldiers came out. 'Blimey, it's packed out here,' said one. 'There's hardly room to stand!' He turned to me, gesturing to the compartment and said, 'Go and sit in there, and I'll take your standing spot. We can swap over later.' I thanked him and took up his kind offer.

Once we'd arrived I looked everywhere for my next host [Edmund Goldschagg] but in vain. In the end I went to the waiting room and telephoned his place of work. I gave my name – Martha Schröder, of course – and he registered surprise. It turned out that Lene's letter about me hadn't arrived, even though she'd written it four days earlier. He promised to come to the station straight away and then to take me home to their flat.

Quarter of an hour later he was there in the waiting room and greeted me most warmly. I hadn't seen him for years and even then only occasionally at the Merkels [Heilmanns], together with his wife Lotte. He was Freiburg born and bred but had always been fondly known as 'Wackes' by Berlin friends due to his having been educated largely in Mulhouse, Alsace, but he took all this in good part even though the name has poor associations on Alsatian territory.[13] I'll refer to him as Wackes here too, for simplicity.

We took the tram and had to change at Bertholdsbrunnen. Wackes said he'd already telephoned his wife about my arrival and that she was about to pop down and say hello as she worked in the building on the corner. And there she was, hardly changed at all since the last time we'd met – tall, good-looking, with blonde hair and grey eyes, and a thoroughly nice person with it! She was far younger than her husband, forty at most, while he was in his late fifties. In spite of the many years she'd now spent away from Berlin, her accent was still there. I knew we'd get on famously.

But now here was the tram that would take us to their home.

'See you at lunchtime, Buddeli!' We'd agreed it would reduce the risk if they always called me by this lovely nickname. 'Wackes, be sure to give her breakfast!'

Their flat was in the attic of a solid two-storey building. The large and attractive living room as well as the study faced on to the street along with a beautiful view of the Black Forest. At the rear were the kitchen and bedroom, looking towards the gentle contours of the Vosges. I was to sleep on the chaise longue sofa in the study, normally used by twelve-year-old Rolf, while he was to move to the second chaise longue located in his parents' room. I met him properly at lunch – a fine-featured lad, tall and slim, with dark blond hair and grey eyes like his mother and a nice demeanour.

'So, this is Buddeli, Rolf. I know you've been excited about meeting her,' said his mother as she introduced him to me. His face was open and honest as he gave me a long look and then welcomed me with a little bow and a firm handshake.

I've always been fond of children, as you know, and find it easy to create a rapport. There was no doubt that he and I would hit it off from the start. I knew things weren't going too well for him at school and had offered to do some work with him via one of Lene's letters to them. That's why he'd been so eager to see what I was going to be like! It was nice for me to sense his obvious relief. His parents had told him that many older people not in active employment were having to leave Berlin because of the bombing, which was actually the case. They'd said that was the reason why I'd left Berlin and that I'd be staying in Freiburg with them for around three months. This version of events would also do when it came to meeting friends of Wackes and Lotte.

In the afternoon I took a gentle stroll through the city, heading first of all to the square to look at the cathedral. I gazed in awe and wonder at this structure which had always seemed to me quite perfect in scale and proportion. The exquisitely elaborate filigree work of the tower appeared to have been executed by some giant goldsmith. The square itself remained impressive with its magnificently patrician department store and the refined elegance of the archiepiscopal palace. At the moment, however, both buildings were lacking decorative detail, it having been removed for safe storage away from the bombing.

I then made my way to the Schlossberg to drink in the view over the city and the glories of the surrounding landscape. I felt touched by a strong sense of gratitude towards the spiritual power that had put everything in place for me, as well as towards all those people who had shown such personal strength and willingness in helping me.

Once Rolf had gone to bed, the three of us sat together well into the evening. I asked Lotte and Wackes to tell me how to conduct myself, whether I should stay indoors as much as possible, hide away from others in the building or let them catch full sight of me.

Wackes replied with a kindly smile, 'The more naturally you move around here, the better. Other people in the building here are quite accustomed to us having visitors, and new faces are a matter of course for folk in Freiburg, what with the university and the favourable location of the place. Lotte will help you gradually to make the acquaintance of everyone living in our building. They're just normal, quiet people with little involvement in politics. We're sure it's quite safe for you staying here with us.'

He got up and went over to switch on a Swiss radio station. 'That's another benefit of being in this locale,' he said. 'We can tune in without fear of the neighbours, and the proximity of our own transmitter means it's a strong signal.'

When the news came to an end, I commented that he probably only ever did this once Rolf was asleep, but he said firmly, 'Oh no, that's where you're wrong. We hide nothing from Rolf. He's fully aware of our own political stance and shares our views. He's completely reliable.'

'You don't feel you might be burdening a child with a little too much? He's barely thirteen, after all. Isn't it hard for him if at home you're saying quite the opposite of what he hears in school and from the Hitler Youth, a group he's doubtless obliged to belong to?'

'Yes, it is a burden, but a burden he must carry. Am I supposed to stand by and do nothing while utterly offensive ideas are drummed into him, harmful in a way that he's not yet able to recognise? No, that to me seems the greatest wrong I could possibly do him. And because he loves and trusts us, he'll believe us more than his teachers and the Hitler Youth. If the parent–child relationship is as it should be, and parents are fully aware of their responsibilities with regard to their children and discuss with them the political ideas that are currently being put about, then these shocking cases you hear of, where children betray their parents, would hardly arise. Now, it's late and I'm sure you won't have got much sleep on your train.'

As we got up to prepare for bed, Lotte added, 'If the air-raid siren goes off, don't be frightened. They go right over our heads here towards Munich or Stuttgart. Freiburg's never had much industry so we don't live in fear of the bombs. When the alarm sounds, we just stay in bed.'

Well, that was fine by me!

Meanwhile I've settled in well. In the mornings I do the housework, shopping and cooking so when Lotte comes in from work around one o'clock, all she has to do is put the finishing touches to the midday meal. On Sundays, weather permitting, there's always some sort of excursion with a friend or two tagging along. We all take food for the day in our rucksacks, usually potato salad and bread, coffee substitute or a herb tea in the Thermos.

The day before yesterday we were up on the Feldberg. All in all we were probably walking for seven hours, and I was thrilled at having been able to do this without too much difficulty. You know Feldberg pretty well, so I can spare you my detailed descriptions. I found myself wishing that I could tell you in person how much a day out like this meant to me after being kept within four walls for so very long. And I mean that quite literally!

In some ways I'm under even greater pressure now, given the separation from you and the children, the absence of any news whatsoever, and the fear and anxiety hanging over so many close to us, and yet it just has to be endured. Night-time is the worst. I hardly get a wink of sleep and when I do drift off, my sleep is plagued by bad dreams. But nowhere is it written that I should somehow not take my share of the burden in this most horrific of wars, in this ocean of misery and suffering that increases by the day. I have two major advantages over most of my unfortunate companions of similar fate and racial background: my own life is not under direct threat, and I can be secure in the knowledge that you and the children are safely away from suffering torment at the hands of the Nazis, from deportation and the horrors of massacre. I have it so easy by comparison.

Rolf must be doing terribly badly at school. When it comes to it, I fear I won't be able to protect him from being forced to stay down a year. He's fallen behind in Maths and English but lacks knowledge in other subjects as well. I told his parents that it would really be better to let him repeat the year as the gaps were now too great to be filled in the short time remaining to us in the current school year. I can only do so much in our daily sessions helping with his homework. When a pupil is kept down a year it means that all the English is gone over again from scratch, and the same goes for German grammar and the maths curriculum. Rolf's father explained to me how there'd been constant changes in teaching staff and that the boy had difficulty in getting used to any new teacher. On top of that his parents didn't have time to do the necessary work with him. At the same time I don't remotely see him as stupid or lacking in ability, more that he's dreamy, slow and unable to concentrate. Nor does he have the level of interest that would actually draw him to the work.

Having said all that, he's good-hearted and is certainly now making an effort. He hardly ever goes to Hitler Youth meetings and if Lotte ever comments on this, he says, 'Not many boys in my class go very often, and no one's fussed 'cos nearly all the group leaders are away in the army now and there are only about three keen Nazis in the whole class. Nothing'll happen, Mutti, let me just be, it'll all be all right.' And with that he'll go off for a swim, whistling cheerily as he goes on his way.

Siegfried's Diary

Oxford, 30 June 1943

Yet more news yesterday! I received a transcript made by Alice with all Else's news as of 30 May. Else is staying with Lene Heilmann and her children. This can only mean Berlin and my thoughts, of course, fly immediately to the risk of major bombardment.

Both she and this particular family are being seen as 'half Aryan', making these lodgings ideal for all concerned. This letter demonstrates a similar confidence to the last, along with her fervent hope that we will at last be reunited after this separation of four, nearly five, years.

Oxford, Sunday, 25 July 1943

Following Allied successes in Sicily over the last fortnight or so, hopes are raised that Italy will soon fall and attacks on occupied Europe may recommence, most especially in the Balkans, with likely assaults coming from east, west and south.

As I stood at my gate that night, I heard aircraft flying overhead, on their way to the continent. Hamburg was their target yesterday. Today they will rain death and destruction on some other place in Germany. The thought leaves me entirely cold. I am untouched by Germany's suffering. It's a dreadful country supporting an unholy regime. [. . .]

Well now, I have just screwed the cap back on my ink bottle for tonight! Dr Mendelssohn, my landlord, has heard on the wireless that Mussolini has been ousted. The same broadcast described this not as the end of the war but the downfall of Fascism and the end of the Fascist war. Just think of the impact this will have on the whole breadth of the continent, and how it will weaken the Nazis!

Letters from Else to Eva Schmidt

Freiburg, 11 June 1943

My dear Eva

I'm starting to notice how much I need solitude again and am relishing my lone walks and excursions as much as someone deprived of water might gulp down their first glass!

Now, about your visit. My host has promised he'll find out whether the hotels you mention are still in business.

Last Sunday our outing comprised what I can only describe as an extended group, including not just the family, of which I now see myself a member, but also two other women, one whose mother is a good friend of my host, the other a woman from my host's office, very pleasant, about your age. We started walking at Hinterzarten, hiking through the most heavenly woods and meadows, the wild flowers out in all their glory . . . Another wonderful feature here is the musical and cultural offering, and lectures too – there's certainly no lack of food for the soul.

It's all still like a dream to me. Even now I find it hard to believe that I'm allowed to see, hear and absorb all of this once again!

Freiburg, 14 August 1943

At times I feel ashamed to be living in such a peaceful and relaxing environment compared with where you and other friends find yourselves. But my feelings of hope and confidence are stronger than they've been for a very long time, and I'm quite sure I'm not fooling myself.

Don't worry yourself over where Lilli's staying. We've taken all necessary steps already and hope soon to know more, but until then I'm at liberty to remain at her guest house whatever happens – her splendid host family reassured me of this yet again only yesterday.

Rolf is feeling more confident but has been kept down a year.

Siegfried's Diary

Oxford, 25 August 1943

This day, my dearest, marks exactly four years since my departure. Saving my own skin but deserting you was the greatest mistake of my life. Today's reports of the devastating air attack on Berlin two nights ago have left me feeling quite in despair. My mind twists and turns, not knowing how or where to picture you, my love. And yet four days back Alice's letter referred to you as 'writing, quite contented, working and hoping to meet again soon in peacetime'. So in July you were still with the Heilmanns in Berlin! None of us here can imagine how it might feel to take refuge in a cellar beneath one of those enormous Berlin mansion blocks that could at any moment be blown to pieces. The bombers' main target seems to have been Siemensstadt, doubtless one of many.

My love, I remember so well how you stood there on the station platform, slowly vanishing from view. With every passing year I have longed and hoped for our reunion.

I am currently counting on help from Hertha and hoping that something may happen soon. Her own background in social work places her right at the heart of plans already being drawn up to provide spiritual and practical support to those left in a Europe decimated by war. [...] I think this work might bring her over to Europe in person as she had so much experience here before. But my mind is drifting from the here and now and this strange lethargy to which we seem condemned and allows me instead to look ahead to an escape from this awful stalemate.

Four years ago at this hour I was travelling overnight towards the Rhine. I had my first glimpse of it at dawn before chugging along its banks for what felt an eternity. One of the last things I was ever able to send to you direct and in person was the telegram I despatched from Nijmegen, just over the border in the Netherlands.

Else's Diary

Freiburg, 26 August 1943

The three months originally planned for my visit here will soon be over but Lotte and Wackes have been urging me to stay on, and I'm only too happy to do so. I feel so well and at ease here with them.

Rolf really is to be kept down a year. At the beginning of the summer vacation he spent a fortnight in Heidelberg with friends of Wackes but soon after his return we started an intensive and systematic programme of work together. He struggled to concentrate at first but we've got past that now. He's finally starting to feel more secure in himself and his almost non-existent self-confidence is slowly coming back. He's one of those children in constant need of encouragement because he has so little faith in himself. His gratitude and obvious attachment to me are very touching, and he's always asking me to promise that I'll be there with them for a good long time.

He and I have become good friends, if the difference in our ages properly allows me to describe us in that way. Rolf knows that I like him and take him seriously. I myself get the impression it would indeed do him a lot of good if I could carry on working with him for a little longer, and his parents feel the same.

Peter Merkel's [Heilmann's] visit over the weekend left us serene in the knowledge that this would likely be the case. He had come down to discuss what was to happen to me next and was full of amazing stories. For me, the most exciting account concerned Belter, the Frenchman he'd mentioned previously. In addition to his ever-increasing dealings on the black market, he'd taken real pride in helping a goodly number of French prisoners of war come by false papers and escape home to France. He was now running quite a large organisation operating in different fields, including a flourishing trade in food and textiles, as well as passes and documents. That's why he'd been more than happy to take my false identity card and pay me for it. The badly reproduced stamp can be removed and the whole card made viable for someone in hiding. I was particularly pleased because we can use the money now to buy food on the black market here.

But poor old Belter had become overconfident and was arrested when police swooped on Alexanderplatz, the heart of black market trading in Berlin. Peter reckoned he'd probably been under suspicion for some time, just that nothing incriminating had ever been found on him or at his home, and the firm had always praised his work to the skies. But it had been serious this time. Among his many German friends was one who had sought out a well-known Nazi lawyer to prepare his defence – and it had worked. He was free once more, but he treated the experience as a warning and immediately vanished from Germany. Peter assumed he'd got hold of false documents, gone to France and joined the French Resistance.

We discussed in depth the political and military situation, all of us hoping that Italy would dispense with Mussolini. Would Germany ever manage to do the same with its own leader? We were greedy for news. Peter had come across some good tales of sabotage. Lene works in the office of a factory making aircraft components and had learned that from a delivery of one hundred new engines, twelve had gone missing. That had happened months ago but the culprit, or culprits, have never been identified. About the same time, another such act occurred while the whole workforce was listening to a lunchtime radio address by Ley. The entire work plan, something of enormous importance to the production schedule and hugely difficult, time-consuming and complicated to draw up – comparable perhaps to the full timetable for a large school – was found in shreds in a waste basket. Nobody found out who was responsible for that either.

In July I had the delight of seeing my friend Eva again. She was here for a few days on the way to Lake Constance where she was off to help someone she knew well with the harvest and fruit processing on his large plot of land. She could provide the necessary proof from the lead farmer for this town that she'd done this several times during the war already, so was given a permit to stay for more than a fortnight – the fixed maximum duration of any official period of rest and recovery otherwise and only available to those in jobs critical to the war effort or in school. People over the age of fifty and in employment are permitted three weeks instead of two. The dates of the stay are entered on the individual's clothing ration card and this has to be presented at any and every health spa to prevent anyone from trying to do this too often.

Something I must add in at this point is that I'd rather hesitantly asked Peter if he saw any possibility of my getting to Switzerland. There was no immediate hurry, for sure, and I needed to help Rolf for a little while longer, but with the approach of winter, and then Christmas coming, I needed to think about changing location again and knew I'd be burning to get to Switzerland by that time and away from this exhausting life in hiding. Peter wasn't able to give me much hope. But he said his girlfriend Hella [Gorn] – who I knew well from earlier visits to the Merkels [Heilmanns] – was most likely aware of an organisation that helped smuggle people out of the country. He was going to talk to her about it and ask her to find some way of contacting the people involved.

But now I really must tell you that I felt daring enough to go to Strasbourg one day. It was Wackes who'd prompted me, saying it was a beautiful city and that we didn't really know for how much longer we'd have access to it. He added that he could see no risk for me, provided I had my postal identity card. And I'm so glad I did it. The city is heavenly and the cathedral made a huge impression on me, as did the equally beautiful historic district.

There was something else that caught my eye. Many of the shops were closed up with similar placards in each window, all bearing a message I'd never seen anywhere else:

DUE TO THE TOTALISATION OF WAR –
CLOSED UNTIL AFTER VICTORY!

What on earth do the people of Alsace feel when they see that? Do they ask themselves what I'm asking myself?

'And whose victory might that be?'

I imagine so.

Letters from Else to Eva Schmidt[14]

Freiburg, 13 September 1943

We've had a visit from my friend Peter this week. He was able to spend a few hours with us, having been despatched by his medical insurance to the sanatorium we'd very much like for Lilli. Peter's promised to write and tell us what it's like and whether they'll have a place for Lilli in the foreseeable future.

Freiburg, 19 September 1943

Lilli isn't wanting when it comes to money. I think I wrote to you about the valuable book she'd sold for such a good price that it'll cover her convalescence costs for the foreseeable future.

Siegfried's Diary

Oxford, 4 September 1943

I received a brief letter yesterday, dated 28 August, from Alice Rosenberg in Lisbon. From her remarks I was able to infer that Else had in fact left Berlin before those two deadly air raids of 22 and 23 August, which were followed by two more. She wrote as follows: 'My sister-in-law is now close by, as feels absolutely right.' Those few words have done so much to calm me.

The papers tell of half a million people now living in temporary accommodation while a further quarter of a million are said to have been forced from their homes. The Russian advance is progressing towards Smolensk and the Black Sea and this, combined with the mass psychological impact from the heavy bombing, gives me a flicker of hope.

Oxford, 16 September 1943

My hopes for a swift conclusion to hostilities in southern and south-eastern Europe are fading. The battle for Italy is growing ever more savage and moving from there into the Balkans is looking far from straightforward. The outstanding performance of the Russian forces may well prove to be the deciding factor here.

Aircraft thunder by overhead. It's a quarter past ten and the skies are illuminated by the constantly scanning searchlights as their outstretched fingers seem to pass messages to one another. I go outside to stand and watch.

Knowing that Peter is taking a few days' leave next week and has plans to see Hanna, I wrote and asked her to spend some of the time with him on deciding where they both stand vis-à-vis the Jewish problem so they can weigh things up when planning their own futures. As far as the refugees are concerned, I can already see two options under consideration, both of them wrong and both rooted in emotion. Namely, that you either turn your back on Judaism, as it's really not that significant in terms of your personal identity, and go over to Christianity; or that you keep a firm hold on it and go even further with the ideal through the pursuit of Zionism. My own reasoning rejects both approaches, fair and square.

It is too late now for Zionism and the creation of a Jewish state, as this offers no security against the outside world and in no way corresponds to my own vision for the future. Most importantly here, I am not really a 'Jews only' sort of man. The Jewish problem will remain after the conclusion of this war, whether it be in England, in Germany, across Europe or in the USA. The next generation also will come up against it.

And how might one solve this, you may ask? By melting into a new national or international community with mixed marriages of Jews and non-Jews? That would certainly bring problems of its own, but over time these would diminish and in at least two generations fade entirely.

The intrinsic motivation here is to find a new place for one's family of the future to call home because the old home has been lost. Members of my own generation, however, will remain for the rest of our lives without that old sense of belonging in one particular location. Reason demands, however, that we all nonetheless embark on the route to establishing a new place to call our own with proper solidity and permanency. For our children the English language presents no obstacle, although it likely will for me and for Else.

Oxford, 16 September 1943

Only the latter part of my daily walk to work affords me any morning sunshine these days, a phenomenon which leads me to reflect further on our respective lives, Else. While here in England we benefit from liberty and light, you have been left in the darkness of servitude. The contrast could not be starker and I blame myself and myself alone for our separation. I was too unquestioning of developments at that time and thinking too much of my own position. Imagining what might still happen to you, Else, is agonising, the closer we draw to the end of the war and all that this will mean for Germany.

The more the Russians push west, now at Kiev and Smolensk, the nearer we do seem to the end. The region impacted by fighting now extends further into the west, covering a host of industries essential to the war effort now being kept going solely under non-German forced labour. Just beyond lies the necessary hinterland for supplies and retreat, with millions of people under evacuation from west and north-west Germany, starting to the west of the River Elbe. On top of all that are the flashpoints within Yugoslavia and on the Adriatic coast. The most obvious outcome is a dangerously seething cauldron, particularly with maltreated Poland now being viewed as nothing more than another hinterland. This might just revive hopes of liberation from the menace that is Germany, given that it now finds itself stretched on all fronts – because that's when the limitations of tyranny become truly apparent. Or is that just my wishful thinking? I think not.

Oxford, Saturday, 30 October 1943

Five weeks since my last entry. A brief note from Alice Rosenberg in Portugal came so quickly this time! With this one it is harder to read between the lines, but she does say that Else is with friends, people she has known for years. Could it the Grossenhains? Please don't let this be anywhere risky – neither Berlin nor any other city likely to fall under direct attack. Alice has become so cautious that she no longer makes reference to any dates or timescales. And yet Else fills my thoughts with every hour of every day. [. . .]

The course of the war is leaving us all in a constant state of suspense, what with favourable daily reports of what is taking place in Russia and specifically, news of progress towards Odessa and Kiev. I found myself agreeing with a recent wireless broadcast by Thomas Mann,[15] when he reminded us that however hard it may be for those of us watching from afar, it is so much worse for all those left in Germany. In the same programme he said there could not possibly remain one single Nazi general or leader who still believes there can be a 'good' outcome, and that all hope now rests on forming a separate peace with Russia. [. . .]

People here in England are generally so much more relaxed about the course of the war, and the same goes for the émigrés here with their families. Our separation has brought me so much misery and only the end of the war can take that away. Maybe my life will then have some meaning again, if only for a few years.

Letters from Else to Eva Schmidt

Freiburg, 1 November 1943

Most of all you need to know how adventurous I'm feeling and that one week from today, I'm off to Montafon for ten days or so. We've found a little rest home there, owned and run by a lady doctor, and it may be a suitable spot for Lilli's longer stay. At the moment, however, it's so difficult to organise anything in writing that I'd rather just take a look at the place myself. Today I've received assurance of a friendly welcome. I'll spend the night in Bregenz, where on the recommendation of the local tourist office I can arrange accommodation by letter with a cash deposit and then travel up on Tuesday. It's beyond Schruns – that's where you get the postbus, and then it's forty minutes from there. The next bit of news will come to you from there. I'll be away for ten days at the most, then I want and need to be back here.

Grete has sent greetings from Uncle Hans, the dear man, who's still there with his house guest. They say the current housing crisis means that nothing else can be found for her.[16]

Freiburg, 17 November 1943

My dear

Have you heard from Annemarie again? I have two big requests to ask of her.

1. I know she had some household soap and wonder if she can spare some if there's any left? I simply can't get clean with this utility stuff we have to use – can't remove the grime from the cracks in my chapped hands, and it just sits there. It's really very unpleasant.

2. In addition, might she have any thick warm socks to spare? They'd be really useful here but especially for Lilli when she comes, as she only has

those short ankle socks you wear in the summer and no warm stockings. No need for the latter if she has good warm socks.

Today is my Hanna's birthday. She's twenty-one. We're thinking of one another, as ever. I wonder if they're all together, celebrating?

Freiburg, 12 December 1943

My dearest

A quick note to say that Lilli's trip isn't happening for the time being. A message came today telling her not come at the moment. Something about an avalanche – all a bit muddled and mysterious. So disappointing for her, as you can imagine.

Freiburg, 28 December 1943

My dear

Just a brief note today as you simply have to know there's great joy here because Peter brought news that Lilli's place has finally come up – the one she's been longing for. She can go in on 15 Jan.

You'll share our delight, I know. She's quite dizzy with excitement – you'll know exactly how she feels. If only we could speak in person.

Siegfried's Diary

Oxford, 24 December 1943

It is quite some time since I last committed my thoughts to paper. Inevitably Christmas Eve is a time for looking back, and the annual leave I am granted at the moment certainly allows me that luxury. Life is always harder in winter and the lack of heating makes any free time spent at home rather unproductive. The grotesque nature of world events takes all my attention and fills the mind. The last three months have seen no attempt to reach into the heart of central Europe and air attacks alone, whatever their increasing force and intensity, can never replace a full-fledged advance on land. Official predictions presume they will eventually have the necessary human impact but their effect on morale will be slow. Such attacks are supposed to drive out from future generations the slightest desire for further warmongering, instilling in them a new outlook fashioned from an acceptance that the devastation has been wrought by war, and war alone. Consider too the ruinous effect that all this destruction has had on material assets, many of which form a substantial part of the national wealth. Take what has been built over many centuries in Cologne, Hamburg, Berlin, Leipzig – these places will never regain their former splendour. I never want to see Germany again. [. . .]

The children will make their way in the world without me – that is clear from everything they are doing and striving for. Look at Peter, still in his old job but hard at work on his five subjects for his Matric and getting himself in a good position to take up something different. And take Hanna, now eighteen months into her nursing training and currently on secondment to a sanatorium. For Christmas I posted her some money and a small book about Leonardo da Vinci, nicely illustrated. She is more purposeful than Peter and highly ambitious, and rightly so, as well as being well thought of by her nursing colleagues, something confirmed by Peter's girlfriend, Ully Simon.

For Christmas I have treated myself to a slightly better oven that uses two units of electricity. It seems reliable and worth the two pounds and ten shillings it cost me. I have had it for two days. [. . .]

Over the last few days my mind has gone back to 65 Wilhelmstrasse with its beautiful blue marble, probably now nothing more than a heap of rubble. It housed a valuable collection of documents, going back one hundred years or so, and I remember the satisfaction of finding there in 1931 or 1932 the papers requested on the matter of a murder case from 1843. (Murder of a woman and her seven children – disgrace over family insolvency, loss of all assets).[17] One of Jakob Wassermann's novels refers to this remarkable trial,[18] noteworthy for the defendant's attempt over several years to gain a pardon. The original death sentence – execution by breaking on the wheel – was eventually transmuted to a life sentence in 1848.

The memories crowd in, starting with 1887 and my first year at Gymnasium. Then in 1893, my father's death just before my Abitur; 1903 professional law exams; March 1904 swearing in as a lawyer; then 1913 and the last year of peace, married life with Gertrud; in 1923 appointed speaker at the Ministry of Justice and counsel to the Court of Appeal; then in 1933, 'Mentenhäusl' in the snow at Oberschönau with Else; and finally in 1943 I find myself in England!

Oxford, New Year's Eve 1943

Two thousand bombs fell on Germany yesterday and thirteen hundred today, bringing a vision of such utter devastation one can barely conceive of. The papers here report on the damage to the Berlin quarters of Neukölln and Königstadt. I try to picture the scene with thousands now homeless, wandering the streets, robbed of all they possess.

I never want to see Germany again. It would be dangerous, suicidal. Anyone who has lived out the war abroad, and especially in England, will always be written off as a good-for-nothing, an enemy of the state, certainly by that large chunk of the population incapable of rational judgment.[19] This means that my dear Else will need to make her way over here if our longed-for reunion is ever to take place.

1944

Siegfried's Diary

Oxford, 5 January 1944

As I write my hands are still trembling with the joy of today's news. I came home from work to find a letter from Alice dated 26 December. She tells me that 'Lene' – by whom she means Else! – has taken on the care of some children in a beautiful mountainous area and is in good health in all respects. This is wonderful news in itself but especially amid the other daily reports of bombing over Berlin and other German cities. I rejoice on her behalf for her being in some haven of safety, for the near future at least. Might this be a good omen for the year ahead? If only that could be true! In the meantime my mind teems with worries over other matters remaining to be dealt with, such as needing to sell some large items of luggage,[1] on top of having to face trouble at work.

Else's Diary

Freiburg, 8 January 1944

The weeks fly by, shaped by that symmetry of work and leisure that I love so much. I know that if instead I measured the passing of time in hopes and wishes, it would pass so painfully slowly.

The latest developments in Italy spell only disappointment, so that our previously soaring hopes of a rapid end to the war are well and truly dashed.[2]

I continue to feel well-placed here. The morning is taken up with housework while my afternoon is dedicated to working with Rolf. He's making good progress. He's formed a strong attachment to me and knows I'm thinking of moving again which is unsettling him, but I tell him he's more than capable now of doing things for himself.

As housekeeper I'm plagued by the food shortages. Even basics like potatoes are rationed and only available in tiny quantities. The lack of vegetables overall is dreadful but we count ourselves lucky that Wackes knows folk out in the countryside, kindly people who sometimes slip in some cabbage and leek for us. And at least we're still drawing on our reserve of potatoes from last autumn, as we received a full entitlement back then. But now that potatoes are the main constituent in our diet this won't suffice.

It's impossible to find unrationed foods anywhere, and the black market is out of the question as we have neither the cash nor the contacts, and in any case there are far fewer sources here than in Berlin. So every evening Lotte and I have long conversations about what I should concoct for lunch the following day.

The physical deterioration caused by our poor diet of bad, indigestible bread and no fat is becoming evident. Lotte suffers from bad pains in the stomach and gut, and I've developed a rash that's so irritable at night that it keeps me awake just when I'm most in need for sleep. Everyone's talking of similar complaints.

Nonetheless, we did try to do Christmas properly. All the preparations Rolf saw me making were quite new to him. His mother and father had always been so busy with work that they'd lost out on this aspect of family life. It therefore gave me a great deal of pleasure to help him think of and make presents for all his nearest and dearest. That wasn't easy as there was barely anything in the shops and when there was something it was soon snapped up. Rolf delighted in visiting every shop he knew on almost a daily basis so he could be sure not to miss anything.

Now and again this paid off. In one of the bookshops he came upon a series of little books produced with soldiers in mind, each containing essays or short fiction by well-known writers. The stationery shop that Rolf would go to for his exercise books – now also rationed and only obtainable with written approval from the school, and with such rough, poor-quality paper that the ink's running out even as you write – yielded up some etchings of Freiburg, and then in a third shop he found some nice little wooden frames. With a haul as good as this, I felt it only right to lend him a hand and for a few pfennigs managed to get some offcuts of coloured paper from the bookbinder. This meant that each of the reading books got an attractive cover and each etching a protective wrapping. And when Rolf was fortunate enough to get hold of a small Christmas tree – with few on the market, that was quite an achievement and well worth a bit of queueing with chilly fingers and toes – his happiness was complete! But candles were going to be a problem. Every family, no matter how large or small, was allocated only one single candle on the household ration card. We managed to turn up some old stumps from previous years and made do with those.

Our Christmas celebration was made all the more wonderful by Rolf's joy at our lamentable little tree with its half-burned candles, something that meant quite as much to him as the huge trees, bathed in the glow of candles galore, had meant to us back in the old days. He took an innocent glee in having something to offer others and in turn accepted their gifts with noisy appreciation! Given the hard times most people simply made a gift out of something of their own.

I hardly need tell you this but later, in the quiet of my room, I held my own little celebration in honour of hope and to remember all those not with me.

A few days later we heard from Peter Merkel [Heilmann] the exciting news that he and his friend Hella were coming to stay for a few days. They arrived in Freiburg quite late and looked worn out, but at least they could enjoy a few days of quiet here with no air raids at night.

They told us about the severe bombing that had been going on over Berlin since the end of November. The raids I had experienced had been bad enough but clearly bore no comparison with these. They related how any business considered essential to the war effort – and that was now virtually everything – had been relocated to quieter areas, and this meant that the workers had had to uproot together along with the company. This had a severe effect on people's personal lives, with families pulled

40. Freiburg's 'silent heroes' photographed at Hinterzarten in the Black Forest, winter 1943/1944: (*from left*) Ernst Ludwig Heilmann, Hella Gorn, Lotte and Edmund Goldschagg, unknown, Else Rosenfeld.

apart as individual members became scattered across a Reich that many were now trying to withdraw from by going underground and, just like we Jews, choosing a life in hiding, something which in their eyes was no life at all.

I couldn't help but think back to something you once said when we saw one of those new billboards for that antisemitic newspaper *Der Stürmer*, do you remember? Emblazoned across the top were the words, 'The Jews are our misfortune'. It was akin to being slapped across the face even back then.

You looked at it and said, 'That's prophetic: "The Jews are our misfortune". But it'll come true in a way that's very different from what the writer intended. What they're doing to us now will be like a boomerang in the hand of the thrower. One day fate will deal them the blows that are raining down on us and will continue to do so.'

At the time I thought you were exaggerating, but now I see you were right. Everything is happening exactly as predicted. Their assets, their houses are being pillaged and destroyed, the people are crammed into emergency billets which soon turn into the most pitiful of lodgings, bearing little or no resemblance to normal human habitation. Their husbands, brothers and sons fight and fall on foreign fields, their wives, sisters and daughters toil for eleven or twelve hours a day and then generally have to trudge home on foot, as did our relatives, because the public transport system has failed. Their children are in temporary homes and it's hard to keep in touch by writing as the unreliable postal service is more stop than go. Women and children are exposed to mass extermination in a way that was once unthinkable. In short, misery and anguish have overpowered the whole population, their consequences driven home as if by incessant hammer blows pounding harder and faster on a people already bent and cowering, numbed and dulled by suffering and with no strength left to defend themselves or to revolt.

But Hella brought me some better news. She'd been able to make contact with an intermediary who works with a people-smuggling organisation in Switzerland.[3] So far she'd not been offered anything definite but was still hopeful that this would prove to be the way to get me over the border.

'Quite when it'll get to that stage, I don't know – it could happen very fast, or might still take another three months or so,' she concluded. 'Once I know the date, I'll come, which'll be easy to arrange as I'm the only one left working in the office, and then I can tell you everything in person. Maybe I can even go a bit of the way with you.'

I felt quietly relieved. In the past autumn I'd often gone foraging for mushrooms and on clear days had gazed across to the Swiss mountains glinting in the distance, and would then feel those old flames of yearning for this free and peaceful country, as well as my hunger to stop living beyond the law, to stop living outside a properly ordered society. Was this longing about to be satisfied? But the door to this place of safety had so often opened to reveal the narrowest sliver of light only to slam shut again, extinguishing any small flicker of hope. Through gritted teeth I told myself to stay calm, wait it out and harbour no great expectations until I could be sure something would come along. But that's easier said than done when those same hopes and wishes are already weaving in secret some new and temptingly soft fabric that envelops and stifles all rational thought. I had no desire to wait longer for the words that would bring me certainty, but I will have to, even though this wears me down and oppresses my spirits. I am no longer in charge of my own destiny.

And then on top of all that, Peter and Hella left five days ago.

Siegfried's Diary

Oxford, 22 January 1944

A fortnight ago I referred to trouble at work but this is sadly no longer a problem. I was summoned yesterday to see the manager who supervises all the German employees. He told me there was no quibble with my work but that my age and limited English meant my current wage level was no longer tenable. He advised a week of paid leave and then not to come back. I asked him if this was a dismissal and he confirmed that indeed it was. And so it was that he bid me a kindly farewell this Saturday, handed me a good reference and eight pounds in lieu of a fortnight's work.

I'm not really angry that it's all ended like this. I had in fact been weighing things up there for quite a while in any case as the working hours were too long for me, my eyesight was suffering and the endless chatter and disturbance from the youngsters more than got on my nerves, and yet the money was always the attraction. Maybe I'll find a half-day of office work somewhere, particularly as I've now worked for one year and seven months without a single day of sickness.

41. Siegfried Rosenfeld, England, early 1940s

Letter from Else to Eva Schmidt

Freiburg, 26 January 1944

Lilli had further news early today but to the effect that she now has to be patient but will be able to get moving before the spring. She's trying so hard to bear it and is in such a difficult position. Her money was all organised in good time, along with everything else, and now all that's gone awry. Thanks to dear Frau Müller she still has enough to last her about a month. She can't bring herself to write. It's hard for me too but I need that feeling of connection with my nearest and dearest quite as powerfully as anyone else needs their daily bread.

Wait, there's one more thing. Did I tell you that poor Grete B[erndt] has lost everything, along with O.H. [Uncle Hans]?[4] I feel so terribly sorry for them both.

Else's Diary

Freiburg, 28 February 1944

And still I'm waiting in vain for the news I long for. I feel ashamed of myself and so sorry for those I'm living with as I'm constantly on edge and full of nerves. I know there's no possibility whatsoever of escape at the moment because the mild January and first half of February has unexpectedly given way to heavy snowfalls. Hella told me that border crossings never took place in snowy conditions as any footprint would immediately give the game away. So here I am still, waiting for the snow to melt.

A week or so ago we heard about a student performance of the *St Matthew Passion* due to take place in the cathedral, but it was already fully booked. I was so disappointed as I would have loved to hear this piece once more. By the most wonderful stroke of luck, however, a ticket came my way, and so I was able to attend after all.

Students from Freiburg University were performing the work in memory of their fallen colleagues. The conductor himself was a student who, having sustained serious injuries in the fighting, was still receiving treatment as an outpatient. He had rehearsed this choir and orchestra composed entirely of fellow students. Only the soloists were professionals, and they'd certainly managed to get hold of first-class performers.

It was a truly special occasion. Anyone who might have reasonably expected some amateur production was in for a big surprise. It was an astonishing achievement that can only be ascribed to the dedication and application of every single participant. You could tell how everything had been studied and then practised to perfection. And the beauty of the cathedral setting, made available by the Archbishop himself, was entirely fitting.

Could these possibly be the same young people who had carried out the appalling atrocities in occupied territories that we'd heard about on foreign radio stations? No, we learned from the student son of a friend of Wackes that in Freiburg as in Munich there had been a substantial element in the student body that had opposed the regime.[5] In Munich the young people who had dared take action openly had been immediately and brutally suppressed. But in spite of the regime's terror tactics it had not destroyed the spirit of opposition. I fancied I could hear it in this performance. Soaring from the choral harmonies and the sounds of the accompanying instruments came the voice of the oppressed divinity who still won the day and of a violated people who eventually triumphed. This was a voice so strong that it stirred anew a feeling of courage among those listening with such rapt attention and gave us all the strength to carry on until the yearned for end to this tyranny, an end which simply must come.

Letters from Else to Eva Schmidt

Freiburg, 13 April 1944

My dear Eva

Warmest thanks for the lovely letter you wrote on Easter Monday. It's just arrived, along with the news that Lilli can start her treatment at the sanatorium next week! You can just imagine how excited she is now that it's happening at long last. I do hope nothing comes along to delay things in the meantime . . .

Lilli will probably be leaving on Thursday. All sorts of things to prepare, of course, so don't be cross if I close now. Do write again when you can.

A million good wishes to you from me

Your E.

Freiburg, 18 April 1944

My dear Eva

Your kind letter dated 14 April has just arrived, and I'm so pleased as I've been waiting to hear your thoughts on Lilli's news. This time it looks as though it really will happen. Lilli won't have to travel alone, as Peter's friend will go with her most of the way. She's arriving early tomorrow and then they'll leave together. You can imagine how reassuring that is for me.

Saying goodbye will be hard for Rolf even though he's had quite some time to get used to the idea. It's really touching to see quite how attached he is to Lilli.

My heart is full and so many emotions are coursing through me that I can't always find the words. You'll know what I mean.

And just think, on top of all this, yesterday brought news from Fritz: good news.

We were overjoyed.

QR Code 22: The escape begins: 20 April 1944

20 April 1944

On the way

My dear

A thousand thanks for your most recent greetings which came this morning. I can only write a couple of lines here but hope you'll get the gist. May everything go well with you, and please pass on my fond regards to Elisabeth and M[agdalena Heilmann] and A[nnemarie Cohen], and could they in turn please convey my best wishes to Sister Ilse and thank her for what she sent me, which came yesterday and has been put to incredibly good use.

Farewell, my dearest, and my warmest wishes to you. You'll be hearing from me again very soon.

Always yours

E.

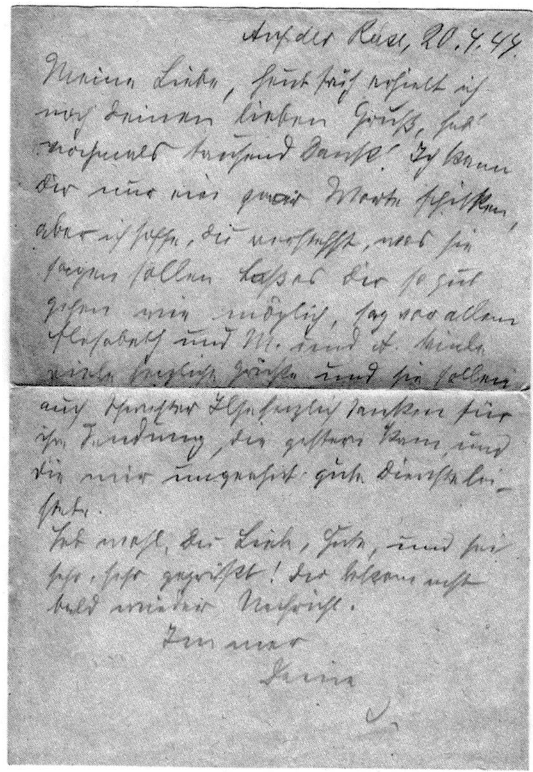

Auf der Reise, 20.4.44.

Meine Liebe, heute früh erhielt ich noch Deinen lieben Gruß, hab' vielmals tausend Dank! Ich kann Dir nur ein paar Worte schicken, aber ich hoffe, Du verstehst, was sie sagen sollen. Lass es Dir so gut gehen wie möglich, grüß vor allem Elisabeth und M. und A. viele, viele herzliche Grüße und sie sollen auch Schwester Ilse herzlich danken für ihre Sendung, die gestern kam, und die mir ungeheuer gute Dienste leistete.

Leb wohl, Du Liebe, Gute, und sei sehr, sehr gegrüßt! Du bekommst recht bald wieder Nachricht.

Immer
Deine
E.

42. Else's letter to Eva the day she left for Switzerland, 20 April 1944.

Else's Diary

Schaffhausen, Switzerland, 24 April 1944

I've been reading the last thing I wrote in February. Yes, for me that oppression is now over and yet everything is still like a dream from which I'm afraid of awakening.

I want to be sure to recount everything to you as accurately as possible.

My patience was more than put to the test. The snow just wouldn't melt and persisted on the ground throughout the whole of March, added to from time to time by fresh falls. Easter approached and the early heralds of spring made their timid appearance, the leaf buds on all the trees and hedges growing fat and shiny. In Freiburg itself the snow had now melted at last but still my longed-for news did not come.

About a fortnight ago Wackes came in from work looking very solemn indeed. Once Rolf had gone to bed, he told me about the following incident. He'd been about to set off for home when he was called in to the local police station by the district police officer, a decent fellow he'd known for many years and who was certainly no friend of the Nazis. There were no other police staff present.

'I wanted to see you on your own,' said the officer. 'You've had in your flat for some time an older lady who fled the bombing elsewhere. You've not registered her with the police in the customary fashion. I know you're going to say that strictly speaking that's no longer always done, and certainly at this station we're happy to turn a blind eye, and where necessary both eyes. But there seems to be someone else in your building who's not so well disposed towards you and must have sensed you're not so keen on the Nazis.' He gave a little smile. 'I can understand all that.'

Wackes wanted to say something at this point but the officer carried on regardless. 'This person clearly wanted to say something to your detriment and took the opportunity to do so while she was here on an unrelated matter. She suggested I take a good hard look at Frau Schröder, this lady who's been living at your flat. It was her belief that Frau Schröder had been heard to say that Germany was no longer up to winning the war, and that it was right for her to intervene as anyone talking in that fashion should be locked up. I managed to placate her somewhat and said I'd look into it. My hope is that she'll calm down if I tell her it's all just been a great big misunderstanding. I'll say that you and Frau Schröder were most indignant that anyone might even suggest that she'd said such a thing. Nonetheless, it would seem advisable for your lady guest to change her place of residence again – not straight away, of course, as that would only result in further idle gossip.'

With that the two men had shaken hands and Wackes had left for home. I was going hot and cold. What next?

'Stay calm, Buddeli. Chin up,' said Wackes, his voice kind and warm. 'I'm quite certain I'd get a second tip-off if there were any real danger. But whereas I wasn't previously all that keen on this plan of yours to escape to Switzerland because of the risks involved, I do now believe it's the right thing to do.'

Lotte stepped in at this point. 'Well, why don't I telephone Hella from work tomorrow? All I need say is that it's high time Buddeli went off to the spa for her convalescence.'

Wackes nodded. 'Good idea.'

Sleep abandoned me that night, as you can well imagine, and in the end I switched on my little bedside lamp to read.

I was on edge all the following day, waiting to hear from Lotte. Yes, she'd managed to speak to Hella, who'd been shocked to hear the news but confirmed that even without the phone call she'd been setting things in motion and I could expect to travel in about twelve days' time. She said that she herself would leave with me and would telegraph the time of her arrival.

'So you see, Buddeli, we're making progress,' Lotte said. 'I'd been rather afraid the whole thing had fallen through but am mighty relieved it's still going ahead.'

The next week was dreadful. Any sudden knock at the door had me on the edge of my seat, ready for action, just like in the days when I lived with Erna and Gustav [Eva and Georg], and not forgetting that whole period with Uncle Karl [Hans]. We'd all agreed that at the slightest strange noise in the evening I should dash into the lavatory out on the stairwell because there was no way to exit the building at the rear. I knew it wasn't a safe place to hide in the event of a really thorough house search, so all I could do was hope it wouldn't ever come to that.

On 18 April the promised telegram came from Hella informing us of her arrival on the following day and telling me to be ready. The strain was by now almost unbearable.

I met Hella at the station. Our departure was set for 20 April, meaning that I'd be crossing the border on Hitler's birthday – Hella was of the opinion that this was deliberate. I asked her how much the journey would cost.

'Well, it was all I could do to persuade them to take German currency. You're going to be the very last one they take over, and they're after a mass of linen and a gold ring into the bargain, but what matters is that we have all that and everything should work out fine.'

'So where do I need to get to and how will it actually work?' I felt incredibly tense over the whole prospect.

'Right, well, I'll tell you. Tomorrow we're heading to Singen. You're not to take a suitcase, just a rucksack at most, nothing too heavy, and one manageable bag. And no hat but you can wear a scarf over your hair. And so they know it's you – don't laugh – you'll need to be carrying a broom.'

I was in no laughing mood, of that you can be sure, but my eyes must have popped out of my head because Hella's reaction was one of mirth. Gripping my hand, she went on. 'Yes, I know it's a strange old way to identify yourself but at least it's safe and sure. And these days it's not easy for anyone to get hold of stuff they need so it won't look the slightest bit odd for a woman to be carrying a broom from one place to another. The tricky bit's getting hold of one in the first place, but what with my coming with you and everything, it means we can just borrow one and then I'll return it to its rightful owner!'

'I'd like a child's play broom,' I said after thinking it over for a moment or two. 'That would be so much better than a full-sized one – far easier to handle and carry.'

'You're right, yes, that'd be much more sensible. We'll ask Lotte where we could borrow one. Now, let me tell you more about what's going to happen. You need to be at Singen for five tomorrow afternoon. You're then to amble along a specified street near the station. Somewhere along there you'll spot a man, who'll give you a discreet signal and then slowly set off. Follow him, and he'll stop where there's no one else around so you can tell him the password and he knows you're the person he has to take. At that point you need to hand over the money, the ring and the collection slip for the parcel of linen that I'll be handing in to left luggage at Singen. He'll tell you everything else you need to know. As far as I'm aware, he'll be passing you on to a second person, and then a third one for the remainder of your route. That's all I can tell you.'

By lunchtime Lotte had had an approach from someone about the play broom. 'Frau M might be able to help, Buddeli. There are children where she lives, she knows you and will do anything she can to offer assistance.'

Luckily for me, Frau M had her little nieces living with her and so had a play broom in excellent condition, and was more than happy to make it available to me.

It took no time at all to pack my rucksack. Shoes, travel slippers, a blouse, nightdress, basic toiletries and my precious diary were all swiftly stowed away. More difficult was what to wear for the journey but my past experiences of deportation meant that I fell all too easily back into the same miserable routine of getting out three sets of underwear, two summer dresses, and finally a skirt and blouse with a winter coat over the top, with last of all the hiking boots given me at the transit camp. I put all these items ready in a pile and Hella said, 'Can you really fit all of that on? Why not try it all out?'

No sooner said than done. What a blessing that I'd weighed a good bit more before all of this started. Once it was all on, yes, I looked a lot more rounded but nothing that would attract attention, or so Hella and Lotte pronounced after looking me up and down.

Saying goodbye the next morning wasn't easy. We'd told Rolf that I was off to work at a children's home in Radolfszell, and he found it a comfort that this wasn't so far away. I'd prepared him long before for a possible sudden departure.

We had to catch the ten o'clock train, due to get into Singen at three in the afternoon. There was a one-hour wait at Donaueschingen so we took the opportunity to track down something hot to eat. I had with me my rucksack plus an old shopping bag and my big leather handbag. Hella was carrying the parcel of linen, her own overnight bag and the play broom. We'd agreed that she'd stay the night in Singen and then return the next day to Freiburg to report back to the others.

I can't tell you how grateful I was to have Hella's company as it made the time pass so quickly with someone to talk to. We arrived in Singen pretty much on time, handed the linen in at left luggage and then meandered through the town together in the opposite direction to where I needed to head later to meet my contact. Once away from the town centre we stopped off at a small beer garden.

Hella broke our silence. 'Are you anxious at all, Buddeli?'

I shook my head. 'Not really, and in fact I feel quite calm. I'm just so relieved that this way of life I've had to adapt to over the last couple of years will finally come to an end by one means or another. Please believe me when I say that if I'd known how long this would all go on for, I'd never have fled to Berlin to live underground the way I did.'

'I believe you,' replied Hella. 'Well, it's high time we were on our way.' We settled our modest bill and wandered back to the station. Hella went into the inn opposite, where we'd arranged that I'd come to look for her if I didn't need to leave straight away. She was of the opinion that I wouldn't be setting off until after dark. We parted quickly.

QR Code 23: Meeting the escape organiser

With the play broom clutched firmly in one hand, I kept a careful lookout as I walked slowly down the prescribed route, rather busy now with a crowd of workers making their way home. And suddenly, over there and quite as if by chance, stood a shortish fellow, sucking on a cigarette as he calmly watched the passers-by. Did I pick up the slightest nod of his head and a wink, almost imperceptible, when he caught sight of me? He turned now and went off down a side street.[6] I set off after him, my heart pounding so hard it might burst! But what was happening now? The man I was watching so intently had turned yet again and walked past me. Was I mistaken then? I couldn't cling to him like a shadow – that would be far too noticeable – so I pottered on a little further in the same direction I'd been following thus far. But what now? My heart skipped a beat when the same man came past me again and then overtook. It was him! I was quite certain of it. The flow of people gradually dissipated, and there were fewer houses here now too, no longer terraced but with gardens and paddocks in between, until before long we'd left it all behind. The man stood there silently, waiting for me to approach.

I gave the password, 'Xaver sent me'.

'You're right, you know where you are with him,' he said approvingly, with an accompanying nod.

What strange creatures we are that this somewhat offhand remark from a stranger left me feeling strangely flattered.

'Do you have the left luggage ticket?' I gave it to him. 'And the other things?' The money and the ring were now in his hands too. 'Good. Come to the station at quarter to nine tonight, stay near the barrier and watch when I go through, then follow me. I'll have your ticket and will get it clipped along with mine. After that, you're to go to the end of the first platform on the right and then walk to the bottom where you'll find a little local train. Get on it and sit tight. It leaves at five past nine.'[7]

I stood there a little while longer and then headed back the way I'd come, suddenly breaking into a cold sweat – had I done the wrong thing by giving everything to that man? What if he disappeared and left me in the lurch? I gave myself a stern talking to and said it had all gone precisely to plan, I just needed to hold my nerve and stay calm! Well, thank goodness Hella was waiting for me, someone who cared about me, and was full of warmth and understanding. Back at the inn opposite the station, I gazed around the lounge bar for Hella and went to sit down with her to let it all spill out. She listened intently and when I voiced my concerns, immediately brushed them off.

'You need have no concerns whatsoever on that account,' she said soothingly. 'You've done exactly what was arranged. Have faith that it'll all go smoothly.'

We sat there a little longer and then took a stroll so that Hella could find a room for the night. The time was dragging. Still two hours to wait.

After a gloomy day with a little drizzle it was now dark but at least there'd been no heavy rainfall. And then there we were, finally at the station, where Hella bought herself a platform ticket before taking up her post near the barrier. There were quite a lot of people about – soldiers, officers and SS men – all doubtless off to mark Hitler's birthday somewhere or other.

Hang on, there he was at last! The small man was making his way slowly towards the barrier so I fell in step behind him. My eyes hadn't adjusted yet after the blinding light of the station concourse, but it was all right because Hella had come to walk alongside me. By now we'd reached a train composed of a very small number of carriages. The small man was standing there already.

'Take this compartment,' he said quietly. 'Here's your ticket. I'll join you after the second stop. It's too risky here with all these people around. I'll go on ahead by bicycle.'

He turned and was gone. Hella had dropped back but now came over to me for a swift farewell. I felt choked with emotion and couldn't speak. And then suddenly she was gone too – this woman who represented the last bridge I had to my past and my previous life. I climbed into the carriage I'd been directed to, which was nearly empty, and dropped into a seat by the door.

The train set off. A few more people had climbed on board before departure. We chugged and rattled along. The ticket inspector came through. I handed him my ticket along with everyone else, but he came back, shone his torch in my face and asked me, 'Where are you getting off?'

Horrified, I realised I had no idea. It had been too dark for me to make out what was printed on the ticket.

'At the third stop,' I ventured.

He went on his way while I sat there in turmoil. We'd gone past the first station, and had already stopped at the second and pulled away. Just then the compartment door opened and someone came in and sat down opposite me.

'Here I am.'

I recognised the voice of the small man. Relieved, I quickly whispered to him the exchange I'd had with the ticket inspector.

'No matter.' He seemed quite unperturbed. 'We're going right to the end of the line – I'll sort it out,' he added soothingly.

I leaned back in my corner. After the third stop the ticket collector came back and said, 'Didn't you say you were getting off at the third station?'

The small man did the talking. 'I think the lady was mistaken and thought Beuren was the third.'

The ticket inspector moved on. I don't know how many more stations there were in all, but it can't have been many. Just before the final one, the small man told me, 'We're here.'

I got off the train after him and thought it seemed even darker outside. You could barely see your hand in front of your face. The man indicated I should wait while he went off to fetch his bicycle from the luggage van. He could easily have abandoned me right there and then, because I'd as good as handed myself over on a platter. The next few minutes felt like an eternity.

But there was his voice again. 'This way.'

We walked on a few steps. 'We're going to rendezvous now with the person who'll take you on the next leg of your journey,' he said softly.[8] We waited until we were joined by someone, who in marked contrast to the first man, seemed really, really tall.

QR Code 24: Journey through the night

43. The 'second man' to guide Else on her escape to Switzerland: escape agent Hugo Wetzstein, 1950s.

The small one handed him something and I heard him say, 'Here's the money. How's it looking?'

The second chap replied curtly, 'Not good,' which really put the wind up me. But then the tall one's voice resounded again in the darkness: 'But we'll try anyway.'

The smaller one replied, 'Good, I'll head off then,' and the darkness swallowed him up.

The tall fellow turned back in my direction. 'Keep about twenty paces behind me, all right?' He lit a cigar, drew on it a few times, making it glow, and then set off. I followed, from time to time seeing the glowing dot of the cigar as the man strode ahead of me. I sensed that we were on a country road. I was pretty sure we were making our way through a village at first, because of the sporadic sound of dogs barking or the occasional lowing of cattle in their sheds.[9] These noises then gave way to a profound silence, in which all I could hear was the dull resonance of the man's footsteps somewhere in front of me. It seemed we'd been walking forever and I lost all sense of time. Eventually we appeared to draw near to a village and I heard muffled human voices floating through the air and then dying away again. We carried on walking. Suddenly I was overcome by mortal fear. I'd lost track of the man, and could neither see nor hear him. What on earth should I do? My heart was thumping, drowning out any other form of sound. I stopped dead in my tracks, but for how long? I have no idea, only that my whole life began to flash before my eyes, back in the far distance with the joyful years of our life together, followed by our separation and all the difficulties I'd faced since, and all I could see was an immense ocean of sorrow, yet shining in it like islands of light all the beauty and nobility that human beings are capable of.

But was there a spectre, a ghostly light taunting me now, or just the glowing spot of the cigar in the man's hand as he came towards me? Yes, that's what it was, and then there he was next to me, and I heard him whisper, 'The third man hasn't come. Hold on to my hand – we need to get away from the road.' I took his hand without saying a word. After this I could sense we were walking in a meadow. We came to a halt.

'There's barbed wire here,' he whispered. Carefully he directed my hand to it. 'Can you feel it?'

'Yes,' I answered.

'Climb over it,' he said. 'I'll help steady you.' I did as I was told and suddenly was standing on the other side of the barbed wire. Then he asked, 'Can you hear the stream below us?'[10] I said I could. He continued, 'We're on a slope running parallel to the stream. Carry on, staying as much as you can at a similar height and the sound of the stream will give you the direction to go in.' He raised his arm and the glowing cigar with it. 'The German Customs House is some distance upstream and on this bank, and further on from there is the border and the Swiss Customs House. That's where you need to get to. Give me your postal identity card and your clothing ration card.'

I gave him both; I'd had them ready in my coat pocket. It had all been arranged that I hand these over so Hella would know that I'd managed to cross the border. But we hadn't got there yet.

'But take me a little bit further,' I said. 'I really can't see in the dark.'

'No. It's too dangerous for me. You'll have to continue on your own. See how you get on.'

And with that he vanished, as if he were a ghost.

I was alone. I could hear the rushing stream below as I went slowly forward, one step at a time. It was clear that I was walking on a sloping meadow which dropped away quite sharply down to the stream at the bottom. I really needed to watch my footing. It was so quiet, and the sounds of the rushing water seemed only to heighten the silence surrounding me. I seemed to be somewhere far beyond the realms of human habitation, in some intermediate zone without a single mortal creature other than myself. I was cut off from my old life and felt as if suspended over a huge chasm with my past on one side and the future on the other. Could I cross that divide or was this the end? Whatever it was that was happening during those minutes, a profound faith in the divine power of destiny brought me the miracle of confidence and drove away the seemingly endless loneliness that had previously possessed me. On I continued, concentrating all my efforts on the need to proceed carefully.[11]

A thump and I was on the ground! A small gully ran across the slope of the meadow at this point and I'd tripped badly but hadn't hurt myself, and was soon back on my feet. But where was my handbag? I'd been carrying it in my left hand in which I didn't have much feeling because of the old weakness. The handbag contained the only photos I had of you and the children, treasured possessions I didn't want to lose. There was also a gold bracelet, the fountain pen I'd been given at the transit camp before the deportations started, a spare pair of spectacles and many other odds and ends. I felt all around me with my right hand, probing everywhere and patting everything. Nothing! But I couldn't stay long in this spot – it was too dangerous to carry on looking and possibly lose my way as a result. I just had to give up on finding the handbag and not cling to material things, so on I went. Somewhere in the distance I heard a church clock striking the hour. I neglected to count the strokes; time had lost all importance.

QR Code 25: Risking life to cross the border

I walked even more slowly, taking ever more careful steps, but then suddenly lost my footing and fell again, coming to with thousands of shining

44. Satellite image from 2011 showing the line of the Swiss border and the old customs house, both are no more than fifty metres from the German border. Drawing and aerial shot supplied by the Swiss Customs office in 2010 showing that the wall where Else fell remains the same. 1: border, 2: Swiss Customs House, 3: German Customs Office, 4: course of the River Biber.

stars dancing before my eyes! I lay quite still for a moment, feeling stone slabs beneath my body. I tried to stand but a sharp shooting pain in my left foot made me collapse on the ground again. It had to be broken, and gingerly feeling around with my fingers, I realised it was severely twisted to the side. If only I knew where I was! All of a sudden, I could hear footsteps and see the light of somebody's lantern or torch. My fall had clearly been overheard in the building alongside the stone-paved courtyard and someone had come to investigate. I called out since it was clearly no use trying to hide any more and I was unable to stand up unaided.

The light drew ever closer. 'Please tell me where I am,' I called out. My voice must have betrayed my fear because the deep voice of a man answered reassuringly, 'Don't worry, you're on Swiss soil here!' I'd landed right in the courtyard of the Swiss Customs House.

Over the last part of the way I'd held strong in my mind the belief that I would be welcomed into Switzerland as a matter of course and with nothing less than kindness. But I could equally well have been seen as some unknown woman who'd crossed the border late at night and caused everyone a whole heap of trouble. I tried now not to lose my nerve, telling myself to accept whatever they decided to do with me.[12] In spite of the severe pain in my ankle I let joy and relief flood over me when I heard the words spoken by the man with the lantern, my messenger from heaven above. He was standing right by me now, and another man had come to join him.

'I think I've broken my foot,' I said after we'd briefly exchanged a greeting.

'Not to worry, we'll look at that right away,' he replied kindly.

With great care and skill the two men lifted me and carried me across to the building. A woman standing at the door welcomed me with great sympathy and then opened a second door through to an office of sorts, where they placed me on a long wooden bench ranged against the wall. She was eager to help and make me comfortable, fetching cushions to place under my head before going off to brew some hot coffee for me. I explained to the customs officials that I'd come from Singen.

'I'll telephone for a doctor from Thayngen and inform the local police,' said one of them.

'Are you in a lot of pain?' asked the other.

I told him I was.

The customs officer's wife now came back with coffee and a rusk for me. I sipped a mouthful of coffee and appreciated its power to revive but couldn't eat. The warmth and kindness I'd met on arrival here did me the power of good though. The woman was amazed that I'd dared make the journey alone and in darkness. I couldn't even have begun to explain how this simply represented the last final link in a long chain of dreadful experiences. I asked for the time. It was almost eleven in Switzerland, one hour different from German summer time.

The doctor and policeman had already arrived by now and greeted me kindly.[13] The doctor, quite a young chap, started a careful examination of the affected ankle. 'I'll have to cut away the boot,' he said. 'It would cause you terrible pain if I simply pulled it off.'

'It doesn't matter, Doctor,' I replied. 'I'll put up with the pain but I really can't do without the boot. Please don't cut it away.'

He thought for a while. 'All right then, I'll give you some morphine so that when I pull your boot off, it'll still hurt but the pain will be easier to put up with.' He set about preparing the injection. 'While it takes effect the police officer will ask you a few questions, unless you don't feel up to it?'

I said I was more than happy to tell him the little I knew. I related very briefly how I knew nothing at all about the middlemen working for the smuggling organisation – the official had taken it as read that this was what we were dealing with here – but that everything had been done through a whole string of people, all of whom were unknown to me, and that I'd simply gone to connect with my contact in Singen. I had nothing to say about the man who'd met me there as I'd been so agitated that I'd paid scant attention to what he looked like. The police officer then asked me to describe the route I'd taken. I related the first fall I'd had on the slope of the meadow and how I'd become separated from my handbag in the process, which had been horribly upsetting.

'It sounds as though you lost the bag on German soil but we'll take a look first thing in the morning. We're right behind the border here,' volunteered the police officer.

(I was later told it was nowhere to be found.)

He took some brief notes along with my name – my real name! This was the first time in two years I'd been able to use it.

'It's a miracle you didn't break your neck rather than your ankle,' marvelled the doctor. 'That wall you came off is about two and a half metres high!' He turned to the policeman. 'And what should we best do for this lady now?'

The two men held a short discussion and agreed that the best thing would be to get me in a splint with some temporary bandaging and then off to the hospital at Schaffhausen.[14]

'They'll wonder why a lady with a lower leg fracture is being brought in as an emergency, but that doesn't matter – it's the right thing to do. I'll telephone for a vehicle myself as I know of one that lends itself well to accommodating anyone with an injury of this type.' He was clearly pleased to have found such a satisfactory solution.

Meanwhile the morphine jab had taken effect and the doctor began to remove my boot. It hurt most dreadfully, but what did that matter after everything else that had happened? The boot was off, the splint was on and the binding in place. The doctor phoned for the transport.

I must have fallen asleep at this point and certainly didn't regain full consciousness as the doctor and the customs man carried me to the car. It's greatly to my regret that I was in no state to thank these kind people properly.

I was driven through the night and can't really say for how long exactly, but later heard that I'd arrived at the hospital around half past midnight. I woke when we came to a halt outside a brightly lit building, and felt myself being lifted from the car and carried up some steps.

Next I remember making out the shapes of two women, one of whom was clearly a deaconess, as they started to undress me. I was vaguely aware of their gentle amusement as they peeled away layer after layer of garments but was far too tired to say anything. I wanted for nothing now. I had achieved my goal. The life I had been leading, devoid of any rights of my own, outside the law – terrifying, full of danger and yet quite extraordinary at times – had finally come to an end.

Letters from Lotte Goldschagg to Eva Schmidt

Freiburg, 21 April 1944

Dear Frau Urtal[15]

I am writing to let you know that I have received news of Lilli. She is on the way to her new place and can write to you herself from there. There is no need for any concern whatsoever. In a week or so I'll have something more conclusive to tell you and will write again then.

In the meantime, best wishes from Lotte Goldschagg.

An acquaintance of Lilli's was able to accompany her part of the way and says it all went well.

Freiburg, 6 May 1944

Dear Frau Urtal

I've just this minute received a card dated 25 April from my sister-in-law in Zürich bringing best wishes to us both from Lilli. My relative has been to Schaffhausen to visit her at the hospital where she was taken on account of the broken leg she sustained on her journey. She's being very good-humoured about it all.

With it being a clean break, she'll soon be able to move to my sister-in-law's home, a nice house with a pretty garden in Zürich's Altstetten. She'll be able to make a full recovery there.

Now we too can feel at ease.

With best regards,

L. Goldschagg

Letter from Siegfried to His Daughter Gustel and Her Husband

Oxford, 14 May 1944

Dear Gustel and Heini

I have the most wonderful surprise news for you! Else has been in Switzerland these last 10–14 days. She's there in Schaffhausen. I heard by telegram from Alice. I cannot begin to imagine how she has managed to do this in the fifth year of the war! Perhaps we'll hear how it all happened, perhaps not. We've been given her address as the Canton Hospital in Schaffhausen, but she's in good health. And Alice has already assured Else that funds are available to her. She'll have arrived there with the absolute minimum, that's for sure. Even if it's only her physical safety she can feel sure of in the first instance – this address is doubtless a camp for refugees – it is to be hoped that the sense of freedom and security she can now gave will help push other matters into the background and be a soothing influence on her mind and spirit. Poor Else, she has been under so much pressure and has lived in constant uncertainty, but now all that is behind her. I have sent her a telegram telling of our joy.

Siegfried's Diary

Lavender Croft, Hitchin

12 November 1944

Ten months without writing a single entry, but I'm finally opening my diary again. For several weeks now I have been here in Lavender Croft, a Quaker house at Hitchin in Hertfordshire.

Turning seventy proved something of a crisis for me, partly down to the effects of working at the Co-op office and partly to the strain of the war and all that goes with it. The two months I spent in hospital helped my physical condition but not my mental state, as being in the constant company of the sick and the dying was extremely lowering.

But then at the end of April came the long-awaited news – Else was safe. It felt like a miracle, all brought about by her personal courage, her admirably capable nature and the help of good friends. She is now in Switzerland, near Zurich, not quite fully recovered but waiting for physiotherapy following a leg injury. This news does somewhat lighten my acute sense of guilt.

From Else herself I have received only one letter in her own hand, dated 1 May, followed by a card she sent via Alice Rosenberg during August – the most important news is that she is no longer in danger, is in reasonable shape both physically and mentally and can now live without the constant threat of death hanging over her. I do hope the fear and unease she has had to live with for so long will now gradually start to fade. I would so love to know everything about her daily life over there! Our hope is to be reunited in 1945, but we cannot begin to imagine how or where. I find myself wondering whether my work in support of the authorities' post-war planning will mean we can get some kind of support in mapping our way through the maze that is always part of any such attempt.

Life in a Quaker house such as this does mean doing without certain luxuries but this is more than compensated for by my improved physical condition, something I owe also to what was once a reasonably sound constitution. The community here is made up of older people from all sorts of backgrounds, many of whom are failing physically and displaying all the somewhat self-centred characteristics that may come with age. As a consequence, they don't make for easy company, and I often choose to remain silent. I have, however, been fortunate enough to be party to two days of productive talks with Mayor Rathbone,[16] and this in itself has given life some direction and lifted my self-esteem.

We need to feel a certain confidence in the likely outcome of the war. Battle is now being waged at Germany's gates and will soon, I trust, drive them asunder.

Hitchin, 30 December 1944

Since my last entry there have been two telegrams from Else! One to mark Hanna's birthday and then another ten days ago with Christmas and New Year greetings. Letters, however, seem not to be getting through in either direction. On top of that we have heard via our contacts in the USA that Else was staying for a time with the Quakers in Geneva and was actually offered a live-in domestic post by their head. I feel some regret that she did not choose to take this up, or felt perhaps unable to, but she seems instead to be committed to accommodation with Pastor Michaelis in Feldis. All the same, the Quakers could arrange her safe passage to England the most speedily, and I have already made contact with their London group to discuss a plan for her this winter. They were the people who tried to create a route out for her in 1939. I still think of her every day, wondering whether she is now fully recovered, wanting to be able to picture her immediate surroundings and whatever work she is currently engaged in. And every day I look out for a letter.

As far as my post-war planning support work goes, I have today written a report on the scale and scope of the Reich Ministry of Justice (within the Nazi-created Akademie für Deutsches Recht) and its activities, with a list of its personnel, including their ages, but am not yet fully satisfied with it. I am refining my own vision of a future civil service – something I would very much enjoy doing more work on, adding to existing information through my perusal of ministerial documents. [. . .]

An end to the war this winter now looks highly unlikely in view of the rather unsatisfactory offensive in the west.[17] The Allies, along with the Russians – no longer fighting on their own soil – are in essence laying siege to a fortress, while the toxic impact of bombing is slowly but surely taking effect through the destruction of armament factories, oil production and rail infrastructure, all of which is expected to bring the enemy to its knees. Saving lives is viewed as more important than saving time. Am I reading the signs with any accuracy, though? Will this all continue into the summer and autumn even? Well, unless something quite unexpected occurs, yes, it looks likely to drag on.

1945

Siegfried's Diary

Hitchin, 26 February 1945

Our exchange of letters is now more an exchange of our innermost thoughts, something we have not been permitted for years. At long last I can picture Else in this peaceful place near the mountains – the Pfarrhaus Michaelis – and can tell that she finally feels unburdened and secure. We both have so many questions over how she might make the journey to England and at last dare to wonder how the future might look for us both – tough at first, with such limited options for employment and accommodation open to us. Simply being together will help us regain our former strength, however. It is bound to be summer in any case before this all comes to fruition, and that will make everything less difficult.

Hitchin, Sunday, 29 April 1945

At long last the Nazi regime is fighting for its life. It has taken the occupation of three-quarters of Germany, immeasurable self-destruction and the decimation of every city to the east and the west for this to come about. How we have hoped and longed for this moment! [. . .]

An English Member of Parliament, Mrs Mavis Tate, has just been on the wireless, reporting on atrocities she and a cross-party group has seen evidence of this week in the concentration camp of Buchenwald. Rapid action taken by the Americans prevented the Nazis from hiding their vile abominations.

National Socialism has breathed its last; the final nail has been driven into its coffin and there can be no resurrection. And here is the reason why. Words and pictures must be used to relate the full horror of the last twelve years to every German who did not already know, and that is quite a few. The enemy of civilisation has been broken, the bloodletting has abated and my spirits are lifting.

Reports are coming in that the Freiheitsaktion Bayern[1] movement is trying to prevent the final decimation of Munich and render futile any attempts by the Nazis to flee into the mountains. Any remaining Nazi

45. From the Rosenfeld family album: the children, mid-1920s, and Else and Siegfried Rosenfeld, 1945.

resistance in Berlin has collapsed thanks to the action of working people as well as some of the military. And fighting in the west has captured a hundred and twenty thousand prisoners of war in the last two days alone. It seems likely that the only people left with the strength of will and sensible ideas for the way ahead will turn out to include those two hundred thousand Germans captured and selected for special training by the Russians, together with other prisoners of war who have had a great deal of unexpected time to gain new skills and experience.[2] The Nazi regime was systematic in its suffocation of all independent thought and action and those it made leaders were merely those who had been easily brought to heel.

Ellen Simon, one of the German Quakers now in London, has estimated that the number of orphaned children in Germany stands at three and a half million, and yet food and housing will be the only matters addressed along with the re-establishment of the postal service and railways, as well as the civil service and other public bodies.

On Wednesday (26 April) I had my second meeting with Colonel Ogelthorpe at 27 Princess Garden to discuss my report on the Reichsjustizministerium. Following that, I met with Ellen Simon herself who recommended me to Erich Hirsch of the Gollancz publishing house, as he himself had previously worked as a social worker in Frankfurt-am-Main. He undertook to talk to people in the Home Office, people with some empathy and influence, about Else coming here to England, and is apparently hopeful of a positive outcome.

Two exciting announcements from the continent! The Russians have designated Karl Renner[3] as Prime Minister of Austria. Mussolini has been executed.

Perhaps May 1 can be renamed as the Day of Germany's Subjugation?

Hitchin, Thursday, 10 May 1945

Two days of victory celebrations are now behind us. Yesterday evening I went to a spot from where I could see the city bathed in floodlights as the crowds danced with joy and relief.

For me this is no celebration of victory as such, more the quiet satisfaction that our enemy, one that loathed us, has at long last been silenced while we survive, and the law will finally prevail over those who have demonstrated their disregard for civilisation. All they wanted to do was show their contempt for and loathing of other human beings. The seeds sown by them have borne fruit more terrible than could ever have been imagined.

In his speech yesterday, Stalin said the aim was not to ruin Germany and then to carve it up, but how can anyone now instil respect for humankind in the minds of those who gave themselves the right to run riot and disdained all those they deemed inferior? Perhaps the English–American occupation can contribute something here, but how will that work with the Russians? More likely is that they will be filled with hatred and a powerful desire for revenge against the gross injustices meted out to their own people and on their land.

The scale of work ahead seems inconceivable, starting with the clearance of sites wrecked in the bombing and the building of new homes. [. . .] I have been asked by the Association of Lawyers if I would be willing to take on specific tasks where my professional knowledge can be of assistance and have, of course, agreed. I don't think much will come of it but if the call came, I would do it if the timing and circumstances were right.

Hitchin, 20 July 1945

I still long for the day of Else's return. So much has been delayed by the snap election here and the current instability of the government. I can't really write to Else about the controversy raging in this country regarding foreigners and refugees, and how influential circles are pressing for all the latter to be returned. The authorities seem worryingly eager to stop the old subsidies. [. . .]

I see that Wolfgang[4] started a letter to me when in Berlin but posted it from Munich on 6 July. True, he described irreversible damage in most cities but went on to comment on the not insignificant number of people whose names demonstrate that there are already well-educated non-Nazis playing a part in municipal administrations, and giving examples of these. This welcome development has also been confirmed in a number of wireless broadcasts. (Hoegner,[5] government minister for Bavaria and prosecutor general, and Goldschagg, top economics official, to name but two.)

And here in the streets the lights shine once more, the wartime barriers constructed from concrete blocks, iron bars and barbed wire – with the intention of hindering any invasion – are in the process of being dismantled, while aircraft can fly overhead without causing alarm! In the evening there is still the occasional sound of a bomber in flight, probably on its way to dispose safely of excess munitions by dumping them in the North Sea, or so the newspapers tell us.

Hitchin, 10 December 1945

No diary entries for five months – but I have at least been free to write to you, Else, and our exchanges are now so regular and uncensored, thank goodness.

But then your diary of what happened to you during the period between 1939 and 1944 arrived here, and as I turned its pages the true horror of what you lived through without me leapt out at me.[6] We have also been receiving, the two of us, personal visits from mutual friends who can add to the accounts we ourselves are giving: Ellen Simon coming to you and Hanna Bertholet[7] to me.

We are now getting ready for your arrival. Money and a roof over our heads are all-important, but it is not easy to see how that can be resolved. Finding a publisher willing to commit to your book would be a happy solution, but will that happen? Frau Bertholet told me you would have preferred another title, something along the lines of 'About the Other Germany'.

But every page, every line surely, actually describes Germany's criminal actions? You no longer want to see the evil side, a state of mind you yourself miraculously overcame through sheer strength of will and your love of others. You shudder to think of Germany's conduct and see only goodness – all those good people who helped you survive.

Whether you intended it or not, your book is first and foremost an indictment, made all the more powerful by the remarkable absence of angry words and hatred on your part. The way you have presented the facts leaves an indelible impression, as do the actions of all those who came to your assistance. And it is also true that you helped yourself by putting aside your own plight in order to aid others. You saw this as a labour of love, and in caring for others were able to bring yourself some degree of comfort. Your personal strength has been exceptional, with so many people able to draw benefit from this and doing so with gratitude.

The people who gave you support amount to this: Tilla, Annemarie, Eva Schmidt, Hanna Schadendorf, Grete Berndt, Uncle Karl, Peter Heilmann and his bride-to-be, and dear Wackes and his wife. Then there is the kindly postwoman, the obliging police officer who checked up on you all at Uncle Karl's place – must I add those two as well? Now the list is complete – and that's all it is – 'The other Germany'.

But even if I were to count all those people twice, look how few they really are in number! Maybe in your shoes I would have seen it differently. You tend to ask very little of others if anything, and it is your own sense of moderation that seems to double or indeed triple in scale any contribution by another person.

Can we really be that subjective in our judgment? How are we to draw far-reaching conclusions from such questions of such enormous import?

One day soon there will be time for you and me to talk these things over and, I hope, through those conversations learn to understand one another fully too.

EPILOGUE TO ELSE BEHREND-ROSENFELD'S DIARIES (1963)

So many readers of my book have asked what happened to us afterwards that I have been moved to add this by way of an epilogue.

During my long spell in hospital at Schaffhausen I experienced nothing but kindness and warmth from all the staff, the other patients and their visitors, not forgetting the six Berliners who had also fled and then read about me in the 'Schaffhauser Zeitung'! I had been billed as 'the refugee who literally fell into Switzerland'. In my three-month stay, not a day went by without at least one of the Berliners at my bedside. They were able to put me in touch with the Swiss charity heading up provision for refugees coming in from all over Europe.

I want to take this opportunity once again to offer up my heartfelt thanks to all at the relief organisation as well as to every Swiss national I came into contact with, as well as my Berlin chums, for every bit of practical and spiritual help. Back then I had forgotten what it was like not to live in perpetual fear. And I'm referring here not to fear for myself because you somehow forget that when you're in constant danger, but to the fear I felt every single day for those risking their lives on my own account and that of their families.

One of the joys of many conversations I had with the lady in the next bed was to pick up news of an old friend of ours, a chaplain who had been based at our most progressive institution for young offenders in Prussia. My husband and I had got to know him through our mutual interest in prison conditions.

But in 1933 he had been removed from his post and his religious beliefs and socialist principles meant he could find no further work of this kind in Nazi Germany. As my husband and I had deliberately broken all ties in order not to put anyone we knew at risk, I was quite unaware of Pastor Michaelis' new post in a little mountain village in the canton of Grisons. He wrote as soon as he heard of my own whereabouts, saying how pleased he was and pressing me to stay at his home once I was discharged from hospital.

Well, it certainly proved to be the ideal place to convalesce and get back my old vim and vigour. The village was high up, well over a thousand metres, and set in beautiful scenery. As was the case in those days for a single gentleman, there was regular domestic help in the form of a good friend of his mother, so I was as well catered for as he was! Another major

46. Else Rosenfeld, Swiss interrogation record, April 1944.

factor in my recovery was the freedom openly to exchange letters with my husband and children. This brought me such happiness.

For the best part of a year I was able to enjoy a simple life in this community of one hundred and fifty hard-working souls, sharing in their joys and sorrows and their charming mountain traditions.

In May 1945 the war in Europe ended and with it a nightmare that had endured for twelve long years. But still this did not bring the reunion that my family and I needed.

I soon found a job as a welfare worker with the Schweizer Arbeiterhilfswerk, one of the charities leading the Swiss post-war support to those countries affected by the long conflict. The fact that I was an experienced social worker, recently arrived from Germany and therefore seen to have a deeper understanding than any local colleagues of the type of support children and young people most urgently needed, meant that I could do a lot to help an organisation that would not normally have been in a position to employ a refugee. For a good six months, and in two out of ten cities, I helped with the groundwork for the organisation of two children's homes and a food

47. Peter and Ursula Rosenfeld, wedding photo, 1 June 1946: (*centre*) Ursula and Peter Rosenfeld; (*right of couple*) Ursula's sister, Hella Simon, who had come to England with the Kindertransport, as had Ursula herself; (*right*) Else and Siegfried Rosenfeld; (*second from left*) Hanna Rosenfeld.

programme for babies and school pupils, working with day nurseries and workshops for youngsters.

It was while I was doing all this that my book was first published. This was in early November 1945.

We had lived apart for almost seven years but it was not until March 1946 that I was allowed to travel to England and did so on a Nansen passport. The moment the aircraft landed on English soil I espied the figure of my husband as he stood there with the children, all waving to me.

There are no words to describe a reunion like this. All the fears and anxieties, all the grief and suffering melted away to create space for a sense of gratitude and joy that was utterly overwhelming.

My husband and I shared two years of happiness, enriched by the close proximity of our children, both contented in their chosen occupations. His sudden death was as he would have wished it. But it was so hard for us to take in.

A few months after my arrival in London, where we had a room with relatives, I had found work. This meant my travelling widely in England and Scotland for over a year, usually for periods of ten days at a time with breaks at home in between. I was employed by the Foreign Office to assist with the hundreds of thousands of German POWs still living in military camps and mostly working on the land. My job was to provide a programme of evening talks for these men but with time for discussion afterwards. I had to go to a number of different locations but the evening commitment left me fairly free during the day so I had time to get to know this beautiful country and its people, its landscape and culture.

My husband took a keen interest in my work and came up with so many good ideas. More than anything he helped me pen replies to the astonishing number of letters that then started to arrive at our home from the men in the camps I had visited. Our correspondents hailed from all over Germany, and all walks of life, and covered a huge age range, probably from as young as eighteen to as old as sixty.

The theme of the evening talks had been education in the penal system with particular reference to young offenders, something my husband and I had worked on before and felt suitable subject matter for this audience. I always started with a brief overview of my own background. Lively and engaged discussions developed on almost every occasion. I was surprised to find that I was always given a free hand with these prisoners and that there was no English presence at all. Perhaps this is what made the discussions flow so freely. Attendance was entirely voluntary. It was rare to find a female speaker doing this kind of work and in many cases I was the first German national to come and talk to them. That explained why so many turned up.

But the men's questions and discussions went far beyond the planned subject matter. The fact that I always opened the evening with an introduction to my own background meant that the issues preoccupying everyone – collective guilt, antisemitism, the atrocities of the concentration camps, the acts of brutality that any normal person struggles to comprehend – were openly spoken about.

I gave them honest replies to the best of my knowledge and conscience. At the start of every talk I would introduce myself as a Jewish Socialist and expected a certain lack of cooperation, if not outright hostility. But over the course of more than one hundred such occasions, I never encountered anything of the kind. All those letters we received – from men whose names I could not have put a face to – told of how they had heard about the brutality but had not believed it, writing off the film footage and talks as enemy propaganda.

I spoke too of the courage of their fellow countrymen who had helped me and carried out acts of resistance. They could see that I was telling them this in all objectivity and honesty and were prepared to believe me. But the truth clearly burdened them. It felt like knowledge they'd rather not have had.

Everything that happened during this time served only to strengthen my belief that it had been right to report on all the positives in my book and not to dwell only on the negatives. I had always emphasised the support I received more than any of the suffering.

I knew that a lot of Germans were ignorant of the crimes committed and had no understanding of the scale of the killings, millions of Jews, practising Christians and Socialists of every hue. Just how many did not know and how many did not *want* to know because it would have been dangerous to do so, nobody will ever be certain. But for as long as the earth turns on its axis we should never forget that the number of true heroes was tiny and their deeds known only to an equally tiny circle. Nor should we ever forget to ask ourselves whether we too would have been capable of such acts of heroism.

It was this knowledge that combined with many other factors to make me want to return home. While I still had the energy to work, I wanted to be part of the developments in prison welfare for inmates and those newly released, something written off by the Nazis as humanitarian nonsense. My nearest and dearest are settled and safe here, while in Germany there were still friends who had demonstrated their loyalty and bravery over and over again in my time of need.

QR Code 26: Else reflects on her experiences

And there's something else. The only explanation I ever found for my survival is that there had to be specific duties awaiting me in however many

48. Families meet up: (*from left*) Edmund Goldschagg, Peter and Ursula Rosenfeld, and Else Rosenfeld with grandchildren, Icking, around 1952.

years I had left. So the obvious path has been to do my bit in ensuring Germany deals properly with its past, and I have done this by sharing my own experiences with the younger generation, at times through writings and at others by giving talks, as well as carrying on with my prison work on a voluntary basis. This seemed a useful way to live the rest of my life.

My children are well and truly grown and have their own families and no longer need the support I gave when I first retired from paid employment and helped with the grandchildren. I have been fortunate enough to go to South America to visit our eldest daughter and will always cherish the memory of my long stay there. Without any obvious livelihood and with my energy failing, I had not previously been in any position to arrange the homeward journey to Germany. But at the end of summer 1952 my widow's pension was authorised and so the time was right.

49. Eva Schmidt (*left*) and Else Rosenfeld in Icking, 1953.

I was sure I would be granted the necessary permission to settle in Bavaria on account of our previous residency there. The arrangements were made surprisingly quickly and the reimbursement of years of lost pension meant I was able to have a little bungalow built on the same plot in Isartal we had occupied before. A friend had made the purchase and then leased me a plot at the far end of the huge garden. I soon found work at the nearby prison which accommodated not only young women but women of other ages serving their first sentence.

Now that I am over seventy I find I can no longer carry out this kind of work and am happy to make way for the young and strong.

My little house sits beautifully in the surrounding countryside and has become my home. Not a day passes without my feeling grateful for the view over meadows and woodland towards the mountains.

I enjoy working in my little garden, all the more so as it is unfenced and my kindly neighbours are close at hand. But the times I love best are when my children and grandchildren come for the holidays, as do friends old and new, all able to rest and relax in this glorious place.

There's plenty of time and quiet for me to read and to keep up with my correspondence, something that has remained a large part of my life. I always spend the winters in England in my children's own homes and enjoy sharing in their lives and those of the tribe of grandchildren.

As for me, I have led an enriching and fulfilling life but however warm and cherished my memories may be, including recollections of those no longer with us, I live in the present with everything that it still holds.

NOTES

1939

1 After the Night of the Pogrom in November 1938, Great Britain declared its readiness to take in from Germany unaccompanied refugee children under the age of seventeen. This meant roughly ten thousand Jewish children were brought to safety. For each child the sum of 50 pounds sterling (now equivalent to around 1,289 pounds) had to be deposited by way of a guarantee. Fast, *Children's Exodus.*

2 On 30 November 1938 the first passage for children departed Berlin for London. In 1939 a total of twelve Kindertransport trains left Munich.

3 The children were permitted one suitcase, one bag and ten Reichsmark. One photograph was allowed. Toys and books were forbidden.

4 Franconia is a region in Bavaria.

5 Emmy Kohn was a kindergarten teacher. After her dismissal in 1933 she worked for the Jewish Community. In 1943 she was deported to Theresienstadt.

6 The Jewish Community Centre in Munich was founded in 1815 after the 1813 edict giving Jews in Bavaria legal status and religious freedom. From 1929 Dr Alfred Neumeyer was its chair in Munich as well as of the Bavarian Association of such community centres. The Jewish Community office looked after services in the three synagogues, teaching in Jewish schools, apprentice training centres, the residential college of housekeeping for young ladies at Wolfratshausen, as well as general welfare, the hospital and cultural events.

7 The first of Else's letters delivered to Eva Schmidt bears the date 12.11.1938, the last 20.04.1944.

8 Else usually calls her husband Fritz, not Siegfried.

9 In November 1932 Siegfried Rosenfeld was relieved of his post and then forced into retirement on 1 May 1933. The two factors at work here were his SPD membership and his Jewish origins. StAM Staatsanwaltschaften 7863, written report by lawyer Willi Walter to the public prosecutor at the Special Court in Munich, 20.6.1934; StAM WB 1a and 4433. Mosse and Paucker, *Entscheidungsjahr 1932*, p. 54.

10 Gustel, Siegfried's daughter from his first marriage, herself married Heinz Behrend, Else's youngest brother. The agricultural training farm at Groß-Breesen was run by Curt Bondy, social education worker. Angress, *Generation zwischen Furcht und Hoffnung.*

11 The River Isar runs through Munich and the railway line follows its course south.

12 In late 1938 the authorities in Upper Bavaria withdrew the Wolfratshausen college teaching permit. StAM LRA 40478. Jörgensen, Krafft and Bäuml-Stosiek, ed., *'Wir lebten in einer Oase des Friedens'.*

13 In Munich the windows of forty-six businesses were smashed and Jewish men arrested. BayHStA Staatskanzlei 6412, Ministry of the Interior, 10 November 1938.

14 Built in 1887, the main synagogue in Herzog-Max-Straße was destroyed on 9 June 1938 on the grounds of 'road improvements'.

15 The National Socialist Party Sturmabteilung (SA) was a paramilitary force. Its members were generally known as Stormtroopers. The Gestapo, short for Geheime Staatspolizei, or secret police, was instrumental in carrying out persecution measures.

16 Dachau had been set up in 1933 as a 'model camp'. As a result of the 1938 pogrom, between thirty and sixty thousand individuals were rounded up and transported by train across the Reich to the camps at Sachsenhausen, Buchenwald and Dachau. Heusler and Weger, *'Kristallnacht'*, pp. 122–138.

17 Lord Ivor Charles Spencer-Churchill was a cousin of Winston Churchill.

18 Dr X is probably an alias for Dr Otto Handwerker; we are grateful to Dr Susanne Wanninger for this information.

19 From 10 November 1938 to 17 March 1939 Jews were banned from borrowing library books. The ban was then lifted, but only until autumn 1941. Wanninger, *Rudolf Buttmann.*

20 The children's home at 7 Antonienstraße was run by the Jewish youth charity and had been in place there since 1926. On 11 April 1942 it was closed down, its warden and all remaining children deported. Grube and Macek, Kinderheim, pp. 87–104. On the Jewish old people's homes, Heusler and Weger, *'Kristallnacht'*, pp. 75f.

21 Dr Gertrud Luckner worked for the German charity Caritas; Rosenfeld and Luckner, eds., *Lebenszeichen aus Piaski*, p. 8; See Glossary of Key People.

22 The Office for Aryanisation at 27 Widenmayerstrasse fell under the Gauleiter, therefore the Nazi Party, not the Gestapo. It was responsible for what was referred to as the 'recovery' of Jewish possessions as well as the allocation of Jews to accommodation in 'Jewish flats' and places of internment.

23 Hans Wegner was in charge of the Office for Aryanisation; Kasberger, Wegner, pp. 230–244.

24 Dr Rudolf and Dr Annemarie Cohen were Munich Quakers. See Glossary of Key People.

25 Ration stamps were issued to all civilians. They were colour coded and covered sugar, meat, fruit and nuts, eggs, dairy products, margarine, cooking oil, grains, bread, jams and fruit jellies.

26 For the urban district of Munich there were twelve shops that Jews and Jewish workers were allowed to use. StAM Gestapo 58, report 18.10.1939.

27 On 2 August 1935 Hitler designated Munich 'the Capital of the Movement'.

28 On 20 September 1939 all Jews had to hand in their radios. This was a requirement under anti-Jewish law.

29 Since April 1939 the law governing tenancies for Jews meant that measures were in place for the eviction of Jews from their property. In the end Jews were forced to make their own arrangements in what came to be called 'Jewish houses' or 'Jewish flats'.

1940

1 The Reichsvereinigung of Jews in Germany was founded in 1933 to represent German Jews. In September 1939 it came under the control of national security, and therefore the Gestapo, and was subject to its orders. All those living in Germany and classified as Jews under the Nuremberg Laws had to join the association and pay contributions. Meyer, Inevitable Dilemma, pp. 297–312.

2 Prior to this there had been two deportations from Vienna, on 20.10. and 26.10.1939. Bundesarchiv Koblenz, ed., Gedenkbuch.

3 These deportations were arranged by SS-Gruppenführer Reinhard Heydrich. Rosenfeld and Luckner, eds., *Lebenszeichen aus Piaski*, pp. 31f.

4 Doctor of philosophy Bruno Finkelscherer, born 1906 in Munich, murdered 1943 in Auschwitz, had been a religious instructor and deputy rabbi at the Ohel Jakob Synagogue since 1933.

5 The despatch of parcels was prompted by reports from those deported to Piaski. Details in Rosenfeld and Luckner, eds., *Lebenszeichen aus Piaski.*

6 The original confirmations are preserved in the Rudolf Cohen private archive. Source: Rudolf Cohen Jr, 18.8.2010.

7 Mighetti is a wartime artificial food (Mi[lch-spa]g[h]etti) resembling rice created from whey, wheat flour and potato starch, mixed with milk.

8 After the Reich-wide Night of the Pogrom, three US representatives of the Quakers in Berlin secured assurances that their organisation's despatch of relief parcels to Jews would not be interfered with. Holl, ed., *Stille Helfer.*

9 Ernst Heilmann, leading politician and chair of the SPD in the Prussian parliament, was murdered at Buchenwald on 3 April 1940.

10 Siegfried Rosenfeld found somewhere to stay in the village of Burcote, near Oxford. His professional legal background could not be recognised in England and, being a foreigner, he was only permitted to take a post that could not be filled by a native. For more on the position of migrants in England see Grenville, *Jewish Refugees*, and Malet and Grenville, *Changing Countries.*

11 Rosenfeld had been working for many years on a history of Jews in different European countries.

12 The Rosenfelds had given thought to a second escape route of emigration to Santo Domingo.

13 Both an entry visa and an immigration permit were obligatory.

14 Hanna Schadendorf lived with her husband, Kurt, and their five children, in Grossenhain, near Dresden.

15 With England's entry into the war, any refugee with a German passport was deemed an 'enemy alien' regardless of where they stood regarding the Nazi regime. These people were interned on the Isle of Man for several months at a stretch.

16 Professor Fritz Heinrich Heinemann, *Biographisches Handbuch der deutschsprachigen Emigration*, vol. II/1, pp. 479f. Dr Rudolf Olden, a prominent lawyer, was until 1933 a leader writer and deputy editor at the *Berliner Tageblatt*; he worked at the *Weltbühne* and on various exile newspapers. Ibid., vol. I, p. 539.

17 Dora Wesley lived in Surrey; now a teacher, she had been a penfriend of Gustel, daughter of Siegfried and his first wife. Quaker records on Siegfried Rosenfeld held by Rudolf Cohen. Mrs Margret Bligh was Hanna's employer from September 1939 to June 1942.

18 Hedi (Hedwig) Kraus was Siegfried Rosenfeld's sister, Hertha her daughter. The family lived near Philadelphia. Marta Rosenbaum was a sister of Siegfried's deceased wife, Frau Gertrud Rewald.

19 Lawyer Friedrich Wittelshöfer, a senior ministry official and SPD member, had left for England in August 1939. *Biographisches Handbuch der deutschsprachigen Emigration*, vol. I, p. 828.

20 The *City of Bernares* was torpedoed in the North Atlantic by a German U-boat on 18 September 1940. It sank and 248 individuals, including 77 children, lost their lives. Thomas Mann's daughter, Monika, was one of the 158 survivors.

21 The Pioneer Corps was apparently the only British military unit in which 'enemy aliens' could serve.

22 At the instigation of the Baden Gauleiter, Robert Wagner and Joseph Bürckel, Rhineland-Palatinate, 6,500 Jews from Baden, Palatinate and Saarland were deported on 22 October 1940 to the French internment camp at Gurs in France. This was the first systematic deportation of Jews out of Germany. Steinbach, Leiden, 109–120.

23 This is likely to be a later entry by Else; the arrest date is not accurate. Lawyer and politician, Otto Hirsch, born 1885 in Stuttgart, was in 1933 co-founder and chair of the Association of Jews. The National Socialists arrested Hirsch in February and took him away to Mauthausen, where they murdered him. Sauer, *Otto Hirsch*.

24 The Bodleian is the principal library at the University of Oxford.

25 James W. Parkes's *The Jew and His Neighbour: A Study of the Causes of Anti-Semitism* had been published by the Christian Movement Press in 1931.

26 Siegfried Rosenfeld could read English but struggled with the spoken language, so he took a number of English courses.

1941

1 For Avigdor see Saint Sauveur-Henn, Landwirtschaftliche Kolonien.

2 Karl Stahl was head of the Jewish Community Centre.

3 Franz Mugler worked at the Office for Aryanisation with effect from 1939.

4 Two internment camps for Munich Jews were set up in Milbertshofen and in Berg am Laim.

5 Käthe Behrend had emigrated in 1939 to Argentina and worked in a textile company in Buenos Aires.

6 Sebastian Haffner (real name Raimund Pretzel), journalist, emigrated in 1938 to England where, in 1941, he published a polemic and indictment of Germany titled *Germany: Jekyll and Hyde*. He was one of the promoters and early writers of *Die Zeitung*, published for German exiles by the British government in 1941–45; since 1942 he had been a journalist on the *Observer* newspaper.

7 On 10 May 1941 Rudolf Hess flew to Scotland as 'representative of the Führer' to meet Douglas Douglas-Hamilton, 14th Duke of Hamilton, the man he believed to be leader of the British peace movement. His plan to negotiate peace ended with his imprisonment.

8 On 22 June the German Reich and its allies attacked the Union of Soviet Socialist Republics. Three million German and 600,000 allied soldiers swept across 1,500 kilometres of the USSR's western border, breaking the 1939 Non-Aggression Treaty.

9 Dr Julius Hechinger was legal advisor to the Jewish Community Centre.

10 Lohhof, essential to the war effort, had been processing flax for its fibres and oil since 1935. Strnad, *Flachs*.

11 This was Irmgard Spiegelberg. Strnad, *Flachs*, p. 59.

12 The internment camp at Berg am Laim in Munich was located at 9 Clemens-August-Straße and officially known as the Residential Facility for Jews, Berg am Laim. The accommodation was in the north wing of the convent and well concealed from public view. Residents had to pay their own expenses.

13 Else Rosenfeld lived at the Berg am Laim internment camp from 4 August 1941 to 15 August 1942 BayHStA LEA 1674 BEG 31409, 1955/62.

14 Aron Albrecht was a teacher at the Jewish primary school in Munich. In April 1942 he was deported to Piaski.

15 Ernst Heilbronner had been a co-owner of a business in the watch and clock trade. On 4 April 1942 he was deported to Piaski.

16 Until 1938 Friedrich Abeles had run an extensive business in tobacco and its various accessories. In 1939 his attempt to migrate to the United States with his two sons failed. He was murdered in Kaunas on 25.11.1941.

17 The Rococo church of St Michael, Berg am Laim, was built by Johann Michael Fischer between 1737 and 1751.

18 Gertrud Lilian Lindauer had moved to Munich in 1934.

19 Hermann (Hersch) Klein, businessman, born 1880, was deported to Piaski on 4 April 1942.

20 The Office for Aryanisation oversaw the wearing of the Star of David with the assistance of the Bavarian office of the Association of Jews in Germany.

21 Many migrants hoped to reach the United States via Cuba. During 1939 Michael von Faulhaber, cardinal in the diocese of Munich and Freising, attempted to smooth the way to Brazil for 'non-Aryan' Catholics.

22 The Reichssicherheitshauptamt (Reich Main Security Office) was headed by Heinrich Himmler as Chief of German Police and Reichsführer SS.

23 Paul N. Cossmann was a publisher and journalist. See Glossary of Key People.

24 Six big deportations had left Vienna since February 1941. Then from October onwards there were deportations from Prague, Trier, Berlin, more from Vienna, Frankfurt am Main, Cologne, Hamburg, Düsseldorf, Brünn, Bremen. The deportation of 1,000 Jews from Munich to Kaunas was the twenty-seventh deportation since February. Bundesarchiv, ed., Gedenkbuch.

25 For her biography see Glossary of Key People.

26 It was a risk for the nuns to have any dealings with internees.

27 The deportation of the Munich Jews was a three-day journey. For organisational reasons the transport did not go to Riga, as planned, but to Kaunas (Kowno) in Lithuania. The Kaunas Fortresses, particularly Forts VII und IX, had been used by German extermination units as places of execution for thousands of Lithuanian Jews since summer 1941. The Munich Jews were locked in cells for two days, then shot by Task Force 3 under the direction of SS Standartenführer Karl Jäger. Only one survived. Porat, Jews, 363–392; Heusler, Fahrt in den Tod, pp. 13–24.

28 Rosenfeld is describing here 'survivor guilt', something he experienced because his family and friends suffered so much and some even lost their lives.

29 On 7 December 1941 the Japanese, allies of the Germans, had attacked and destroyed the American Pacific fleet at Hawaii without warning and without any declaration of war.

1942

1 Ludwig Altschüler, a respected Bavarian businessman and a bank director in Neustadt, had been forced into retirement in 1937, and had lived thereafter with his wife and son in Krün, Upper Bavaria. Krauss, ed., *Kommerzienräte*, p. 394.

2 Rosenfeld's first wife died in 1916 after the birth of their daughter, Gustel. Else's marriage to Siegfried, deemed a '*Volljude*', fully Jewish, under Nazi laws, meant that she too was categorised thus. Before her marriage she had been deemed a '*Mischling*' because of her parents, although only her father had been Jewish.

3 Dr Walter Breslauer, lawyer and association official. The AJR was the most important support organisation for migrants.

4 Salomon Adler-Rudel was a professional social worker, writer and publisher, and co-founder in 1941 of the AJR. *Biographisches Handbuch der deutschsprachigen Emigration*, vol. I, pp. 8f. Adolf Schoyer was an entrepreneur and administrator, and co-founder and chair of the AJR. Ibid., vol. I, pp. 666f.

5 Else Rosenfeld, looking back in 1963, related how they had all promised to write but no news came: 'That made us suspicious, but we didn't know that they had all been killed.' Rosenfeld, *Four Lives*, p. 98.

6 These are the words of the inscription on the memorial in Berg am Laim at the gates of the former camp. It is near to the school where co-editor Erich Kasberger was a long-standing history teacher.

7 During checks like this it was common for jewellery, cash, documents, and anything in short supply, such as expensive clothing and food, to be confiscated. StAM Staatsanwaltschaften 29499, Bl. 118. Such activity lined Gestapo pockets.

8 Numerous attempts were made to get names removed from the Gestapo transport lists, but mostly in vain. An example is StAM Staatsanwaltschaften 29499/1, witness statement, Julius Bauer, 25.8.1950.

9 For Dr Frank Bienenfeld see Glossary of Key People.

10 Emanuel (Manny) Shinwell was a Jewish trade union official who became a Labour member of parliament. Cowling, *Impact of Hitler*, p. 416.

11 Walter Geismar survived and emigrated to Australia in 1946 with his parents. Macek, Walter Geismar, pp. 160–162.

12 The indignation of these 'Aryan' women doubtless stemmed from their sense of unassailability. In Munich there was no open resistance of the type shown by the women in Berlin's Rosenstrasse in 1943.

13 Nobody survived the 4 April 1942 transportation to Piaski.

14 In 1942 in June and July alone there were twenty-two transports from Munich to Theresienstadt and one to Poland. A total of 1,100 people were deported.

15 Dr Karl Kupfer was deported to Auschwitz on 13 April 1943.

16 The date of this letter indicates that Tilla's journey to Eva Schmidt at Lake Constance actually occurred two weeks earlier than Else recorded (Else puts the date at 05.08.1942). In this letter she uses her own coded way of telling Eva that she would like now to go underground, something she had previously rejected and was still questioning in her diary entry of 26.07.1942. That was a week after Else's letter. Presumably only a very short time elapsed between request and actual escape on 15.08.1942.

17 There had been some cases of suicide before Frau Schulmann's death: Martha Pilliet killed herself in view of deportation to Kowno, Moritz Schilling on 4.2.1942; Martin Mordechai Neumeyer and his wife Lina took their own lives on 17.7.1942.

18 After Else's escape from the camp there were further attempts; StAM Staatsanwaltschaften 29499, witness statement, Julius Bauer, 25.8.1950.

19 For more about the children in the Antonienheim see Grube and Macek, Kinderheim, p. 97.

20 In August and September 1942 there were five further transports out of Munich involving 285 people.

21 Dr Oskar Cossmann, physicist, was brutally treated when he was recaptured. On 8 June 1953 Johann Grahammer was sentenced to eight months in prison for causing grievous bodily harm. StAM Staatsanwaltschaften 29499/1, Bl. 146 f. Statement by Dr Margarete Cossmann 14.8.1950.

22 This was Theodor Koronczyk, who took over the work of the Jewish Community Centre after the deportation of its board members. Kasberger, Hans Wegner, pp. 230–244.

23 In Germany it was rare for men to take care of their own domestic tasks. An unmarried man would usually take lodgings in the home of a woman who would

then act as housekeeper, looking after his room and keeping everything in order, as well as providing breakfast. The midday and evening meal would always be eaten out in the equivalent of a public house.

24 Else uses a code in her letters to avoid being found out. A 'change of air' or a 'stay in a sanatorium' means in reality a change of accommodation. In this letter she is really asking if she can come and stay with Eva in Weimar for a few days.

25 Henny Rewald was the first wife of Arthur Rewald, brother to Gertrud, Siegfried Rosenfeld's deceased wife. She lived in Berlin.

26 Eva Kunkel was Gustel's teacher at primary school; Irma refers here to the secondary school teacher Irmgard Beer. Conversation with Hanna Cooper, 11.4.2010.

27 For the situation in Berlin see the following: Gross, *Last Jews in Berlin*; Strauss, *Over the Green Hill*; Friedlander and Schwerdtfeger, *'Versuche dein Leben zu machen'*.

28 Grete Berndt.

1943

1 'Hopf' is probably an alias for Hofmann.

2 For more about life underground see Lutjens, Jews in Hiding in Nazi Berlin, 268–291; and Schrafstetter, Life in Illegality, pp. 69–85.

3 Hella Gorn was a Quaker. For more about Hella see Strauss, *Over the Green Hill.* Peter and Hella married after the war and lived in East Germany.

4 Peter Heilmann, son of Ernst Heilmann, chair of the SPD parliamentary group in the Prussian state government. See Glossary of Key People.

5 This was the family of Social Democrat, Edmund Goldschagg.

6 Dr Charlotte Bamberg (1890–1967), formerly the most senior civil servant in her department; Bamberg, Erinnerung, 803–808.

7 Ibid.

8 After free trade unions were dissolved in 1933, the German Labour Front became the association for any employee.

9 Else calls herself 'Lilli'. She sells the field glasses to a major for much needed income.

10 Else calls herself 'Anni'.

11 Fritz Kucharski had studied with Else in Jena. Gertrud was his second wife.

12 The day after the police visit Kollmorgen's flat was checked over by the Kripo, the criminal police department; all the Jewish lodgers moved back in. In November 1943 Kollmorgen was ordered to present himself to the Gestapo but managed to worm his way out of the situation. Bamberg, Erinnerung, 804f.

13 The name Wackes is used in a derogatory or mocking way by the Germans and Swiss-German border residents about the Alsatians and Mosellans.

14 There are no diary entries between September and December 1943. In this period Peter Heilmann was looking into possible escape routes to Switzerland. Else shares this with Eva, but in her form of code.

15 The writer Thomas Mann, who had left Germany, addressed a German audience via the BBC. Anyone listening to an 'enemy broadcaster' in Germany risked severe

punishment, but it was only through channels of this kind that people could be sure of getting any reliable information.

16 This refers to Jews still in hiding at Hans Kollmorgen's flat; Bamberg, Erinnerung.

17 Rosenfeld's recollections of the assembly hall in the Prussian Ministry of Justice represent his personal sense of mourning for the destruction of the previously robust, well-organised state and system of justice that he had served all his life.

18 Jakob Wassermann (1873–1934) was one of the most popular German writers of his time.

19 Rosenfeld is quite direct here about how things are likely to play out post-war. Many Germans tried to make those who had left the country take responsibility for their own misfortune. Krauss, *Heimkehr in ein fremdes Land.*

1944

1 Rosenfeld had been able to take a few possessions to England with him, such as porcelain and some more portable items of furniture, all of which were still in storage and costing him money.

2 On 3 September 1943 Italy and the Allies agreed the Armistice of Cassibile. German troops exploited this opportunity to disarm the Italians, but on 13 October Italy declared war on the German Empire.

3 This refers to the escape organisation Luise Meier had set up with locksmith Josef Höfler and Elise, his Swiss-born wife. Lotte Strauss was saved by the same group. Strauss, *Over the Green Hill.*

4 Kollmorgen's factory was badly bombed; he relocated the facility to Coburg and Grete Berndt went with him. Bamberg, Erinnerung, 806.

5 Reference to the activity and arrest of members of the White Rose Group early in 1943. The student resistance network extended as far as Baden.

6 This is probably Josef Höfler.

7 The suburban train went five stations from Singen to Beuren am Ried. The rest of the way was covered on foot.

8 In Beuren-Büsslingen the first smuggler took leave of Else and handed over to Hugo Wetzstein, a junior member of customs staff and resident in that settlement. Conversation with Wetzstein's daughter, Frieda Schuster, 26.03.2019.

9 The route went first through Büsslingen and then through the border settlement of Hofen. Six refugees managed to reach Switzerland along this route: Hannchen Stein, Jizchak Schwersenz, Jacheta Wachsmann, Lotte and Walter Heskle, and Elsbeth Rosenfeld. Battel, *'Wo es hell ist'*, p. 211n.136.

10 The Biber is a small river on the border between Germany and Switzerland.

11 The convoluted course taken by the German-Swiss border at this point made it quite confusing, and this meant that a number of escape attempts failed when Jewish refugees lost their way.

12 Since August 1942 Switzerland had been turning back all Jewish refugees, nearly 25,000 in total, but after autumn 1943 it softened its isolationist stance. Battel, *'Wo es hell ist'*, p. 147.

13 Else Rosenfeld was questioned several times, but described her first encounter as the kindest. This had been with Swiss national, Private Oskar Brunner. Rosenfeld, *Four Lives*, p. 126f. The record of her first interrogation in Switzerland states: 'I was also told that I had to have on me anything that I was bringing in payment, things like cash, jewellery, bits of nice linen. Outside the station I was to hand over the money to someone who would speak to me. The cash, which amounted to around 3,000 Reichsmark, and the linen, had all been gathered up by various friends in Berlin and brought to me in Freiburg. The jewellery had been decided in advance and consisted of a gold ring set with one small diamond, one of the last pieces I had left. As far as money went, I had nothing more to offer. I'd had no money for a long time.' BAB, E4264(-) 1985/196 vol. 1902, Dossier-No.: 22262, Rosenfeld-Behrend Elsbeth, Report by Private.O. Brunner, Polizeikommando Schaffhausen. Politische Abteilung, 30. April 1944.

14 Else Rosenfeld had literally fallen into the yard of the Customs House at Hofen, badly injuring her leg. That same night, 21.4.1944, she was taken to the hospital at Schaffhausen where she was diagnosed with a complicated fracture and severe exhaustion. BayHStA LEA 1674 BEG 31409, 1955/62, Else Rosenfeld, affirmation in lieu of an oath.

15 Lotte Goldschagg writes to Eva, addressing her as Frau Urtal, discreetly informing her of Else's successful escape.

16 This was almost certainly Eleanor Rathbone, British MP, founder of the National Committee for Rescue from Nazi Terror, member of the Advisory Board to the Foreign Office Refugee Section and of the Parliamentary Committee on Refugees.

17 The unsuccessful German Ardennes Offensive of 16 December 1944 – 25 January 1945.

1945

1 In April 1945 the Bavarian resistance group Freiheitsaktion Bayern, led by Hauptmann Rupprecht Gerngross, aimed to end the senseless blood-letting, but their attempt was crushed. Diem, *Freiheitsaktion Bayern*.

2 England, the United States and the Soviet Union trained German POWs, selected for their political balance, to carry out work in post-war Germany.

3 Karl Renner was president of the Austrian National Assembly from 1931 to 1933 and president of Austria from 1945 to 1950.

4 Wolfgang Kraus was Rosenfeld's nephew.

5 Social Democrat Wilhelm Hoegner was in exile in Switzerland; in 1945 he became minister president of Bavaria; Edmund Goldschagg, the man who had sheltered Else in Freiburg, was one of the first licence holders for the *Süddeutsche Zeitung*.

6 Else's diary was first published in 1945 by Büchergilde Gutenberg in Zurich.

7 Hanna Bertholet was an editor at Büchergilde Gutenberg.

QR CODES

1 Rosenfeld, *An Old Lady Remembers*, BBC Radio, April/May 1963
2 Early life among Jews and Christians
3 Siegfried's career in the Ministry
4 Reasons not to leave
5 Foreign countries and the persecution of Jews
6 In the ghetto at Berg am Laim
7 Life underground
8 Life underground in the air war
9 Arrival in England, 1946
10 Courage
11 Kindertransport
12 Deportation
13 Siegfried's departure for England
14 The outbreak of war, 1939
15 The first deportation, 1941
16 Reprieve at the eleventh hour
17 Cultural life in the ghetto
18 Attacks on Jews
19 Inhumanity and abuse of power
20 Encouragement and consolation
21 Emotion and life underground
22 The escape begins: 20 April 1944
23 Meeting the escape organiser
24 Journey through the night
25 Risking life to cross the border
26 Else reflects on her experiences

GLOSSARY OF KEY PEOPLE

This glossary is ordered alphabetically by surname. The principal references used to create it are as follows: *Biographisches Handbuch der deutschsprachigen Emigration 1933–1945*; *Biographisches Gedenkbuch der Münchner Juden 1933–1945*, www.muenchen.de/rathaus/gedenkbuch/gedenkbuch.html (last accessed 11 August 2020); *Gedenkbuch: Opfer der Verfolgung der Juden unter der nationalsozialistischen Gewaltherrschaft in Deutschland 1933–1945*, www.bundesarchiv.de/gedenkbuch/chronicles.html.de?page=1 (last accessed 11 August 2020).

Dr Frank Rudolf (Rudi) Bienenfeld, born Vienna 1886, lawyer, 1938 migrated to Switzerland, then in 1939 to England. In 1936, writing as Anton van Mueller, he published 'Deutsche und Juden' ('The Germans and the Jews', 1939), an analysis of the relationship between Jews and Germans under Hitler. He was a member of the Association of Jewish Refugees (AJR), board member of the World Jewish Congress, London, and later worked on the UN Charter of Human Rights.

Adunka, 'Franz Rudolf Bienenfeld'

Dr Rudolf Cohen, born 1864 in Hamburg, and Dr Annemarie Cohen led the Munich Quakers. Rudolf was a physicist, sometimes working to assist Wilhelm Röntgen. The Cohens created a file index to record the details of more than three hundred Jews and Christians in need of help, and facilitated the acquisition of visas and sureties, and assisted with travel and passport fees as well as the search for employment abroad.

Zahn, ed., *Hilfe für Juden*

Paul N. Cossmann, born 1869 in Baden-Baden, was a publisher and journalist. During 1924 his magazine *Süddeutsche Monatshefte* addressed the '*Dolchstoss*' myth, an assertion promulgated since World War I by right-wing politicians and high-up military leaders that the 1918 revolution had been 'a stab in the back', robbing the previously undefeated German Army of victory. As a staunch Catholic, he rejected Hitler and National Socialism and advocated the restoration of the monarchy in Bavaria. As early as April 1933 he was seized by the Gestapo for being a political opponent and a Jew. Freed in 1934, he was arrested again in 1938 and from autumn 1941 was interned at Berg am Laim, Munich. He was deported to Theresienstadt in 1942 and died there the same year.

Selig, 'Cossmann'

Eva Fischer, born 1901, and husband Georg, a chemist, lived in Berlin-Tempelhof at 120 Manfred-v.-Richthofenstraße. Eva, Else's sister, was protected by virtue of being married to Georg, an 'Aryan'. Else, however, had married Siegfried, who was considered to be fully Jewish under National Socialist racial laws. Else Rosenfeld lived at the Fischers' home from 15 August to 8 December 1942. Georg died in tragic circumstances after the war, shot dead as he shielded his wife from marauding Russians. Eva Fischer and her daughter subsequently left for Argentina to be near relatives.

Conversation with Hanna Cooper (Else's daughter), 11 April 2010

Edmund Goldschagg, born 1886 in Freiburg, was a Social Democrat and a journalist. He and Ernst Heilmann had been close friends since 1914. During the 1920s Goldschagg was an editor for the Social Democrat newspaper the *Münchener Post*, but from 1933 onwards was forbidden by National Socialist laws from carrying out this profession and returned to his home city with his wife, Lotte, and young son, Rolf. There he found work helping out at his brother's printing business. It was during 1943–1944 that Else lived with them, but very much in hiding. In August 1945 the Americans made Goldschagg one of the licence holders for the *Süddeutsche Zeitung* in Munich, and he became co-publisher and chief editor.

Goldschagg, *Leben des Journalisten*, p. 166

Magdalena (Lene) Heilmann, born 1894, was the widow of Ernst Heilmann, who had been chair of the Social Democratic Party's parliamentary group in the Prussian state government. Ernst was murdered in 1940 at Buchenwald. Lene was a social worker and co-founder of the Arbeiterwohlfahrt, the workers' welfare charity. Ernst Heilmann and Siegfried Rosenfeld first met in 1919. The Heilmann family hid Else and other Jews and Social Democrats, including Friedrich Stampfer, former chief editor of *Vorwärts*, Gustav Noske, politician, previously chief editor of the *Volksstimme* in Chemnitz, and social reformer Marie Juchacz, politician.

Sandvoß, *Widerstand am Kreuzberg*, pp. 74–76

Peter Heilmann, born 1922 in Berlin, son of Social Democrat politician Ernst Heilmann and his wife, Magdalena. Designated as 'half Jew', he was sent to a work camp that was part of the Todt organisation. After the war he became a member of the German Communist Party and studied in East Berlin, becoming secretary to the central council for the Freie deutsche Jugend (Free German Youth). He and Hella Gorn married, but in 1951 the couple were seized during Stalin's purges and sentenced to five years' detention, 'officially' because he had paid a visit to his mother in West Berlin. After serving their sentences, Hella and Peter divorced. In 1956 Peter was recruited by the Stasi, the East German national security organisation, and travelled to the West. While working as course leader at the Evangelical Academy in Berlin, he and his second wife, Charlotte, who was the most senior PA at the institution, acted as informants. For more than twenty years they supplied the Stasi with undercover reports – a lucrative activity – on Berlin society and the Protestant Church. This eventually led to them appearing in court in 1999. Both received suspended sentences.

Conversation with Hanna Cooper, 11 April 2010; Knabe, *Unterwanderte Republik*; Strauss, *Over the Green Hill*

Hans Kollmorgen, manufacturer, whose business F. A. Optische Anstalt Hans Kollmorgen was essential to the war effort, lived in an apartment on Bülowstraße in Berlin-Schöneberg. This is where Else Rosenfeld was in hiding from 9 December 1942 to 15 March 1943. Kollmorgen also helped Paul Szillat by employing him as his warehouse stock controller in 1940–1945. In 1933 Szillat had replaced Ernst Heilmann as SPD chair in the Prussian state parliament, but was eventually sent to Oranienburg. Due to bomb damage, Kollmorgen's manufacturing facility later moved to Coburg, where he died early in 1948. BayHStA LEA 1674 BEG 31409, 1955/62.

Sworn statements of Dr Tilla Kratz 2.1.1956 and Else Rosenfeld 21.12.1955; Bamberg, Erinnerung, 804–806

Dr Tilla (Mathilde) Kratz, born in Breslau in 1897, married a Mr Levi, but the couple divorced. An art historian by training, she worked as a teacher in Elmau. From 1939 she lived in Icking, where she gave private tuition and was a good friend and companion to Else Rosenfeld, supporting her during her time at Berg am Laim, and then helping her go underground. She died in Lauben (Allgäu) in 1985.

Residents' Registration Office for Icking, 25 August 2020

Dr Hertha Kraus, born 1897, was Siegfried Rosenfeld's niece and a social scientist. She became a Quaker after her student days when she was a contemporary of Else Behrend, and it was through her that Else met her future husband, Siegfried. From 1923 she worked in Cologne as director of the Welfare Office, but in 1933 she was dismissed and migrated to the United States, where she worked as a lecturer, becoming a professor of social work and social research in 1936 in Philadelphia. She played an active role in the Quaker support programme for refugees, and after the war made frequent visits to Germany as a representative of the American Friends Service Committee.

Schirrmacher, *Hertha Kraus*; Hauff, ed., *Deutsches Reich und Protektorat*, doc. 73, p. 250

Dr Hildegard Lion was born in 1893 in Hamburg, studied economics, and was awarded her doctorate in Cologne. From 1929 to 1933 she was principal of the Berlin-based Deutsche Akademie für soziale und pädagogische Frauenarbeit, where female academics trained women wishing to enter the social work profession, then migrated to England where, with Quaker help and support, she founded in Haslemere, Surrey, a school primarily for refugee children. She remained in charge of Stoatley Rough School until its closure in 1960.

Goldenstedt, Pionierinnen sozialer Arbeit

Dr Gertrud Luckner, born 1900 in Liverpool, England, studied economics in Königsberg, Frankfurt am Main, and at Woodbrooke College, a Quaker institution in Birmingham, England. In 1938 she was awarded her doctorate by the University of Freiburg im Breisgau. A committed pacificist, she was a member of the Quakers from 1931 to 1934, but then converted to Catholicism. From 1933 onwards she was actively engaged in supporting German Jews by helping with migration, delivering money and other necessities as well as helping with escape plans. Together with Else Rosenfeld, she lent her support to Jews deported to Piaski. In March 1943 she was arrested and taken to the Ravensbrück concentration camp. She survived, and after the war, working on behalf of the Freiburg branch of the charity Caritas, led the welfare work for those who had suffered persecution.

Rosenfeld and Luckner, eds., *Lebenszeichen aus Piaski*

Luise Meier, born 1885, lived with her husband from 1936 onwards in Berlin, and during this time was committed to helping those in need. In spring 1943 she met Josef Höfler, a locksmith, together with his Swiss-born wife, and they jointly planned and organised escape routes. But in the middle of 1944 they were found out and arrested. The case got as far as the Special Court and the People's Court, but the war ended before any sentences were passed. In 2001 Luise Meier and Josef Höfler were posthumously honoured and their names added to the Righteous among Nations list at Yad Vashem, the World Holocaust Remembrance Centre.

Battel, '*Wo es hell ist*'; Strauss, *Over the Green Hill*

Franz Mugler, SA Sturmführer, worked in the 'Aryanisation Office' from 1939 onwards, but in 1942 was sentenced to one year in prison for the misappropriation of Jewish property and excluded from the Nazi Party one year later.

BArch Berlin BDC PK Mugler, Franz, born 28.5.1894

Dr Alfred Neumeyer, *Oberlandesgerichtsrat* (senior official at the Higher Regional Court) was head of the Jewish Community in Munich. In 1941 he migrated with his wife to Argentina to live on their son's farm, where they both died in 1944.

Biographisches Handbuch, vol. 1, p. 531

Heinz Pringsheim, born 1882 in Munich, was brother-in-law of the author Thomas Mann. Under the National Socialists he was banned from working as a music critic, but after 1945 he became head of music at the Bayerischer Rundfunk, the Bavarian Broadcasting Company, as well as music critic for the *Süddeutsche Zeitung*.

Prinz, ed., *Trümmerzeit in München*, p. 433

Dr Eva Schmidt, teacher, born 1897 in Ottmachau, Silesia, died in Weimar in 1988. She grew up in Berlin, studied German, biology and geography in Jena, and eventually became a senior teacher at the Friedrich-Schiller-Oberschule in Weimar. Eva was to become the most important of Else's supporters and helpers in the quest for survival. Two hundred and thirty letters written by Else to Eva during this period have been passed to us, and they demonstrate how much Else depended on Eva, especially during her life underground. After her retirement from teaching in 1952, Eva became a significant force in Weimar when it came to research into regional history and biographies.

Kühn-Stillmark, Autorin; Elke Minckwitz, Weimar; Jens Riederer, Weimar City Archive

Ludwig Schrott had a delicatessen business during the 1920s but was out of work in 1933 and became a member of the National Socialist Party. In 1938 he joined Vermögensverwaltung GmbH, a property management company in Munich that later became the 'Aryanisation Office'. He remained there intermittently until 30 June 1943.

StAM, Spruchkammerakten (Denazification Tribunal records) K 1919: Wegner, Hans, born 7.8.1905

Dr Magdalena Schwarz, born 1900 in Berlin, was a medical doctor with her own practice in Munich. In accordance with Nazi racial laws, her Jewish origins meant that as of 1938 she was no longer permitted a full licence to practise. Like fourteen other Jewish doctors in Munich, she was authorised to treat Jewish patients, and Jewish patients only, such as in the Jewish hospital and the internment camps at Berg am Laim and Milbertshofen. In 1945 she managed to evade deportation when the head of psychiatry at Munich's Schwabing Hospital hid her away on his locked ward.

Wertheimer, Magdalena Schwarz, p. 449f.

Dr Julius Spanier, born 1880 in Munich, was a paediatrician and senior consultant at the Jewish Hospital in Munich until its closure. He was also responsible for medical care at the residential facility at Berg am Laim. In 1942 he and his wife were deported to Theresienstadt. They both survived. From 1946 to 1955 Spanier was senior consultant at the Children's Hospital in Lachnerstrasse, and from 1947 to 1953 he was chair of the Regional Association for Jewish Communities in Bavaria as well as a member of the Bavarian senate.

Spies, Erinnerungen an Dr. Julius Spanier, pp. 130–135

Karl Stahl, engineer and director of the Federation of Vintners, became head of the Munich Jewish Community in 1938. He and his wife were deported to Theresienstadt on 16 June 1942. In 1944 both died at Auschwitz.

Biographisches Gedenkbuch der Münchner Juden

Hans Wegner, born 1905, joined the National Socialist Party in 1929. The SA opened up opportunities for promotion that he craved, and in 1943 he was elevated to *Sturmbannführer* for 'services rendered' in persecuting Jews.

Kasberger, Wegner

BIBLIOGRAPHY

Archives

Bundesarchiv (BArch) Berlin, Berlin Document Center (BDC)
Bundesarchiv Bern (BAB)
E 4264-1985/196 Bd. vol. 1902, Dossier 22262
Bayerisches Hauptstaatsarchiv München (BayHStA)
Landesentschädigungsamt
Staatskanzlei
Staatsarchiv München (StAM)
Finanzamt (FA)
Gestapo
Landratsamt (LRA)
Regierungsakten (RA)
Spruchkammerakten
Staatsanwaltschaften
Wiedergutmachungsbehörde (WB)
Geheimes Preußisches Staatsarchiv Berlin-Dahlem – Preußischer Kulturbesitz (GStA PK)
I HA Rep 84a D
I HA Rep 169 D Landtag I J, 32 e
I HA Rep 169 D, XI d G Nr. 4 adh. 3
Rep. 90a, Protokolle des Staatsministeriums MF
Preußischer Landtag, Stenografische Protokolle 1920–1933
Stadtarchiv Freiburg (StadtAF)
Nachlass Stefan Meier
Stadtarchiv Weimar
Leo Baeck Foundation, New York
Ernest Hamburger Collection
Institut für Zeitgeschichte (IFZ)
MA 1500
Archiv der Friedrich-Ebert-Stiftung
SPD Parteivorstand
Nachlass Willi Eichler
Nachlass des Deutschen Landarbeiter-Verbandes
Archiv der Barmherzigen Schwestern München (ABSchM)
0.8.02. III Reich
Privatarchiv Hanna Cooper
Privatarchiv Helmut Kolmeder

Primary Sources

Amtsblatt der Landeshauptstadt München, no. 6/1997, Straßenbenennung.

Andreas-Friedrich, Ruth. *Berlin Underground 1939–1945*, London: Latimer House, 1948.

Der Schattenmann: Tagebuchaufzeichnungen 1938–1945, Frankfurt am Main: Suhrkamp, 1986.

Association of Jewish Refugees in Great Britain: Refugee Voices. Online audio-visual database, Association of Jewish Refugees, Holocaust Testimony Archive, http://www.refugeevoices.fu-berlin.de/sammlung/index.html (last accessed 17 August 2020).

Bamberg, Lotte. Erinnerung ans Dritte Reich: An der Oberfläche untergetaucht. *Frankfurter Hefte*, 10 (1955), 803–808.

Behrend-Rosenfeld, Else. *Ich stand nicht allein: Erlebnisse einer Jüdin in Deutschland 1933–1944s*, Hamburg: Europäische Verlagsanstalt, 1949.

Ich stand nicht allein: Leben einer Jüdin in Deutschland 1933–1944, Munich: C. H. Beck, 1988.

Leben und Sterben der Münchner Gemeinde 1938–1942. In Hans Lamm, ed., *Vergangene Tage: Jüdische Kultur in München*, pp. 452–457. Munich: Langen Müller Verlag, 1982.

Verfemt und verfolgt: Leben einer Jüdin in Deutschland 1933–1944, Zurich: Büchergilde Gutenberg, 1945.

Bettelheim, Bruno. *Surviving and Other Essays*, New York: Vintage, 1980.

Boehm, Eric. *We Survived: Fourteen Histories of the Hidden and Hunted in Nazi Germany*, Boulder, CO: Westview Press, 2003.

Degen, Michael. *Nicht Alle waren Mörder: Eine Kindheit in Berlin*, Munich: Econ, 1999.

Deutschkron, Inge. *Ich trug den gelben Stern*, Munich: Dt. Taschenbuch-Verlag, 1995.

Dietz, Edith. *Den Nazis entronnen: Die Flucht eines jüdischen Mädchens in die Schweiz: Autobiografischer Bericht 1933–1942*, Frankfurt am Main: Dipa, 1990.

Fittko, Lisa. *Mein Weg über die Pyrenäen: Erinnerungen 1940/41*, Munich: Deutscher Taschenbuch-Verlag, 1989.

Friedlander, Margot and Schwerdtfeger, Malin. *'Versuche dein Leben zu machen': Als Jüdin versteckt in Berlin*, Berlin: Rowohlt-Taschenbuch-Verlag, 2010.

Gershon, Karen, ed. *We Came as Children: A Collected Autobiography of Refugees*, London: Victor Gollancz, 1966; London: Macmillan-Papermac, 1989.

Goldschagg, Edmund. *Das Leben des Journalisten, Sozialdemokraten und Mitbegründers der 'Süddeutschen Zeitung'*, retold by Hans Dollinger, Munich: Süddeutscher-Verlag, 1986.

Gross, Leonard. *The Last Jews in Berlin*, New York: Carroll & Graf, 1999.

Gurewitsch, Brana. *Mothers, Sisters, Resisters: Oral Histories of Women Who Survived the Holocaust*, Tuscaloosa: University of Alabama Press, 1998.

Heilmann, Peter, ed. *So begann meine Nachkriegszeit: Männer und Frauen erzählen von Mai 45*, Berlin: Wichern-Verlag, 1985.

Jalowicz-Simon, Marie. *Gone to Ground: One Woman's Extraordinary Account of Survival in the Heart of Nazi Germany*, translated by Anthea Bell, London: Profile Books, 2016.

Underground in Berlin: A Young Woman's Extraordinary Tale of Survival in the Heart of Nazi Germany, Boston: Little, Brown, 2015.

Jalowicz-Simon, Marie and Stratenwerth, Irene, eds. *Untergetaucht: Eine junge Frau überlebt in Berlin 1940–1945*, Frankfurt am Main: Fischer-Verlag, 2014.

Klemperer, Victor. *Ich will Zeugnis ablegen bis zum letzten: Tagebücher*, 2 vols. Berlin: Aufbau-Verlag, 1995.

Laak, Gert van. *Die Nazis nannten sie Sara*, Munich: Pendo, 2000.

Lamm, Hans, ed. *Vergangene Tage: Jüdische Kultur in München*, Munich: Langen Müller Verlag, 1982.

Lewyn, Bert and Saltzmann-Lewyn, Bev, eds. *Versteckt in Berlin: Eine Geschichte von Flucht und Verfolgung 1943–1945*, Berlin: Metropol-Verlag, 2009.

Orbach, Larr and Orbach-Smith, Vivien. *Soaring Underground: A Young Fugitive's Life in Nazi Berlin*, Berlin: Kowalke, 1998.

Parkes, James W. *The Jew and His Neighbour: A Study of the Causes of Anti-Semitism*, London: Christian Movement Press, 1931.

Prinz, Friedrich, ed. *Trümmerzeit in München: Kultur und Geschichte einer deutschen Großstadt im Aufbruch 1945–1949*, Munich: C. H. Beck, 1984.

Regierungsblatt I 1939

Rosenfeld, Elsbeth. *The Four Lives of Elsbeth Rosenfeld as Told by Her to the BBC, with a Foreword by James Parkes*, London: Victor Gollancz, 1965.

Rosenfeld, Else, *An Old Lady Remembers*, BBC Radio, April/May 1963, interviewer Charles Parker.

Rosenfeld, Else and Luckner, Gertrud, eds. *Lebenszeichen aus Piaski: Briefe Deportierter aus dem Distrikt Lublin 1940–1943*, Munich: Biederstein, 1968.

Ruch, Martin, ed. *'Inzwischen sind wir nun besternt worden': Das Tagebuch der Esther Cohn (1926–1944) und die Kinder vom Münchner Antonienheim*, Norderstedt: Books on Demand, 2006.

Sachse, Carola, ed. *Als Zwangsarbeiterin 1941 in Berlin: Die Aufzeichnungen der Volkswirtin Elisabeth Freund*, Berlin: Akademie-Verlag, 1996.

Sozialistische Mitteilungen der London-Vertretung der SPD, issued by the London Representative of the German Social Democratic Party, nr. 96/97 (1947), p. 18. Friedrich-Ebert-Stiftung Library, http://library.fes.de/fulltext/sozmit/1947-096.htm (last accessed 8 August 2021).

Hallo – Berg am Laim (Munich), 16 January 1987.

Strauss, Lotte. *Over the Green Hill: A German Jewish Memoir 1913–1943*, New York: Forham University Press, 1999.

Es wird weiter gesaeubert, *Vossische Zeitung*, 4 September 1932.

Weber, Hermann and Weber, Gerda. *Leben nach dem 'Prinzip links': Erinnerungen aus fünf Jahrzehnten*, Berlin: Links, 2006.

Weiss, Helga. *Und doch ein ganzes Leben: Ein Mädchen, das Auschwitz überlebt hat.* Cologne: Lübbe, 2013.

Wegner, Hans. Tätigkeits- und Abschlussbericht zum 30. Juni 1943. In Stadtarchiv München, ed., *'... verzogen, unbekannt wohin': Die erste Deportation von Münchner Juden im November 1941*, n.p. Document no. 2. Munich: Pendo, Dokument, 2000.

Secondary Sources

Adunka, Evelyn. 'Franz Rudolf Bienenfeld: Ein Pionier der Menschenrechtsgesetze'. In David, Jüdische Kulturzeitschrift (website), 45 (2000), http://david.juden.at/kulturzeitschrift/44-49/menschenrecht-45.htm (last accessed 14 October 2020).

Aly, Götz. *Hitlers Volksstaat: Raub, Rassenkrieg und nationaler Sozialismus*, Frankfurt am Main: Fischer-Verlag, 2005.

Aly, Götz and Heim, Susanne. Forced Emigration, War, Deportation and Holocaust. In Jonathan Frankel, ed., *The Fate of European Jews 1939–1945: Continuity or Contingency?*, pp. 56–73. New York: Oxford University Press, 1997.

Andritzky, Michael, ed. *Oikos, von der Feuerstelle zur Mikrowelle: Haushalt und Wohnen im Wandel: Ausstellungskatalog*, Gießen: Anabas-Verlag, 1992.

Angress, Werner T. Auswandererlehrgut Gross-Breesen. *Leo Baeck Institute Year Book*, 10(1), 1965, 168–187, doi.org/10.1093/leobaeck/10.1.168

Generation zwischen Furcht und Hoffnung: Jüdische Jugend im Dritten Reich, Hamburg: Christians, 1985.

Bajohr, Frank. German Responses to the Persecution of the Jews Reflected in Three Collections of Secret Reports. In Susanna Schrafstetter and Alan E. Steinweis, eds., *The Germans and the Holocaust: Popular Responses to the Persecution and Murder of the Jews*, pp. 41–58. New York: Berghahn, 2016.

Bajohr, Frank and Pohl, Dieter. *Massenmord und schlechtes Gewissen: Die deutsche Bevölkerung, die NS-Führung und der Holocaust*, Frankfurt am Main: Fischer-Verlag, 2008.

Barkai, Avraham. Exclusion and Persecution: 1933–1938. In Michael A. Meyer, ed., *German-Jewish History in Modern Times*, vol. IV, pp. 197–230. New York: Columbia University Press, 1998.

Jewish Life under Persecution. In Michael A. Meyer, ed., *German-Jewish History in Modern Times*, vol. IV, pp. 231–257. New York: Columbia University Press, 1998.

Battel, Franco. *'Wo es hell ist, dort ist die Schweiz': Flüchtlinge und Fluchthilfe an der Schaffhauser Grenze zur Zeit des Nationalsozialismus*, Zurich: Chronos-Verlag, 2000.

Baumel-Schwartz, Judith Tydor. *Never Look Back: The Jewish Refugee Children in Great Britain 1938–1945*, West Lafayette, OH: Purdue University Press, 2012.

Beer, Susanne. *Die Banalität des Guten: Hilfeleistungen für jüdische Verfolgte im Nationalsozialismus 1941–1945*, Berlin: Metropol-Verlag, 2018.

Benz, Wolfgang. Die jüdische Emigration. In Claus-Dieter Krohn and Patrik von zur Mühlen, eds., *Handbuch der deutschsprachigen Emigration 1933–1945*, pp. 5–16. Darmstadt: Primus-Verlag, 1998.

Solidarität und Hilfe für Juden während der NS-Zeit: Eine Einführung. In Beate Kosmala and Claudia Schoppmann, eds., *Überleben im Untergrund*, pp. 9–16. Berlin: Metropol-Verlag, 2002.

Benz, Wolfgang, ed. *Solidarität und Hilfe für Juden während der NS-Zeit*, 4 vols., Berlin: Metropol-Verlag, 1998–2004.

Überleben im 'Dritten Reich': Juden im Untergrund und ihre Helfer, Munich: C. H. Beck, 2003.

Benz, Wolfgang and Dahm, Volker, eds. *Die Juden in Deutschland 1933–1945: Leben unter nationalsozialistischer Herrschaft*, Munich: C. H. Beck, 1998.

Berger, Franz and Holler, Christiane. *Überleben im Versteck: Schicksale in der NS-Zeit*, Vienna: Ueberreuter, 2002.

Berghahn, Marion. *German-Jewish Refugees in England: The Ambiguities of Assimilation*, London: Macmillan-Papermac, 1984.

Bergmann, Martin S., Milton, Jucovy E. and Kestenberg, Judith S., eds. *Kinder der Opfer, Kinder der Täter: Psychoanalyse und Holocaust*, Frankfurt am Main: Fischer-Verlag, 1998.

Biographisches Gedenkbuch der Münchner Juden 1933–1945, edited by Stadtarchiv München, online database, Munich 2003, www.muenchen.de/rathaus/gedenkbuch/gedenkbuch.html (last accessed 11 August 2020).

Biographisches Handbuch der deutschsprachigen Emigration nach 1933, edited by the Institut für Zeitgeschichte München / Research Foundation for Jewish Immigration New York, gen. eds. Werner Röder and Herbert A Strauss, Munich, among others, 1980–1983, vols. I, II/1 and II/2.

Bonavita, Petra. *Mit falschem Pass und Zyankali: Retter und Gerettete aus Frankfurt a. Main in der NS-Zeit*, Stuttgart: Schmetterling-Verlag, 2009.

Bosco, Andrea. *Federal Union and the Origins of the 'Churchill Proposals': The Federalist Debate in the United Kingdom from Munich to the Fall of France 1938–1940*, London: Lothian Foundation Press, 1992.

Brewer, W. F. What is Biographical Memory? In D. C. Rubin, ed., *Autobiographical Memory*, pp. 25–49. Cambridge: Cambridge University Press, 1988.

Brinson, Charmian et al., eds. *'England? Aber wo liegt es?' Deutsche und österreichische Emigranten in Großbritannien 1933–1945*, Munich: Iudicium, 1996.

Bröckling, Ulrich, Paul, Axel T. and Kaufmann, Stefan, eds. *Vernunft – Entwicklung – Leben: Schlüsselbegriffe der Moderne*, Munich: Wilhelm Fink, 2004.

Bronowski, Alexander. *Es waren so Wenige: Retter im Holocaust*, Stuttgart: Quell, 1991.

Broszat, Martin, Fröhlich, Elke and Mehringer, Hartmut, eds. *Bayern in der NS-Zeit: Herrschaft und Gesellschaft im Konflikt*, 6 vols., Munich: Oldenbourg, 1977–1983.

Buchholz, Marlis and Kwiet, Konrad. Judenhäuser in Germany. In Guy Miron, ed., *The Yad Vashem Encyclopedia of the Ghettos during the Holocaust*, pp. 999–1001. Jerusalem: Yad Vashem, 2009.

Bundesarchiv Koblenz, ed., Gedenkbuch Opfer der Verfolgung der Juden unter der nationalsozialistischen Gewaltherrschaft in Deutschland 1933–1945, www.bundesarchiv.de/gedenkbuch/ (last accessed 25 September 2020).

Burrin, Philippe. *Hitler und die Juden: Die Entscheidung für den Völkermord*, Frankfurt am Main: Fischer-Verlag, 1993.

Büttner, Ursula. *Die Deutschen und die Judenverfolgung im Dritten Reich*, Hamburg: Christians, 1992.

Caplan, Jane. *Ausweis bitte!* Identity and Identification in Nazi Germany. In Ilsen About et al., eds., *Identification and Registration Practices in Transnational Perspective*, pp. 224–242. Basingstoke: Palgrave Macmillan, 2013.

Chappell, Connery. *Island of Barbed Wire: Internment on the Isle of Man in World War Two*, London: Robert Hale, 1984.

Charny, Israel, ed. *Holding on to Humanity: The Message of Holocaust Survivors*, New York: New York University Press, 1992.

Christoph, Jürgen. *Die politischen Reichsamnestien 1918–1933*, Frankfurt am Main: Peter Lang, 1988.

Cowling, Maurice. *The Impact of Hitler: British Policies and Policy 1933–1940*, London: Cambridge University Press, 1975.

Cox, John M. *Circles of Resistance: Jewish, Leftist, and Youth Dissidence in Nazi Germany*, New York: Peter Lang, 2009.

Craig-Norton, Jennifer. *The Kindertransport: Contesting Memory*, Bloomington: Indiana University Press, 2019.

Culbert, David H. *Mission to Moscow*, Madison: University of Wisconsin Press, 1980.

Diem, Veronika. *Die Freiheitsaktion Bayern: Ein Aufstand in der Endphase des NS-Regimes*, Kallmünz: Verlag Michael Lassleben, 2013.

Düring, Marten. *Verdeckte soziale Netzwerke im Nationalsozialismus*, Berlin: De Gruyter, 2015.

Edwards, Ruth D. *Victor Gollancz: A Biography*, London: Victor Gollancz, 1987.

Eschelbacher, Max. *Der zehnte November 1938*, Essen: Klartext, 1998.

Fast, Vera. *Children's Exodus: A History of the Kindertransport*, London: I. B. Tauris, 2011.

Fogelman, Eva. *Conscience and Courage: Rescuers of Jews during the Holocaust*, New York: Anchor Books, 1994.

Fox, Anne L. and Abraham-Podietz, Eva. *Ten Thousand Children: True Stories Told by Children who Escaped the Holocaust on the Kindertransport*, West Orange, NJ: Behrman House, 1999.

Friedländer, Saul. *Nazi Germany and the Jews: The Years of Persecution 1933–1939*, New York: HarperCollins, 1997.

Nazi Germany and the Jews, vol. ii, *The Years of Extermination 1939–1945*, New York: HarperCollins, 2007.

Political Transformations during the War and Their Effect on the Jewish Question. In Herbert A. Strauss, ed., *Hostages of Modernization: Studies on Modern Anti-Semitism 1870–1933/39, 3/1*, pp. 150–164. Berlin: De Gruyter, 1993.

Garbarini, Alexandra. *Numbered Days: Diaries and the Holocaust*, New Haven: Yale University Press, 2006.

Genizi, Haim. American Interfaith Cooperation on Behalf of Refugees from Nazism 1933–1945. *American Jewish History*, 70(3), 1981, 347–361.

Gerhard, Ute. *Unerhört: Die Geschichte der deutschen Frauenbewegung*, Hamburg: Rowohlt, 1995.

Gestrich, Andreas and Krauss, Marita, eds. *Zurückbleiben: Der vernachlässigte Teil der Migrationsgeschichte*, Stuttgart: Steiner, 2006.

Gilbert, Martin. *Endlösung: Atlas of the Holocaust*, Hamburg: Rowohlt, 1995.

What Was Known and When. In Yísra'el Gutman and Michael Berenbaum, eds., *Anatomy of the Auschwitz Death Camp*, pp. 539–553. Bloomington: Indiana University Press, 1994.

Gillman, Peter and Gillman, Leni. *'Collar the Lot!' How Britain Interned and Expelled its Wartime Refugees*, London: Quartet Books, 1980.

Ginzel, Günther, ed. *Mut zur Menschlichkeit: Hilfe für Verfolgte während der NS-Zeit*, Cologne: Rheinland-Verlag, 1993.

Goeschel, Christian. *Suicide in Nazi Germany*, Oxford: Oxford University Press, 2009.

Goldberg, Amos. The History of the Jews in the Ghettos: A Cultural Perspective. In Dan Stone, ed., *The Holocaust and Historical Methodology*, pp. 79–100. New York: Berghahn, 2015.

Goldenstedt, Christiane. Pionierinnen sozialer Arbeit, Alice Salomon (1872–1948) und Hilde Lion (1893–1970). *Spirale der Zeit. Geschlechterdemokratie in Deutschland*, 5, 2009, 73–77.

Goldhagen, Daniel. *Hitler's Willing Executioners: Ordinary Germans and the Holocaust*, New York: Vintage, 1997.

Göppinger, Horst. *Juristen jüdischer Abstammung im 'Dritten Reich': Entrechtung und Verfolgung*, 2nd ed., Munich: C. H. Beck, 1990.

Graevenitz, Karoline v. Verlust eines Freundes: Zum Tode von Eduard Goldstücker. *Uni'kon: Journal der Universität Konstanz*, 1, 2001, 28–29.

Greenspan, Henry. *On Listening to Holocaust Survivors: Recounting and Life History*, Westport: Praeger, 1998.

Grenville, Anthony. The Association of Jewish Refugees. In Grenville, Anthony and Andrea Reiter, eds., *'I Didn't Want to Float; I Wanted to Belong to Something': Refugee Organizations in Britain 1933–1945*, pp. 89–112. Amsterdam: Rodopi, 2008.

Jewish Refugees from Germany and Austria in Britain 1933–1970: Their Image in AJR Information, London: Mitchell, 2010.

Grenville, Anthony and Reiter, Andrea, eds. *'I Didn't Want to Float; I Wanted to Belong to Something': Refugee Organizations in Britain 1933–1945*, Amsterdam: Rodopi, 2008.

Grossmann, Atina. *Jews, Germans, and Allies: Close Encounters in Occupied Germany*, Princeton: Princeton University Press, 2007.

The Survivors Were Few and the Dead Were Many: Jewish Identity and Memory in Occupied Berlin. In Marion Kaplan and Beate Meyer, eds., *Jüdische Welten: Juden in Deutschland vom 18. Jahrhundert bis in die Gegenwart*, pp. 317–335. Göttingen: Wallstein-Verlag, 2005.

Grube, Werner and Macek, Ilse. Das Kinderheim der Israelitischen Kultusgemeinde e. V. in der Antonienstraße 7. In Ilse Macek, ed., *Ausgegrenzt – Entrechtet – Deportiert: Schwabing und Schwabinger Schicksale 1933–1945*, pp. 87–104. Munich: Volk-Verlag, 2008.

Gruner, Wolf. Die Berliner und die NS-Judenverfolgung: Eine mikrohistorische Studie individueller Handlungen und sozialer Beziehungen. In Rüdiger Hachtmann, Thomas Schaarschmid and Winfried Süß, eds., *Berlin im Nationalsozialismus: Politik und Gesellschaft 1933–1945*, pp. 57–87. Göttingen: Wallstein-Verlag, 2011.

Einleitung. In Wolf Gruner, ed., *Die Verfolgung und Ermordung der europäischen Juden durch das nationalsozialistische Deutschland 1933–1945*, vol. 1, *Deutsches Reich 1933–1937*, pp. 13–50. Munich: Oldenbourg, 2008.

Der Geschlossene Arbeitseinsatz deutscher Juden: Zur Zwangsarbeit als Element der Verfolgung 1938–1943, Berlin: Metropol-Verlag, 1997.

The Persecution of the Jews in Berlin 1933–1945: A Chronology of Measures by the Authorities in the German Capital, Berlin: Stiftung Topographie des Terrors, 2014.

Widerstand in der Rosenstraße: Die Fabrikaktion und die Verfolgung der 'Mischehen' 1943, Frankfurt am Main: Fischer-Verlag, 2005.

Gruner, Wolf, ed. *Die Verfolgung und Ermordung der europäischen Juden durch das nationalsozialistische Deutschland 1933–1945*, vol. 1, *Deutsches Reich 1933–1937*, Munich: Oldenbourg, 2008.

Gruner, Wolf and Pegelow, Thomas, eds. *Resisting Persecution: Jews and Their Petitions during the Holocaust*, New York: Berghahn, 2020.

Hachtmann, Rüdiger, Schaarschmidt, Thomas and Süß, Winfried, eds. *Berlin im Nationalsozialismus: Politik und Gesellschaft 1933–1945*, Göttingen: Wallstein-Verlag, 2011.

Hajak, Stephanie and Zarusky, Jürgen eds. *München und der Nationalsozialismus: Menschen, Orte, Strukturen*, Berlin: Metropol-Verlag, 2008.

Halbauer, Manuel. Fluchthelfer an Hochrhein. In Wolfram Wette, ed., *Stille Helden: Judenretter im Dreiländereck während des Zweiten Weltkriegs*, pp. 179–194. Freiburg: Herder–Verlag, 2014.

Hammel, Andrea, ed. *The Kindertransport to Britain 1938/39: New Perspectives*, Amsterdam: Rodopi, 2012.

Harris, Mark Jonathan and Oppenheimer, Deborah. *Into the Arms of Strangers: Stories of the Kindertransport*, New York: Bloomsbury, 2000.

Kindertransport in eine fremde Welt: Mit einem Vorwort von Lord Richard Attenborough, Munich: Goldmann, 2000.

Hauff, Lisa, ed. *Die Verfolgung und Ermordung der europäischen Juden durch das nationalsozialistische Deutschland 1933–1945*, vol. XI, *Deutsches Reich und Protektorat Böhmen und Mähren April 1943–1945*, Munich: Oldenbourg, 2020.

Hecker, Hans, ed. *Grenzen: Gesellschaftliche Konstitutionen und Transfigurationen*, Essen: Klartext, 2006.

Heiber, Helmut. Aus den Akten des Gauleiters Kube. *Vierteljahrshefte für Zeitgeschichte*, 1, 1956, 67–92.

Heiliger, K. H. Retter und Gerettete – Fluchthilfe für Juden im Gottmadingener Grenzgebiet während des Zweiten Weltkrieges durch Josef und Elise Höfler und Andere. Gottmadingen, lecture paper, 14 March 2003 (Masch. Manuscript).

Heim, Susanne. Einleitung. In Susanne Heim, ed., *Deutsches Reich 1938–August 1939*, pp. 13–63. Munich: Oldenbourg, 2009.

Refugees' Routes: Emigration, Resettlement and Transmigration. In Simone Gigliotti and Hilary Earl, eds., *A Companion to the Holocaust*, pp. 363–379. Hoboken, NJ: Wiley Blackwell, 2020.

Die Verfolgung und Ermordung der europäischen Juden durch das nationalsozialistische Deutschland 1933–1945, vol. II, *Deutsches Reich 1938–August 1939*, Munich: Oldenbourg, 2009.

Heim, Susanne, ed. *Die Verfolgung und Ermordung der europäischen Juden durch das nationalsozialistische Deutschland 1933–1945*, vol. VI, *Deutsches Reich und Protektorat Böhmen und Mähren Oktober 1941–März 1943*, Munich: Oldenbourg, 2019.

Heim, Susanne, Meyer, Beate and Nicosia, Francis R., eds. *'Wer bleibt, opfert seine Jahre, vielleicht sein Leben': Deutsche Juden 1938–1941*, Göttingen: Wallstein-Verlag, 2010.

et al., eds. *The Persecution and Murder of the European Jews by Nazi Germany, 1933–1945*, 3 vols., Berlin: De Gruyter/Oldenbourg, 2019.

Heusler, Andreas. Fahrt in den Tod: Der Mord an den Münchner Juden in Kaunas (Litauen) am 25. November 1941. In Stadtarchiv München, ed., *'... verzogen, unbekannt wohin': Die erste Deportation von Münchner Juden im November 1941*, pp. 13–24. Munich: Pendo, 2000.

Verfolgung und Vernichtung (1933–1945). In Richard Bauer and Michael Brenner, eds., *Jüdisches München: Vom Mittelalter bis zur Gegenwart*, pp. 161–184. Munich: C. H. Beck, 2006.

Heusler, Andreas and Sinn, Andrea, eds. *Die Erfahrung des Exils: Vertreibung, Emigration und Neuanfang*, Munich: Bayerische Landeszentrale für politische Bildungsarbeit, 2016.

Heusler, Andreas and Weger, Tobias. *'Kristallnacht': Gewalt gegen die Münchner Juden im November 1938*, Munich: Buchendorfer-Verlag, 1998.

Hilberg, Raul. *The Destruction of the European Jews*, 3 vols., New Haven: Yale University Press, 2003.

Perpetrators, Victims, Bystanders: The Jewish Catastrophe 1933–1945, New York: HarperCollins, 1992.

Hirschfeld, Gerhard, ed. *Exil in Großbritannien: Zur Emigration aus dem nationalsozialistischen Deutschland*, Stuttgart: Klett-Cotta, 1983.

Holl, Oskar, ed. Stille Helfer, Die Quäker in der NS-Zeit: Das Hilfsnetz von Annemarie und Rudolf Cohen in München, 2009, www.yumpu.com/de/document/read/6914543 (last accessed 10 August 2020).

Holtman, Tasha. 'A Covert from the Tempest': Responsibility, Love and Politics in Britain's 'Kindertransport'. *The History Teacher*, 48(1), 2014, 107–126.

Hopkinson, Deborah. *We Had to be Brave: Escaping the Nazis on the Kindertransport*, New York: Scholastic, 2020.

Johnson, Eric A. *Nazi Terror: The Gestapo, Jews, and Ordinary Germans*, New York: Basic Books, 1999.

Jörgensen, Kirsten, Krafft, Sybille and Bäuml-Stosiek, Dagmar, eds. *'Wir lebten in einer Oase des Friedens': Die Geschichte einer jüdischen Frauenschule 1926–1938*, Munich: Dölling & Galitz, 2009.

Jünger, David. *Jahre der Ungewissheit: Emigrationspläne deutscher Juden 1933–1938*, Göttingen: Vandenhoeck & Ruprecht, 2017.

Kaplan, Marion. *Between Dignity and Despair: Jewish Life in Nazi Germany*, New York: Oxford University Press, 1999.

Hitler's Jewish Refugees: Hope and Anxiety in Portugal, New Haven: Yale University Press, 2020.

Jewish Daily Life in Germany 1618–1945, Oxford: Oxford University Press, 2005.

Jewish Women in Nazi Germany: Daily Life, Daily Struggles 1933–1939. In Peter Freimark, ed., *Juden in Deutschland: Emanzipation, Integration, Verfolgung und Vernichtung*, pp. 406–434. Hamburg: Christians, 1991.

Der Mut zum Überleben: Jüdische Frauen und ihre Familien in Nazi-Deutschland, Berlin: Aufbau-Verlag, 2001.

Kasberger, Erich. Die Barmherzigen Schwestern. In Christl Knauer-Nothaft and Erich Kasberger, *Berg am Laim: Von den Siedlungsanfängen zum modernen Stadtteil Münchens*, pp. 286–291. Munich: Volk-Verlag, 2007.

Hans Wegner und Theodor Koronczyk – zwei Pole des Täterspektrums. In Marita Krauss, ed., *Rechte Karrieren in München von der Weimarer Zeit bis in die Nachkriegsjahre*, pp. 230–244. Munich: Volk-Verlag, 2010.

Die 'Heimanlage für Juden Berg am Laim'. In Christl Knauer-Nothaft and Erich Kasberger, *Berg am Laim: Von den Siedlungsanfängen zum modernen Stadtteil Münchens*, pp. 341–380. Munich: Volk-Verlag, 2007.

Karrierewege Münchner Gestapobeamter aus dem 'Judenreferat': Eine Kollektivbiographie. In Marita Krauss, ed., *Rechte Karrieren in München von der Weimarer Zeit bis in die Nachkriegsjahre*, pp. 189–229. Munich: Volk-Verlag, 2010.

Die nationalsozialistische Gewaltherrschaft und München Berg am Laim, ihr Ende und ihre Folgen. Dokumentation, 2nd ed., Munich, the author, 1985.

Kasberger, Erich, and Michaeli-Gymnasium, in Zusammenarbeit mit der Klasse 11d. Heimanlage für Juden Berg am Laim. In Landeshauptstadt München, ed., *Verdunkeltes München: Geschichtswettbewerb 1985/86. Die nationalsozialistische Gewaltherrschaft, ihr Ende und ihre Folgen*, pp. 21–50. Buchendorf: Buchendorfer Verlag, 1987.

Keller, Stefan. Emigrantenschmuggler an der Schweizer Grenze. In Wolfram Wette, ed., *Stille Helden: Judenretter im Dreiländereck während des Zweiten Weltkriegs*, pp. 195–214. Freiburg: Herder-Verlag, 2014.

Keller, Thomas. *Lieux de migrations – lieux de mémoires franco-allemand*, Aix-en-Provence: PUP, 2007.

Kellerhoff, Sven Felix. In München wachsen Stolpersteine jetzt in die Höhe, *Die Welt*, 31 July 2018, www.welt.de/geschichte/article180269598/Erinnerungspolitik-In-Muenchen-wachsen-Stolpersteine-jetzt-in-die-Hoehe.html (last accessed 8 September 2020).

Kershaw, Ian. Reaktionen auf die Judenverfolgung. In Martin Broszat and Elke Fröhlich, eds., *Bayern in der NS-Zeit: Herrschaft und Gesellschaft im Konflikt*, vol. II, pp. 281–348. Munich: Oldenbourg, 1983.

Kestenberg, Judith. *Children Surviving Persecution: An International Study of Trauma and Healing*, Westport, CN: Praeger, 1998.

Kieval, Hillel J. Legality and Resistance in Vichy France: The Rescue of Jewish Children. *Proceedings of the American Philosophical Society*, 124(5), 1980, 339–366.

Klatzkin, Jakob. *Encyclopaedia Judaica*, vol. IV, Berlin, the author, 1929.

Klein, Anne. *Flüchtlingspolitik und Flüchtlingshilfe 1940–1942: Varian Fry und die Komitees zur Rettung politisch Verfolgter in New York und Marseille*, Berlin: Metropol-Verlag, 2007.

Knabe, Hubertus. *Die unterwanderte Republik – Stasi im Westen*, Berlin: Propyläen, 1999.

Kompisch, Kathrin, ed. *Täterinnen: Frauen im Nationalsozialismus*, Cologne: Böhlau, 2008.

Kosmala, Beate. Mißglückte Hilfe und ihre Folgen: Die Ahndung der 'Judenbegünstigung' durch NS-Verfolgungsbehörden. In Beate Kosmala and Claudia Schoppmann, eds., *Überleben im Untergrund: Hilfe für Juden in Deutschland 1941–1945*, pp. 205–222. Berlin: Metropol-Verlag, 2002.

Nichts wie raus und durch: Lebens- und Überlebensgeschichte einer jüdischen Berlinerin, Berlin: Metropol-Verlag, 2019.

Sie blieben unsichtbar: Zeugnisse aus den Jahren 1941 bis 1945, Berlin: Förderverein Blindes Vertrauen, 2006.

Stille Helden. *Politik und Zeitgeschichte*, 14, 2007, 29–34.

Zwischen Ahnen und Wissen: Flucht vor der Deportation (1941–43). In Birthe Kundrus and Beate Meyer, eds., *Die Deportation der Juden aus Deutschland: Pläne – Praxis – Reaktionen. 1938–1945*, pp. 135–159. Göttingen: Wallstein-Verlag, 2004.

Kosmala, Beate and Schoppmann, Claudia, eds. *Überleben im Untergrund: Hilfe für Juden in Deutschland 1941–1945*, Berlin: Metropol-Verlag, 2002.

Kosmala, Beate and Verbeeck, Georgi, eds. *Facing the Catastrophe: Jews and Non-Jews in Europe during World War II*, Oxford: Berg, 2011.

Krauss, Marita. Grenze und Grenzwahrnehmung bei Emigranten in der NS-Zeit. In Andreas Gestrich and Marita Krauss, eds., *Migration und Grenze*, pp. 61–82. Stuttgart: Franz Steiner Verlag, 1999.

Heimkehr in ein fremdes Land: Geschichte der Remigration nach 1945, Munich: C. H. Beck, 2001.

Zurückbleiben und Abschied: Das Beispiel NS-Zeit. In Andreas Gestrich and Marita Krauss, eds., *Zurückbleiben: Der vernachlässigte Teil der Migrationsgeschichte*, pp. 27–48. Stuttgart: Steiner, 2006.

Krauss, Marita ed. *Die bayerischen Kommerzienräte: Eine deutsche Wirtschaftselite von 1880 bis 1928*, Munich: Volk-Verlag, 2016.

Rechte Karrieren in München von der Weimarer Zeit bis in die Nachkriegsjahre, Munich: Volk-Verlag, 2010.

Sie waren dabei: Mitläuferinnen, Nutznießerinnen, Täterinnen im Nationalsozialismus, Göttingen: Wallstein-Verlag, 2008.

Krauss, Marita and Gestrich, Andreas, eds. *Migration und Grenze*, Stuttgart: Franz Steiner Verlag, 1999.

Krauss, Marita and Kasberger, Erich, eds. *Leben in zwei Welten – Else und Siegfried Rosenfeld: Tagebücher eines jüdischen Paares in Deutschland und im Exil, Hörbuch*, Munich: Volk-Verlag, 2011.

Krauss, Marita and Will, Herbert (2006). Innensichten: Grenzüberschreitungen bei Emigranten der NS-Zeit in interdisziplinärer Annäherung. In Hans Hecker, ed., *Grenzen: Gesellschaftliche Konstitutionen und Transfigurationen*, pp. 57–72. Essen: Klartext, 2006.

Krohn, Claus-Dieter et al. Zufluchtsländer: Arbeits- und Lebensbedingungen im Exil: Einleitung. In Claus-Dieter Krohn and Patrik von zur Mühlen, eds., *Handbuch der deutschsprachigen Emigration 1933–1945*, pp. 129–134. Darmstadt: Primus-Verlag, 1998.

Krohn, Claus-Dieter and Mühlen, Patrik von zur, eds. *Handbuch der deutschsprachigen Emigration 1933–1945*, Darmstadt: Primus-Verlag, 1998.

Krüger, Maren et al. Alltag im Berliner Untergrund 1943 bis 1945. In Rainer Erb and Volker Berbüsse, eds., *Antisemitismus und jüdische Geschichte: Studien zu Ehren von Herbert A. Strauss*, pp. 295–312. Berlin: Wissenschaftlicher Autoren-Verlag, 1987.

Kühn-Stillmark, Uta. Autorin. In Eva Schmidt, ed., *Jüdische Familien im Weimar der Klassik und Nachklassik und ihr Friedhof: In memoriam Dr. Else Behrend-Rosenfeld*, 2nd ed., pp. 139–143. Weimar: Ständige Kommissionen Kultur der Stadtverordnetenversammlung, 1993.

Kulka, Otto Dov, ed. *Deutsches Judentum unter dem Nationalsozialismus*, vol. 1, *Dokumente zur Geschichte der Reichsvertretung der deutschen Juden 1933–1939*, Tübingen: Mohr Siebeck, 1997.

Kuller, Christiane. *Bürokratie und Verbrechen: Antisemitische Finanzpolitik und Verwaltungspraxis im nationalsozialistischen Deutschland*, Munich: Oldenbourg, 2013.

Kundrus, Birthe. *'Dieser Krieg ist der große Rassenkrieg': Krieg und Holocaust in Europa*, Munich: C. H. Beck, 2018.

Kundrus, Birthe and Meyer, Beate, eds. *Die Deportation der Juden aus Deutschland: Pläne – Praxis – Reaktionen, 1938–1945*, Göttingen: Wallstein-Verlag, 2004.

Kushner, Tony. *The Holocaust and the Liberal Imagination: A Social and Cultural History*, Oxford: Blackwell, 1994.

Kwiet, Konrad and Eschwege, Helmu. *Selbstbehauptung und Widerstand: Deutsche Juden im Kampf um Existenz und Menschenwürde 1933–1945*, Hamburg: Christians, 1984.

Lafitte, François. *The Internment of Aliens, 1, Great Britain: Aliens, Internment, London 1940*, 2nd ed., London: Libris, 1988.

Longerich, Peter. *'Davon haben wir nichts gewusst!' Die Deutschen und die Judenverfolgung 1933–1945*, Munich: Siedler, 2006.

Holocaust: The Nazi Persecution and the Murder of the Jews, Oxford: Oxford University Press, 2010.

Politik der Vernichtung: Eine Gesamtdarstellung der nationalsozialistischen Judenverfolgung, Munich: Piper, 1998.

Löw, Andrea. Einleitung. In Andrea Löw, ed., *Deutsches Reich und Protektorat September 1939–September 1941*, pp. 13–64. Munich: Oldenbourg, 2012.

Die Verfolgung und Ermordung der europäischen Juden durch das nationalsozialistische Deutschland 1933–1945 vol. III, *Deutsches Reich und Protektorat Böhmen-Mähren September 1939–September 1941*, Munich: Oldenbourg, 2012.

Löw, Andrea, Bergen, Doris and Hajkova, Anna, eds. *Alltag im Holocaust: Jüdisches Leben im Großdeutschen Reich 1941–1945*, Munich: Oldenbourg, 2013.

Löw, Konrad. Deutsche Geschichte(n): Juden unerwünscht. *Frankfurter Allgemeine Zeitung*, 1 March 2007, p. 7.

Die Münchner und ihre jüdischen Mitbürger 1900–1950 im Urteil der NS-Opfer und -Gegner, Munich: Olzog, 2008.

Luise Meier (1885–1979). Gedenkstätte Stille Helden: Wiederstand gegen die Judenverfolgung 1933–1945, www.gedenkstaette-stille-helden.de/biografien/bio/meier-luise/ (last accessed 24 September 2020).

Lustiger, Arno, ed. *Rettungswiderstand: Über die Judenretter in Europa während der NS-Zeit*, Göttingen: Wallstein-Verlag, 2011.

Lutjens, Richard N. Jews in Hiding in Nazi Berlin 1941–1945: A Demographic Survey. *Holocaust and Genocide Studies: An International Journal*, 31(2), 2017, 268–291.

Submerged on the Surface: The Not-So-Hidden Jews of Nazi Berlin, New York: Berghahn, 2019.

Macek, Ilse. Walter Geismar (South Caulfield, Australien): 'Man konnte nicht glauben, dass Deutsche das tun'. In Ilse Macek, ed., *Ausgegrenzt – Entrechtet – Deportiert: Schwabing und Schwabinger Schicksale 1933–1945*, pp. 155–168. Munich: Volk-Verlag, 2008.

Werner Grube: 'Mitzunehmen sind sämtliche Kinder mit Gepäck zwecks Wohnsitzverlegung nach Einsatzort'. In Ilse Macek, ed., *Ausgegrenzt – Entrechtet – Deportiert: Schwabing und Schwabinger Schicksale 1933–1945*, pp. 128–144. Munich: Volk-Verlag, 2008.

Macek, Ilse, ed. *Ausgegrenzt – Entrechtet – Deportiert: Schwabing und Schwabinger Schicksale 1933 bis 1945*, Munich: Volk-Verlag, 2008.

Malet, Maria and Grenville, Anthony. *Changing Countries: The Experience and Achievement of German-speaking Exiles from Hitler in Britain from 1933 to Today*, London: Libris, 2002.

Malettke, Klaus (1969). Heilmann, Ernst. *Neue Deutsche Biographie*, 8, 1969, 260–261, www.deutsche-biographie.de/pnd118547879.html#ndbcontent (last accessed 24 September 2020).

Matthäus, Jürgen. Evading Persecution: German-Jewish Behaviour Patterns after 1933. In Francis R. Nicosia, ed., *Jewish Life in Nazi Germany: Dilemmas and Responses*, pp. 47–70. New York: Berghahn, 2010.

Maurer, Trude. From Everyday Life to a State of Emergency: Jews in Weimar and Nazi Germany. In Marion Kaplan, ed., *Jewish Daily Life in Germany 1618–1945*, pp. 271–373. Oxford: Oxford University Press, 2005.

Mehringer, Hartmut. *Waldemar von Knoeringen: Eine politische Biographie. Der Weg vom revolutionären Sozialismus zur sozialen Demokratie*, Munich: Saur, 1989.

Meyer, Beate. *A Fatal Balancing Act: The Dilemma of the Reich Association of Jews in Germany 1939–1945*, Oxford: Berghahn, 2016.

Handlungsspielräume regionaler jüdischer Repräsentanten (1941–1945). In Beate Meyer and Birthe Kundurs, eds., *Die Deportation der Juden aus Deutschland: Pläne – Praxis – Reaktionen: 1938–1945*, pp. 63–85. Göttingen: Wallstein-Verlag, 2004.

The Inevitable Dilemma: The Reich Association (Reichsvereinigung) of Jews in Germany, the Deportations, and the Jews who Went Underground. In Moshe Zimmermann, ed., *On Germans and Jews under the Nazi Regime: Essays by Three Generations of Historians*, pp. 297–312. Jerusalem: Hebrew University Magnes Press, 2006.

Jews in Nazi Berlin: From Kristallnacht to Liberation, Chicago: University of Chicago Press, 2009.

'Jüdische Mischlinge': Rassenpolitik und Verfolgungserfahrung 1933–1945, Hamburg: Dölling & Galitz, 1999.

Tödliche Gratwanderung: Die Reichsvereinigung der Juden in Deutschland zwischen Hoffnung, Zwang, Selbstbehauptung und Verstrickung 1939–1945, Göttingen: Wallstein-Verlag, 2011.

Michalski, Franz. *Als die Gestapo an der Haustür klingelte: eine Familie in 'Mischehe' und ihre Helfer*, Berlin: Metropol-Verlag, 2013.

Mikhman, Dan and Schramm Lenn J. *The Emergence of Jewish Ghettos during the Holocaust*, Cambridge: Cambridge University Press, 2011.

Moore, Bob. *Survivors: Jewish Self-help and Rescue in Nazi-occupied Western Europe*, Oxford: Oxford University Press, 2010.

Moorhouse, Roger. *Berlin at War: Life and Death in Hitler's Capital, 1939–1945*, London: Vintage, 2011.

Mosse, Werner and Paucker, Arnold. *Entscheidungsjahr 1932: Die Judenfrage in der Endphase der Weimarer Republik*, Tübingen: Mohr, 1965.

Mühlen, Patrick von zur. Lateinamerika: Übriges. In Claus-Dieter Krohn and Patrick von zur Mühlen, eds., *Handbuch der deutschsprachigen Emigration 1933–1945*, pp. 297–307. Darmstadt: Primus-Verlag, 1998.

Mühlfenzl, Martin. Erinnerung an vergessene Verbrechen. *Süddeutsche Zeitung*, 4 February 2020, www.sueddeutsche.de/muenchen/landkreismuenchen/unterschleissheim-in-der-ns-zeit-erinnerung-an-vergessene-verbrechen-1.4783397 (last accessed 8 September 2020).

München – Hauptstadt der Bewegung, exhibition catalogue, Münchner Stadtmuseums, Munich, 1994.

Nachama, Andreas, Schoeps, Julius H. and Simon, Hermann, eds. *Jews in Berlin*, Berlin: Henschel-Verlag, 2002.

Nigbur, Werner, ed. *Wenn im Amte, arbeite, wenn entlassen, verbirg dich – Prof. Dr. iur. Dr. phil. Rolf Grabower 'Dreiviertejude': Überlebender der Shoa, Theresienstadt. In Zeugnissen aus der Finanzgeschichtlichen Sammlung der Bundesfinanzakademie. Ein Lesebuch und Materialband.*, Brühl: Bundesfinanzakademie im Bundesministerium der Finanzen, 2010.

Noakes, Jeremy. The Development of Nazi Policy towards the German-Jewish 'Mischlinge' 1933–1945. *Leo Baeck Institute Year Book*, 34(1), 1989, 291–354, doi.org/10.1093/leobaeck/34.1.291

Ofer, Dalia and Weitzman, Lenore J., eds. *Women in the Holocaust*, New Haven: Yale University Press, 1998.

Oldfield, Sybil. 'It is Usually She': The Role of British Women in the Rescue and Care of the Kindertransport Kinder. *Shofar-Ashland*, 23(1), 2004, 57–70.

Oliner, Samuel P. and Oliner, Pearl M. *The Altruistic Personality: Rescuers of Jews in Nazi Europe*, New York: Free Press, 1992.

Oppenheimer, John F. *Lexikon des Judentums*, Gütersloh: Bertelsmann, 1971.

Pabst, Martin. *U- und S-Bahnfahrzeuge in Deutschland*, Munich: GeraMond-Verlag, 2000.

Palmer, Kelly D. Humanitarian Relief and Rescue Networks in France, 1940–1945, unpublished PhD dissertation, Michigan State University, 2010.

Paucker, Arnold. Speaking English with an Accent. In Charmian Brinson et al., eds., *'England? Aber wo liegt es?' Deutsche und österreichische Emigranten in Großbritannien 1933–1945*, pp. 21–32. Munich: Iudicium, 1996.

Paul, Axel. Sohn-Rethel auf dem Zauberberg: Über phantastische Ideen, intellektuelle Isolation und den Abstieg der Philosophie zur Wissenschaft. In Ulrich Bröcklung, Axel T. Paul and Stefan Kaufmann, eds., *Vernunft – Entwicklung – Leben: Schlüsselbegriffe der Moderne*, pp. 73–96. Munich: Wilhelm Fink, 2004.

Peitsch, Helmut. *'Deutschlands Gedächtnis an seine dunkelste Zeit': Zur Funktion der Autobiographik in den Westzonen Deutschlands und den Westsektoren von Berlin 1945 bis 1949*, Berlin: Edition Sigma, 1990.

Picard, Jacques. *Die Schweiz und die Juden 1933–1945*, Zurich: Chronos, 1994.

Porat, Dina. Jews from the Third Reich in Kovno. *Tel Aviver Jahrbuch für deutsche Geschichte*, 20, 1991, 363–392.

Radcliffe, James. Bishop Bell of Chichester and Non-Aryan Christians: The Role of the Berlin Quakers, the Paulusbund, the Grüberbüro and the German Jewish Emigration Office. *Kirchliche Zeitgeschichte*, 21(2), 2008, 277–286.

Rademacher, Michael, Deutsche Verwaltungsgeschichte von der Reichsvereinigung bis zur Wiedervereinigung 1990: Die Länder des Deutschen Reichs 1871–1945, Bayern, Kreis Berchtesgaden, http://treemagic.org/rademacher/www.verwaltungsgeschichte.de/index.html (last accessed 20 February 2021).

Reichling, Norbert. Mit Kant gegen die Nazis: Der 'Bund' und sein vergessenes 'Judenhilfswerk' im Rhein-Ruhr-Gebiet. In Arno Lustiger, ed., *Rettungswiderstand: Über die Judenretter während der NS-Zeit*, pp. 59–63. Göttingen: Wallstein-Verlag, 2011.

Religiöse Gemeinschaft der Freunde (Quäker), ed. *Lebensbilder deutscher Quäker während der NS-Herrschaft 1933–1945: Sammlung von Schicksalen aus der Erinnerung, aus Briefen, Zeitungsartikeln und anderen Dokumenten*, Bad Pyrmont: Religiöse Gesellschaft der Freunde (Quäker) Deutsche Jahresversammlung, 1992.

Ritchie, James M. Exile in Great Britain. In Charmian Brinson et al., eds., *'England? Aber wo liegt es?' Deutsche und österreichische Emigranten in Großbritannien 1933–1945*, pp. 9–20. Munich: Iudicium, 1996.

German-speaking Exiles in Great Britain, Amsterdam: Rodopi, 2001.

Roell, Wolfgang. *Sozialdemokraten im Konzentrationslager Buchenwald 1937–1945: Unter Einbeziehung biographischer Skizzen*, Göttingen: Wallstein-Verlag, 2000.

Roseman, Mark. *The Past in Hiding: Memory and Survival in Nazi Germany*, New York: Picador, 2002.

Surviving Undetected: The Bund, Rescue and Memory in Germany. In Jacques Semelin, Claire Andrieu and Sarah Gensburger, eds., *Resisting Genocide: The Multiple Forms of Rescue*, pp. 465–480. New York: Columbia University Press, 2011.

Rosenfeld, Gavriel D. *Architektur und Gedächtnis: München und Nationalsozialismus: Strategien des Vergessens. Aus dem Amerikanischen von Uli Nickel und Bernadette Ott*, Munich: Dölling & Galitz, 2004.

Munich and Memory: Architecture, Monuments, and the Legacy of the Third Reich, Berkeley: University of California Press, 2000.

Saint Sauveur-Henn, Anne. Landwirtschaftliche Kolonien deutsch-jüdischer Emigranten in Argentinien. In Karl Kohut, *Alternative Lateinamerika: Das deutsche Exil in der Zeit des Nationalsozialismus*, pp. 155–166. Frankfurt am Main: Vervuert, 1994.

Sandvoß, Rainer. *Widerstand in Kreuzberg: Reihe Widerstand in Berlin 1933–1945, 10*, Berlin: Gedenkstätte deutscher Widerstand, 1997.

Sasse-Voswinckel, Ulrike and Berninger, Frank, eds., *Exil am Mittelmeer: Deutsche Schriftsteller in Südfrankreich 1933–1941*, Munich: Allitera-Verlag, 2005.

Sassin, Horst. Überleben im Untergrund: Die Kinderärztin Dr. Erna Rüppel (1895–1970), Memorial Book Dedicated to the Victims of NS in Wuppertal (website), www.gedenkbuch-wuppertal.de/sites/default/files/doc/ueberleben-im-untergrund-die-kinderaerztin-dr-erna-rueppel-1895-1970-von-horst-sassin.pdf (last accessed 25 September 2020).

Sauer, Paul. *Für Recht und Menschenwürde: Lebensbild von Otto Hirsch (1885–1941)*, Gerlingen: Bleicher, 1985.

Schieb, Barbara. Möglichkeiten und Grenzen der Helferforschung heute – Quellen und exemplarische Fragestellungen, Podiumsbeitrag in der 3. Internationalen Konferenz zur Holocaustforschung Helfer, Retter und Netzwerker des Widerstands, Berlin, 27–28 January 2011.

Schilde, Kurt. Grenzüberschreitende Flucht und Fluchthilfe (1941–1945): Ereignisse, Interessen, Motive. In Beate Kosmala and Claudia Schoppmann, eds., *Solidarität und Hilfe für Juden während der NS-Zeit, vol. v, Überleben im Untergrund. Hilfe für Juden in Deutschland 1941–1945*, pp. 151–190. Berlin: Metropol-Verlag, 2002.

Schirrmacher, Gerd. *Hertha Kraus – Zwischen den Welten: Biographie einer Sozialwissenschaftlerin und Quäkerin (1897–1968)*, Frankfurt am Main: Peter Lang, 2002.

Schmitt, Hans H. *Quakers and Nazis: Inner Light in Outer Darkness*, Columbia: University of Missouri Press, 1997.

Quaker Efforts to Rescue Children from Nazi Education and Discrimination. The international Quakerschool Eerde. *Quaker History*, 85(1), 1996, 45–57.

Schoppmann, Claudia. Die 'Fabrikaktion' in Berlin: Hilfe für untergetauchte Juden als Form des humanitären Widerstandes. *Zeitschrift für Geschichtswissenschaft*, 53 (2), 2005, 138–148.

Fluchtziel Schweiz: Das Hilfsnetz um Luise Meier und Josef Höfler. In Wolfgang Benz, ed., *Überleben im Dritten Reich: Juden im Untergrund und ihre Helfer*, pp. 205–219. Munich: C. H. Beck, 2003.

'Fortgesetzte Beihilfe zur illegalen Auswanderung von Juden nach der Schweiz': Das Hilfsnetz um Luise Meier und Josef Höfler. In Wolfram Wette, ed., *Stille Helden: Judenretter im Dreiländereck während des Zweiten Weltkriegs*, pp. 163–178. Freiburg: Herder-Verlag, 2005.

Das war doch jenseits jeder menschlichen Vorstellungskraft: Hilfe für verfolgte Juden im deutsch besetzten Norwegen 1940–1945, Berlin: Lukas-Verlag, 2016.

Schrafstetter, Susanna. *Flucht und Versteck: Untergetauchte Juden in München – Verfolgungserfahrung und Nachkriegsalltag*, Göttingen: Wallstein-Verlag, 2015.

'Life in Illegality Cost and Extortionate Amount of Money': Ordinary Germans and German Jews Hiding from Deportation. In Frank Bajohr and Andrea Löw, eds., *The Holocaust and European Societies*, pp. 69–85. London: Palgrave Macmillan, 2016.

Schröder, Wilhelm Heinz, Biographien sozialdemokratischerParlamentarier in den deutschen Reichs- und Landtagen 1867–1933, BIOSOP online, http://zhsf.gesis.org/biosop_db/biosop_db.php (last accessed 25 September 2020).

Schwarzmüller, Alois. Garmisch-Partenkirchen und seine jüdischen Bürger 1933–1945. Ludwig und Margarete Altschüler, 2006/2013, www.gapgeschichte.de/juden_in_gap_vortrag_1993/kapitel_7.htm#_ftn6 (last accessed 25 May 2021).

Selig, Wolfram. 'Cossmann, Paul Nikolaus.' In Wolfgang Benz, ed., *Handbuch des Antisemitismus*, vol. II/1, *Personen A–K*, pp. 149–150. Munich: Saur, 2009.

Seyfert, Michael. 'His Majesty's Most Loyal Internees': Die Internierung und Deportation deutscher und österreichischer Flüchtlinge als 'enemy aliens': Historische, kulturelle und literarische Aspekte. In Gerhard Hirschfeld, ed., *Exil in Großbritannien: Zur Emigration aus dem nationalsozialistischen Deutschland*, pp. 155–182. Stuttgart: Klett-Cotta, 1983.

Sinn, Andrea. *'Und ich lebe wieder an der Isar': Exil und Rückkehr des Münchner Juden Hans Lamm*, Munich: Oldenbourg, 2008.

Sogos, Giorgia and Fry, Varian. 'Der Engel von Marseille': Von der Legalität in die Illegalität und zur Rehabilitierung. In Gabriele Anderl and Simon Usaty, eds., *Schleppen, schleusen, helfen: Flucht zwischen Rettung und Ausbeutung: Mandelbaum*, pp. 209–220. Vienna: Mandelbaum-Verlag, 2016.

Spies, Gerty. Erinnerungen an Dr. Julius Spanier. In Hans Lamm, ed., *Vergangene Tage: Jüdische Kultur in München*, pp. 130–135. Munich: Langen Müller Verlag, 1982.

Spitta, Arnold. Argentinien. In Claus-Dieter Krohn and Patrik von zur Mühlen, eds., *Handbuch der deutschsprachigen Emigration 1933–1945*, pp. 143–162. Darmstadt: Primus-Verlag, 1998.

Steinbach, Peter. Das Leiden – zu schwer und zu viel: Zur Bedeutung der Massendeportation von südwestdeutschen Juden. *Tribüne – Zeitschrift zum Verständnis des Judentums*, 49(195), 2010, 109–120.

Steinweis, Allan A. *The Germans and the Holocaust: Popular Responses to the Persecution and Murder of the Jews*, New York: Berghahn, 2016.

Kristallnacht 1938: Ein deutscher Pogrom, Stuttgart: Reclam, 2011.

Steinweis, Allan A., Bannasch, Bettina and Schreckenberger, Helga, eds. *Exil und Shoah*, Munich: Edition Text+Kritik, 2016.

Steinweis, Allan A., Heusler, Andreas and Smith, Dana, eds. *Judenverfolgung in München*, Munich: Lehrstuhl für Jüdische Geschichte und Kultur, 2014.

Stent, Ronald. *A Bespattered Page? The Internment of His Majesty's 'Most Loyal Enemy Aliens'*, London: Andre Deutsch, 1980.

Strempel, Rüdiger. Letzter Halt Marseille – Varian Fry und das Emergency Rescue Committee. In Winrich C.-W. Clasen and W. Peter Schneemelcher, eds., *Mittelmeer-Passagen*, pp. 185–196. Rheinbach: CMZ-Verlag, 2018.

Strnad, Maximilian. Die Deportation aus München. Alan E. Steinweis, ed., *Judenverfolgung in München: Münchner Beiträge zur jüdischen Geschichte und Kultur*, 8(2), 2014, 76–96.

Flachs für das Reich. Das jüdische Zwangsarbeiterlager 'Flachsröste Lohhof' bei München, Munich: Volk-Verlag, 2013.

Zwischenstation 'Judensiedlung': Verfolgung und Deportation der jüdischen Münchner 1941–1945, Munich: Oldenbourg, 2011.

Taylor, Jennifer (2009). The Missing Chapter: How the British Quakers Helped to Save the Jews of Germany and Austria from Nazi Persecution, online article, October 2009, http://remember.org/unite/quakers.htm (last accessed 28 August 2020).

Tennstedt, Florian. Arbeiterbewegung und Familiengeschichte bei Eduard Bernstein und Ignaz Zadek: Hilfswissenschaftliche Mitteilungen zu persönlichen Aspekten von Revisionismus und Sozialreform bei deutschen Sozialdemokraten. *IWK Internationale Wissenschaftliche Korrespondenz zur Geschichte der deutschen Arbeiterbewegung*, 18, 1982, 451–481.

Unabhängige Expertenkommission Schweiz – Zweiter Weltkrieg, Die Schweiz und die Flüchtlinge zur Zeit des Nationalsozialismus, Bern, 1999.

Varese, Federico and Yaish, Meir. 'The Importance of Being Asked': The Rescue of Jews in Nazi Europe. *Rationality and Society*, 12, 2000, 307–334.

Wanninger, Susanne. *'Herr Hitler, ich erkläre meine Bereitwilligkeit zur Mitarbeit': Rudolf Buttmann (1885–1947). Politiker und Bibliothekar zwischen bürgerlicher Tradition und Nationalsozialismus*, Wiesbaden: Harrassowitz, 2014.

Zwischen Politik und Bibliothek: Die Karriere des Dr. Rudolf Buttmann – eine Musterkarriere, unpublished PhD thesis, Munich, 2011.

Watts, Irene N. *Escape from Berlin: 75th Anniversary of the Kindertransport*, Toronto: Trunda Books, 2013.

Wertheimer, Waltraut. Magdalena Schwarz. In Ilse Macek, ed., *Ausgegrenzt – Entrechtet – Deportiert: Schwabing und Schwabinger Schicksale 1933–1945*, pp. 449–450. Munich: Volk-Verlag, 2008.

Wette, Wolfram, ed. *Stille Helden: Judenretter im Dreiländereck während des Zweiten Weltkriegs*, Freiburg: Herder-Verlag, 2005.

Wetzel, Jakob. 32 neue Stolpersteine auf einmal, Erinnerungskultur in München. *Süddeutsche Zeitung*, 29 October 2018, www.sueddeutsche.de/muenchen/stolpersteine-muenchen-verlegung-1.4188023 (last accessed 25 May 2021).

Wietog, Jutta. Bevölkerungsstatistik im Dritten Reich. In Statistisches Bundesamt, ed., *Wirtschaft und Statistik*, 7, Wiesbaden: Statistisches Bundesamt, 2001.

Wollasch, Hans-Josef. Hilfe für Verfolgte: Die Freiburgerin Gertrud Luckner, eine 'Botschafterin der Menschlichkeit'. In Wolfram Wette, ed., *Stille Helden: Judenretter im Dreiländereck während des Zweiten Weltkriegs*, pp. 67–86. Freiburg: Herder-Verlag, 2014.

Wollenberg, Jörg and Pribic Rado. *The German Public and the Persecution of the Jews 1933–1945: No One Participated, No One Knew*, Amherst: Humanity Books, 1998.

Wriggins, Howard. *Picking up the Pieces from Portugal to Palestine: Quaker Refugee Relief in World War II: A Memoir*, Lanham, MD: University Press of America, 2004.

Zahn, Christine. Von einem Quartier zum nächsten: Eine Odyssee im Berliner Untergrund. In Wolfgang Benz, ed., *Überleben im Dritten Reich: Juden im Untergrund und ihre Helfer*, pp. 229–238. Munich: Dt. Taschenbuch-Verlag, 2006.

Zahn, Peter, ed. *Hilfe für Juden in München: Annemarie und Rudolf Cohen und die Quäker 1938–1941*, Munich: Oldenbourg, 2013.

Zellinger-Kratzl, Hildegard. *175 Jahre Barmherzige Schwestern in Bayern 1832–2007*, ed. Kongregation der Barmherzigen Schwestern, Munich: Don Bosco, 2007.

Websites

Bodleian Library and Radcliffe Camera, ed., History of the Bodleian, www.bodleian.ox.ac.uk/bodley/about/history (last accessed 15 August 2010).

Melián, Michaela. Memory Loops, www.memoryloops.net (last accessed 8 September 2020).

INDEX OF NAMES

INDEX OF PLACES